PRAISE FOR
THE FOUNDERS

"[Soni] is balanced and fluid in this solo outing, making mundane projects like the creation of an online 'button,' or the dawn of CAPTCHA, somehow literary. . . . [He] also has a knack for the wry or lovely phrase . . . [and] appends a coda about the power of 'PayPal's Mafia' to inspire that left this reader, at least, in sobs."
—*NEW YORK TIMES*

"A gripping account of PayPal's origins and a vivid portrait of the geeks and contrarians who made its meteoric rise possible. His richly reported narrative includes corporate intrigue, workplace hijinks, breakthrough innovation, and first-class nerdiness."
—*WALL STREET JOURNAL*

"Illuminating."
—TYLER COWEN,
Marginal Revolution

"Spellbinding . . . What an achievement by Jimmy Soni in telling the essential story of PayPal, and the amazing people who made it happen."
—*FORBES*

"Engrossing."
—*BUSINESS INSIDER*

APTEKAR

"A dramatic business story about the payment company's rise . . . Also a human tale about [Elon] Musk, Peter Thiel, and Max Levchin before they went on to greater fame and fortune. In *The Founders*, Jimmy Soni captures the heady days of the dot-com bubble."
—REUTERS

"Gripping . . . An engrossing glimpse of the 'PayPal Mafia's' riotous early days."
—*ECONOMIST*

"[An] entertaining history . . . Soni's account memorably renders the personalities involved and engages with ideas about financial sovereignty, open-source technology, and the place of politics in Silicon Valley." —*NEW YORKER*

"A masterpiece of reporting and storytelling by a deeply intuitive writer who gained access to the most important—and elusive—minds of our generation. In *The Founders*, Soni has produced more than just a bona fide business thriller. He has written a book with the power to change how we see the world, and one that reminds us that America's most beautiful instinct is to embrace original thinkers who are willing to risk everything in the name of innovation. The best book I have read in ages."
—ROBERT KURSON, author of
Shadow Divers and *Rocket Men*

IMBACH

NOSEK

NATIONAL BESTSELLER

"Anyone who has used the internet in the last decade will find *The Founders* a revealing and sometimes shocking look inside today's tech revolution and the very human wizards who have transformed our lives—for good and ill."
—KATI MARTON, author of *The Chancellor: The Remarkable Odyssey of Angela Merkel*

"This is a fascinating page-turner about the brilliant and competitive innovators who created PayPal and went on to shape our digital world. The colorful cast of characters—including Thiel, Musk, Hoffman, and Levchin—is amazing. Deeply reported and bracingly written, this book is an indispensable guide to modern innovation and entrepreneurship."
—WALTER ISAACSON, author of *The Code Breaker*

"The real secrets of Silicon Valley are the tight networks of friendship and business that propel new ideas, companies, and personalities into the world. The most consequential of these networks in recent decades is the one that began at PayPal. Here Jimmy Soni delivers a start-up hustle story for the ages, revealing why their wild entrepreneurial ride did so much to build Silicon Valley's supersized present."
—MARGARET O'MARA, author of *The Code: Silicon Valley and the Remaking of America*

"You may think you know something about the early careers of Elon Musk, Peter Thiel, and Max Levchin, but until you read this extraordinary and meticulously reported book, you really don't. *The Founders* not only explains the veiled histories and inner workings of Silicon Valley's influential 'PayPal Mafia'—it explores the profound questions of how world-changing networks of technology, talent, and innovation come together."
—JON GERTNER, author of *The Idea Factory* and *The Ice at the End of the World*

"With this book, Soni joins the ranks of Eric Ries and Ben Horowitz as the author of a canonical must-read for all start-up founders. Readers will discover not only rich characters, but unflinching and trend-proof insights into what it takes to start a company that changes history."
—AMANDA CASSATT, founder of Serotonin and former CMO of ConsenSys

"Short of getting into a time machine, it's hard to imagine how you'd get closer to capturing PayPal's rise—and understanding the lives of its creators. A brilliant book chock-full of wisdom and lessons for business and life."
—NIR EYAL, bestselling author of *Hooked* and *Indistractable*

"[A] punchy origin story full of wheeling, dealing, and political machinations . . . Soni tells the story with novelistic verve."
—*PUBLISHERS WEEKLY*

"This deep dive into PayPal's history will intrigue readers from the beginning. Soni, an award-winning author, had unprecedented access to Elon Musk and internal PayPal documents. Readers will be surprised by how much personalities, company culture, and people shape revolutionary innovation. Those with entrepreneurial spirits will want to add this to their reading list."
—*BOOKLIST*

ALSO BY JIMMY SONI

Jane's Carousel
(with Jane Walentas)

A Mind at Play: How Claude Shannon Invented the Information Age

Rome's Last Citizen: The Life and Legacy of Cato
(with Rob Goodman)

THE
FOUNDERS

THE STORY OF PAYPAL AND THE ENTREPRENEURS
WHO SHAPED SILICON VALLEY

JIMMY SONI

SIMON & SCHUSTER PAPERBACKS

NEW YORK   LONDON   TORONTO   SYDNEY   NEW DELHI

An Imprint of Simon & Schuster, LLC
1230 Avenue of the Americas
New York, NY 10020

First Simon & Schuster trade paperback edition February 2024

SIMON & SCHUSTER PAPERBACKS and colophon are
registered trademarks of Simon & Schuster, LLC

Simon & Schuster: Celebrating 100 Years of Publishing in 2024

For information about special discounts for bulk purchases, please contact
Simon & Schuster Special Sales at 1-866-506-1949 or
business@simonandschuster.com.

The Simon & Schuster Speakers Bureau can bring authors to your live event.
For more information or to book an event, contact the
Simon & Schuster Speakers Bureau at 1-866-248-3049 or
visit our website at www.simonspeakers.com.

Interior design by Ruth Lee-Mui

Manufactured in the United States of America

1   3   5   7   9   10   8   6   4   2

Library of Congress Cataloging-in-Publication Data has been applied for.

ISBN 978-1-5011-9726-0
ISBN 978-1-5011-9724-6 (pbk)
ISBN 978-1-5011-9725-3 (ebook)

To my daughter, Venice, who arrived just as this project started,
and to my late editor, Alice, who left us just as it finished.

Contents

It ought to be remembered that there is nothing more difficult to take in hand, more perilous to conduct, or more uncertain in its success, than to take the lead in the introduction of a new order of things. Because the innovator has for enemies all those who have done well under the old conditions, and lukewarm defenders in those who may do well under the new. This coolness arises partly from fear of the opponents, who have the laws on their side, and partly from the incredulity of men, who do not readily believe in new things until they have had a long experience of them.

—Niccolò Machiavelli, *The Prince*

"Those who have learned to walk on the threshold of the unknown worlds, by means of what are commonly termed par excellence the exact sciences, may then, with the fair white wings of imagination, hope to soar further into the unexplored amidst which we live."

—Ada Lovelace

Introduction

"Fuck, you're making me rummage around the attic," said Elon Musk.

We sat in his living room, but the metaphor still fit. Musk was about to tell me the story of PayPal.

At the moment we met, in January 2019, PayPal—a company he cofounded some two decades earlier—was likely the furthest thing from his mind. The day before, he had announced significant layoffs at Tesla Motors, the electric car company he has led since 2003. And just the week before that, he had cut one-tenth of the workforce at SpaceX, the aerospace manufacturer and transportation firm he started in 2002. With all this present swirl, I didn't know how much Musk would want to delve into the past, and I was ready for him to trot out a few familiar talking points and send me on my way.

But as he spoke about the internet's development and PayPal's origins, the stories spilled out. About his first internship at a Canadian bank. About building his first start-up, then his second. About what it felt like to be overthrown as CEO.

By the end of the afternoon—nearly three hours later—I suggested we pause. We had only scheduled an hour together, and though Musk had been generous with his time, I didn't want to wear out my welcome. But even as he stood to show me out, he launched into another PayPal story. Forty-seven years old, Musk spoke with the enthusiasm of someone older asked to relive his glory days: "I can't believe it's been twenty years!"

■ ■ ■

It *was* hard to believe—not just the years that had passed, but how much PayPal's alumni had accomplished in them. If you have used the internet at all in the last twenty years, you've touched a product, service, or website connected to the creators of PayPal. The founders of several of our era's defining firms—the creators of YouTube, Yelp, Tesla, SpaceX, LinkedIn, and Palantir, among others—were early PayPal employees; others occupy top posts at Google, Facebook, and Silicon Valley's leading venture capital firms.

Both in the foreground and behind the scenes, PayPal's alumni have built, funded, or counseled nearly every Silicon Valley company of consequence for the last two decades. As a group, they constitute one of the most powerful and successful networks ever created—power and influence captured in the controversial phrase the "PayPal Mafia." Several billionaires and many multimillionaires have emerged from PayPal's ranks; the group's combined net worth is higher than the GDP of New Zealand.

But to look only at their wealth and impact on technology is to miss the group's wider imprint: PayPal's alumni have built world-changing micro-lending nonprofits, produced award-winning films, written bestselling books, and advised politicians at every level—from the state house to the White House. And they're far from done: Today, PayPal alumni have taken as a mission everything from cataloging the world's genealogical records to restoring three billion acres of forest ecosystems to "scaling love"—bringing their PayPal experience to bear in each case.

They've also been at the center of the biggest social, cultural, and political controversies of our age, including bitter fights over free speech, financial regulation, privacy in technology, income inequality, the efficacy of cryptocurrency, and discrimination in Silicon Valley. For its admirers, PayPal's founders are a force to be emulated. For its critics, the group represents everything wrong with big tech—putting historically unprecedented power into the hands of a small clutch of techno-utopian libertarians. Indeed, it is hard to find a lukewarm opinion about PayPal's founders—they are either heroes or heathens, depending on who offers the judgment.

■ ■ ■

And yet, despite all that, the PayPal days themselves are usually glossed over. If the early years come up at all, they are typically granted a polite paragraph crediting PayPal for making the later, splashier achievements possible. The group's subsequent successes are so legendary—and their controversies so conspicuous—that they steal the oxygen from the origin story. Space travel, after all, makes for better copy than payment services.

But this seemed odd to me. It was as if these people had grown up in the same tiny town, and no one had bothered to ask what was in the water. It also seemed a shame: To skip PayPal's creation is to neglect the most interesting stuff about its founders. It is to miss the defining experience of their early professional lives—one that defined so much of what came later.

As I began poking around, asking questions about PayPal's beginnings, it became clear just how much of the story had been overlooked— and how many of its central figures were absent from the retellings. More than one person I spoke to had never previously been asked about their PayPal tenure at length. And their stories were as rich and revealing as those of the household names.

Indeed, it's in the recollections of scores of engineers, UX designers, network architects, product specialists, fraud fighters, and support personnel that the story of PayPal comes to life. As one former employee put it, "You have folks like Peter Thiel, Max Levchin, and Reid Hoffman. But when I first got to the company, it was the database administrators who were thought of as gods."

Whether known or unknown, the hundreds of individuals who worked at PayPal from 1998 to 2002 consider the experience a watershed. It influenced their approach to leadership, strategy, and technology. Several PayPal alumni observed that they'd spent the rest of their careers seeking a team of comparable intensity, intellect, and initiative. "There was something really special, and I think we may not have all realized it at the time," one member of the product team said. "But now, when I go into teams, I'm just looking for what is that magic that we saw in the early days of PayPal. And it's rare, but it's what we keep searching for."

One employee remarked on PayPal's butterfly effect—not just in the achievements of people like Musk, Levchin, and Hoffman, whose creations have touched millions, but in the lives of the hundreds present at the creation. "It is . . . something that defines me and my life, and probably will for my entire life," he said.

Understanding the PayPal years helps shed light on a remarkable period in technological history and the remarkable people who brought it into being. The more I learned, the more convinced I became that "the attic" was worth rummaging through.

■ ■ ■

PayPal's founding is one of the great, improbable stories of the internet age. Two decades later, living and shopping in an era in which the "e" in "e-commerce" is redundant, it's easy to take a service like PayPal for granted. When a couple taps can summon a car to our doorstep, sending money over the internet hardly seems groundbreaking. But it's a mistake to assume that the technology underlying digital money transfer was easily built, or that PayPal was destined for success.

The PayPal we know today resulted from the fusion of two companies. One—originally called Fieldlink and renamed Confinity—was founded in 1998 by two unknowns, Max Levchin and Peter Thiel. In the course of finding itself, Confinity built a framework linking money to email, a service dubbed "PayPal" that found an enthusiastic audience on the auction website eBay.

But Confinity wasn't the only company working on digital payments. Fresh off the sale of his first start-up, Elon Musk had founded X.com, a company that also helped users email money. That wasn't close to the extent of his original ambition, though. Musk was convinced that financial services needed upending, and that X.com would be the platform to do it. He pitched his new start-up as the single-letter finance website to rule them all, offering every financial product or service available. But a series of strategic shifts led X.com to target the same online payments market as Confinity, with digital payments as the gateway for a bigger financial services play.

Confinity and X.com fought fiercely over eBay market share, a contest that raised the competitive ire of both teams and ended in a fractious merger. For the next several years, the company's survival was an open question. Sued, defrauded, copied, mocked—from the outset, PayPal was a start-up under siege. Its founders took on multibillion-dollar financial firms, a critical press and skeptical public, hostile regulators, and even foreign fraudsters. In the space of just four years, the company survived the bursting of the dot-com bubble, investigations from state attorneys general, and a copycat product built by one of its own investors.

PayPal also faced a spectacularly competitive market. During its formative years, PayPal saw well over a dozen new entrants to the payments space, while simultaneously defending against entries from legacy players—credit card associations like Visa and Mastercard as well as multibillion-dollar banks. And because it emerged as the primary payment platform for eBay, PayPal found itself a hook in the craw of eBay's executives, who thought of PayPal as an intruder skimming service fees rightly owed to eBay. eBay acquired and launched its own payments platform to unseat PayPal, a rivalry that defined PayPal's earliest years.

■ ■ ■

Perhaps unsurprisingly, stormy seas without did not engender peace within the company. "Calling us a mafia is an insult to mafias," joked John Malloy, an early board member. "A mafia is far better organized than we were." During its first two years of existence, PayPal cycled through three CEOs, and its senior management team threatened to resign en masse—twice.

Not that PayPal's senior management had much seniority in the traditional sense. Many of its founders and early employees joined the company in their twenties; most were fresh out of college. Working at PayPal was their first taste of the professional world. A young workforce alone wasn't uncommon in late 1990s Silicon Valley, awash in young technologists looking to make a fortune. But even by Valley standards, PayPal's was an iconoclastic culture. Its earliest hires included high school dropouts, ace chess players, and puzzle champions—often chosen because of their eccentricities and peculiarities, not in spite of them.

At one point, the company's office featured both an indicator called "The World Domination Index," which tracked the day's users, and a banner bearing the words "Memento Mori," Latin for "Remember that you will die." PayPal's oddball team was out to dominate the world—or die trying.

Most observers predicted the latter outcome. In the late 1990s, only 10 percent of all online commerce was conducted digitally—the vast majority of transactions still ended with the buyer sending a check by mail. Many people were dubious about entering personal credit card or banking information online, and sites like PayPal were often thought to be portals for illicit activity like money laundering or the sale of drugs and weapons. On the eve of its IPO, a prominent trade publication declared that the country needed PayPal "as much as it does an anthrax epidemic."

Bad press could be ignored. World-shattering events could not. Just as PayPal's founders prepared to take the company public—finalizing the terms of what should have been their greatest triumph—two planes screamed through the New York sky, striking the Twin Towers. PayPal was the first company to file for its IPO after September 11, 2001, as the country and the financial markets were only just beginning to recover from the attack.

On the way to its IPO, PayPal faced a raft of lawsuits and an SEC on the prowl following several high-profile accounting scandals at other companies. After nearly endless setbacks—a brutal merger, tens of millions of dollars lost to fraud, and a tough climate for technology stocks—PayPal pulled off the improbable: a stunningly successful IPO, and its acquisition, the same year, by eBay for $1.5 billion.

■ ■ ■

Musk would later correct an interviewer who offered that PayPal was a hard company to create. The company wasn't hard to create at all, he said. Rather, "it was a hard company to keep alive." Twenty years later, PayPal can claim a rare triumph for companies of its era: it still exists.

Eventually, eBay spun PayPal out on its own, and today it's worth roughly $300 billion—making it one of the largest companies in the world.

Less than two years passed between the X.com-Confinity merger and PayPal's initial public offering on the Nasdaq, but many employees felt as though they'd worked a lifetime. Many remembered the company as a crucible—cutthroat as it was creative, and unforgivingly intense. One employee saw it vividly on the first hour of her first day. Walking over to her PayPal cubicle, she spotted an industrial-sized cache of Tylenol on her right. On her left, in the next cubicle over, she overheard another employee chastising a frustrated spouse. "I remember her talking to her husband, 'Listen, I'm not going to get home tonight! So stop asking me!'"

Employee after employee described the era as a "blur"—a haze of exhaustion, adrenaline, and anxiety. One engineer slept so little during this period that he totaled not one but two cars driving home late at night from the PayPal office. The company's CTO described the group as feeling "like veterans of an intense military campaign."

Still, PayPal's former employees waxed nostalgic. "It was crazy exciting," observed Amy Rowe Klement, "I don't think we even fully realized the rocket ship we were on when we were on it." Several said they did their life's finest work during this period. "I felt like I was part of something grand, and I'd never had that before," said one quality assurance analyst, Oxana Wootton. "To this day," remarked a fraud analyst, Jeremy Roybal, "I still bleed PayPal blue."

■ ■ ■

Many who ended up working at PayPal came to the company circuitously. This project emerged in a similar way. In the course of writing my last book—a biography of the late Dr. Claude Shannon, the founder of the field of information theory and one of the great, forgotten geniuses of the twentieth century—I examined his employer, Bell Laboratories. Bell Labs was the research arm of the Bell Telephone company, and as a group, Bell's scientists and engineers won six Nobel Prizes and invented, among other things, touch-tone dialing, the laser, cellular networks, communications satellites, solar cells, and the transistor.

I began to wonder about other Bell-like constellations of talent—including tech companies like PayPal, General Magic, and Fairchild Semiconductor, but also non-technological cohorts like the Fugitive Poets, the Bloomsbury Group, and the Soulquarians. The British musician and producer Brian Eno once said that as a visual art student he was taught that artistic revolution came from solitary figures—Picasso, Kandinsky, Rembrandt. But as he looked into these revolutionaries, he discovered them to be products of "very fertile scenes involving lots and lots of people—some of them artists, some of them collectors, some of them curators, thinkers, theorists . . . all sorts of people who created a kind of ecology of talent."

Eno called it "scenius." "Scenius," he said, "is the intelligence of a whole . . . operation or group of people. And I think that's a more useful way to think about culture, actually." It's also a useful way to think about the PayPal story, properly understood as a narrative about the lives, intersections, and interactions of several hundred individuals, set at a moment in time when the consumer internet took shape.

Modern technology tales are usually told as stories of individual achievement—more "genius" than "scenius." Jobs is inseparable from the Apple narrative, as is Bezos from Amazon, Gates from Microsoft, or Zuckerberg from Facebook. PayPal's success is a story of a different kind. There is no single hero or heroine. At different moments in the company's history, various team members produced critical, company-saving breakthroughs; remove any one of them, and it's possible that the whole thing would have collapsed.

Moreover, many of PayPal's signature achievements emerged from the productive friction of the group—the tension among the product, engineering, and business teams yielding pearls of innovation. The company's early history was marked by deep disagreements, and yet, as early engineer James Hogan observed, "There was some way where we just were not stepping on each other's toes, interpersonally and emotionally, in a way that really spiraled into dysfunction." At PayPal, disharmony produced discovery.

I wanted to grasp this ecology, the fertile mix of the people involved, the challenges they faced, and the moment in technological history in which they faced them.

■ ■ ■

For the prospective author, PayPal's origin tale is thrilling—though daunting—to write. I began with an exhaustive look at what had already been said and written on the subject. Thankfully, many of those who built the company had prolific public profiles; they had written books, launched podcasts, and spoken about PayPal at conferences, on television, on the radio, and in print. I reviewed hundreds of hours of their prior commentary and the hundreds of articles written about PayPal during its formative years, as well as a small number of books and academic papers that included the company as a case study.

I also tried to contact many of PayPal's pre-IPO employees, and I interviewed hundreds during the course of this project. I was grateful to have spoken to and interviewed all of the company's original cofounders and most of its board members and earliest investors. I also talked with outsiders who provided invaluable perspectives: the company's technical advisors, the person whose firm birthed the "PayPal" name, would-be investors who almost pulled the trigger, and the leaders of competing firms, among many others. I am grateful to all who generously allowed me to rummage through their collections of notes, documents, photos, memorabilia, and tens of thousands of pages of email correspondence from PayPal's earliest days.

In many cases, I uncovered previously untold PayPal stories—including harrowing accounts of the near-breakdown of the Confinity-X.com merger, and how close the company came to collapse at several critical points. I also tried to understand how—through the mayhem—PayPal's internet innovations came to be and came to form today's internet landscape.

What emerged from those years of research is a tale of ambition, invention, and iteration. From a period of duress came a generation of entrepreneurs, whose later creations bear PayPal's imprint. But the first triumph—the success of PayPal—was hard-won. Properly understood, PayPal's story is a four-year odyssey of near-failure followed by near-failure.

It's fitting, then, that PayPal's story starts with an historic technological breakdown—a disaster thousands of miles from Silicon Valley that exposed a future PayPal founder to computer technology for the first time.

PART 1

SICILIAN DEFENSE

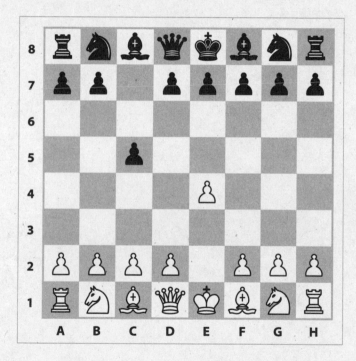

BUILDING BLOCKS

The February 1986 issue of *Soviet Life* included the ten-page glossy spread: "Peace and Plenty in Pripyat." Pripyat was, per the article, a cosmopolitan idyll. "Today the town is made up of people belonging to more than 30 different nationalities from all over the Soviet Union," the authors wrote. "The streets abound in flowers. The blocks of apartments stand in pine groves. Each residential area has a school, a library, shops, sports facilities, and playgrounds close by. In the morning there are fewer people around. Only young women pushing baby carriages stroll along unhurriedly."

If the town had any problems at all, it was only that it lacked sufficient space for new arrivals. "Pripyat is currently experiencing a baby boom," the mayor observed. "We've built scores of day-care centers and nursery schools, and more are on the way, but they still can't cope with the demand."

The demand was understandable, because Pripyat was home to a Soviet technological marvel: the Chernobyl nuclear power plant. The plant was a significant employer, and, per the article, it provided good-paying jobs and energy that was "ecologically much cleaner than thermal plants that burn huge quantities of fossil fuel."

And what of safety concerns? A Soviet minister was asked directly about this matter, and he replied with all the confidence and assuredness of officialdom. "The odds of a meltdown," he boasted, "are one in 10,000 years."

Just months after *Soviet Life* gushed about Pripyat living, of course, the town was left a smoldering, radioactive ruin. At 1:23 a.m. on April 26, 1986, the number 4 reactor at the Chernobyl nuclear power plant melted down, causing an explosion that ripped the building's thousand-ton roof clean off. Soon, Pripyat's skies pulsed with more than four hundred times the radioactive material dropped on Hiroshima.

Maksymilian "Max" Rafailovych Levchin was ten years old, and he was sleeping ninety miles away when Chernobyl exploded. He'd awaken to a life transformed and shaped by the disaster. In those first anxious moments, his parents shipped him and his brother away on a train. During the trip, he was scanned for radiation with a Geiger counter—and set off the machine's alerts. A rose thorn stuck in his shoe turned out to be the radioactive culprit, but for a moment, he panicked when he considered the possible amputation of his foot.

■ ■ ■

Levchin's whole family was affected by the Chernobyl disaster, including his mother, Elvina Zeltsman. She was a physicist and worked in the radiology metrics lab at the Institute for Food Science.

Before Chernobyl, this was a sleepy post. According to her son, she spent her days verifying the safety of Ukraine's (nonradioactive) bread supply. But after Chernobyl, as radioactive food began emerging from Northern Ukraine, her responsibilities grew—as did the urgency of her efforts.

To aid her work, the Soviet government sent Elvina's office two computers: a Soviet DVK-2 and an East German Robotron PC 1715. Levchin occasionally accompanied his mother to work, and at first, he found the computers boring and clunky. That is, until a game arrived for the DVK-2: Stakan (one name given to Tetris, which was created in 1984 by engineers at the Academy of Sciences of the Soviet Union). He was hooked.

Levchin's curiosity soon turned to the Robotron. It came with a Pascal compiler—a program that turned human code into machine commands. Also in the box was a pirated Turbo Pascal version 3.0 manual, which explained the compiler's use. Such texts were rare in the Soviet Union, and for Levchin, the manual became scripture.

Before long, Levchin could write rudimentary programs—and he was entranced. "This notion of you can tell a machine to do things in the future that you're only going to know about later on was this profound realization," he said years later. "From now on, I don't have to know everything to get stuff done. I can just start writing it down, and it'll happen on its own later." Before, Levchin aspired to become a math teacher; now, he boasted that he'd program computers when he grew up.

Levchin relished his early coding and gaming, but the computers weren't there for his enjoyment. They were supposed to help Elvina report radiation in Soviet food. Seeing that her son's technical skills surpassed her own, she put him to work and cut him a deal: the computers were all his—once her tasks were complete.

That didn't leave Levchin much time for leisure-coding. So to preserve precious Robotron time, he devised a system: writing code with a pencil and paper. At the park near his family's home, he'd draft and edit his programs longhand. Once his mom's tasks were complete, Levchin transferred the contents of his notebook into the computer. Then came the machine's verdict: "If I type it out verbatim from my notebook, does it compile and run at start—or do I have to debug it?"

This learning process left exacting standards. "My standard self-definition as a programmer had always been that I started with these decrepit computers," Levchin said. "It was all . . . very procedural programming in various different assembly languages. . . . [It] probably made me slightly more elitist, but certainly made me very tenacious as a developer. I never really had an option to take the easy way out, I guess."

■ ■ ■

Not taking the easy way out was a Levchin family tradition. As Jewish people living in an anti-Semitic state, they worked doubly hard for their achievements—and faced obstacles others did not. One morning, Levchin's father awoke to find a Star of David graffitied on their front door. They told their son that because of his religion, becoming valedictorian of his high school would be his only shot at getting into a top college.

Despite these barriers, the family had accomplished much, with Levchin's maternal grandmother leading the way. Dr. Frima Iosifovna Lukatskaya was a four-foot-eight force of nature who had earned graduate degrees in astrophysics and worked at Kiev's Main Astronomical Observatory of the Academy of Sciences. She advanced the field of astronomical spectroscopy, the science of measuring "eclipsing variables" from stars, and her lengthy papers on the "Autocorrelative Analysis of the Brightness of Irregular and Semi-Regular Variable Stars" and "Properties of Optical Radiation of Variables and Quasars" ran in prestigious journals.

For Levchin, she was fortitude personified—a woman who triumphed in a male-dominated field and a Jewish person who succeeded in a hostile country. Her grit seemed to him almost supernatural. The year Max was born, Lukatskaya was diagnosed with a rare and aggressive form of breast cancer. "She basically said, 'I can't die. I have my grandson here.' So she willed herself to live for another twenty-five years," Levchin said. "I had this living example of someone who'd never surrender under any circumstances."

In the early 1980s, just years after Levchin was born, the Soviet economy was in freefall and the Politburo was in panic. Lukatskaya began to feel the disquieting echoes of World War II, the horrors of which she had seen firsthand. As best as the family could tell, the KGB was monitoring Levchin's father, and the prospect of the government disappearing him loomed large.

Lukatskaya applied for funding from a Jewish refugee agency and made arrangements for the Levchins to immigrate to America. The family's departure was kept a closely guarded secret. "It was one of these crazy years where I knew for about twelve months we were going to leave the country and I couldn't tell anybody," Levchin recalled.

The family left for the airport, pared-down possessions in tow. Despite the balmy July weather, the Levchins arrived at the terminal wrapped in down winter coats to avoid having to declare them. After a final exit interview with a Soviet border agent—who reminded them, in no uncertain terms, that their emigration would be final—they boarded their flight to the United States.

■ ■ ■

Still cloaked in coats, the Levchins disembarked at Chicago's O'Hare International Airport on July 18, 1991, one day before a deadly heat wave struck the city. They sold the coats to an underground dealer for just pennies on the dollar. But the limited proceeds made a big difference. Just before leaving Ukraine, the value of the ruble had collapsed, reducing the family's few-thousand-dollar nest egg to just several hundred dollars.

For his family, immigrating to the United States was risky, but for Levchin, who had just turned sixteen, it was the first step on an epic quest—and the adventure started right away. Levchin had been a strong student, and he wanted to get his Ukrainian high school transcripts verified by the Chicago Board of Education. Rather than ask his parents for help, Levchin hopped on a city bus by himself to complete the mission.

After getting off at the wrong stop, Levchin found himself in the middle of the Cabrini-Green housing projects, then one of the city's deadliest neighborhoods. "I just kind of strolled through and thought, *Oh, there's no one who looks like me here. Hello, fine American people,*" Levchin remembered. "I was completely oblivious . . . I was a skinny Jewish kid with a giant 'fro, and I looked like I wore clothes from the Lenin factory in St. Petersburg—which I did."

Levchin assimilated in fits and starts. Shortly after arriving in America, he fished a broken television out of the trash, which his physicist family fixed up. He could now watch the sitcom *Diff'rent Strokes*, and as he told journalist Sarah Lacy years later, he modeled his English on Gary Coleman's Harlem-raised Arnold Jackson. "Where did you learn English?" one of Levchin's teachers asked him, curious about Levchin's New York–meets–Kiev lilt. "Watchu talkin' 'bout, Mr. Harris?" he replied. The teacher gently suggested Levchin broaden his media diet.

The language and culture were new, but one thing remained: Levchin's love for all things computers. And in America, he finally got one to use at his leisure. It was a gift from a relative, and it did something his old machines didn't: connect to the internet. Levchin soon became consumed by the world wide web and found networks and forums full of kindred digital spirits.

He found them at school, too. At Stephen Tyng Mather High School, on the north side of Chicago, Levchin joined the chess club, helped run the computer club, and played clarinet in the school band along with a friend and later PayPal colleague, Erik Klein, who played trombone. At Mather, Levchin showed the early signs of his hallmark intensity. A friend and later PayPal employee, Jim Kellas, recalled that he and Levchin were once left alone in the back of art class. Bored, they decided to hurl X-ACTO knives into the wall like darts. "Max . . . is a perfectionist. He always wants to be the best at everything he does. And so he's sitting there, and he's putting his finger on it and like, measuring the weight and saying, 'Oh, this would be the perfect position to try to throw them,'" Kellas recalled. "And I'm like, 'No, no, no. Just whip it harder.'"

Levchin excelled in his math and science classes, so when college application season arrived, he approached the Mather guidance counselor brimming with ambition: Levchin wanted to go to "MTI." "I said, 'I really want to get into MTI. You have to get me into MTI.' She's like, 'What the hell is MTI?'"

Levchin was referring, of course, to MIT. His college counselor recommended that he apply to the nearby University of Illinois at Urbana-Champaign (UIUC) instead. Here, too, there was an issue: Levchin had missed UIUC's application deadline. But scanning the requirements, he noticed that the deadline for international students hadn't passed yet. He saw an opening: "I'm international-ish," he said. "I'm not a citizen, came to the US less than two years ago, who is to say?" And under that pretense, UIUC said yes to Levchin.

■ ■ ■

Tired of living at home, Levchin moved to the university two weeks early. The dining halls were still closed, so Levchin ate his first collegiate meal at McDonald's on Green Street. He also tried to keep a low profile.

Before arriving on campus, Levchin had received a letter informing him that a welcoming committee would greet new international students at nearby Willard Airport. It didn't sound optional.

"I was terrified that they would out me as someone who snuck in," he recalled. So, on the day the welcoming committee was to greet him, he left campus and went to the airport, carrying two repacked suitcases in hand. He feigned wide-eyed wonder—as if arriving for the first time to his home of two years, America. "The whole scheme—or scam—was fairly elaborate," Levchin said.

Scam or not, Max Levchin's UIUC admission was a serendipitous product-market fit: a budding, energetic technologist entered one of the world's computing epicenters. For decades, UIUC researchers pioneered digital technology and built some of the world's first social networks. And just as Levchin was playacting the foreign arrival, the UIUC-based National Center for Supercomputing Applications (NCSA) announced a new web browser called Mosaic. Among other improvements, Mosaic added graphics to the web and simplified the browser installation process, changes that mainstreamed the internet and accelerated its growth—with UIUC at the center of it all.

For freshman Max Levchin, the university's computing triumphs were notable, but at the time, he sought what all new college students want: belonging and diversion. He found both at campus Quad Day, where student organizations pitched new arrivals. Levchin spotted a group of people who had all the trappings of nerds, standing next to a computer with a cardboard box around the monitor. The box shielded the screen from the sun—and signaled to future Association for Computing Machinery (ACM) members that sunshine wouldn't interfere with screen time. "These are my people," Levchin concluded.

Indeed, they were. Founded in the mid-1960s, the UIUC ACM chapter quickly became the hub for all things computing on campus and the de facto home for generations of comp sci undergrads. By the time Levchin arrived on campus, the ACM's various special interest groups—known as "SIGs"—tinkered with everything from advanced networking to immersive virtual reality. "I've seen entire [computer science] departments," one ACM-er from that era boasted, "with less computing power than we have in our ACM office alone."

Levchin felt at home here and soon occupied the ACM office in the Digital Computer Lab (DCL) more than his dorm room at Blaisdell Hall. "I can tell you that Eric Johnson's 'Ah Via Musicom' guitar instrumental is exactly how long it is to ride from Blaisdell to DCL on a bicycle at seven o'clock in the morning. I did that many, many times," he confessed to the university's alumni magazine, years later.

■ ■ ■

At ACM, Levchin also met two undergraduates who would later play pivotal roles in his life and at PayPal: Luke Nosek and Scott Banister. They first met when Nosek and Banister walked into the ACM office late one night. They found Levchin pounding away at the keyboard, largely oblivious to their presence. By then, Levchin had become such a fixture there that they became curious about him.

"What are you working on?" Nosek asked.

"I'm making an explosion simulator," Levchin said.

"But what does it do? What purpose does it serve?" Banister asked.

"What do you mean? It's beautiful," Levchin replied. "It's in real time, and it recomputes a random explosion every time."

"Okay, but why?" Nosek asked.

"I don't know. It's cool?" Levchin said.

"It's Friday night. Don't you have somewhere to be?" Banister said.

"No . . . I love this. Don't *you* have somewhere to be?" Levchin answered.

"We're going to go start a company. You should come with us," Nosek replied.

Like Levchin, Luke Nosek grew up in an immigrant family that had fled communism. Originally from Poland, he arrived in the United States in the 1970s.

Nosek was bright, with a technical bent and a love of learning, but he found school stifling. "I started to shift into thinking that my education was about the things that I do—not the things that they're making me do," Nosek said. His mother promised that college would be a freer and more independent learning experience.

Nosek chose UIUC because of the application's brevity, but he wasn't there long before formal education disillusioned him again. "By the end of that [first] year, I was trying to figure out how to get out of class," he said. Nosek dissected the registrar's handbook and determined a degree's minimum requirements. And whenever possible, he allowed his test results to compensate for unexcused absences.

He hunted for others of like mind and soon found ACM. "ACM was . . . a little anti-education rebel group," Nosek said. Even among student organizations, Nosek felt ACM stood apart. "We noticed that the people who were joining other student groups were using them as stepping stones to stay within the system." ACMers didn't care for the system, but they united rebellion with creation by making innovative prototypes and trying niche experiments.

One involved taking the ACM office soda machine online. "We thought one of the more interesting uses of the internet was to put our office pop machine—in the Midwest, it's pop, not soda—on [it]," Nosek said. The machine was nicknamed "Caffeine," and per the Department of Computer Science newsletter, the ACMers had "installed a microcontroller on a vintage Dr Pepper vending machine and hooked it up to the internet so that students could buy soda by swiping their student ID cards."

Nosek and other ACMers were proud of the smart soda machine—both its design and the difficulty of designing it. "It was very difficult to hack into a pop machine and put it on the internet," Nosek said, "We probably could've built eBay in the time it took us to do that."

■■■

Before they met Levchin, ACM had also brought Nosek and Scott Banister together. Banister would become the first in their trio to set off to Silicon Valley, the first to sell a start-up, and an investor in the earliest iteration of PayPal, ultimately serving as a founding board member.

Hailing from Missouri, Banister took to technology early. In high school, and then college, he kindled a passion for creating websites and came to UIUC because of its exceptional reputation in computer science.

By the time he and Nosek first met, Banister also chafed against the confines of traditional education, and he began to treat college as a target to hack. He devised workarounds to UIUC rules, including an audacious scheme in which he created a company, hired himself as an intern, then used the internship to earn course credit.

Iconoclastic, intense, soft-spoken, and with "Jesus-like hair," Banister became a guiding light for both Nosek and Levchin, and the three became fast friends and collaborators. Their first joint venture was a T-shirt for the 1995 Engineering Open House, a student-organized annual conference whose keynote speaker that year was Apple cofounder Steve Wozniak. The trio bonded over producing something small, and it gave them confidence that they might one day make something big.

As they got to know one another, Nosek and Banister gave Levchin a crash course on libertarianism. The two had cofounded a libertarian student group, and Banister coded the group's website. Together they tried to indoctrinate Levchin, encouraging him to attend various libertarian events and read books like Ayn Rand's *The Fountainhead* and Friedrich Hayek's *The Road to Serfdom*. "[Nosek and Banister] were the subversives of our group," Levchin said. "They were burning libertarian love. And I was just like, 'Guys I just want to write some code.' I always felt a little bit like the dumb Beatle."

Levchin's domain was software engineering. Banister would, on occasion, try to write his own code in Perl, a functional but inelegant programming language, half-jokingly referred to as "the internet's duct tape." Levchin was horrified. "Don't bring that near me," he said. "That's gross." For his part, Banister was happy to pass code-writing on to Levchin. "Max is the person that convinced me not to be a programmer," Banister admitted, "because he was so good."

They pooled their respective talents for the group's first serious project, called SponsorNet New Media, an attempt to build classified advertising for websites. The team ran the business off their meager savings, and then, when that money ran out, credit cards. SponsorNet did bring in revenue, though, enough that the team hired employees and signed a lease on office space at the bottom of Huntington Tower, a minor Champaign landmark. "We were students. And so for us to actually go and get an office," Banister remembered, "was . . . a fairly big deal."

To focus on SponsorNet, Banister took the semester off from classes. Levchin and Nosek moonlighted, precariously balancing studies with their SponsorNet duties. The business lasted a little over a year. "We burned through Scott's reasonable, Luke's meager, and my nonexistent personal capital in the course of that year," Levchin later wrote of SponsorNet's demise, "and were now coming up toward the inevitable wall. Multiple fundraising forays proved futile, and our trivial earnings were not enough to keep the server lights on."

Despite its failure, SponsorNet was formative, their first go at hiring a team, creating a product, selling it, and making—or in this case losing—money. "I don't think PayPal would have been possible without it," Nosek said.

■ ■ ■

Levchin—the last remaining believer in school among the three—remembered the SponsorNet and UIUC days fondly: "I was a very happy nerd. I went to all my classes and I loved them. . . . If there's school, programming, girlfriends, and sleep, I traded the last two for the first two."

Levchin's class schedule was thick with technical coursework, but one of his nontechnical courses left a lasting imprint. In a film class, Levchin studied some of the twentieth century's critically acclaimed motion pictures, and he became obsessed with Akira Kurosawa's *Seven Samurai*. "I thought that it was the best movie ever," he remarked. "I'd never seen anything like it."

During a college summer, Levchin binged the three-hour-twenty-seven-minute black-and-white film with abandon. "All you've got is you, the TV, and air-conditioning . . . I watched *Seven Samurai* at least twenty-five times during the course of that summer. I got addicted." As of this writing, Levchin claims to have watched Kurosawa's classic over one hundred times—and calls it his sole source of "management training."

On the social front, Levchin did eventually manage to "acquire a girlfriend," but his devotion to coding complicated the romantic commitment. "I remember once coming over to her house and, right when I got there, going into the bathroom to write code." Knocking on the door, his girlfriend asked, "What are you even doing here?"

"What? We're dating," he replied, confused at the question.

"No, this is not dating. You are coding in my bathroom."

For Levchin, writing code—wherever he did it—was a singular source of wonder and insight. For the world, writing code was becoming a path to wealth and influence.

A fellow UIUC alumnus, Marc Andreessen, helped clear that path. As an undergrad, he cut his teeth at the university's National Center for Supercomputing Applications (NCSA). There, he helped create the Mosaic browser, before taking his talents west and launching the company Netscape. Soon, Netscape landed on the Nasdaq, and Andreessen landed on the cover of *Time* magazine.

"Perhaps nowhere are our young alumni so prominent right now than in the internet arena," a mid-1990s Department of Computer Science newsletter reported. "When we started tracking the original Mosaic developers after they left NCSA, it was possible to keep a file of press clippings on them. In a short time, this task became a full-time job, and eventually we gave up." The clips confirmed the internet's rising cultural clout: in 1994, *Fortune* magazine dubbed Mosaic a product of the year—"right alongside the Wonderbra and Mighty Morphin Power Rangers."

UIUC's comp sci department was suddenly abuzz. "I came to U of I *because* of Marc Andreessen," admitted Jawed Karim, a future PayPal employee and later cofounder of YouTube. In high school, Karim was a Mosaic devotee, and when he learned the browser's origins, he trained his sights on UIUC for college. He got in, and even before freshman classes started, Karim took a job at the NCSA.

Andreessen's rise inspired this generation of Illini engineers: here was evidence that the internet was an economic force, not just an eccentric hobby. "One thing that really shaped me—and probably a lot of other people at Illinois—was this constant sense of opportunity in the air because of Mosaic and subsequently Netscape," Levchin would later tell the UIUC alumni magazine. "It was this notion that students like us built these amazing tools that were not at all contemplated by the industry."

■ ■ ■

Scott Banister became convinced that the internet gold rush was too tempting to miss, and he dropped out of UIUC to pursue his ambitions. Luke Nosek wasn't quite willing to quit college outright, but he redoubled his efforts to earn his diploma and venture west.

With his two close friends California-bound, Levchin had designs on dropping out as well to pursue entrepreneurship full-time. Of course, there was the matter of telling his education-oriented family. The conversation was short: "Your grandma's already dying," his parents told him. "Do you want to accelerate the process?" For the Levchins, a bachelor's degree was simply the first rung on the educational ladder. "Higher education in the Levchin family is . . . a PhD," Levchin told the *San Francisco Chronicle*, years after his parents' admonishment. Shut down, he returned to UIUC to finish his degree.

His West Coast dreams on hold, Levchin had plenty to occupy him. SponsorNet had no sooner failed when Levchin launched his next venture—NetMomentum Software—creating white-label classifieds for newspaper websites. But that venture didn't last long either. The project brought Levchin his first experience of a bitter founder divorce, as he and his cofounder disagreed over the product and its development.

Short on cash, he launched a consulting company to give a professional mien to his one-off programming gigs. He repurposed NetMomentum's remains—its "NM" logo—and called the firm NetMeridian Software, cofounding it with a fellow UIUC student Eric Huss.

A NetMeridian project became one of Levchin's first commercial successes. NetMeridian's ListBot was a primitive email list manager and spiritual predecessor of Mailchimp and SendGrid. The product launched—then thrived, so much so that Levchin and Huss's server was pushing its limits. To keep up with demand, they invested in a several-thousand-dollar Solaris server, which weighed 200 pounds and arrived on a big-rig truck.

NetMeridian scored a second success with a project called Position Agent. Even in the pre-Google days of the late 1990s, the top spots on a Lycos, AltaVista, or Yahoo search were coveted. Position Agent helped website administrators track their rankings. It featured a Levchin engineering coup: a ranking counter, which updated without the user having to reload the webpage.

But NetMeridian's success was both a blessing and a curse. As users grew, infrastructure had to keep pace, but Levchin didn't have cash for ever-bigger servers. So he revisited a funding model he first used during the lean SponsorNet days: he daisy-chained credit cards to finance the company's growth, which saddled him with high-interest debt and marred his credit rating for years.

■ ■ ■

Nominally, Levchin was the founder of NetMeridian, a promising software-as-a-service start-up. In reality, he was an indebted twenty-year-old struggling to stay solvent. Thankfully, coders who could work around the clock were in high demand, and Levchin landed a lucrative gig from John Bedford, the head of a firm called Market Access International (MAI).

Levchin credited Bedford with his "extraction from poverty," through programming jobs that paid several thousand dollars per week. MAI's primary product was a CD-based subscription database of competitive intelligence for consumer products and packaged goods. The money was welcome, even though Levchin found the Microsoft-based software "unbearably bad."

In addition to MAI, Levchin found programming work with the US Army Corps of Engineers, whose research outpost was near campus.

"I got an army-issued ID and got to go into a real army installation," Levchin said. "I'd roll up on a bike and lock it up outside." The pay was fourteen dollars per hour, and Levchin's work gave him a rare vantage point—a chance for the young programmer to bounce around military bases and hobnob with helicopter pilots.

His purview was audio software built into the army's air traffic control system. "By the time I got there, they had this enormous piece of code, built in Pascal, of all things," he said. The original creator of the software was gone, so it fell to Levchin to maintain it. "I got to learn how real systems were built."

The software's users were hardened base commanders—an audience happy with paper-and-pencil flight procedures and skeptical of automation. To address their hesitation, Levchin crafted a user experience that mimicked the paper-and-pencil method. "I once spent a week figuring out how to make a form that would be the exact dimensions of the paper strip," he said.

Levchin's form appeared to scroll as the user typed, but he worried that the jittery screen animation looked too "psychedelic" and "insane." His superiors, though, dubbed it "perfect." "Our people will use it because they know it," they told Levchin.

■ ■ ■

At the Corps, Levchin faced another new experience: aesthetic criticism of his work. "They would tell me that [my program] was perfectly functional—but not cool . . ." Levchin said. That's when he dusted off an old creation: the explosion simulator. By making it his software's screensaver, he added a dash of cool to the dull work of displaying flight patterns.

By now, Levchin had earned a dash of cool, too. He would travel to army bases—Fort Drum in New York and Camp Grayling in Michigan, among others—and return with colorful tales to tell. His time as a grunt contractor also exposed him to darker realities of military life. At one point, he learned about two service members, a gay man and a lesbian woman, who were legally married to each other—but lived with other partners. "It's called an 'army marriage,' " a friend at the base explained to

Levchin. In the days before Don't Ask, Don't Tell—when gays, lesbians, and bisexuals were forbidden from serving in the military—such "army marriages" were common. "I grew up a lot by watching all this," Levchin said.

Soon, one dark reality hit close to home. During Levchin's tenure, the Army Corps of Engineers grew concerned about foreign employees and information security. Unfortunately for the research outpost at Urbana-Champaign, that meant potentially losing the vast share of its programming talent and leaving a complex computer system in the hands of staff unfamiliar with its upkeep.

Levchin was on the chopping block as well, but his manager intervened: Levchin would continue working on his helicopter software, and he'd receive off-the-books payment in the form of computer parts. This worked in the interim, and the Corps ultimately kept its foreign workers, though with a troubling stipulation: non-US citizen contractors would have to wear yellow identification tags. "If you wear one of these badges, you were monitored closely. You could not leave your desk. And if you did, you would have to be escorted," Levchin recalled.

For a Jewish refugee, the badges evoked painful parallels. "I didn't *have* to do this, but I had relatives who did," he said. Levchin quit the US Army Corps of Engineers, though he kept the tag, a fraught relic from the strangest of his college side hustles.

■ ■ ■

By graduation, Levchin was running NetMeridian while simultaneously cramming for final exams and mulling his next step. While his friends prepared for their lives away from Urbana-Champaign, Levchin found himself tethered. NetMeridian was successful, but in a world before cloud computing, the company relied on its massive, immobile server. As long as the server was stuck in Illinois, so was he.

A lifeline came from Scott Banister. By this point, Banister had built and sold a company in Silicon Valley. From his new perch, he brokered the sale of NetMeridian's ListBot and Position Agent products in August 1998. Levchin had officially achieved "an exit" and could now "escape to California"—the first steps of an entrepreneurial journey that would forever alter the digital world.

It began humbly, with Levchin refusing to pay for movers. Instead, he walked into Penske Truck Rental and rented their second-largest truck. He and his roommate, Eric Huss, loaded up everything from the office, including gently used IKEA desks and chairs. They packed the truck and Huss's Toyota Tercel to the brim and began the journey west. "We did zero sightseeing anywhere. I just wanted to get to Palo Alto as quickly as possible," Levchin said.

2

THE PITCH

By his own admission, Peter Andreas Thiel spent his childhood checking off all the right meritocratic boxes: first excelling in high school and then earning admission to Stanford University for his undergraduate and law degrees. "I had been competitively tracked from middle school to high school to college," Thiel later said in a commencement speech, "and by going straight to law school, I knew I would be competing at the same kinds of tests I'd been taking ever since I was a kid, but I could tell everyone that I was doing it for the sake of becoming a professional adult."

His success continued after law school as he won a prestigious appellate court clerkship. But then came a consequential failure: Thiel interviewed for a Supreme Court clerkship and was turned down. For Thiel, the court's rejection was cataclysmic. "It seemed just like the end of the world," he later said. This prompted Thiel's "quarter-life crisis trying to find myself," during which he exited the law, joined Credit Suisse as a derivatives trader, and, in 1996, returned west.

In California, he began anew, raising money from friends and family to launch a hedge fund called Thiel Capital, which focused on global macroeconomic strategy and currency investing. Two years later, as Thiel began the search for the fund's first employee, he leveraged a familiar talent pool. As a Stanford sophomore, Thiel and fellow undergraduate Norman Book had launched an independent student newspaper called the *Stanford Review*.

The *Review*'s first issue established its unrepentant contrarianism: "First of all, we would like to present alternative views on a wide range of current issues in the Stanford community." Thiel was responsible for fundraising, editing, and soliciting pieces. He also penned editorial essays to open each issue, tracts titled "Open or Empty Mind?," "Institutionalized Liberalism," "Western Culture and Its Failures," and "The Importance of Being Honest," among others.

For its supporters, the *Review* offered a breath of fresh air to Stanford's stifling political correctness. For its detractors, the *Review* engaged in disingenuous devil's advocacy, opting for provocation over substance. The *Review* became famous on campus for its political heterodoxy. Its inaugural editor-in-chief would later become infamous in Silicon Valley for his.

The *Review* survived the graduation of its creators, and for Thiel, it proved a lasting link to campus. He attended *Review* events from time to time after graduating, and that's where he first connected with a Stanford senior from Texas named Ken Howery. They chatted briefly and kept in touch.

Soon after, Thiel left Howery a voicemail about joining Thiel Capital. The two met for dinner at a steakhouse in Palo Alto to talk things over. Several hours into the dinner, Howery was impressed—not just by Thiel's depth of knowledge, but also by his range. Howery returned to his dorm and said to his girlfriend, "Peter might be the smartest person I've met in my four years at Stanford. I think I might work for him for the rest of my life."

To Howery's girlfriend, friends, and family, this was a ridiculous declaration. Howery had received lucrative offers from top East Coast financial firms and he would turn all that down for . . . what? Thiel's fund had no employees other than Thiel himself. It didn't even have an office.

But Howery was intrigued nonetheless—if more by the man than his nascent firm. Howery, whose eventual goal was to become an entrepreneur himself, nursed an interest in start-ups and technology, and Thiel seemed plugged in to those worlds. Here was someone worth taking a chance on. So upon graduation, Ken Howery signed up with Thiel Capital.

■■■

Soon thereafter, the dot-com boom began—and right in Thiel and How-ery's backyard. Internet firms started listing themselves alongside legacy American companies on stock exchanges, and billions of dollars came pouring westward. While Thiel had found some success as a global macro investor, he saw in the craze for all things internet a lucrative opportunity to invest in promising technology start-ups.

If Thiel were to flourish in this arena, he believed his firm needed the right address, namely on Sand Hill Road in Menlo Park, the home of Silicon Valley's preeminent venture capital firms. Thiel put Ken Howery on the hunt for office space—Howery's first Thiel Capital assignment. It wasn't an easy one. With the internet land grab underway, Sand Hill Road's low-slung buildings had waiting lists and leased for sums higher than Manhattan offices with sweeping views of Central Park.

Howery traversed Sand Hill Road by foot, hoping in-person so-licitations might generate leads. After a frustrating day of rejections, he came to his final stop—3000 Sand Hill Road—where he saw an older gentleman trimming the hedges. Howery approached him, asking who he might speak to about leasing. As it turned out, the hedge trimmer was also the building's owner—seventy-seven-year-old Tom Ford, a World War II veteran and local real estate baron who could occasionally be found sprucing up his own properties.

Ford led Howery inside 3000 Sand Hill where he pulled out a build-ing schematic. He slid his fingers over the rows of already-filled offices but paused over what looked to Howery like a blip on the page. "Well, I don't have an office," he said, "but there is this broom closet that might work."

Ford walked Howery to the closet. A broom, a mop, several buck-ets, and assorted cleaning supplies lined the walls. Howery accepted on the spot, and Ford put together an unfussy, one-page lease. Howery set to work decorating Thiel Capital's new headquarters. "We got some metal numbers from a hardware store and nailed them to the outside wall," Howery recalled, "so it looked a little less like a closet." In lieu of windows to connect them to the outdoors, Ford gifted his new tenants two wildlife posters to gaze at.

■ ■ ■

By 1998, Thiel Capital had an associate and a Sand Hill Road "office," and it had begun making technology investments. One of its earliest start-up bets: an investment in a company started by a promising University of Illinois graduate named Luke Nosek.

Following graduation, Nosek had trekked to California and crashed on couches as he got situated. Gregarious as ever, he snagged invites to the Valley's countless dot-com parties. At one, he struck up a conversation with a partygoer who had a contact at Netscape, and before long, Nosek had earned himself a job in Netscape's business development department.

For this new job, he attended every conference and tech meet-up he could find. At one such get-together—a gathering of the Silicon Valley Association for Startup Entrepreneurs—Nosek's friend Scott Banister sat on a panel about education reform. After the presentation, a fellow panelist mentioned that Banister and Nosek would enjoy meeting his college roommate, Peter Thiel.

The four met at Hobee's, a local fast-casual chain, the first get-together leading to more. In his emails, Nosek winkingly referred to these gatherings as "the billionaires' breakfast club." "We all believed that the others were going to build big things," Nosek explained. Over meals, they'd discuss the latest developments in technology, philosophy, education, start-ups, and their predictions for the future. It was here that Nosek learned of Thiel's interest in start-up investing.

Well before joining Netscape, Nosek had been bitten by the start-up bug. Once he became a full-time company employee at a big company, the infection grew worse. "I did nothing [at Netscape]," he confessed. One year later, he was let go amid layoffs at the company.

But joblessness opened the door to creating a company of his own. His idea was called Smart Calendar, a digital upgrade for the dead-tree relic of yesteryear, and Nosek persuaded Thiel to invest. "In retrospect, just about everything was wrong with it," Thiel later said of Smart Calendar. The saturated e-calendar space had "like two hundred companies" competing for dominance. Facing headwinds from without and conflict within—Nosek had a falling out with his cofounder—Smart Calendar shuttered.

Unlike other failures, Nosek agonized over Smart Calendar, in part because it had cost his new friend Peter Thiel money. "In my mind, it hurt my relationship with Peter, because I lost his money," Nosek recalled. But for Thiel, the value of Smart Calendar wasn't as an investment so much as a crash course in start-ups. Nosek had shared the blow-by-blow account of the company's rise and fall, walking Thiel through the intricacies of internet marketing, customer acquisition, and product design.

Thiel would later cite his Smart Calendar investment as a rich vein of learning, a failure whose lessons—including choosing cofounders wisely and minimizing competition—paved the way for PayPal's success. For Nosek, Thiel's willingness to continue to speak to him in the aftermath of Smart Calendar's demise was a lesson, too: it illustrated that losing money in Silicon Valley wasn't like losing money elsewhere. Here, you earned points for effort—not just for an exit.

■ ■ ■

With Nosek busy building his company and Thiel his fund, Max Levchin searched for a more basic asset: air-conditioning. His Palo Alto efficiency apartment wasn't equipped, so he had to improvise. Levchin discovered that if he milled about Stanford's campus and attended lectures open to the public—where he'd sit in the back and close his eyes—he could enjoy a reprieve from the heat.

On one such A/C mission, Levchin saw an advertisement for a lecture by Peter Thiel. The lecture topic—financial markets and currency trading—didn't especially grab Levchin's interest, but he had heard about Thiel from Luke Nosek and knew that Thiel invested in start-ups. When Levchin arrived at the classroom in Stanford's Terman Engineering

Center, he was surprised to find a smaller crowd than anticipated, with the handful of attendees sitting seminar-style around Thiel.

Small crowd notwithstanding, Thiel's talk impressed Levchin. *Wow, if I ever do anything in the financial world*, Levchin thought, *that's the dude I want to hang with*. He saw in Thiel's financial acumen a reflection of something else, too: *This is obviously not a computer scientist*, Levchin thought, *but he is a nerd*.

After the lecture finished, Levchin hung around to try to bend Thiel's ear. Locked in what looked to be a painful, impromptu fundraising pitch, Levchin could see that "[Thiel] needed to be bailed out," so he intervened. "Hey, Peter, I'm Max . . . I'm friends with Luke."

The other interlocutor took the hint, and Thiel turned his attention to Levchin. "So what do you do?" he asked.

"I'm probably going to start a company. That's what I did in Illinois," Levchin said, explaining that his most recent venture, NetMeridian, had recently been acquired.

"Oh great! We should have breakfast," Thiel replied.

The next morning, Levchin misjudged the distance to the agreed-upon meeting spot—Hobee's. Sprinting to make up time, he arrived drenched in sweat and gasped an apology. Already nursing his favorite Hobee's smoothie—a Red, White & Blue—Thiel looked unfazed. Levchin sat down, and Thiel commenced grilling him about his start-up ideas.

Levchin's first pitch was an upgrade on a product sold by Market Access International, the firm that gave him contract work in college. MAI sold insights on physical and retail goods, and Levchin thought there might be a market for online advertising databases, too. "Somebody ought to scrape the web and get these banners collected and package them into a database. There's an opportunity to create Market Access [for advertising] online," he said.

"Okay. Interesting," Thiel replied.

Sensing Thiel's muted reaction, Levchin moved to his next concept. During college, he had built an application for the PalmPilot—then the world's hottest handheld device—to solve a problem for friends who ran big computer systems. These system administrators relied on credit-card-sized key cards for security. Each computer was tied to a key card, which spit out a onetime passcode, but this left Levchin's sysadmin friends carrying a bulky assortment of key cards.

Levchin called his creation SecurePilot, and it turned the password generation of multiple key cards into a single application on a handheld device. "I basically emulated the whole thing on a PalmPilot so my friends were able to throw out their stupid devices," Levchin said.

This was no small feat. The key cards did complex cryptography and produced codes quickly. SecurePilot had to keep up to avoid annoying users, but the PalmPilot's weak processor made speed a technical challenge. "There is some art involved in how you speed [the program] up—both from the user interface perspective and the math perspective," he later told interviewer Jessica Livingston. "In math you have to see how much you can squeeze out of it, and in the user interface, you have to make it feel like it's not taking that long."

SecurePilot conquered both math and art—and earned paying customers to boot. Levchin charged $25 per download, and by the time he sat down at Hobee's with Thiel, Levchin had built a profitable product. Levchin explained to Thiel that SecurePilot's modest success hinted at something bigger—a business opportunity at the intersection of handheld devices and mobile security. He prophesied a future in which the PalmPilot and similar handheld devices would become indispensable.

Thiel was skeptical. "I've seen these devices," he said, "but what are they good for?"

"Well, right now they're good for note-taking," Levchin conceded, "but I believe one day these things will replace the notebook, the Dictaphone, email-reading on the desktop . . ." At some point, he suggested, everyone would be carrying a supercomputer in their pockets.

Thiel pressed further. "So what's the point?"

"The point is right now there's no encryption. If someone steals my PalmPilot and knows my PIN, I'm screwed. They'd get everything," Levchin explained. "You need to encrypt this stuff."

Thiel began to see the potential. But he had a question, a core challenge in the field: It was one thing to generate single-use passwords, but could the PalmPilot's processor handle encrypting emails, documents, and other files? Did Levchin's ideas outstrip the technology at hand?

"That's exactly my point," replied Levchin. As a student, he had pored over the academic research on small-device cryptography, and he'd brought it to life with SecurePilot. Efficient mobile encryption had become an obsession and an area in which Levchin felt he had a competitive advantage.

All of this, it seemed, persuaded Thiel, who flipped from skeptic to supporter. "That's a good idea. You should do that. And I'd like to invest."

■ ■ ■

Levchin and Thiel met regularly for the next several weeks—meetings Levchin later called "ultra-nerd dates." One took place at Printers Inc. Bookstore in Palo Alto, where they spent hours volleying brain teasers back and forth. "I'd throw one at him and see if I could make him squirm," Levchin remembered, "and then he'd throw one at me."

The tone was friendly, but with a competitive undercurrent—which foreshadowed the later culture at PayPal. Both Thiel and Levchin honed their puzzle-solving prowess, and neither liked to lose. Levchin recalled one problem Thiel posed early on: *Take any positive integer. Some have an odd number of unique divisors, and some have an even number of unique divisors. Describe the subset of all z integers that have exactly an even number of divisors.**

Levchin wrestled with it for four or five minutes. He remembers "initially over-complicat[ing] it" and accidentally "giving a subset of the subset," but eventually, he arrived at the right answer. Even with his extra half-step, Thiel was impressed.

Then, Levchin fired one back: *Imagine you have two ropes of variable*

---

*Answer: Find the number of perfect squares less than z and subtract that number from $z - 1$.

density. If you set either rope on fire, despite burning at varying speeds, it will be entirely gone in one hour. Using the two ropes, measure exactly 45 minutes.*

Thiel answered correctly.

This elaborate sussing-out went on for hours: brain teasers met by math problems one-upped by logic questions. Levchin and Thiel discovered a common, quirky interest—it was a particular kind of person who turned math into sport. "Peter wasn't technical," Nosek said of Thiel, "but he was an intellectual in the way that Max was in that they were both always trying to understand things. They enjoyed pushing themselves to the limits of their own minds."

Thiel and Levchin's early meetings foreshadowed the process Pay-Pal would use to evaluate candidates. Some questions, like the burning ropes, became staples of the company's interviews. "They sound like cute puzzles," Levchin explained, "but underneath they are very base computer science problems . . . It behooves you to step back and think: This is a puzzle; it's meant to be solved quickly. If you're digging deep, you're doing it wrong."

Levchin recalled one interview with a promising candidate who had a PhD in mathematics. Given a puzzle, the mathematician began scribbling, his calculations occupying an entire whiteboard and then the office's glass door. For Levchin, the candidate's long and winding process was a definitive knock. *This is your future as a software engineer: You'll get it right, but it will probably take too long*, he thought.

Using esoteric puzzles in interviews didn't make PayPal unique—plenty of technology firms made candidates suffer through them. And not all of PayPal's alums believed this process ideal. "I'm not a great puzzle solver . . . but I like solving problems," PayPal engineer Erik Klein admitted. "There is a difference between puzzles and problems. We did do a lot of puzzles in interviews, but I feel like the puzzle solving might have filtered away people that were good problem solvers." Klein remembered

---

*Answer: Simultaneously light both ends of one rope and one end of the other rope. The first rope will burn out in 30 minutes. When it does, light the unlit end of the other rope. When the second rope burns out, 45 minutes will have passed.

being "all-in on it" at the time but reflected that "the elder version of me sees that that was probably not the best way to hire."

One engineer, Santosh Janardhan, could see the pros and cons of live-action puzzle solving. "We probably lost out on good people, because somebody was having a bad day. But the people we ended up hiring were at least extremely high IQ and thought like us. So we might have lost out on some really good talents, but the people who ended up coming in . . . instinctively gelled. So maybe it was groupthink, but for a small group of people to achieve something and achieve it really fast, it was actually, in hindsight, a masterful thing to do."

Advantageous to hiring or not, what made PayPal different was that the puzzle-solving spirit pervaded its corporate culture. One UX designer remembered the engineering team's love of problem solving. "It's just really, like, the joy of coming up with a beautiful solution," she said. To spark such joy, the company included brain teasers in its weekly employee newsletter, correct answers earning shout-outs in the next issue.

■ ■ ■

Several rounds of coffee and puzzles later, Thiel Capital issued a $100,000 bridge loan in December 1998 to seed Levchin's nascent firm. It wasn't much, but it was a start. Levchin now had an angel investor and the makings of a company. He also had in mind the perfect CEO: John Powers, an IT expert who worked at the software company JD Edwards.

They had met at a mobile technology conference in Oak Brook, Illinois, while Levchin was still in college. At the conference, Powers was standing in line at the Motorola booth, armed with questions; nearby, he heard Levchin addressing his queries. *It seems like this kid over here knows more than the guys running the booth*, Powers remembered thinking.

They grabbed coffee nearby, where Levchin sketched an impromptu framework for the problem Powers had planned to pose to the Motorola people. Powers was struck by Levchin: college students weren't exactly regular attendees at enterprise technology conferences, nor were they this sharp.

Levchin remembered Powers as "tall, gangly, wacky . . . and a good-hearted guy," someone who "was always a decade ahead of his time." Powers had come to the conference because of his interest in mobile computing. The first generation of mobile devices—the PalmPilot, the Apple Newton, the Casio Cassiopeia, the Sharp Wizard, and so on—had just burst onto the scene. When he met Levchin, Powers had begun reading up on wireless standards and mobile device security. "You could see the evolution coming," he remembered.

Shortly after the conference, Powers pitched the idea of starting a mobile enterprise consulting practice to his bosses at JD Edwards. But promising though it all seemed to him, the field of mobile computing was in its infancy, and his bosses demurred. Still, Powers remained excited by mobile, even if his employers were not, and he took a leave of absence to start a consulting firm.

In need of an associate, Powers called Levchin and offered him mobile programming contract work at $15 per hour, which Levchin gladly accepted. Their first client was the Hyster Company, a lessor of forklifts and tow tractors. Hyster's service technicians needed a way to bill clients while in the field, and Levchin wrote software for the field techs to track time and money spent on parts.

More companies soon hired the young firm, including Peoria, Illinois-based Caterpillar Inc., and another company from a wholly different industry: Avon cosmetics. It was Avon, Powers recalled, that saw the smoothest roll-out of its program. In a short time, Levchin's software facilitated makeup sales *and* forklift repairs.

With paying clients, Powers began arranging investor meetings. He and Levchin pitched the company to dozens of Chicago investors, but found no takers. "They were happy to fund a company that was somehow going to use the internet to send pet food or make T-shirts, but we got nothing, zilch," Powers recalled.

In retrospect, the pair was making a tough sell: In 1998, many businesses had only just begun to swap paper-and-pencil for keyboards-and-mice, and low-power, handheld devices like the PalmPilot felt like an even bigger leap—untried, unworkable, and potentially unsafe. "We were kind of naïve," Powers admitted.

Though their pitches amounted to nothing, presenting their ideas and winning small contracts was instructive for Levchin. At one point, the duo were invited to the headquarters of Palm Computing—the then-Mecca of mobile computing.

Powers arrived in a blue blazer, khaki pants, and a necktie. Levchin strolled into the meeting sporting shorts, flip-flops, and a T-shirt bearing the words "WINDOWS SUCKS." Before the meeting, Powers expressed concern about Levchin's attire—but Levchin pushed back on substantive grounds. "John, you don't understand," Levchin replied, "they don't like Microsoft either."

Indeed, they didn't—the Palm Computing office hosted many ex-Apple employees, who shared Levchin's dim view of Microsoft. Any concerns regarding Levchin's casual appearance were also put to rest as he rattled off answers to difficult technical questions. He calculated problems put to him about device throughput and processor speed with ease. Even the most seasoned technologists in the room sensed that his outfit belied his talent.

Still, the Palm meeting ended like the others, with good wishes and ample enthusiasm—but not much else. As Levchin finished up college and shipped out west, he and Powers stayed in touch and continued working on one-off consulting projects.

■ ■ ■

In late 1998, Levchin reached out to Powers again—their mobile company finally had a backer. It was time to build the security products they had always envisioned. Powers began commuting back and forth between Palo Alto and his home in Illinois.

This effort arguably represented PayPal's earliest iteration: revived after multiple rejections, the company now boasted an angel investor with a closet-office (Thiel), a CTO without air-conditioning (Levchin), and a CEO with a 2,100-mile commute (Powers).

Powers suggested calling the company Fieldlink, which captured the gist of the Avon and Hyster projects and sounded credible. Thiel, Levchin, and Powers began brainstorming the company's products and pitching prospective investors.

Fieldlink's trio quickly gelled as a team. For work breaks, Levchin, Thiel, and Powers played chess and card games, and in these casual contests, Powers saw a striking similarity between Thiel and Levchin: cutthroat competitiveness. Once, sitting at Printers Inc., Powers bested Thiel at a coin game called 3-5-7 (also known as "the matchstick game"). Frustrated, Thiel paused the contest to run the game's underlying math with paper and pencil. Calculations complete, Thiel beat Powers in every subsequent round. "I learned a lot about Peter from doing that," Powers recalled. "He's going to make decisions based on some type of scientific basis, rather than just shooting the gun and see where it goes later."

Powers was enjoying his time out west building a budding technology start-up—but he was also running himself ragged. He would land in California on Friday night, where he spent the full weekend grinding away with Levchin and Thiel. Then, on Sunday evening, he'd take a red-eye back to Chicago, stopping home in the early morning to greet his wife and change clothes before heading back to work.

This early structure suited Levchin: with Thiel and Powers handling business and fundraising, he was left alone to write code. But weeks in, Levchin saw the strain on Powers, and he concluded that the company needed a full-time, local CEO. The trio—Thiel, Levchin, and a tired Powers—went to dinner at Caffe Verona in Palo Alto. Levchin left it to Thiel to start the difficult conversation, and Thiel gently told Powers that if he couldn't move out to Palo Alto, he wouldn't be able to continue as CEO. Thiel acknowledged the difficulty of uprooting a newly settled life (Powers had recently married) for the uncertainty and chaos of a start-up across the country.

Powers took it as well as he could. "I was a little upset, because I liked the intensity and the fun of it," he said, "but looking back, it was completely sensible." Things ended amicably, and as the company expanded,

Levchin and Thiel even turned to Powers to vouch for their credibility. He did so with enthusiasm.

In this first employee transition, Levchin saw firsthand the skills Thiel brought to the table. Early on, Levchin and Powers divided the company equity equally. But with Powers's departure along with Thiel's investment came a thorny issue: they would each have to dilute their ownership stake, and the company would need enough equity available to dole out to prospective recruits.

Levchin turned to Thiel to handle the sensitive negotiation, and Thiel did so. "I thought, *Wow, that's what a hard-core Jedi mind trick looks like*. I basically said nothing for three hours, and I just watched Peter explain why [John] has to have less equity." Levchin began to wonder whether Thiel might play a bigger role than just as a Fieldlink angel investor.

"CEOs and founders have to have someone they can actually trust," John Malloy, a later PayPal investor, observed. "There are so many people who are good at being good to you when things are great, but when shit's not really working, who do you objectively talk to? [Levchin and Thiel] had each other. They burn so brightly, and so differently. They are one of the best examples of a great partnership."

3

THE RIGHT QUESTIONS

Elon Musk's adventures in finance began in college. He and his brother, Kimbal, had emigrated from South Africa in the late 1980s, and together they attended Queen's University in Kingston, Ontario. To fill their empty Rolodex, they started cold-calling people they read about in the newspaper.

At one point, Elon came across an article about Dr. Peter Nicholson, an executive at the Bank of Nova Scotia. Nicholson was educated in physics and operations research and brought his scientific acumen into the world of politics, policy, and finance. He was elected to Nova Scotia's House of Assembly and served as the deputy chief of staff for policy in the Office of the Prime Minister of Canada. Over a diverse career, Nicholson had worked on everything from punch-card computer problems to rights-sharing agreements among Canada's fishing companies.

Musk was intrigued, so he contacted the article's author, who shared Nicholson's phone number, which Musk promptly dialed. "I think it's fair to say that Elon is the only person who ever called me out of the blue and asked me for a job," Nicholson remembered. Impressed by Musk's gumption, he agreed to meet Elon and Kimbal for a meal.

Over lunch, they discussed "philosophy, economics, the way the world works," and Musk confirmed his perception from the article that Nicholson was "super smart . . . a giant brain." They broached the subject of an internship, and Nicholson said he had one spot on his small

Scotiabank team. Feeling that Nicholson's scientific interests mirrored his own, Elon chose to take the spot, and Nicholson took him under his wing as his sole intern.

Peter Nicholson earned a distinction, too. He'd serve as one of Elon Musk's only bosses.

■ ■ ■

Musk joined Scotiabank because of Nicholson, not to become a financier. Nicholson joined the bank for similar reasons, lured not by finance but by the firm's CEO, Cedric Ritchie. Ritchie had installed Nicholson at the head of a small internal consulting team. "We were a little like DARPA [the Defense Advanced Research Projects Agency]," Nicholson remembered. "We were this little crazy organization off to the side."

For Musk, the unit's nineteen-year-old intern, it was an opportunity to see finance from the top perch, and he showed early promise. "He was very bright, very curious," Nicholson recalled, "and he was already a very, very big-picture thinker." Outside of work, Nicholson and Musk would spend "a lot of time talking about puzzles, talking about physics and the meaning of life and the essence of the universe." Even then, Nicholson recalled, one of Musk's interests stood above the rest: "His real love was space."

Over the course of Musk's internship, Nicholson gave him progressively more demanding assignments, including a research project on Scotiabank's Latin American debt portfolio. Throughout the 1970s, North American banks had lent billions to developing countries, including several in Latin America, believing the emerging markets' swift growth would earn them a tidy profit. But growth never came, and by the 1980s, both banks and countries faced a looming debt crisis.

Several proposed fixes failed. Many experts, including Nicholson, believed the best solution was to convert the bad debt into bonds—to securitize it. The banks would agree to an extended repayment period at a fixed interest rate. In exchange, the new bonds would be tradeable on the open market and could theoretically increase in value if growth returned. Even if it didn't, this scenario was preferable to the disastrous alternative: dozens of countries and banks defaulting, sending the global economy into a tailspin.

The US Treasury secretary, Nicholas Brady, put his support behind the proposal, and the resulting bonds were dubbed "Brady Bonds." Denominated in US dollars, they were backstopped by the US Treasury, the IMF, and the World Bank. In 1989, Mexico reached the first Brady Agreement, and other countries followed suit. "A secondary market developed for them quite quickly," Nicholson said.

■ ■ ■

In truth, Nicholson didn't imagine much coming of the Latin American debt assignment, but he felt it was complex enough to occupy his unit's hyperkinetic intern. However, no sooner had Musk begun his deep dive into the market for Brady Bonds when he spotted an opportunity.

He calculated the theoretical backstop value of one country's bonds but found that the debt itself could be purchased from rival banks for much less. Unbeknownst to Nicholson, Musk dialed up US firms—Goldman Sachs, Morgan Stanley, and others—to ask about the debt's pricing and availability. "I was literally, like, nineteen or something," Musk remembered. "[I would say] 'I'm calling from the Bank of Nova Scotia, and I'm curious as to what you would sell this debt for . . .'"

Musk saw a lucrative arbitrage: What if Scotiabank bought bad, cheap debt from other banks and then waited until it converted into Brady Bonds? The gains could be in the billions, and it was theoretically guaranteed by the US Treasury, the IMF, and the World Bank. He took the idea to Nicholson. "I was like, 'We just buy up all this debt. These people are fools. It's a no-lose proposition,'" Musk said. "'We could just instantly make $5 billion. Right now.'"

The powers that be didn't see it that way. While other Canadian banks sold their developing-world debt at steep losses, Scotiabank had bucked convention and held, with red ink to show for it. In its CEO's view, the bank had plenty of Brazilian and Argentinian debt—to the tune of billions of dollars. Having already taken heat from his board for the exposure, he wasn't about to ramp up risks—particularly for a bet on new and uncertain Brady Bonds.

Musk was dumbfounded. In his view, the past was no guide; Brady Bonds *were* new, and that was the point. "In fact, that was why the debt was for sale—because there were so many other bank CEOs who had that same absurd notion," Musk said. "It blew my mind that there was this massive arbitrage opportunity just lying there, and they did nothing."

Nicholson offered a more charitable assessment of Ritchie's decision. Because it had held on to its Latin American debt, Scotiabank was far more exposed than its competitors. "What Elon may not have fully appreciated at the time," Nicholson said, "was that it was bad enough that Scotia wasn't prepared to sell its debt at a loss. But to think of buying? That would have been a bridge too far."

To Nicholson, both Ritchie and Musk demonstrated similar foresight—Ritchie in his conviction that Scotiabank keep its developing-world debt, and Musk in his belief that they acquire more. Both were eventually proven right: between 1989 and 1995, thirteen more countries reached Brady deals to exchange debt for tradeable bonds.

For Musk, the Scotiabank internship proved "how lame banks are." Fear of the unknown had cost them billions, and in his later efforts at X.com and PayPal, he'd return to this experience as evidence that the banks could be beaten. "If they're this bad at innovation, then any company that enters the financial space should not fear that the banks will crush them—because the banks do not innovate," Musk concluded.

■ ■ ■

Musk left Scotiabank with a dim view of banks, but with a lifelong friend and mentor in Peter Nicholson. He even followed in Nicholson's footsteps, blending science and business studies in school. Musk transferred from Queen's to the University of Pennsylvania and pursued dual degrees in physics and finance.

Later, Musk admitted to studying business as a hedge. "I was concerned that if I didn't study business, I would be forced to work for someone who did study business, and they would know some special things that I didn't know," he told the American Physical Society newsletter. "That didn't sound good, so I wanted to make sure that I knew those things, too." If he redid his studies, he admitted, he might have ditched the business classes altogether.

Physics, he felt, was rigorous. "I was in an advanced securities analysis class," Musk recalled, "and they were teaching people what matrix math is. I was like, *Wow, okay. If you can do physics math, then business math is super easy.*" Crucially, Musk's physics classmates also shared his extracurricular interests: for someone who once referred to himself as "Nerdmaster 3000," it was a relief to find others who relished Dungeons & Dragons, video games of every kind, and computer programming.

Though he studied it formally at UPenn, Musk's passion for physics predated college. "I had an existential crisis when I was twelve or thirteen," he later said, "and trying to figure out what does it all mean, why are we here, is it all meaningless—that sort of thing." In the midst of this crisis, Musk discovered a science fiction novel that offered hope: Douglas Adams's *The Hitchhiker's Guide to the Galaxy*.

The novel's protagonist, Arthur Dent, survives Earth's destruction and begins an intergalactic quest to locate the planet Magrathea. During his adventures, he learns of an old species of "hyperintelligent, pandimensional beings" who had constructed a computer dubbed "Deep Thought" to seek an answer to the "Ultimate Question to Life, the Universe, and Everything." *The Hitchhiker's Guide to the Galaxy* soothed Musk's existential worries by suggesting that framing the right questions was as important as divining the answers. "A lot of times," Musk explained, "the question is harder than the answer, and if you can properly phrase the question, then the answer is the easy part."

To Musk, physics asked the right questions. After Adams, he started to read the work of Nobel Prize–winning physicist Dr. Richard Feynman, among others. Once Musk started college, he immersed himself in physics further; in his Wharton business classes, he wrote well-received papers on the financial case for ultracapacitors and space-based energy systems.

Musk relished physics questions in his classes, but he worried about the reality of physics work after graduation. "I thought I might get stuck in some bureaucracy at a collider," he said, "and then that collider could get canceled like the Superconducting Super Collider, and then that would suck." But what were his alternatives? Many Wharton classmates were cashing in their signing bonuses as new recruits for banks and consulting firms. He'd been there and done that; those traditional routes were even less appealing to him than grinding away in a hapless collider's hierarchy.

Ultimately, Musk selected a path embraced by indecisive undergraduates since time immemorial: graduate school. He applied and was admitted to Stanford's graduate degree program in materials science and engineering.

■ ■ ■

Dr. Elon Musk. This was the ticket—or was it? Musk knew he wasn't cut out for corporate life, but even as he gained admission to the prestigious program at Stanford, he considered alternatives to academia.

During his later collegiate summers, Musk worked two Silicon Valley internships simultaneously. By day, he worked at Pinnacle Research Institute, a company researching space-based weapons, advanced surveillance systems, and alternative fuel sources for cars. At night, he was off to the buzzy video game start-up Rocket Science Games. "He was the 'disc flipper' that came in at night while the game software was rendering," noted his supervisor, Mark Greenough.

These internships exposed Musk to the world of technology start-ups, and he found people who, like him, labored around the clock, relished video games, and solved math puzzles for fun. As in his physics classes, to be a nerd here was a feature, not a bug. Most importantly for Musk, though, he saw how his work could marry ideas with impact. At Pinnacle, the researchers weren't publishing-or-perishing; they were *producing*—crafting technologies to change cars forever.

Musk's Bay Area summer spawned blue-sky brainstorming with his brother, Kimbal—they briefly considered building a social network for medical doctors. While the idea amounted to nothing, it planted the start-up seed. And they were keenly aware of the opportunity sprouting all around them. Mere months before Musk came west, Stanford graduate students Jerry Yang and David Filo toiled in a trailer and created "Jerry and David's Guide to the World Wide Web," which they renamed "Yet Another Hierarchical Officious Oracle" and later shortened to "Yahoo." In 1994, an ex–hedge funder left New York, moved to the Seattle suburbs with his wife, and launched Cadabra Inc. in their garage. He, too, would later rechristen his company—Amazon.com.

Computer programming wasn't new to Musk—he'd been coding since boyhood. At age thirteen, Musk sold a coding project, a video game called Blastar, in which the player must "destroy an alien space freighter, which is carrying deadly Hydrogen Bombs and Status Beam Machines." Entrepreneurship was old hat for Musk, too. During his Canada years, he founded Musk Computer Consulting, which sold computers and word processors. The company was "STATE OF THE ART," per an ad in the Queen's student newspaper, and implored customers to call "anytime day or evening."

From where he sat, the brains behind Yahoo and Amazon were just a few years older than him and surely no wiser. But starting his own venture still felt risky, particularly with a Stanford graduate school acceptance in hand. So Musk sought a middle ground by applying for a job at the hot dot-com of the moment: Netscape.

Musk didn't receive a reply from Netscape—but he also wasn't rejected outright. So he decided to venture to Netscape's offices and loiter in the lobby. Perhaps there, he could start a conversation that would lead to something. This didn't pan out either. "I was too shy to talk to anyone," he later told Digg founder Kevin Rose. "So I'm just, like, standing in the lobby. It was pretty embarrassing. I was just sort of standing there trying to see if there was someone I could talk to and then I was too scared to talk to anyone, so then I left."

Netscape off the table, he wrestled with whether to attend grad school or start an internet company. "I was trying to think, *What would most influence the future? What are the problems we have to solve?*" he said. While at UPenn, he made a short list of the impactful fields of the near future: the internet, space exploration, and sustainable energy. But how would he—Elon Musk—best position himself to influence the fields that would "influence the future?"

He approached Peter Nicholson for guidance. They discussed Musk's next steps on a long walk around Toronto. Nicholson told him, "Look Elon, the dot-com rocket is ascending. The time is perfect to take your good idea and take a risk with it, because you can always go back and do your PhD. That opportunity is going to stay on the table." Coming from Nicholson—a Stanford PhD himself—the advice carried weight.

Still, Musk left the University of Pennsylvania in the summer of 1995 intending to start his Stanford graduate program. But upon returning to the Bay Area, Nicholson's advice grew harder to ignore. "I would spend several years watching the internet go through this incredibly rapid growth phase and that would be really difficult to handle—so I really wanted to be doing something," Musk said. He requested a deferment from Stanford to begin his program in January 1996 instead of September 1995.

Though cast today as one of business's consummate risk-takers, the Musk of 1995 was conflicted about abandoning grad school. "I'm not a born risk-taker," he told an interviewer for UPenn's *Pennsylvania Gazette* just years after. "I also had a scholarship and financial aid, which I'd lose." Upon receiving his deferral, Musk's Stanford department contact reportedly told him, "Well, give it a shot, but I'll bet we'll see you in three months."

■ ■ ■

In 1995, Musk began writing software for a website uniting vector maps, point-to-point directions, and business listings. Musk brought his brother on board, and together they bootstrapped the company with their own savings and several thousand dollars from Greg Kouri, a Canadian businessman they had befriended, who came aboard as a cofounder.

Kouri had been approached by Maye Musk, Elon and Kimbal's mother, who told him about her sons and their ambitions. Kouri passed away in 2012 at age fifty-one, but his widow recalled her late husband sharing the story of his bet on the Musk brothers. "Maye told him, 'I have these two sons and they have this idea . . . ,'" Jean Kouri shared. In time, Kouri would play a vital role in the business—and in the lives of the Musk brothers. Several years older and with a nose for business, he lived with Kimbal and Elon during these early formative years. "I think Elon and Kimbal loved him like a big brother," said Jean Kouri, "because he became like their big brother." Musk spoke of Kouri with affection. "Greg was really one of my closest friends," he recalled. He called Kouri "a trickster with a heart of gold," someone who "used his powers for good."

The team rented a spartan Palo Alto office space, drilling a hole through the floor to secure internet access from their downstairs neighbors. Musk slept at the office and showered at the nearby YMCA. (In this, Musk mimicked his maternal grandfather, a chiropractor named Dr. Joshua Haldeman. "During [World War II], Dr. Haldeman was so busy with his political and economic research that he had little time for his practice and lived at the YMCA.")

The Musks named their new company Global Link Information Network and formally registered the business in early November 1995. The company's first-ever press release demonstrated the brothers' inexperience—they had failed to settle on a name for the product before announcing it. The February 2, 1996, edition of the *San Francisco Chronicle* ribbed them: "The new product is called either Virtual City Navigator or Totalinfo, which we keep wanting to read as Totalfino, the name of a new Italian soft drink," the item in the Datelines section read. "The accompanying letter says it is Global Link's first news release, and this is evident in a number of ways, not the least being that it's hard to tell whether the product is named Totalinfo or Virtual City Navigator."

Whatever was in a name, the *San Francisco Chronicle* gave the two unknowns their first mention in American media: "The lads are from South Africa, where, Kimbal said, they owned the third IBM PC in the country, an XT with a mere 8K of memory and no hard drive. Datelines is suitably awed." Sarcasm aside, the Musk brothers had reason to be proud—they had earned national press coverage within months for something they'd built.

Things moved rapidly from there. After multiple failed pitches for venture capital, Global Link secured a $3.5-million investment round led by Mohr Davidow Ventures. In fundraising, yet again, the brothers' greenness showed. "They were originally asking for a ten-thousand-dollar investment for 25 percent of their company," investor Steve Jurvetson later shared with author Ashlee Vance for his biography of Musk. "That is a cheap deal! When I heard about the three-million-dollar investment, I wondered if Mohr Davidow had actually read the business plan." Musk was astonished, too. "I thought they were on crack," he said to a journalist two years later. "They don't know anything about us and they're going to hand over $3.5 million?"

The brothers ditched Global Link, Totalinfo, and Virtual City Navigator, and a branding firm devised a new name for the company, Zip2. They registered the www.zip2.com URL on March 24, 1996, and recruited an experienced CEO, Rich Sorkin, to run the business.

At first, they had set out to build a consumer website—an aspiring Yahoo, Lycos, or Excite—with a focus on neighborhood shops and stores. But selling internet ads to small businesses proved a challenge in 1996, with many mom-and-pops uninterested. So Zip2 pivoted and explored partnerships with big telecom companies like Pacific Bell, US West, and GTE to help them expand their internet ad offerings. In July 1996, Kimbal Musk told a trade publication that "telecom companies have a lot of experience and strength in marketing, but not a lot in developing internet technology." Zip2 could provide the telecoms with internet bench strength, but when the telecom companies signaled that they wanted to run internet advertising in-house, the Zip2 team abandoned that approach, too.

Zip2 then recast itself as "a world-class technology platform that enables media companies to extend their local franchise and dominate on-line local advertising." In practice, this meant boosting media companies' digital ad sales and building local city guides. The concept showed promise—Zip2 signed deals with big players like Knight Ridder and Landmark Communications. One influential trade publication declared Zip2 "Newspaperdom's new superhero," writing that the "mild-mannered software firm has muscled its way to the front of the online directory pack to lead the newspaper industry's counter-attack against the Telcos and Microsoft."

■ ■ ■

At the start of their North American lives, Elon and Kimbal Musk hustled to meet the subjects of Canadian newspaper stories. Now, only a few years later, they were being heralded as the American newspaper world's white knights. The next few years blurred together as Zip2 raced to compete against Microsoft, Citysearch, AOL, and Yahoo for a slice of the $60 billion local advertising pie. Musk had his first real taste of start-up life during this period, with its requisite highs and lows.

Zip2's innovations—working digital maps, a free email service, even a feature to reserve a seat at a restaurant via fax machine—thrilled Musk. The general-purpose programming language Java launched in January 1996; by September, Musk and his technology team had put Java at Zip2's core. Dr. Lew Tucker, a senior director at JavaSoft, sang Zip2's praises. "Zip2's groundbreaking maps and directions are some of the most powerful real-world applications of Java on the internet today," said Dr. Tucker in a (much-improved) Zip2 press release. "The true convergence of advanced technology and everyday practicality."

Zip2 grew throughout late 1996 and 1997, as Knight Ridder, Soft-Bank, Hearst, Pulitzer Publishing, Morris Communications, and the New York Times Company invested millions. Only two years into its existence, the company powered sections of 140 different newspaper websites. "By mid-1997 . . . Zip2 had become an entity that, in effect, functioned as a kind of mini-Microsoft," wrote one industry observer.

The growth came at a price, though. In the fall of 1996, Musk clashed with his investors and fellow executives, who raised questions about his leadership. Impatient and perpetually sleep-deprived, he was prone to setting unreasonable deadlines, chewing out other executives and colleagues in the open, and retooling code written by other people without asking first.

Later, Musk acknowledged these weaknesses and explained that until Zip2, he had never run much of anything, had "never been a sports captain or a captain of anything or managed a single person." He recalled to biographer Ashlee Vance a moment in which he publicly humiliated a colleague by correcting his work in front of others—thereby poisoning the relationship. "Eventually, I realized, 'Okay, I might have fixed that thing, but I've made that person unproductive.' It just wasn't a good way to go about things," he said.

Zip2 kept Musk on as its CTO and allowed him to remain chairman of the board. But as the company expanded, his influence over its strategic direction shrank. In his diminished role, Musk grew frustrated with what he saw as the company's narrowed ambitions. He had envisioned Zip2 as the next Yahoo, but it had now become a glorified shill for the newspaper industry. "We developed awesome technology that essentially got captured by the traditional media industry and the VCs," Musk remembered. "I was like, 'Wait, we've got essentially the equivalent of an F-35 joint strike fighter, and the way that the media company wants to use them is by rolling them down the hill at each other.'"

Musk lobbied unsuccessfully to change course. He pushed for Zip2 to buy the site "city.com," and in 1998, he took the fight to the press, pointedly telling the *New York Times*, "We think the real battle is with Yahoo and AOL to become a local portal." But Zip2's board, investors, and executive team disagreed. In their view, the media companies were paying, powerful customers; becoming the next Yahoo was a fantasy. "It wasn't a philosophical issue," said Rich Sorkin, the company's CEO. "We went where the money was."

Zip2 struggled throughout 1998. A proposed merger with its biggest rival, Citysearch, went awry. The *Charlotte Observer*, an early and prominent client, canceled its Zip2 city guide, complaining of slowing ad sales. The *Observer*'s complaints were emblematic of an industry-wide problem. "Despite all the interest from advertisers," the *New York Times* wrote in September of 1998, "no city guide has consistently shown a profit."

■ ■ ■

It all came to a conclusion early the following year. In February 1999, Zip2 sold to Compaq Computer for $307 million in cash. For Compaq, the acquisition united its AltaVista search engine with Zip2's local listings and ad business. For Musk, the purchase meant a $21 million payday.

To this day, that moment astonishes him—the amount as well as the means of delivery. The millions arrived by check. "Literally, to my mailbox. I was like, 'This is insane. What if somebody. . . ? I mean, I guess they'd have trouble cashing it?' But it still seems a weird way to send money." The deal let him move on from Zip2. "My bank account went from, like, $5,000 to $21,005,000," he said. He was twenty-seven years old.

After his exit, Musk became a figure of interest in the media, a role he embraced. "Although he speaks rapidly and dresses as casually as any Silicon Valley techie," one writer observed of Musk, "he has the clean-cut appearance and impeccable manners of a Mormon missionary." With his fresh millions, Musk bought himself a condo in Palo Alto and a $1 million McLaren F1 sports car.

Money and fame were welcome, but Musk felt that Zip2's success came with an asterisk. The company had triumphed financially, but Musk felt it was handicapped technologically. He took deep pride in Zip2's innovations—creating some of the first working online maps, for instance. But those technological pearls, Musk believed, were cast before swine. Zip2's products had not exhibited the awesome potential of the internet—at least not to the extent he'd hoped. "I knew how to develop technology," he observed, "but I hadn't seen it flourish, and it had been stifled."

Musk admired both capitalists and scientists—but as in his days at UPenn, his fascination with science prevailed. The business types treated the internet as the twentieth century's latest, garish gold rush. Musk saw it differently. "I thought it was something that would fundamentally change the world," he said. "It was like a nervous system for the world that would potentially make humanity somewhat of a superorganism."

To Musk, this "nervous system" fused science fiction with hard science—a cocktail of Adams and Feynman—and he spoke of it with unselfconscious amazement. "Previously we could only communicate by osmosis. One person would physically have to go to another person. For a letter, someone has to carry the letter," he observed. "And now, you could be in the middle of the Amazon jungle, and if you had just one satellite signal to the internet, you'd have access to all the world's information. That's unreal."

Unreal—yet being *made real* all around him. Musk craved the chance to do more. He wanted to be responsible, as he put it, for constructing the internet's "building blocks." Zip2 was now behind him. More than a little cash lay before him. It was time for his next venture.

4

"WHAT MATTERS TO ME IS WINNING"

As an intern in 1990, Musk couldn't get over Scotiabank's unwillingness to innovate. But through the intervening decade of rapid technological progress, big banks across the board seemed only to have doubled down on their intransigence.

The internet was everywhere, yet bank leadership eyed it with all the wariness of the small business owners to whom Musk had unsuccessfully tried to sell Zip2's digital ads. In 1995, when Musk was still building Zip2, "online banking" was a contradiction in terms. Even as more banks stepped into the digital world, their online offerings were barely more than brochures bolted onto the internet.

One example: Wells Fargo's website, circa late 1994. A site visitor saw a carefully sorted catalogue of information, all beneath images of the bank's iconic stagecoaches—that is, if they could open the site at all. "Unfortunately, with dial-up internet access the norm," a historian at the bank later admitted, "the colorful stagecoach pictures downloaded one line at a time and took several minutes to load the whole site." Wells Fargo customers lodged complaints—and asked a sensible product question: "When can I check my account balance on the website?"

Of course, Musk wasn't alone in thinking that offline banks were too slow to move online. By the late 1990s, the digital finance and banking space swarmed with start-ups. But Musk found those services lacking in one respect or another—he wasn't keen on launching just *another* dot-com bank. Musk's vision for his new financial services firm was—unsurprisingly—ambitious.

What if, he wondered, a single entity unified a person's entire financial life? In some of his earliest investor pitches, he described this idea as finance's one-stop shop, offering not just standard-issue savings and checking accounts, but everything from mortgages to lines of credit, stock trading, loans, and even insurance. Wherever money went, Musk believed his new company should go, too.

His vision was both eminently logical and impossibly grandiose. Musk wasn't just pitching a new company—he was pitching half a dozen companies in one. Money's underlying infrastructure, he felt, was long overdue for an upgrade. He'd describe both banks' and governments' "bunch of mainframes, ancient mainframes, running ancient code, doing batch processing with poor security, and a series of heterogeneous databases—like this herky-jerky frickin' monstrosity."

Translation: 1990s-era banking infrastructure was bad. He saw its primary operators—bankers—as armies of middlemen charging big fees and offering little of merit in return. "There was a desire [among banks] to build very large buildings, for some reason," Musk joked. "They're very into having adjectives in front of 'vice president.' *Senior* vice president. *Executive* vice president. *Senior Executive* vice president."

Musk's critique extended even to seemingly vital financial infrastructure like stock exchanges: "I said, 'Well, why don't we just allow people to trade with each other? So if I want to send you stock, why don't I just send you a share of whatever?' I don't need to go through anything. The exchange is unnecessary." The right code, in other words, could obsolete even the Nasdaq.

But someone had to write that code—someone had to build, run, and own the databases that would replace high finance's tall buildings, richly titled personnel, and the exorbitant fees funding it all. Musk believed that someone could be him.

■ ■ ■

One of the first people Musk pitched his idea to was Harris Fricker, a Canadian financial executive. Musk and Fricker had been introduced by Peter Nicholson while Musk was working at Scotiabank. "They're both intensely bright guys," Nicholson said of his protégés. "I thought the two of them would make a pretty potent brain trust."

Fricker hailed from Ingonish, a rural community in Nova Scotia. The son of a construction worker and a nurse, he excelled in university and earned one of the eleven Rhodes Scholarships awarded to Canadian students. In England, he studied economics and philosophy, and afterward returned to Canada to work in banking. As Musk achieved his dot-com success, Fricker flourished in finance, becoming the head of a securities firm in his late twenties.

Like others, Fricker was intrigued by the emergence of the internet. In late 1998, Musk pitched Fricker his idea for a new kind of financial services firm. "He's one of the greatest salesmen I have ever met," Fricker said of Musk's entreaties. "Like a Steve Jobs. When he articulates something, he tends to find the kernel that will appeal to a broad mass intuitively." By early 1999, Fricker was sold. He gave up his million-dollar salary and moved to Palo Alto.

Soon thereafter, Fricker recruited a third cofounder: Christopher Payne. Payne graduated from Queen's University in Ontario, after which he worked in finance and private equity, then pursued an MBA at Wharton. He also nurtured an amateur interest in computers, tinkering with hardware and writing elementary code on nights and weekends. His day job was quickly becoming technology packed, too. At BMO Nesbitt Burns, the private equity firm he joined following Wharton, Payne's desk overflowed with business plans for internet start-ups.

Payne met Fricker when they both worked at BMO Nesbitt Burns, and years later, when Fricker left private equity to join a Silicon Valley dot-com, Fricker lobbied Payne to come with him. "What do you want to tell your children twenty years from now [when they ask] where you were at the birth of the internet: at a stodgy old bank, or on the front lines?" Payne remembers Fricker telling him.

In 1999, Payne packed for Palo Alto—where he soon got his first impression of Musk. "Very high energy," Payne remembered. "Very much *let's go, let's get going and do something, build something, achieve something.*" At Musk's home one day, Payne walked into the bedroom. "The room was literally filled with books—biographies or stories about business luminaries and how they succeeded," Payne said, "In fact, I remember sitting there and at the top of this stack was a book about Richard Branson. It kind of clicked to me that Elon was prepping himself and studying to be a famous entrepreneur. He had some superordinate goal that was driving him."

■ ■ ■

Rounding out the cofounder cohort was Ed Ho, a Musk recruit. Ho had earned degrees in electrical engineering and computer science at Berkeley and worked at Oracle following graduation. Later, Ho joined Silicon Graphics, a great hub of engineering talent. But by the mid-1990s, Ho's colleagues started fleeing their plum Silicon Graphics jobs for positions at internet start-ups.

The exodus swept up Ho's boss, Jim Ambras, who left for a company called Zip2—and recruited Ho to join him. Ho enjoyed Zip2's engineering challenges, including a final, memorable project: building apps for the era's primitive mobile phones. "Imagine you could type in two addresses—which is a real pain on those cell phones!—and then you get directions on your phone," Ho said.

At Zip2, Ho also got his first exposure to Musk's leadership style. "Every time I pushed an idea," Ho recalled, "Elon would say, 'Go do it.'" He appreciated that Musk acted less like an executive and more like a line engineer, remembering how he would throw himself into all-night sessions of the video games StarCraft and Quake—where his competitive streak showed through. "He's Mr. StarCraft," Ho said.

Video games soon led to a friendship. "You stay late," Ho remembered, "and then eventually you start playing games, and then you become friends." Before the ink had dried on Compaq's Zip2 acquisition,

Musk had begun pitching Ho on his next start-up. "In retrospect, you're not supposed to do that," Ho said. Technically, Musk was bound by Zip2's noncompete clauses, but he regularly ran afoul of such rules—often with relish. Ho recalled Musk's jubilance when Silicon Graphics finally sent a formal complaint about Zip2 poaching from its ranks.

In the early months of 1999, Musk's new company was essentially some ideas in Musk's mind, but Ho joined enthusiastically as employee number four. "There's a wave, right?" Ho said. "And you either catch the wave, or you can sit there waiting—and Yahoo goes by." The original team of four divvied up responsibilities: Musk and Ho would drive technology and product, while Fricker and Payne handled the company's financial, regulatory, and operational elements.

■ ■ ■

Even before they had a product, Musk chose the venture's name: X.com. This was, Musk believed, simply "the coolest URL on the internet." He wasn't the only one who thought so. In the early 1990s, a pair of engineers, Marcel DePaolis and Dave Weinstein, had bought www.x.com for their company Pittsburgh Powercomputer. They sold the company—but held onto the X.com URL, using it for their personal email addresses.

Over the years, DePaolis and Weinstein turned down bids to sell the URL, underwhelmed by the various offer terms. In early 1999, they received fresh interest. "Under the looming shadow of Y2K, we were approached by Elon Musk," they said. This time, the deal terms proved more interesting. They sold X.com to Musk in exchange for cash and 1.5 million shares of the company's Series A stock. The negotiation drew the interest of the *Wall Street Journal*, which included it in a story about start-up equity—a story that, as chance had it, included another young entrepreneur, Max Levchin, explaining how he used stock to secure office space.

Musk came out of the deal sporting, among other things, a memorable corporate email address: e@x.com. Musk believed deeply in the X.com URL and company name, even in the face of criticism that it sounded confusing or sinister. To him, X.com was novel, intriguing, and open-ended enough to capture the company's gist—a place for all banking and investment services to coexist. Just as *X* "marked the spot" on a treasure map, so X.com marked the spot where money would be kept online. He also enjoyed pointing out that the URL was rare, one of only three single-letter .com URLs in the world at the time (the other two: q.com and z.com).

Musk had a practical rationale for the name, too. He believed the world would soon be overrun with handheld devices—pocket-sized computers with index-card-sized keyboards. In this world, X.com was the ideal URL because a customer was only ever a few thumbstrokes from their full financial life.

Musk's conviction about X.com also stemmed from his consternation with the name "Zip2." "First of all, what the hell does it mean? It's literally one of the worst URLs you could possibly have. Because is it Zip, the digit '2'? Or is it Zip t-w-o? Or Zip t-o? Or Zip t-o-o?" Musk said. "You just picked the homonym with the most number of variations. And websites don't work with homonyms. So it's dumb in every possible way."

Heads down writing Zip2's code, Musk had outsourced the renaming of Global Link—and regretted it. "I deferred brand and marketing and whatever to people I thought were domain experts," Musk said. "And then discovered subsequently that you just have to use common sense. And that's actually a better guide."

To Musk, X.com's name was everything Zip2's wasn't—and he was convinced X.com would become everything Zip2 hadn't. "He was really passionately inspired by that letter," Payne recalled.

■ ■ ■

Musk rolled much of his Zip2 windfall into X.com, investing $12.5 million and purchasing the X.com domain with personal funds. "At the time, I thought, *He's nuts.* Honestly, that's risk!" Ho said. Indeed, staking so much of one's net worth on a new start-up was noteworthy—in large part because Musk didn't have to. A successful exit like Musk's from Zip2 generated its own halo, and others were now readily willing to invest in

Musk's new venture. "[He] could get a meeting on a phone call's notice," Payne remembered.

Serious venture firms—New Enterprise Associates, Mohr Davidow Ventures, Sequoia Capital, Draper Fisher Jurvetson, among others—were eager to hear his vision for an online financial services firm. Fricker—with his traditional finance background—was astonished at how casual it all seemed. The team would arrive at pitch meetings without so much as a presentation prepared, and they'd successfully draw interest. "One of the things that Elon was highly adept at, which frankly I underestimated . . . was on the VC side," Fricker said. "He would articulate what was wrong with the industry. You know, the big monoliths, the lack of democracy in pricing . . . everybody would get all fired up."

Despite the venture capitalists' enthusiasm, Musk stuck to his own funding for the time being. His commitment to self-funding had two virtues. First, it gave Musk full ownership and operational control over X.com—this time (at least for now), there would be no investors to sideline him. Second, Musk's personal investment made for a winning recruitment pitch. "I'd make a phone call for recruiting or whatever," Ho remembered, "and say, 'Oh, he's got thirteen million in.'" With the competition for engineers reaching a fever pitch, every bit of buzz mattered—up to and including a high-profile founder betting his fortune on the company.

X.com's recruitment efforts paid off on both the engineering and financial talent fronts. Steven Dixon, an executive from Bank of America, joined as CFO. Julie Anderson, a former analyst at Deutsche Bank, joined the business team as well. On the product and engineering teams, X.com added See Hon Tung, a friend of Fricker's and Payne's from Canada; Harvey Tang, X.com's principal architect; Doug Mak, a software engineer; and Chris Chen, a former insurance analyst from Hawaii and a friend of Ed Ho's.

Musk also courted an attorney, Craig Johnson, to be an X.com advisor. "Craig was a legal tour de force in the valley at the time," Fricker said. Landing Johnson sent loud signals about X.com's seriousness. It was also time for a serious address, and the team moved into a leased office space at 394 University Avenue.

From its new vantage, X.com trained its sights on other retail and dot-com bank competitors. "There were a few other internet banks out there in the marketplace at the time. And they were trading for roughly four times book value per share. And the regular banks are trading around two times. So there's this huge premium for [internet banks]," one early X.com employee recalled. "And so Elon's business plan was basically 'I'm an internet guy. I can do this. This will be the first Silicon Valley–funded bank, so therefore, it will be more successful than all the others.'"

One of the team's online targets was NetBank, which was founded in 1996 and advertised itself as the digital bank of the future. In mid-1997, the company went public at $12 per share; by 1999, NetBank's stock price was seven times higher. Despite NetBank's success, Ho remembered the confident tone around the X.com office: "We're just going to crush them."

But it was more hope and hype than plan. "Basically our thought process—and this is kind of negative to say—is that those banking guys knew nothing. They might know banking. They know nothing about technology and the consumer," Ho said. Partly, they were responding to comments from NetBank's founder. "We are a bank and we are regulated," he told one reporter in 1998. "Amazon.com—no one looks at their ratios." He wanted the world to know that his company was a genuine bank and not a fly-by-night dot-com. As if to prove the point, NetBank operated out of Georgia—not Silicon Valley.

For Musk and X.com, this amounted to clear evidence that NetBank and its competitors in the digital banking space weren't "techy" enough. X.com was techy alright—and would defeat them by getting to market fast, lowering fees and minimums, and aggressively acquiring customers. To achieve their speedy go-to-market, the team opted to work with third-party vendors, using existing software that had been licensed to and approved by traditional banks—then building products atop that code. "The tradeoff is that you don't own the core software," Ho recalled, "but the good side is that all the accounting and the regulatory issues are handled."

■■■

Even with its adaptations of third-party software, X.com soon entered a regulatory hellscape. Lines of credit, cash advances, mortgages, bonds, stock trading, even the mere storage of money were all subject to complex state and federal rules, governed by long-standing agencies like the FDIC, who were hardly accustomed to dealing with jeans-wearing Silicon Valley execs.

The team hired the law firm Dechert Price & Rhoads to take on these regulatory issues, but even with that support, the team was up against regulatory headwinds. The fact that X.com's CEO had committed to a revolution in finance—integrating all types of financial services under one roof—made matters more difficult.

Revolution and regulations didn't mix well. Musk wanted to fuse retail banking with investment banking, for example, which the Glass-Steagall Act of 1933 expressly forbade. Only in April 1999 was legislation introduced to allow the two entities to mix, and it would still be months before President Bill Clinton signed the bill into law.

To Musk and others, laws made during the Great Depression's bust didn't suit the digital economy's boom. "What can be very frustrating is that regulation is often irrational," Musk would say later. "And you can try to convince them those rules don't make any sense but they won't listen to you." (Well into his SpaceX years, Musk would propose a solution to this problem for a future Mars government, suggesting that all Martian laws include automatic sunset clauses.*)

---

*"Most likely the form of government on Mars would be direct democracy, not representative," Musk elaborated at the Recode Code Conference in 2016. "So it would be people voting directly on issues. And I think that's probably better because the potential for corruption is substantially diminished in a direct versus a representative democracy. So I think that's probably what would occur. I would recommend some adjustment for the inertia of laws. That would be wise. It should probably be easier to remove a law than create one. That's probably good. Laws have infinite life unless they're taken away. So I think my recommendation would be something like 60 percent of people need to vote in a law, but at any point greater than 40 percent of people can remove it. And any law should come with a built-in sunset provision. If it's

At the time, Musk decided that X.com should plow ahead. "We shouldn't be afraid to break a few eggs along the way," Musk told Payne. X.com's attorney supported Musk, reportedly telling the team that when the time was right, they would approach the relevant regulators.

The key, per the team's attorney, was banking venture capital money—and squaring circles later. "When approached with the conundrum that we have in terms of the desire not to misrepresent ourselves to potential venture capitalists, [Johnson's reply] was 'The deer is almost in the box. Don't spook the deer. Business plans change all the time,'" one early X.com employee remembered.

The finance veterans on the team worried about this strategy. In this industry, they knew, regulations were not to be ignored. "You have capital requirements, reporting requirements, privacy requirements—on and on and on," Payne said. "We have to be responsible and sensitive that this is a regulated industry." Some early employees grew concerned that the company and its officers could face legal trouble if they played fast and loose with financial rules.

■ ■ ■

Fricker and Musk, in particular, began to butt heads—a fissure that defined X.com's first several months. On top of Musk's regulatory approach, Fricker took exception to his hiring of a public relations firm to generate headlines for the fledgling company and his use of equity to purchase the X.com domain. To Fricker, these were expensive extravagances that didn't advance the core work of the business. To Musk, these were essential costs to compete successfully in a crowded market.

Fricker also became flummoxed by Musk's promise that X.com would handle everything under the financial sun. "The description of what we were doing was . . . 10x what we were actually doing. And if there was frustration . . . it was that I wanted to get something built, regulated, and

---

not good enough to be voted back in . . . That would be my recommendation. Direct democracy where it's slightly harder to put laws in place than to take them away and where laws don't automatically just live forever."

productized," Fricker said. "The more we described what we were going to build, the more difficult the project became to do that."

Fricker tried to narrow the company's scope. In his conception, X.com would succeed by focusing on two specific services: marrying traditional banking offerings to index funds and providing financial advice. Needless to say, Musk was less than receptive. From his point of view, that strategy clipped X.com's wings unnecessarily. Financial advisory also added a cost- and labor-intensive human element to what Musk saw as a primarily digital company.

Fricker and Payne had run models about X.com's growth and revenue, but the numbers on the financial superstore model didn't seem to add up. "This was all a little bizarre to me. My training was very classic Wall Street. Very fact-based. Very numerical. Very much spreadsheets and sort of forced complexity around what you thought the future was going to be," Payne said. "It was logical and mechanical, especially around how I thought you analyze risk and opportunity."

To Musk, the models didn't add up because the assumptions baked into the models were false. "What was more potent than the mathematical exercise was the story," Payne would appreciate later, "and Elon was very good at pointing to the future—just as he is today—and saying *the objective is over there, and I know it's over there, and we should all go over there*." Even in hyperrational Silicon Valley, vision weighed as much as data. "There's a reason why entrepreneurs who succeed in the technology world get paid as well as they do—it's because it's not a straight line between *I build the factory and the widgets come out and the widgets get sold*," Payne said.

Fricker grew increasingly frustrated by the engineering team that Musk led—specifically its unwillingness to deliver even preliminary widgets. To X.com's engineers, the work wasn't "incomplete" so much as "in progress." Programming, like writing, was halting and uncertain—less paint-by-numbers than most appreciated. "It's not linear, and you might burn three hours going this way, and you go, *aw, shit*, and you don't want to tell someone you went down the blind alley," Ho said.

But those blind alleys mattered: At Zip2, Musk had learned that start-up success wasn't just about dreaming up the right ideas as much as discovering and then rapidly discarding the wrong ones. "You start off with an idea, and that idea is mostly wrong. And then you adapt that idea and keep refining it and you listen to criticism," he'd tell an audience years later. "And then engage in sort of a recursive self-improvement . . . keep iterating on a loop that says, 'Am I doing something useful for other people?' Because that's what a company is supposed to do." Too much precision in early plans, he believed, cut that iterative loop prematurely.

■ ■ ■

Fricker, on the other hand, had grown up in finance. Precision marked every facet of his life. He'd arrive at the X.com office early—the financial markets opened at 6:30 a.m. PST, by which time Fricker would already be hard at work. By contrast, Musk would regularly conclude his work day at three or four in the morning with a catnap on his office floor—just hours before Fricker would arrive.

To Fricker, this was a sign of Musk's disconnection from the company, but to Musk, late nights were just how start-ups operated. It became yet another source of friction between them. The mounting tensions spilled into meetings, fueled by Fricker's and Musk's intense and impatient personalities.

Some coworkers found the conflict confusing. Ed Ho, for instance, was perplexed at how quickly things went sour between Fricker and Musk: "Whenever they'd get into these fights, I'd ask, *Why are you guys so antagonistic? Isn't he your friend?*" Others were less surprised. Musk and Fricker had both run the show in prior roles; power-sharing wasn't a particular strength for either of them. "They were just never going to work together successfully," Payne concluded early on in the partnership.

Fricker resented what he saw as Musk's insufficient commitment to X.com, but he attempted to repair the breach. On May 9, 1999, he wrote a long email to Musk, concluding with, "Elon, please rejoin us in the trenches at X . . . As smart as you are, we are smart enough to know when it is not fully engaged—the curse of competent partners." He reminded

Musk that the opportunity to work together had motivated his move to California in the first place.

Musk responded graciously—but rejected Fricker's premise that he was asleep at the wheel. "Well said, although I think you may misread me a little. My mind is always on X by default, even in my sleep—I am by nature obsessive-compulsive," Musk wrote back. "What matters to me is winning, and not in a small way." Musk suggested they get dinner together that evening and signed off "Your friend and partner in turn, Elon."

Over the course of May and June of 1999, the fissures continued to widen. "There were livid discussions," Ho said. The X.com team divided into camps: the Silicon Valley veterans—Musk and Ho—in one, and the financial veterans—Fricker, Payne, and Dixon—in the other. By several accounts, in July of 1999, the finance camp tried to shift X.com's strategy—and shelve Musk as CEO.

During this period, Peter Nicholson received a late-night phone call from Musk. His former intern was apoplectic, telling Nicholson that Fricker was trying to push him out of the company. He leaned on his mentor to "set things right." Nicholson had no formal involvement with X.com, but out of concern for the protégés he had introduced years before, Nicholson assured Musk he would get in contact with Fricker the next day.

Nicholson recalls Fricker saying, "The team we put together is having a great deal of difficulty coping with Elon's management style." Fricker feared they might quit en masse. He also told Nicholson that Musk was brilliant, his ideas were farsighted, "but you've got to be able to execute."

Wisely, Nicholson chose to recuse himself from the conflict. "I decided at that point that there was no point in me getting involved in this," Nicholson said. "I really liked them both. I have a great deal of respect for them both. I have no idea what the inner machinations are, much less what it was like day to day at this start-up."

With or without Nicholson, things soon came to a head. Musk still held a controlling interest in X.com, and at the height of the drama,

Musk called a meeting with Fricker and the company's lawyer. Other employees left the office in advance of what they anticipated would be a fiery discussion. "We knew something was happening," Payne said. "We left because we didn't want to be eavesdropping." The shouting began as they departed.

In the end, Musk fired Fricker. In an unceremonious dismissal, Fricker arrived at the office one day to discover that his computer had been wiped and his access to X.com files suspended.

■ ■ ■

Cofounder Chris Payne was stunned. "When it all fell apart, you have to scratch your head and think, *What the hell just happened?*" he said. In the chaotic aftermath, rumors spread that Fricker was starting a new company—and that he wanted much of the X.com team to join him.

To head this off, Musk met with the remaining X.com employees, asked them each to stay, and promised a chunk of additional equity if they did. "Elon sat everyone down in the conference room . . . was basically saying, 'Look, are you in or are you out? Because if you're in, you're in, and we're going to build this thing,'" engineer Doug Mak recalled. Chris Chen remembered that in his one-on-one with Musk, the X.com CEO emphasized that the additional equity was going to "be worth a lot of money one day."

Musk lobbied Payne to stay—a gesture that Payne appreciated. "He was being very open and wanting me to stay," Payne said. Payne had always had positive interactions with Musk, but he felt loyal to Fricker; it was Fricker who had urged him to move to California. Out of respect, he thought it best to leave.

Cofounder Ed Ho also departed—despite having been recruited by Musk. "It kind of rattled Ed," Musk said. By Ho's own account, he "loved working with Elon," but he had grown weary of months of infighting. He was also disenchanted by the X.com product road map—the idea of "taking someone else's software and painting on top of that" didn't thrill him. Ho briefly considered joining Fricker's next venture but ultimately ended up creating his own start-up.

Several others sided with Musk, including Doug Mak, an engineer who had left IBM to join the company just weeks before the blowup. Now, with three-quarters of X.com's cofounders gone, Mak wondered if he had chosen wisely. What persuaded Mak to stay—and gave him hope for the company's future—was Musk's pitch. "There's something about Elon that I knew . . . if he's going to make something happen, he would bet his last penny to make that happen," Mak said. "He wants to revolutionize how people do banking. He's going to do it."

X.com employee number 5, Julie Anderson, stayed with X.com as well. An Iowa native, Anderson came to the Bay Area after being rejected from the Peace Corps because of a back injury. She joined Deutsche Bank's Technology Group as a junior analyst, working under Frank Quattrone and joining just as Deutsche Bank started to become a high-profile underwriter of technology IPOs, including Netscape, Amazon, Intuit, and many others.

Anderson and her colleagues worked nonstop for the next two years as the internet came into its own. But the early thrills gave way to burnout. "I sort of looked around, and everybody seemed to be getting cancer early," Anderson said. She left Deutsche Bank and apprenticed with a stained-glass maker out of a garage in San Mateo. When her savings ran out, a friend mentioned that she knew someone who had just sold a company and was starting another. Anderson was introduced to Musk over email, and she went to lunch at Palo Alto's Empire Tap Room with the entire four-person X.com team—Musk, Fricker, Ho, and Payne.

The four now reduced to one, Anderson opted to stay with Musk anyway. At Deutsche Bank, she witnessed her share of start-up executive turnover as companies prepared to go public. "People are getting overthrown all the time, and the chances that your senior-level people are going to stay through is very, very small," Anderson said. "Finding the right personalities is really, really hard."

Like Mak and Chen, she was also inspired by Musk. "I like to have something to believe in," she said, "and Elon was always about changing the world or doing something good for humanity." She also appreciated Musk's quirks. "When he has a hard problem on his mind—at least back in those days—he would spend a lot of time looking at his computer, like he was reading something or doing something, but I don't actually think he was reading something. He was just thinking. Or more like just waiting for the answer to come," Anderson said.

■■■

Two decades later, Musk offered only brief reflections on the early chaos at X.com, calling it "a hot minute" in PayPal's history. "There's always drama in start-ups," he said.

Harris Fricker regretted how things ended. "I would have handled things very differently," he said. He believed he should have been more open to Musk's strategy of courting investors and the press with a vision of what could be—as opposed to what was already built. "Where I was wrong is that I should have suspended my traditional business judgment and realized that wasn't all that odd back then."

Fricker's deeper regret was personal. He and Musk were more than coworkers; they had been friends. "One of the biggest disappointments of my professional life was the blowing up of our relationship. We never addressed it," Fricker said. Following his divorce from X.com, Fricker tried to launch a financial advisory start-up, whatifi.com. When it failed, he returned to Canada and found success again as a financial executive, including serving as CEO of GMP Capital.

Looking back, Musk and Fricker's mutual mentor Peter Nicholson sensed a breakdown may have been unavoidable. "They were two titanic talents," Nicholson said. "Or maybe one was the iceberg—and one was the ship."

5

THE BEAMERS

Fieldlink—Levchin's mobile device security start-up—needed a CEO. Levchin briefly considered doing the job himself but decided that he preferred the CTO role. A self-described "engineer's engineer," Levchin felt his strengths lay in writing code rather than managing a business and pitching investors.

But if not himself, then who? Levchin wasn't a natural networker, and his Valley contact list remained sparse. He had asked Luke Nosek to introduce him to a few prospects, but none panned out. John Powers interviewed two candidates at Northwestern's Kellogg School of Management, and both were promising. The company extended them offers; both turned Fieldlink down. "We didn't have much money," he remembered, "and [the candidates] were looking at $100K+ starting salaries, which we couldn't come close to matching."

That left Levchin with Peter Thiel—"The only guy I knew who wasn't currently busy and could be CEO." Thiel hadn't lobbied for an expanded role at the company outside of his investment, but Levchin had watched him deftly handle the Powers departure. Levchin called Thiel from his "big-ass brick cell phone" and popped the question: Would Thiel consider becoming Fieldlink's CEO?

Initially, Thiel was uninterested. "He was huffing and puffing, like Peter tends to do," Levchin remembered. "It wasn't coerced, but I definitely had to work to persuade him." Thiel wanted Fieldlink to be successful, but he had no interest in a CEO's administrative and managerial duties—he preferred sticking to markets and money.

But Thiel could also see the value in operating experience—time in the CEO chair could fine-tune his investor antennae. So he proposed a compromise: he would serve as Fieldlink's "ramp-up CEO," doing the job until the business found its footing. Then, he would depart the position, remaining an advisor and letting someone else steer the business. Levchin agreed.

Thiel called Ken Howery, his fund's first employee, to let him know that he would be joining Fieldlink as CEO. Howery was enthusiastic, and given that his goal was to join a start-up, he was pleased when Thiel suggested precisely that, bringing Howery on as Fieldlink's VP of Operations. Despite their new start-up executive positions, the pair continued to run Thiel Capital Management on nights and weekends.

■ ■ ■

As Fieldlink's new CEO, Thiel stepped up the pressure to launch the company. As he surveyed the market, he saw a gathering blizzard of activity—every minute, it seemed another start-up was born. Thiel emphasized the need for swiftness—in hiring, fundraising, and releasing products. One day, Thiel pushed Levchin to recruit more engineers.

"Well, yeah, but I'm coding," Levchin remembers telling him.

"But you need to hire more engineers. You're the CTO," Thiel said.

"Sure, but I don't know anyone."

"You just graduated from one of the better computer science programs in the country. You don't know anyone?" Thiel replied.

"Oh, well, I guess I know some . . ."

Levchin considered two of his former UIUC classmates: Yu Pan and Russel Simmons. He had worked with both before, subcontracting one-off programming projects to them when his plate was full.

Following graduation, Yu Pan moved to Rochester, Minnesota, to work at IBM. But he second-guessed his decision after surviving his first Minnesota winter. Simmons described Pan's bleak existence: "He would go to work, come home, eat rice with oyster sauce every day for dinner, and then play online video games. . . . It was totally sad."

In the winter of 1998, Levchin pitched Pan on Fieldlink—and the prospect of moving to California. Despite the draw of a more temperate climate, Pan was wary. He had made good money from Levchin's subcontracted programming work, but he thought of Levchin as a flake. After graduation, Levchin had abruptly left for California, without much warning to Pan and other friends. Several of Pan's emails to Levchin went unanswered. "He just disappeared. . . . *What the hell happened to him?*" Pan remembered thinking. "Am I going to get paid or anything? . . . In my head, it was like, 'Max—unreliable.'"

Levchin reassured him that Fieldlink was a real, funded company—and he'd stick around this time. Initially, Pan gave Levchin a resolute no: "I was like 'F-U, I'm not coming out. This is the most idiotic thing I've ever heard. I am not going to trust you.'" But Levchin kept selling the upsides of working at a start-up as well as Palo Alto's balmy climate and vibrant ultimate Frisbee scene.

Pan slowly came around, but there was another obstacle: Pan's family. Like Levchin and Thiel, Pan's parents were immigrants. They viewed Pan's IBM job as a solid, stable opportunity conveniently located close to home. To them, Levchin's start-up was the opposite in every way that mattered: a company no one had ever heard of, run by a college friend of their son's, far away from Illinois. "They needed a little convincing," Pan said.

Pan asked Levchin to come to Chicago to do exactly that. Levchin hopped on a flight, went to Pan's home, and sold the family on the opportunity. The elder Pans satisfied, Yu Pan agreed to join Fieldlink as a senior engineer.

■ ■ ■

Russel Simmons proved an easier recruit. Levchin had met Simmons working on ACM projects. Even in college, Levchin remembers Simmons standing out: "Russ is brilliant. An outlier. Genius-level IQ. He can learn anything he sets his mind to in half the time you expect him to."

Post-college, Simmons enrolled in graduate school at UIUC for computer science. "I'm not very strategic about anything in my life," Simmons said, "and I haven't even thought about getting a job, and I am just like, 'I guess I'll go to grad school?' . . . I had no interest in starting companies or Silicon Valley or anything like that."

When Levchin reached out in September of 1998, Simmons had grown bored with his master's program. In emails, he confessed to Levchin that he was considering quitting for a programming job in Texas. Levchin encouraged him to come to California instead. "This place rocks and you should move here and work on cool stuff," he wrote. By the end of the year, "cool stuff" meant Fieldlink.

Like Yu Pan, Simmons remembered needing some reassurance: "I knew [Levchin] was smart, but it was like, 'Is this dude for real? Am I going to actually have a job when I get out there?' " Another point of concern: Levchin told Simmons he'd have to pay a nominal sum to buy equity in Fieldlink. While this was standard in the start-up world, Simmons was suspicious and, similar to Pan, he consulted his mom. "[She] was like, 'Whoa, whoa, whoa, you haven't even started or gotten a salary, and they're asking you to send them money? . . . This sounds like a scam.' "

In spite of his reservations, Simmons decided to go for it. Simmons and Pan agreed to a "Levchin pact"—if Levchin bailed on them, they'd look out for each other. Besides, they saw little risk—the market for engineering talent in Silicon Valley was booming. Pan and Simmons flew west from Chicago on the same, low-cost American Trans Air flight, and Levchin greeted them at the airport.

■ ■ ■

Just as Levchin hustled to recruit employees, so did Thiel. In addition to Ken Howery, Thiel asked Luke Nosek to join Fieldlink. Like Pan and Simmons, Nosek was reluctant. For one thing, he was already developing a new start-up in the aftermath of Smart Calendar: an online news betting platform, a sort of futures market for ideas. Thiel cautioned against it when Nosek brought it up, warning him of the onerous regulations surrounding gambling and securities markets. Thiel told Nosek he should join Fieldlink instead.

Nosek was unsure. "I thought security for handheld devices was really boring, and kind of a dumb business idea," Nosek said. Both Thiel and Levchin told Nosek that they'd iterate until they landed on a concept that struck sparks. More persuasive to Nosek was the team's alchemy, as well as the chance to work once more with Levchin, whom he knew well from their enterprising UIUC days. "I decided to work on it because of this feeling that, together, we're going to do something amazing," Nosek said. "Even if they had been wanting to do something completely different, I would have wanted to work with this group."

Nosek was in—but Levchin raised a key concern: What exactly would Nosek *do*? His fellow Illinois grad was technically competent, but he wasn't a programming superstar. When Levchin posed the question to friends, another UIUC alum, Scott Banister, provided the answer: "That's obvious. He's going to do 'Luke things.' "

Over time, "Luke things" would acquire a loose shape—Nosek would generate an endless flow of counterintuitive ideas, mostly related to marketing and customer acquisition. "Luke . . . was one of those people who could walk around and just bump into brilliant ideas. And they somehow were only visible to him," Levchin said. "He'd suggest something and we'd say, 'Well, that's insane,' and then it turned out that it was this gem of an idea. He often sees loopholes that other people pass by—almost like spotting dollar bills on the ground that are inexplicably still there."

Nosek was given the title Vice President of Marketing and Strategy, and he, Russ Simmons, Yu Pan, and Ken Howery were all named company cofounders.

■ ■ ■

The work took place in cofounder apartments at 469 Grant Avenue, until Howery—once again tasked with securing real estate—found an office at 394 University Avenue. Howery outfitted the office with furniture from Nosek's previous start-up and Levchin's Illinois IKEA collection. Howery and Nosek hand-assembled the cubicles. "That's when I learned that

Ken always finds a way to enjoy anything," Nosek said. "He was the most enthusiastic person about the office assembly process."

With a new home, Levchin decided it was time to change the company's name. He had never loved Fieldlink and decided to blend the words *confidence* and *infinity* to form Confinity. Soon, Levchin had naming remorse. "Everybody I told about it was like, 'Con . . . So, is it like a great con? Like a company that's going to con people out of money?' That was the last time I named a company," Levchin said.

The company's renaming—ill-advised or not—reflected a strategic reorientation. In its previous incarnations, Fieldlink had focused on connecting mobile workers securely, building on Levchin's and Powers's consulting work and Levchin's SecurePilot product. But as Levchin and Thiel began to see, Fieldlink wasn't the only player in the mobile security space.

Levchin had been working to ingratiate himself with 3Com—the parent company of PalmPilot—for years. He was a regular attendee at the company's conferences and became PalmPilot's 153rd registered developer. He had also befriended Griff Coleman, Palm's product manager for enterprise solutions. Levchin's goal: get Palm to change its codebase to support Levchin's security software.

At one point, Levchin pulled a daring attempt at cold outreach. He attended a developer conference at 3Com's office, and he followed Palm CEO Jeff Hawkins outside after Hawkins finished his conference keynote. Levchin approached him and asked for a ride home. Hawkins agreed, believing Levchin to be a stranded 3Com employee. Levchin gave vague directions in order to lengthen the ride, but a few confusing turns later, Hawkins had reached the limits of politeness, asking, "Can I just drop you off here?"

"Well," Levchin responded gently, "can you just talk to me for a few more minutes about the security that your operating system will need very soon?"

Levchin says Hawkins told him that Palm had already partnered with a Canadian company called Certicom for its security needs. "I thought, *Oh fuck, they have someone else working on this*," Levchin said.

There were other concerning signs, too. Levchin and Thiel were having a hard time selling enterprise customers on the need for mobile security. "We realized that, even though the theory was pretty much logical, the move of the enterprise to handheld devices was not actually forthcoming," Levchin said later, "kind of like the early Christians in the first century were all really hard at work waiting for the second coming. Still waiting . . . 'Any minute now, there'll be millions of people begging for security on their handheld devices.' It just wasn't happening." The company would need to change course.

■■■

Confinity's original plan had succeeded in one important sense: earning funding. The team closed a $500,000 funding round in February 1999, raised largely from friends and family. Thiel's fund contributed $240,000, and Scott Banister provided another $100,000. Families helped as well: an additional $35,000 came from Thiel's parents, and $25,000 from Ken Howery's parents. Another $50,000 came from friends of Thiel's: $25,000 from Edward Bogas, a musician and chess player from San Francisco, and $25,000 from Norman Book, Thiel's Stanford classmate and the *Stanford Review* cofounder.

A final $50,000 came from the investment firm Gödel Capital. Gödel, run by Australia natives Peter Davison and Graeme Linnett, was new to the American technology scene. With few connections, Davison and Linnett "went looking for deals with a little hair on them," as Linnett put it. "I didn't know anything about start-ups, hadn't ever done a thing in investment, and we were just going to be venture capitalists," Davison said. The pair found Confinity through Kevin Hartz, a Stanford connection of Thiel's who was working with Gödel. Confinity was Gödel's first venture capital deal, which it agreed to close only after Thiel included a two-week, penalty-free out clause.

On February 26, 1999—the day *after* closing its investment round—Confinity sent Davison, Linnett, and its other investors an eighteen-page document outlining a strategy shift. Selling business-to-business mobile security was not working; instead, the company would pivot to become consumer-facing. Confinity would launch a "Mobile Wallet" for handheld devices, an attempt to obsolete physical wallets. Mobile Wallet would secure financial information and allow users to send currency and conduct e-commerce—all from a PalmPilot.

As a blueprint for the mobile future, Confinity's February 1999 business plan holds up surprisingly well. The company planned on riding the growth of the handheld computer and electronic finance markets. "Today's handheld computer market shares certain characteristics with the Internet of 1995 and the home computer market of 1980," the plan stated. "New applications and lower costs are shifting demand from a core group of technologists toward the general public."

In theory, the expanding number of handheld devices would grow Mobile Wallet usage, and users would install the Mobile Wallet because their friends and family already had one. The business plan anticipated the obvious question: "How will the Confinity network ever come into being if its value to each particular customer depends on the prior existence of the whole network?" The team developed two approaches to addressing this tautology: top-down and bottom-up. From the top down, Confinity would find and target prime business and market candidates. The bottom-up approach would see users inviting members of their own networks. "Confinity," its founders wrote, "will combine these two approaches, albeit with the major initial emphasis on the second, grassroots model."

Then, Confinity believed, the market would be theirs for the taking—and keeping. It was only a matter of scaling, linking vendors and merchants, creating credit cards, and offering internet banking, *et voilà*: "As the Confinity network grows, the cost of transition to other authentication companies will become prohibitively high, creating an effective barrier to new entrants." The company sought $4 million in its next round of fundraising to see this vision through and build out the team and the product, which was expected to launch six months later in August 1999.

At the time of the plan's writing, Confinity consisted of not much more than six people, $500,000, a leased office space above a bakery, and some used IKEA furniture—but the team was swinging for the fences. Once the Mobile Wallet achieved ubiquity, "Confinity's default exit strategy consists of an acquisition by a financial institution or technology company, which would be best positioned to take advantage of Confinity's customer network."

Or the alternative: "A successful and aggressive leveraging of the e-finance platform could turn Confinity into a global financial institution, offering a complete suite of customer banking services. Under this scenario, Confinity would push all the way to an IPO."

■ ■ ■

In the plan, the preamble to the founders' biographies offered a window into how Thiel and Levchin thought about building start-up teams at the time:

> In bringing together Confinity's founders we have been driven by two overriding considerations. The first is to identify people who are highly talented and individually diverse, so that each of them is capable of taking on several different business and technology tasks. The second is to form a group that will work well as a team. Each of Confinity's founders has worked with at least one other founder in some past startup context. As a result we are aware of both the strengths and weaknesses of each member of the core team. We know who is best at what and how to allocate the various tasks. This common history enables Confinity to execute with efficiency and celerity.

Later, in his role as an investor and advisor, Thiel emphasized the importance of a team's "prehistory"—the bonds of work and friendship that exist prior to starting a venture. At least on Levchin's end, Confinity's prehistory was long. Nosek, Pan, and Simmons were friends from Illinois; other early employees came through that network and Thiel's Stanford contacts. There were downsides to this approach, too, of course. Hiring friends risked a cloistered, exclusionary monoculture and made it exceptionally hard to let people go.

But Thiel's view was that trust among teams was hard to build, and that friends-turned-employees came preinstalled with trust. "It was this network hiring sort of effect where we had a great deal of trust that everybody was reasonably bright, and trying to work toward making this successful," early employee David Wallace recalled. Trust produced speed. "We could be at a much faster cycle than a lot of companies where you have to take a month to sort of message things throughout the company before you could say what you were trying to say."

Wallace, a mild-mannered personality, also felt a "comfort level" speaking up at Confinity. "If I had been walking into somewhere where I didn't know anybody, I wouldn't have been talking that way."

Engineer Santosh Janardhan didn't join the PayPal team until 2001, but he got a fast education in how the company's senior leaders trusted even fresh hires. In the first few hours of his first day on the database team, Janardhan was given the root password for PayPal's database. "[His boss, Paul Tuckfield,] was like, 'Play around with it and let me know if you have questions.'"

Soon thereafter, Janardhan saw Tuckfield and the company's CTO, Levchin, approaching him. "So Paul and Max walk over, and they're like, 'Hey, what are you doing?' [And I said,] 'I'm looking around trying to understand the layout of the databases, looking at the tables and stuff. I was doing some database queries.' They're like, 'The site just had a blip. Did you just take it down?' I'm like, 'Fuck no.' And they both look at each other and go, 'Cool.' And walk back."

Janardhan was amazed. "If you think through this . . . five minutes into me joining, they gave me the root password for the site. The amount of either foolhardiness or trust it takes is amazing, right? On the flip side, when I said I didn't [take the site down], they just said 'Okay' and walked away. There was no grilling. There was no 'Show me what you're doing.' In a weird way, I felt more in the trust circle than anything else they could have ever done."

Janardhan had not been a friend-of-friend, nor a University of Illinois or Stanford graduate, and he joined the company later in its life cycle. But he, too, sensed the power in hiring for trust. "They hired really good people, gave them a lot of trust, and so people ran at their own pace, just made sure that they checkpointed to make sure we were in sync occasionally. And then we would just keep on running. So they got the best out of some very, very smart people."

■ ■ ■

In many ways, the wisdom of PayPal's hiring only became apparent later—after the company's success validated the early team design. At the time, the founders' logic was more practical than philosophical and driven more by expediency than experience. "We had to recruit our friends because no one else would work for us," PayPal's future COO David Sacks would later say.

From 1994 to 1999, the internet talent pool had gone pro. Companies like Amazon, Google, and Netscape that famously launched in garages, trailers, and dorms now labored from spacious offices. They offered generous salaries, ample benefits, and stock options worth actual— rather than just theoretical—money. They could also afford expensive recruiting firms to source the best talent in Silicon Valley and elsewhere.

By contrast, Confinity had no reputation, no products, and no traction. "It was a challenge because basically it was very hard to recruit people into this totally untried company," Thiel said. Vince Sollitto had been working as a communications director for a senator in Washington, DC, when David Sacks approached him about working at Confinity. Sollitto remembered his wife's skepticism—and the couple's truce. "We can do it," he remembered her saying. "We're not going to sell our [Washington] house. We're going to rent our house out for a year . . . and then when this thing flames out in a year, we have to come home. That's the bargain."

Confinity was also competing for talent against any number of "totally untried companies" that mushroomed during the internet boom—a period of rapid growth that caused an unprecedented demand for software engineers. As Janardhan put it, "If you had a pulse, you got a job. It was that kind of thing in 1999."

That environment forced Levchin and Thiel to recruit friends and close contacts. One of Confinity's earliest engineers, Tomasz Pytel, was a prototypical case. As teenagers, Pytel and Levchin first met as Delph (Levchin) and Tran (Pytel), the handles they used in a computer art subculture called "demoscene."

Groups of demoscene coders competed to showcase cutting-edge digital graphics, and Pytel had become a legend in this community for his breathtaking visualizations. "I did have a lot of time to dedicate to [demoscene]," Pytel recalled, "because I was always cutting school. In fact, I dropped out of high school—because it was just pointless."

Pytel was a Polish immigrant to the United States, and his computing baptism resembled Levchin's in its rigor:

My mother bought me a computer when I was in the fourth grade. It was a Commodore 16 with a datasette—not a disk drive, a datasette—which promptly broke after a couple of months. Which means that every time I turned on the machine, whatever I was playing around with, I had to write from scratch, basically. So I guess in terms of programming practice, that would be the software equivalent of maybe Rocky Balboa hitting a side of beef. And I was hooked, from then on.

By the time he left high school in his sophomore year, Pytel had already cobbled together different contract programming jobs to pay the bills, including writing code for the video game software firm Epic Games.

Years later, he was traveling across the country when he stopped in Palo Alto to see Levchin, Simmons, and Pan. "He was a true vagabond nomad," Levchin remembered of Pytel. When he arrived at the Confinity office during his stop in California, Pytel wore a pair of tattered water slippers. "His toes were sticking out," Simmons said. Later PayPal employees recalled that the decrepit footwear stuck around even as the company thrived. ("They were the most comfortable shoes I'd gotten in a while," Pytel remembered, "and I just loved them so much that I just wore them everywhere.")

Odd shoes were no matter—at Confinity, the eccentricities of the talented were easily excused. Levchin made an aggressive effort to bring Pytel aboard the team, and when he agreed, it gave Simmons and Pan hope. "The fact that he joined the team was a big deal," Simmons said. For Pytel, the decision was invested with far less significance. "At that point in your life, when you're that young, you don't really pay attention to risk," he recalled. "It's just like, *Yeah, okay, this looks cool. Let's do this for a while.*"

Confinity's Tom Pytel was talented enough to earn a doctorate, but too defiant to replace worn footwear. He had time on his hands. And he tolerated the team's notions about world-beating PalmPilot wallets. Brilliance, nonconformity, availability, and the willing suspension of disbelief—these qualities defined Confinity's first hires and formed the foundation of its culture.

■ ■ ■

Almost right away, Confinity's Mobile Wallet pitch ran into the same market problem as the Fieldlink security software: people weren't begging to swap actual wallets for virtual ones. Even as they coded furiously, the team wondered about the Mobile Wallet's efficacy. That prompted a series of team discussions in the spring of 1999, reflecting on their creations and considering alternative use cases.

The question was less technical than it was logical—what information was better stored inside a PalmPilot than a normal wallet? One idea: passwords. Passwords on paper slips tucked into a real wallet were vulnerable to theft. "If you store them in your PalmPilot, you could secure it further with a secondary passphrase that protects it," Levchin said. This was a promising concept and, indeed, a forerunner of today's password managers. But at the time, the handheld device market was still small and the market for PalmPilot password managers even smaller.

Compounding the challenge for Confinity, passwords lacked glamour. The era's dot-coms were busily pitching technological revolution—promising to do everything from deliver groceries to play Cupid. Even Levchin admitted that Confinity's pitch for a password manager seemed dull by comparison.

The password concept, though unsuccessful, gave rise to a vital question: What were other protectable slips of paper? One possible answer was bank checks and paper money. "The next iteration was this thing that would cryptographically secure IOU notes. I would say, 'I owe you $10,' and put in my passphrase," Levchin recalled. The digital IOUs would be stored until the user docked their PalmPilot to a computer, at which point the payments would clear.

Essentially, Confinity had created primitive digital checks, marrying handheld devices and finance. But as with the earlier ideas, PalmPilot-based IOUs didn't represent a stop-the-presses breakthrough. That is, until the team tweaked the product yet again.

For its 1998 generation of Palm IIIs, Palm tucked a half-inch sliver of red plastic into the corner. Palm pitched this infrared (IR) port as a way for PalmPilot users to beam information, but even as IR-bearing PalmPilots shipped, it wasn't exactly clear what users would beam. "Not all applications can use the beaming feature. Even the built-in programs, such as Palm Mail and Expense, can't beam items," *Palm Pilot for Dummies* noted. "But more and more Palm add-on programs include a beaming feature as time goes on, so you can start to plan on beaming things that you create from your Palm to another."

The ports proved notoriously glitchy. "Two Palm devices lose sight of each other when they're about four feet apart," the same guide noted, "and they also have some trouble communicating at less than three inches or so."

But such novelties were catnip to early adopters, and software engineers filled forums with possible use cases. "While the port is not powerful enough to act as, say, a remote control for a television," one developer wrote, "it does have enough power to support Palm-to-Palm communications of most any kind of data." What followed was a several-thousand-word guide on how to configure the IR port to play Battleship.

The IR port foreshadowed a future of pocket-sized devices in fluid communication. But in 1999, the port was a clever feature without a concrete purpose. However, the Confinity team—early adopters all—had such a purpose in mind: beaming money.

■ ■ ■

Picture the scene: A few technophiles are at lunch in Palo Alto. The check arrives, and the onerous task of dividing up the bill begins. One diner reminds the group that they have PalmPilots, which include a calculator and Confinity's money-beaming software. Presto: debts beamed, tab divided.

Confinity would reorient the company, its software, and its pitch around beaming money from PalmPilot to PalmPilot. This idea had two virtues. First, it leveraged the thousands of lines of cryptographic handheld device code they'd already written. Second, it was a new thing in the world. To date, no one had made much use of the PalmPilot IR ports, other than swapping notes or sinking battleships. In beaming money, Confinity had an IR port use case.

In retrospect, Levchin chuckled at the idea, calling it "quaint and silly." Years later, he joked to Jessica Livingston, author and founder of the seed stage venture firm, Y Combinator, "What would you rather do, take out five dollars and give someone their lunch share, or pull out two PalmPilots and geek out at the table?" But at the time, Levchin remembered that the idea had freshness: "It was so weird and innovative. The geek crowd was like, 'Wow. This is the future.'"

Lauri Schultheis was a paralegal at Wilson Sonsini Goodrich & Rosati, the law firm that Levchin and Thiel used to incorporate and handle their financing paperwork. She, too, was initially skeptical of her clients' money-beaming ambitions. "I remember thinking, *This is a really weird idea. Like, I don't know that people are going to go for this because all that [PalmPilot] technology was new*," Schultheis said. She dutifully filed the company's incorporation papers, even as she wondered about their prospects. (Later, Schultheis left the law firm to join PayPal as an office manager and rose to become a company vice president.)

From Thiel's perspective, beaming money gave the company a glitzy new story. By piggybacking on the moment's futuristic technology, the company could make a convincing fundraising pitch. The half a million dollars Confinity had raised from friends and family wouldn't go very far, especially as they staffed up. So, the team prepared a PowerPoint pitch deck, focused on this product evolution.

Beaming money via PalmPilot, the deck boasted, was a billion-dollar opportunity—"better than cash," "better than checks," and "better than credit cards." More importantly, Confinity would "capture part of seigniorage as it shifts from the US Treasury." Seigniorage is the difference between the face value of money and its production cost—an ancient concept. If it costs the royal mint £100 to mint coins using £100 worth of silver, but the face value of those coins is £110, the £10 difference is seigniorage—tax the king takes for transforming raw silver into currency.

Thiel hypothesized that technology companies, rather than the government, could serve as the intermediary—and keep this tax for themselves. It was a bit of an abstruse concept. "To this day, I don't fully understand what he meant," Levchin admitted. But the numbers were real: per the estimates in the deck, seigniorage was worth almost $25 billion per year in the US. If Confinity captured even a modest 4 percent of that, the company would net $1 billion.

Thiel and Levchin envisioned a cashless mobile world, with Confinity linking central banks, credit card companies, and retail banks. The company hoped to turn PalmPilots into the default form of payment and money transfer, replacing cash and checks. By 2002, if all went according to plan, Confinity projected $25 million in annual revenue from the success of its Mobile Wallet and beaming products.*

■ ■ ■

Compelling as the concept seemed to the team, they struggled—once again—to sell it. In February 1999, Levchin attended the International Financial Cryptography Association conference. Hosted in Anguilla, a sliver of a Caribbean island, the annual gathering drew the leading

*As it turns out, their revenue estimate was off by about a factor of eight—eight times too low.

players in academic cryptography and digital currencies. (To this day, Thiel, who attended the 2000 conference, harbors a theory that Satoshi Nakamoto—the mysterious founder of the cryptocurrency Bitcoin— was among the attendees. "I think if you try to figure out who Satoshi is, "Thiel reflected, "there are basically two frameworks. One is that he came from inside the sort of cyberpunk crypto anarchist world. Or he or she was some sort of idiot savant, completely disconnected from everybody. [With the] second theory, it's impossible to figure out. So just like you have to look for the lost keys under the lights, you have to assume the first theory is true, if you have any hope of solving it. And then if the first theory is true, then he would have been in Anguilla.")

At the conference, Levchin wanted to test the waters for his idea of a cashless, all-digital, PalmPilot-based money system. The academics were unimpressed—they had been thinking about this problem for a long time. "It is hard to understate the degree of anger and resentment that the people felt," Thiel said.

Unfortunately, Confinity was pitching its concepts amid a series of spectacular digital currency failures, including the recent bankruptcy of DigiCash. To the assemblage of financial crypto experts, Thiel and Levchin came off as arrogant, uninformed outsiders, unaware of the decade of wasted effort before their arrival on the scene.

Academics weren't the only ones giving Confinity the cold shoulder. Mark Richardson was a consultant who had connected with Thiel, helped revise the early business plans, and made introductions to some of his contacts in financial services. Richardson recalled a JP Morgan Chase banker's dismissive response to the money-beaming pitch: "He said, 'We've looked at, we've tested, we've tried to get people to use money in a different way than an ATM or a credit card. And there's been all kinds of thoughts about how to get that done, and tests, and pilots. We just don't see people being comfortable getting away from cash, ATMs at the time, and credit cards.'"

Venture capitalists, too, were unenthused. During what Thiel called "an excruciating process," the team presented over one hundred times— with pitch after pitch falling flat. Would-be investors asked sensible questions: *Would people really beam money from handheld devices? What were the odds that four separate lunchtime companions would all own PalmPilots and have Mobile Wallet installed? Also, what exactly was seigniorage, and could Confinity really make money, as Thiel put it, "off the float"?*

As the rejections piled up, the team grew desperate. They began cold outreach to venture firms beyond Silicon Valley. Luke Nosek used contacts to earn a meeting with the venture division of the European mobile company Nokia.*

The meeting with the head of Nokia Ventures, John Malloy, got off to a rocky start. Levchin and Nosek both arrived in shorts and flip-flops. "You just didn't do that shit with VCs in that day," Malloy said of their attire. The team also seemed distracted. "They were so excited about being able to send device-to-device payments by infrared that they wouldn't stop doing it! I'm trying to have an adult conversation with them, and it was crazy. It was like 'Guys, okay . . . !'" Malloy said. "I called them 'the Beamers.'"

Malloy worked for Nokia—a mobile device company. But even to him, some of Confinity's claims seemed a long shot. "Peter looked me dead in the eye and said, 'We're going to be the dominant payment system for the Palm economy,'" Malloy recalled. He remembered thinking, *Really? Shit, c'mon man, what kind of objective is that?* Still, Malloy and his partner at Nokia Ventures, Pete Buhl, left the meeting intrigued. Nokia had been circling around mobile payments, and they believed in the technology's future. Confinity was on to something.

Far more impressive to Buhl and Malloy was the team itself. "There was a unique energy about them. . . . They just so stood out," Malloy said. Buhl agreed: "You have Peter, this super smart business guy. Max, the allegedly super smart technical guy. And then Luke, the ideas guy." Malloy anticipated that Confinity's PalmPilot ideas wouldn't work out as pitched, but that the team possesed the raw material to find something that would.

---

*Incidentally, John Powers had pitched John Malloy on Fieldlink months before the Malloy-Nosek connection—to no avail. "[Nokia] had a bunch of good ideas on adopting the Palm OS," Powers remembered.

Buhl and Malloy signaled their interest, and they ran due diligence on the team. Buhl approached two Stanford professors, Dr. Dan Boneh and Dr. Martin Hellman, who served as Confinity technical advisors. Boneh was a young professor at Stanford known for his work on handheld device cryptography; Hellman was renowned as the inventor of public-key cryptography. They told Buhl that Levchin was the "real deal." "In a way," said Buhl, "the real insurance policy was how incredible Max was by reputation."

Malloy set up a meeting between Levchin and the president of Nokia, Dr. Pekka Ala-Pietilä. Malloy didn't need Ala-Pietilä's approval to invest in Confinity, but he wanted to give Nokia's president the chance to connect with this young Silicon Valley engineer—which had been one of Nokia's goals in seeding start-ups in the first place.

Levchin, though, didn't get the memo. He interpreted the time with Ala-Pietilä as more final exam than meet-and-greet, with Confinity's future hanging in the balance. Adding to the pressure, Ala-Pietilä was the leader of one of the world's foremost technology companies— one that actually built and sold mobile technology to millions of people. In the weeks leading up to the meeting, Levchin mainlined mobile knowledge.

When they finally met face-to-face, Ala-Pietilä dove in with technical questions—including how Levchin could get low-power PalmPilots to perform highly complex calculations. A well-prepared Levchin summarized the differences between different cryptographic standards—the algorithms used to secure systems—and explained how he'd get maximum security at minimum processing speed.

Coming into the meeting, Levchin thought Ala-Pietilä might render an instant judgment on Nokia's investment. But as the discussion ended, Ala-Pietilä simply thanked Levchin for coming in. It felt concerningly anticlimactic. When Thiel asked Levchin how he did, Levchin answered honestly, "I don't know. I think I did fine, but I wouldn't know if I failed."

Shortly after the meeting, Malloy received a positive review on Levchin from Ala-Pietilä. Nokia Ventures would draft terms for its investment in Confinity.

■ ■ ■

In the Silicon Valley venture capital pecking order, firms backed by corporate partners like Nokia ranked near the bottom. At the time, Nokia Ventures had another knock against it: Buhl and Malloy's small operation had no investing track record—no lengthy list of exits and IPOs.

Which is why Confinity briefly flirted with an offer of investment from a better-known firm. Draper Fisher Jurvetson (DFJ) had found some success with consumer internet investments, including an early stake in the breakthrough email service Hotmail. But despite the temptation of its superior reputation, Thiel persuaded the team to stick with Nokia Ventures, which offered a larger sum of money on more favorable terms.

In 1999, Nokia Ventures made its third-ever investment, leading a $4.5 million dollar investment round in Confinity. The funding gave Thiel and Levchin the semblance of a professional operation—they could now boast venture-backing, a tentative road map, and a board of directors.

Nokia's John Malloy and Pete Buhl joined the company's board and engaged deeply with its people and operations. Over the years that followed, Malloy would find himself at the center of the company's highest-profile and most sensitive controversies, and he'd take on the role of investor-therapist, with execs and employees alike turning to him to air their grievances. "John was a great presence for us," Scott Banister said. Levchin went one step further and described him as "the unsung hero of the PayPal story."

Malloy's involvement began ominously. Malloy and Thiel hammered out the final details for the investment on the phone, just as Malloy was taking Nokia's president, Ala-Pietilä, sailing. By Malloy's account, the boat's owner "had bought himself too much boat," and the craft hit high winds and choppy seas. The propeller malfunctioned, and they retreated gingerly to the dock. "That ride becomes a total shitshow," Malloy remembered. "It was a tumultuous day."

6

HOSED

Throughout the spring and early summer of 1999, Confinity and X.com occupied adjoining office suites at 394 University Avenue in Palo Alto. After the fact, much was made of the two companies' cohabitation, but it started as mere coincidence. X.com and Confinity were neither competitors nor collaborators—Confinity pursued mobile money transfer and cryptography while X.com went about building its financial services superstore.

Each company thought the other was misguided. Musk was unreserved in his criticism of PalmPilot money beaming. "I'm like, *That's a dumb idea. They're doomed,*" he remembered thinking. Meanwhile, Confinity expected X.com to sink in regulatory quicksand.

Despite divergent approaches to financial technology, the companies' CEOs shared an obsession: getting noticed. Just as Musk courted media attention for X.com, Thiel made generating headlines a top priority. He had just closed Confinity's investment deal with Nokia Ventures, and he wanted a big, splashy event to trumpet the deal—and demo the team's breakthrough beaming technology.

The team chose Buck's of Woodside for the event. Buck's—whose kitschy decor included porcelain cowboy boots, an authentic Russian cosmonaut suit, and a scaled-down Statue of Liberty—earned frequent visits from the technology set—and a storied place in tech lore. Buck's was one of the first US restaurants with public WiFi, and Hotmail was reportedly incorporated at one of its tables.

Confinity hoped to add another chapter to Buck's history—Thiel planned to use PalmPilots to beam the $4.5 million investment from Nokia Ventures's bank account to Confinity's in real time. But the "Beaming at Buck's" would be easier said than done. "[The infrared technology] didn't work for shit," Levchin remembered. Nonetheless, Levchin insisted that the beaming be a real, encrypted transaction—not a facsimile.

Despite the engineering team's hard work, its codebase was far from finished. "The stuff was barely working," Pan admitted. To prepare for the Beaming at Buck's, Levchin had to hastily create his own security protocols and update the app's user interface, including its buttons. He copied most of the buttons from a different PalmPilot calculator application and frantically coded a brand-new "Send" button for the demo.

Soon, the team faced a more harrowing problem than hastily built buttons. In order for a programmer's code to work, it had to be compiled—the process that turns coded commands into a language machines can comprehend. It's during compiling that programming errors are discovered and fixed. Mere days before the Buck's event, Russ Simmons discovered that Yu Pan hadn't compiled his code—for months. "And of course, we try to compile, and he has something like a thousand errors," Levchin said.

A dead sprint followed. "From that point on, the insane mad rush to the Buck's Beaming begins. The three of us did not sleep at all. Yu Pan was basically near catatonic by the end of the third day," Levchin recalled. Scheduled for the morning of Friday, July 23, 1999, Levchin and the team pulled back-to-back all-nighters, double- and triple-checking code until just before the event.

As the sun rose that Friday, Levchin realized he'd been wearing the same pair of pants several days in a row. *I need to change my pants*, he thought to himself. So Levchin got in his car, drove home, and swapped out pants. Pants upgraded, he raced to Buck's.

■ ■ ■

When Levchin arrived, Thiel was already there, hobnobbing with Pete Buhl from Nokia Ventures. Thiel had managed to attract several local television stations to cover the event, and their satellite trucks idled nearby.

Levchin had prepared two PalmPilots for the transaction. He handed one to Buhl and the other to Thiel. Standing before the cameras, Buhl took his device and used the stylus to enter Nokia's payment: 4-5-0-0-0-0-0. He positioned his infrared port next to Thiel's, and pressed Levchin's freshly coded Send button. Levchin held his breath—if something were to fail, it would fail now.

But Thiel's PalmPilot beeped and displayed a message saying that it had successfully received the payment—which he proudly held up for the cameras to see. The entire Confinity team heaved a sigh of relief.

For all the anxiety leading up to the Beaming at Buck's, Buhl remembered the main event as "anticlimactic." Afterward, one of the television crew members came over to ask Thiel and Levchin if they could repeat the transaction—his camera hadn't quite caught it. "No! We cannot do it again," Levchin cried. "It's millions of dollars moving from one bank to the other. We can't just do it again." At the cameraman's request, Thiel and Buhl playacted the exchange.

Levchin didn't have the energy to register his frustration. Instead, he wandered off to a corner table, sat down, and laid his head on the table. Sometime later, he awoke, finding his Confinity colleagues gone and a cold omelet next to him. The waiter told him that his teammates had left but paid for his breakfast. *Should I be angry at Peter for not waking me up?* Levchin wondered. *Or should I be thankful that he was so caring to let me sleep?*

Thoughtful or otherwise, Thiel was pleased with the event. "It was a phenomenal way of breaking through the clutter," he said. Confinity earned some valuable press coverage, which in turn spurred several job applications and some investor interest—neither of which had come easily in the past.

Despite the attention, the event didn't succeed in winning users—no one was calling the Confinity office asking how to beam money from their PalmPilots. "This was one of the lessons we had about PR early on," Nosek remembered. "It was much more important for recruiting and for perception among investors than it is about actual product adoption."

Arguably the most important signal from the Beaming at Buck's was internal. In just months, Levchin, Thiel, and their small group had created an app worth covering—even worth televising! It boosted the team's confidence. "I think we needed to believe where things would go," Nosek said.

■ ■ ■

As the internet boom began, start-up superfluities flooded the Bay Area: expensive team retreats, parties with limitless alcohol, and pricey billboards. None of it, Thiel and Levchin thought, credibly advanced a given company's products or mission. They would not use Nokia Ventures's millions for such excesses. The funds did, however, allow them one luxury: a better name for the beaming product.

"Confinity" sufficed as a corporate name, but for a consumer product, they worried that four syllables beginning with *con* wouldn't inspire trust. Besides, "Just Confinity the money to me" didn't exactly float off the tongue.

A consumer products company needed a name with mass appeal, and the task of finding that name fell to Nosek—who turned to the internet for guidance. He typed www.naming.com into his browser and discovered the website of a naming firm, Master-McNeil. "We figured they owned the URL 'naming.com,' so that was promising," Nosek explained.

SB Master, the firm's founder, had earned a triple major from UC Santa Cruz in economics, music, and a self-designed course of study called "the history of the book." Following an MBA at Harvard, she founded the naming division of a branding company behind the names Touchstone Pictures and Westin Hotels. Then she set off on her own, creating Master-McNeil and advising companies on what to call themselves.

Master married a poetic sensibility with hard-nosed business skills. Too many start-ups, she believed, treated naming as a mere exercise in

wordplay, "a kind of bounce it off the wall, somewhat random, purely creative process." She believed that naming was as crucial a business decision
as any other and merited analytic rigor.

In June 1999, Confinity signed Master-McNeil to name its beaming
product. Master and her team interviewed Thiel, Levchin, Nosek, and
other Confinity employees. Together, the group solidified what the name
should suggest:

1. Convenient, easy, simple to set up/use
2. Instant, fast, instantaneous, no waiting, time-saving, quick
3. Portable, handy, always with you
4. Transmit, "beam," exchange, send/receive, give/get
5. Money, accounts, financial transactions, numbers, moving
   money around

Confinity's discussions with Master-McNeil revealed an important question about the product's trajectory. Money beaming appealed to the
American tech crowd, but how would Confinity grow to markets beyond
them? The team didn't have an answer yet, but they urged Master-McNeil
to split the difference and to find a name that was both not overly "techy"
and yet "appropriate for anyone who uses a portable electronic device
(PDA, cell phone), with emphasis on early adopters," as well as a name
"appropriate for use in the US, France, Germany, Spain, Italy."

Criteria and naming objectives in hand, the Master-McNeil team set
to work generating dozens of potential names, a list they winnowed to
the eighty "most promising" names, and following a check of trademarks,
URLs, and common law, a dozen recommended ones. Among them were
eMoneyBeam, Zapio, MoMo, Cachet, and Paypal. eMoneyBeam and
MoMo were shelved quickly. Zapio was playful and spoke to the core
product—"zapping" money—but the Confinity team didn't warm to it. Initially, they thought Cachet was the best option, but Master herself thought
it was not. Tough to spell and pronounce, Cachet also had a "highfalutin'
tone," said Master, and wouldn't translate easily to other languages. Another
strike against it: the domain www.cachet.com was claimed.

Then there was Paypal. Master-McNeil's presentation slide offered six rationales for its selection:

- Conveys money, accounts, financial transactions, moving money around
- Suggests friendly, accessible, simple, easy
- Suggests always with you, portable, handy
- Repeated pa- structure memorable, fun
- Particularly short, symmetrical (an ascender at either end, two descenders in the middle)
- .com available

Master believed Paypal to be the clear winner. It was one syllable shorter than Zapio and far less likely to be mispronounced than Cachet. "If people don't know how to say something, or if they are fearful of saying it incorrectly," Master said, "they will do anything to avoid saying it. Embarrassment is a very strong emotion."

Master also felt that Paypal engendered trust. Confinity had been Levchin's awkward attempt to bestow confidence, but Master believed the disarming quality of *pal* in Paypal achieved that objective more gracefully: "Your pal is more than a friend. A pal has their arm around you. You're with each other. You really trust each other," she explained.

To top it all off, Paypal featured two *p*s. "We love these sounds, called plosives," Master explained. "To produce [them], you stop the air and then you release it." Plosives hung in the ear for an extra fraction of a second—more time to remember the brand. "To create a name that has two plosives really takes maximum advantage of this," said Master.

Master was sold on Paypal, but many on the Confinity team, including Thiel, were not. "I remember all of us talking about it . . . and thinking, *Paypal?* That sounds like the dumbest name ever," engineer Russ Simmons remembered. "It was definitely not a unanimous decision," Jack Selby, employee number eleven, said. Board member Pete Buhl believed it sounded too playful for a financial product. "People are not going to trust 'Paypal.' I thought it was the stupidest idea," he said. "Guys, a Paypal? You're going to trust your money with a Paypal?"

But as they sat with Paypal, the team became convinced of its virtues. "The initial way we were thinking about [the product] was so much about reimbursing each other at lunch, and that kind of use case. PayPal just naturally fit that use case more than the others did," recalled David Wallace, who had joined the company to handle customer service and operations.

The verb form—"Just Paypal it to me"—won them over, as did its simple spelling. Some early board members advocated for it—including Scott Banister: "I said, 'I think that's a great name. It's alliterative. It's very memorable.'" Because the domain www.paypal.com was unclaimed, the team would face no protracted, expensive negotiations to acquire it. They did so on July 15, 1999.

Though Thiel had originally preferred Cachet, he, too, came around to Paypal. In fact, he would later reference it to illustrate the value of friendly, generous-sounding company monikers, using it to argue for "Lyft" over "Uber" and "Facebook" over "MySpace." In the near term, Thiel and many others would argue that—next to Paypal—X.com sounded ominous.

Confinity selected PayPal—with a stylization, capitalizing the middle *p*. This intercap *P* stuck—forever after, Paypal would be written PayPal. A note in Master's files records the adoption of the intercap *P*—a quick entry with the phrase "Chose PayPal"—but Master couldn't recall the edit's origins, nor if she, a graphic designer, or the Confinity team was the source.

■ ■ ■

Name in hand, the company now needed to expand in order to bring its beaming product to life. Just like X.com, Confinity had to compete in a white-hot market for engineers, and even with ample funds and some press attention, hiring remained difficult.

The team's collegiate connections paid some dividends, as did several of the early engineers' ties to the Illinois Mathematics and Science Academy (IMSA), a prestigious public magnet high school in Aurora, Illinois. As more engineers came aboard from both University of Illinois and IMSA networks, new product and business team members came by way of Stanford.

To speed things up, the team instituted a several-thousand-dollar referral bonus for recruiting engineers. One hire, James Hogan, recalled his IMSA-UIUC friend and Confinity engineer, Steve Chen, reaching out. "He was very excited [about the referral bonus]," Hogan said, chuckling. "He was pinging anyone he had known in his life who had some sort of software development experience. I was as much a dollar sign for the referral bonus as anything else."

To win recruits over, the team crafted an edgy sales pitch. Years later, Levchin described the approach to a Stanford computer science class:

> Engineers are very cynical people. They're trained to be. And they can afford to be, given the large number of companies that are trying to recruit them in Silicon Valley right now. Since engineers think any new idea is dumb, they will tend to think that your new idea is dumb. They get paid a lot at Google doing some pretty cool stuff. Why stop indexing the world to go do your dumb thing? So the way to compete against the giants is not with money. Google will outbid you. They have [an] oil derrick that spits out $30 billion in search revenue every year.
>
> To win, you need to tell a story about cogs. At Google, you're a cog. Whereas with me, you're an instrumental piece of this great thing that we'll build together. Articulate the vision. Don't even try to pay well. Meet people's cash flow needs. Pay them so they can cover their rent and go out every once in a while. It's not about cash. It's about breaking through the wall of cynicism. It's about making 1% of this new thing way more exciting than a couple hundred grand and a cubicle at Google.

For Hogan, that argument landed. He was living in Dallas and working "as a cog in a very large machine" at Nortel Networks. "I was quite unhappy and quite ineffective," he admitted. Confinity's pitch hit home.

Despite their honed recruiting spiel, hiring moved slowly. Some of this was by design. "There was a huge, huge worry in engineering that any one bad hire could destroy the codebase," engineer Erik Klein said. "That's partially our doing, because it's bad that a codebase can be destroyed so easily. But if you're coding fast and loose, that's the codebase that you build. And you create the problem—but then you have to hire people to fit within that problem."

Levchin kept the bar for talent exceedingly high, engineer Santosh Janardhan noted, even if that came at the expense of speedy staffing. "Max kept repeating, 'As hire As. Bs hire Cs. So the first B you hire takes the whole company down.'"

Additionally, Confinity's leaders mandated that all prospects meet with every single member of the team. Once the lengthy round-robin of interviews was completed, the team discussed the candidate as a group, asking whether they passed the so-called "aura test."

With tech firms hiring left and right, future recruits performed "aura tests" of their own—and more than one employee cited the team as the main draw, more than the product vision or promise of success. Skye Lee had cut her teeth at Netscape and Adobe, and she was working at another start-up when a former colleague who had joined Confinity suggested she meet David Sacks. She agreed, despite reservations—her current start-up wasn't faring well, and she didn't want to repeat that experience.

Sacks invited Lee to visit the Confinity office at 10 p.m., and given the hour, she expected to "stop by—and then move on." But a short meet-and-greet was not to be. "It was a *full-on* interview," she recalled, "which I was not prepared for." By the time she left at 2 a.m., she had spoken to nearly every Confinity employee.

She also learned about Confinity's PalmPilot money transfer product. When Sacks pitched the concept, Lee noticed a problem: "I'm like, 'But it's not beaming *actual* money. Because you're just syncing on the desktop, right?'" She was right, of course, as technically a transaction only took place once a PalmPilot was nestled into its desktop cradle. "I thought I was missing something," Lee recalled. Sacks confessed that Lee wasn't missing anything and that her questions were justified.

Despite the lengthy late-night interview and the limitations of infrared money beaming, Lee left intrigued by the team. "I can't really put words on it, because I go by my gut," she said, "but the *energy* there, I hadn't felt that before. And I'm like, 'There's *something* here.'" After an additional interview, she joined Confinity, where she would play a key role in designing the company's signature products.

Denise Aptekar, a member of the product team, had worked at another start-up for several months when she met Luke Nosek at a party—where he grabbed a napkin and drew Confinity's money-beaming master plan. Aptekar was taken—not so much by the idea, but the way Nosek spoke about it.

She came in to meet the team. "I left the interview not being able to tell you anything exactly about the product or much [else]—other than, those are the people I want to work with," Aptekar recalled. "*Clearly* hypercompetitive. *Clearly* workaholics. *Clearly* want to change the world. It was like, *I found my people*."

Benjamin Listwon, a technical designer, was happily employed and not looking for "his people" when he met David Sacks and Max Levchin. After they met, Sacks invited Listwon to lunch at Confinity. "Lunch turned into seven hours," Listwon recalled.

The spontaneous several-hour jam session about design practices hooked him. "I already feel like I'm actually in the room whiteboarding . . . if *this* is their interview, imagine what working here must be like!" he remembered thinking.

■ ■ ■

Early on, Thiel instituted an informal no-firing rule. "Firing people is like war," he explained, "and war is bad, so you should try not to do it." The no-firing rule set a high bar for talent, but it also caused underperforming employees to be shuffled around the company, rather than efficiently dismissed. "We probably should have fired more people," one early employee admitted.

The aura test and no-firing rule were imprecise and inefficient, but the deliberate recruiting process was designed to speed the company up. In Confinity's early days, Levchin observed that the number of people in a room correlated positively to friction in basic communication. "If you're alone," he explained, "you just work really hard and hope it's enough. Since it often isn't, people form teams. But in a team, an n-squared communications problem emerges. In a five-person team, there are something like twenty-five pairwise relationships to manage and communications to maintain."

To minimize such chafe, Levchin wanted engineers who saw the world as he did. For example, when early on Levchin chose C++ as PayPal's programming language—which even he referred to as a "kind of crappy language"—he expected the founding engineers not to complain. "Anyone that did want to argue about it," Levchin said, "wouldn't have fit in. Arguing would have impeded progress."

Still, both he and Thiel were cautious to avoid groupthink. "Arguing about smart marketing moves or different approaches to solving tactical or strategic problems is fundamental. These are the decisions that actually matter," Levchin said. "A good rule of thumb is that diversity of opinion is essential anytime you don't know anything about something important. But if there's a strong sense of what's right already, don't argue about it."

Finding that balance wasn't easy, and the team faced its share of frustrations—as well as a few violations of the no-firing rule. But they also notched some hiring wins. During this period, Confinity landed its first "out-of-network" hire: Chad Hurley. He would go on to become one of the cofounders of YouTube, but in 1999, Hurley was a new college graduate with a fine arts degree and no prior connection to the Confinity team. He had seen a press mention of the Beaming at Buck's and sent a cold email expressing his interest, which earned him a meeting. After a flight delay, a late arrival, and an all-night interview, Hurley was extended an offer to join Confinity as its first graphic designer.

His first assignment: designing the logo for Confinity's PayPal product. He landed on a blue-and-white image, with a stylized letter P set in a swirl. Levchin also asked Hurley to design a team T-shirt, and he gave Hurley the seed of an idea: What if the T-shirt riffed on the Sistine Chapel ceiling? Instead of God sending the spark of life to Adam through his fingertips, the Almighty could instead send him money through a PalmPilot. As the years passed, this T-shirt featuring Hurley's Michelangelo remix became a treasured team memento.

With the addition of Hurley and several others, Confinity outgrew its cramped headquarters at 394 University Avenue. The team found a space available just five minutes down the road, at 165 University Avenue. The building carried special significance, as its most recent tenant was the most-talked-about company in town: Google. Confinity inherited the search giant's ping-pong table, which, for a time, doubled as its boardroom table.

The change in offices also eliminated an important rite of passage. At 394 University, each new hire was required to assemble their own IKEA desk. A bonding and democratizing ritual, it also paid homage to Levchin's early IKEA furnishings. In a fatal blow to tradition, Confinity's new offices at 165 University Avenue came mostly furnished.

■ ■ ■

A new name, new offices, and new employees—it all looked like progress. But an old, central question still bedeviled the company: How exactly would people discover the PalmPilot beaming product? And more importantly, would they use it?

At some level, the team assumed demand would exist—if they built it, the beamers would come. It was an easy mistake to make, given their surroundings. Handheld devices like the PalmPilot and its technological cousin, feature phones, were all the rage in Silicon Valley. "I was very bullish on [the PalmPilot] platform," Scott Banister admitted. "Many, many people out here were." By 1999, more than five million people owned Palm devices, and 3Com, Palm's parent company, was even exploring a Palm spin-off IPO.

The Confinity team felt confident it could surf this handheld device growth wave. The team purchased advertising in magazines devoted to the handheld market, and team members took to various internet tech forums to trumpet the PayPal product. During this period, Nosek also proposed an unorthodox marketing idea: seeing the shabby state of the office awning, he suggested that Confinity replace it—with a strobing infrared light built in to beam messages about PayPal.

The "awning strobe light ad" never did come to pass, but it illustrated the lengths the team was willing to go to win users—indeed, it showed how far they'd *have* to go. Because despite all their hard work, beamers weren't beaming, and by the summer of 1999, advisors and friends of the company probed the product's viability.

"We are living in the heaven of PalmPilots," observed Reid Hoffman, a Stanford friend of Thiel's and early Confinity board member, "and we could walk into every single restaurant and go to each table and ask how many people have PalmPilots." He guessed the answer was between zero and one per restaurant. "And that means your use case can only be used between zero and one times, per restaurant, per meal cycle! You're hosed! It's over on this idea."

At one of many late-night product debates that summer, Reid Hoffman raised another critical stumbling block: What if one of these hypothetical PayPal users forgot their PalmPilot and needed to execute a transaction? Levchin proposed a workaround, suggesting the PayPal .com website be set up to send money via a user's email address. Users had to use the website anyway to download the PayPal software for syncing their handheld devices to their computers. The site could have an email system as a backup to the PalmPilot money-beaming option.

When emailing money was first suggested, few recognized it as a eureka moment. Quite the opposite: Levchin intended it to be a throwaway demo—buried in a corner of the main site for the unlucky souls who forgot their PalmPilots. To him, emailing money was a far cry from PayPal's primary use case. This feature, if it could even be called that, was a concession to Hoffman's critique, not a core product.

This "concession" quickly became useful in ways Levchin hadn't predicted. Before the emailing money demo, he'd perform an elaborate ritual to test PayPal's plumbing: He'd beam money from one PalmPilot to another, sync both devices in their cradles, and then check two dummy accounts to confirm a funds transfer. The email money demo dramatically simplified this sequence—Levchin could now test transfers with a few mouse clicks. Within weeks, Levchin had become an avid user of the afterthought product, even as he remained committed to the vision of the original. "That should have been a clue," he said.

Erik Klein remarked on the team's fortunate timing. "Things happen on the internet like a snowball effect. It rolls quickly. It went from nobody really knowing about websites to everybody knowing about websites in what seemed like a year," he said. "And so the idea was business professionals were using their PalmPilots to pay—and we were going to catch *that* wave. But the wave of the web just tsunami-ed all over that concept. And we were just lucky that we ended up having both."

■ ■ ■

Another person who severely doubted money beaming's viability was a recent hire who would play a pivotal role in the company's success: David Sacks. Thiel and Sacks had attended Stanford together, and after graduating, Sacks went to law school at the University of Chicago before heading to the management consultancy McKinsey & Company.

In mid-1999, Sacks and Thiel were having regular discussions about Confinity and its products. Thiel urged Sacks to leave consulting and join Confinity. Sacks was interested, and entrepreneurship ran in the family. Sacks's grandfather had moved from Lithuania to South Africa in the 1920s to launch a candy factory. But his grandson, while intrigued by his friend Thiel's company, thought the PalmPilot idea a dud.

He came west for an interview nonetheless—which was not a success. "Sacks definitely didn't pass the aura test," one early Confinity team member said. The team objected, in part, to Sacks's total dismissal of the PalmPilot product. "It was a dumb idea," Sacks remembered. "There were two problems: one is that there are only five million Palm users, so unless you're with somebody who also had a PalmPilot, the app is useless. And then there's the other problem: even if you're with somebody who's got a PalmPilot, what would you use it for? Nobody could really come up with anything better than splitting dinner tabs."

Sacks told Thiel he'd join the company—if the email product was given primacy. "I said, 'If that's what the company's going to do, I'll quit my job at McKinsey tomorrow,' because that sounded to me like a killer idea," Sacks said.

Thiel assured him that email would take precedence over beaming, and Sacks agreed to join the company. But that assurance was unknown to most of the rest of the team—who still thought beaming was the priority. When Sacks arrived and began deprioritizing the PalmPilot product, the engineers were surprised—and incensed. "[Levchin] knew, but no one else on the team knew," Sacks said, "so I think their perception of me was that I was the guy coming in there and telling them everything they were doing was wrong." Thiel brokered a compromise: both products would be built side by side.

In hiring David Sacks, Thiel pulled rank and overruled the team's objections. This was a rare move for Thiel, who believed Sacks a rare candidate: After all, few people would come into an interview guns blazing *against* their prospective employer's flagship product. Thiel valued bracing honesty, and he trusted that Sacks would speak candidly. "Peter said, 'I need people here I can scream at,'" Sacks remembered.

Within the company, Sacks earned a reputation for being tough and tough-minded, and many in the company credited him with focusing the team and sharpening the product. "For as much as people gave [David Sacks] shit for arguing, it was always *good* arguing. It was good trouble," recalled Giacomo DiGrigoli. "It was never ad hominem or shitty or entitled. It was always about the idea. It was always about, *Look, what are we trying to do? What does the customer need? Why are we even here?*"

■ ■ ■

Much of that summer's discussion was hypothetical. Confinity didn't yet know how the public would receive its products, because its products hadn't yet been released. The Beaming at Buck's was a showcase, not a launch. Thiel wanted another opportunity to tell the world about Confinity, not only to prove the value of Confinity's creations to investors, but also to give the company a second chance at press attention.

Accordingly, he pushed Levchin to launch. "We worked seven days a week, twenty-hour days, just writing code, trying to get this thing to work," Levchin remembered of that summer. During this period, the team had to quickly educate itself on financial services, among other topics. "None of us had ever interacted with a bank before and never done any of this code," engineer Erik Klein recalled, "and our poor CFO, David Jaques, had to sit us down and tell us how banks work. And then we had to write the software four weeks before we went live."

It was one thing to beam money between two Confinity-owned PalmPilots for television cameras; it would be another when real users began crowding the airwaves with real dollars. "It's kind of funny in retrospect because we didn't know anything about payments . . . we had never written code that had interacted with a database. . . . We didn't know well enough to know that we should be more intimidated by the problem," Simmons said.

As news of PalmPilot money beaming made its way onto technology forums like Slashdot, the company faced its first set of critics. One Slashdot poster wrote a post about the technology, bracingly titled "What an amazingly bad idea":

Bad idea becauses there's at least three points at which to break in and subvert the system.

- On the IR level, such as copying someone's transaction from a distance.
- At the software level, such as getting a legit payment, then hacking the software on the Palm to up the amount by a large number.
- At the return the data to Confinity, such as sending them records of transactions that never actually occured in the first place.

Plus probably more. Admittedly, all these three can be fixed with the right kinds of encryption, but I doubt they worried about that too much when writing the software.

Just don't use this for anything important for about a year or two, giving them time to work out the bugs. Probably vaporware anyway.

Slashdot's tech-savvy users were sharply—and often comically—critical. One commenter wrote an "Extract From Galactic Encyclopedia, May 2010," describing robberies of the future "And from that point on, robbers had PalmPilots in their equipment, along with switchblades and guns. When they robbed somebody, their usual words were: 'point your Pilot to mine and beam all your money and nobody gets hurt.'"

The team hustled to write a technical FAQ, in which they acknowledged the criticism: "Was this technical FAQ created in response to the postings on Slashdot?" Their response: "Yes. This was written in a hurry to address posters' concerns ASAP. Please forgive the lack of organization, formatting and indexing."

In response to "What is the flavor/strength of your crypto?" the team's reply was both technical and candid:

> Currently we use 163-bit ECDSA for signatures on payments, DESX for encrypting data on handheld devices, Diffie-Hellman key exchange algorithm for exchanging [sic] keys for IR transmissions, DESX for encrypting IR transmissions, and ECC-based TLS for securing connections from the desktop to the server during a sync. We bang on the keyboard for half an hour or so to get enough entropy to seed our random number generator.

The team's inexperience showed in other ways as well. At one point, Levchin and his team learned that they neglected to use double-entry accounting in the PayPal system. Double-entry accounting is a centuries-old cornerstone of bookkeeping, by which any credit or debit has an equal and opposite record. "If you're an engineer, and you've never encountered accounting," Levchin said, "you don't really understand why it might be helpful to have two copies . . . I thought 'double-entry' accounting was some weird accountant fiction." He asked Confinity's CFO for an accounting crash course, and the team rebuilt the database accordingly.

The product itself pivoted rapidly before launch. Thiel had been doing some preliminary press in New York. "After Peter had had his first round of interviews, he calls . . . and basically tells us, 'Hey, guys, I told everybody that this is gonna be totally free. Take off all the fees,'" David Wallace recalled. The team had to update all the website language to remove fees, though Wallace briefly questioned the wisdom of promising a free product in perpetuity.

Approaching problems fresh and feeling the pressure to launch, the team had to devise solutions quickly, but that approach left the engineers with an operating style that served them well in PayPal's near future and in their later work. "Even in the current work I'm doing, we'll be in standups talking about the situation we're in, and your mind goes to *How can I solve this situation? What is some invention?* You learn to 'invent' instead of 'research and implement,'" Erik Klein observed.

During this period, the company also experienced the closest of close calls. In moving hard drives from one server to another, Confinity's system administrator inadvertently wiped out the codebase. *No problem*, Levchin thought, *let's just fire up the backup.* That's when the team discovered, to its horror, that the same system administrator had failed to retain a backup. Thousands of lines of code and eight months of work had vanished. "For a moment it looked like PayPal was done for," Thiel said.

Then another engineer, David Gausebeck, spoke up. He had replicated the company's entire source code. "We were all developing on a shared server, and we were running out of space there," Gausebeck explained, "and we had set up a new one where people could move everything over. I did that—and I was apparently the only one who had done that at the time the original one died." Gausebeck's backup saved the team from rebuilding its code line by painful line. "It was the closest shave we had," Levchin remembered. The system administrator became a rare exception to the no-firing rule.

■ ■ ■

Summer turned to fall, and the team's preparations for PayPal's debut dragged on. Levchin was forced to petition Thiel for repeated extensions to the launch date—leaving Thiel exasperated. "It was a rocky run-up to the launch," Levchin recalled.

During this period, Levchin sought a security check on the product.

PalmPilot code was in its infancy, and cryptographic code for Palm-Pilot even more so. To speed up the PayPal application, Levchin had employed a method of public-key cryptography known as "elliptic-curve cryptography"—but here, too, he was in new territory. "Palm had such a paucity of crypto code, especially elliptic curve, that we had to build some of it ourselves," Levchin recalled.

By creating these elements from scratch, Levchin risked vulnerabilities. "You don't ever want to build your own primitives . . . you want it to be done by someone who's got nothing else in the world to do other than just building the crypto primitives," Levchin shared.

Levchin had been trading thoughts on cryptographic security with, among others, Confinity's technical advisor and Stanford professor Dr. Dan Boneh. Boneh and Levchin were both enthused about mobile technology and cryptography and enjoyed playing ultimate Frisbee together. Crucially, Boneh was as passionate about PalmPilots as Levchin. "I have to say, for many years, even after the iPhone came out, I was so in love with my PalmPilot that I resisted the iPhone," Boneh joked. He and his Stanford colleagues had even taken a page out of Nosek and the UIUC ACM book: They connected a PalmPilot wallet to a Stanford vending machine. "There was a cryptographic protocol between the two," Boneh remembered, "Money would transfer between the two."

Expert in securely expanding PalmPilots to the world of vending machines and elsewhere, Boneh was the person that Levchin turned to when he wanted a speedy code check that fall. "So I was like, *Well, what's the closest thing to a security audit that I can do in twelve hours?* So then I thought, *Hey Dan, how would you like to come by and read my code?* And he's like, 'Of course, anything for you, man. Happy to,'" Levchin recalled.

Both Boneh and Levchin assumed they would be doing a quick scan, after which Boneh was due to celebrate his thirtieth birthday. Soon, however, Boneh caught an issue. "He reads through the code, and he's like, 'Dude, what is this?'" Levchin recalled. The issue was in how Levchin and the team were "packeting" certain bits. Per Levchin, Boneh said, "'No, no, no, look at how you are packeting it.' And I'm like, *'Oh my God!'*

And he's like, 'This is not random. Like this is the opposite of random. I could break it with a pencil. I don't need a supercomputer to break this.'"

What followed was a mad, all-night scramble in which the two had to go through every line of code and fix the mistake. At one point, Boneh recalled, he went home to briefly celebrate his birthday, then returned to the office where he remained with Levchin until 5 a.m.

Birthday interruptions and frantic all-nighters notwithstanding, the Confinity team put the finishing touches on its first release. In late October and early November, its small group of employees began sending emails to their friends and family. They announced that their company's first product was now available for download and use. PayPal was live.

7

MONEY TALKS

In the late summer of 1999, Elon Musk's X.com was a pale shadow of the digital finance behemoth he envisioned—and that PayPal would later become. At the time, X.com had no finished products and a hollowed-out team. After the departure of Canadian financier Harris Fricker and company, X.com's employee directory contained a mere five names. Missing were the company's founding president and COO, CTO and VP of product development, CFO, principal architect, and VP of corporate development.

A young engineer named Scott Alexander had a front-row seat to the turmoil. Fresh from Berkeley with a major in computer science and a minor in business administration, Alexander had watched his classmates throw themselves headlong into anything with a dot-com suffix attached. Alexander opted to take his time, carefully scrutinizing start-up business plans. "Even though there was this fever in 1999," he remembered, "I didn't believe that a mail-order dog food company was really going to sustain its billion-dollar value."

Alexander found X.com through a recruiting site. He applied and earned an interview with Musk, which he remembered distinctly: "Near the end of the interview, [Musk] said, 'I want you to understand this is a start-up company, and a lot is going to be expected of you. Like you can't just come in and work a forty-hour workweek. I expect really long hours until we succeed, and you're going to be asked to do the impossible.'"

One day after his interview, Alexander received an urgent email from Ed Ho, the X.com cofounder. Ho told Alexander that X.com was splitting up and that he and other senior managers were leaving to start new companies. He ended by wishing Alexander luck with X.com. Shortly after, Alexander found another email from Ho—this time from a personal address—asking him to come work for his new company.

Alexander found the recruiting war "weird" and left for a long-planned vacation to Cabo San Lucas, hoping to leave it behind. Musk, however, had other plans. "I come back and [there were] like six messages on my answering machine," Alexander said. "[Musk] said, 'Please give me a call. You've heard the bad news, but I've got some good news.'" Musk told Alexander that he had secured venture capital funding and that he was putting millions of his own money into X.com.

Alexander found Musk's personal commitment convincing. "Elon really impressed me," he remembered. "Money talks." He joined X.com in August 1999.

■■■

Until that point, Musk hadn't taken on outside investment for X.com, despite interest. After feeling burned by Zip2's investors, he wanted to be deliberate this time around.

Still, Musk talked with venture capitalists interested in X.com. Two factors influenced him. First, the staggering sums pouring into internet start-ups, a mania he called "happy gas." Even just in the period from 1998 to 1999, the amount of venture capital invested in internet start-ups increased considerably as the buzz about all things internet reached its apex. Though X.com was well funded by Musk, it held a risky position. If competitors down the street caught a whiff of happy gas, they could expand rapidly and leave X.com in the dust.

Then there was the story. While Musk continued to boast of his huge personal stake in the company, he, like Thiel, was also aware of the signaling value of outside investment. "We didn't need the money," Musk said, "it was more like the imprimatur of a top VC." To that end, Musk courted a high-profile general partner at the Valley's marquee firm, Michael Moritz at Sequoia Capital.

Moritz cut an unconventional figure in Silicon Valley; an Oxford graduate with a Welsh accent, he was a former *Time* magazine journalist with limited technical background. But his years of reporting honed his instinct for talent and ambition. He went on to spot what would become the era's biggest internet companies when they were just saplings. In one famous deal, he secured a 25 percent stake in Yahoo.com for $1 million, when its founders were still working from a trailer.

Moritz couldn't recall exactly how he first connected with Musk, in part because 1999, he recalled, was "the venture equivalent of a hurricane. We'd gone from the thirty-five-hour-a-week business to a business where there were more opportunities than you could possibly conjure up, where everybody wanted to start a company, where everybody could do no wrong."

Still, X.com stood out from the crowded field. Moritz found its story interesting, and its chief salesman—Musk—convincing. "Elon, as the world knows today, is a very gifted storyteller," Moritz said, smiling. "And some of the stories even come true." Moritz also recalled meeting a big bank executive at the time, Citicorp's John Reed, and seeing the truth in X.com's critique of the industry: "I remember thinking, *We can get him. Absolutely.*"

Importantly for Musk, Moritz was also sold on the X.com name. "It was like Yahoo. Or . . . Apple," he said. "I think there's a benefit to having a name that, once you've heard it, is memorable, and doesn't seem like it came out of the kitchen mixer, or the brand-naming entities that someone like Toyota might hire."

In August of 1999, Sequoia Capital became a backer of X.com, purchasing $5 million worth of X.com shares from Musk and installing Mike Moritz on the company's board. Sequoia had insisted that Musk step back his original personal investment. "[Moritz] was like, 'Dude, you should not have basically everything except your house and car in a company,'" Musk remembered. (Musk reinvested his personal funds later—though at a higher valuation.)

Had Moritz and Sequoia known precisely what they were signing up for—the years of difficulty ahead, both for the company and the tech ecosystem in general—he wondered if they'd have signed up at all. "I think we waded into it perhaps the same way that Elon and then Peter and Max waded into it, with a level of ignorance . . . ," Moritz remembered. "There was certainly an element of wanton adventurism associated with the decision."

Steve Armstrong interviewed for a financial comptroller position during this period and remembered Musk's own adventurism on vivid display. "He's like, 'We're gonna do this online bank! And we've got insurance services! And we've got the broker dealer to go set up! And we just bought a bank! . . . And we're going to put Bank of America out of business! And I've got $5 million in the bank from Sequoia Capital!' He shows me the checkbook, and he just hands it to me and says, 'Your job is to make sure I don't lose it all.' And I'm like, 'Alright, I'm in.'"

■ ■ ■

Funding secured—but a crucial question remained: What exactly had Moritz and Sequoia Capital purchased a piece of? "There was almost no product. There were a lot of ideas thrown around and a little bit of code," Alexander remembered of the company's progress when he started in August of 1999. X.com was a bank without deposits; an investment firm without assets under management; a digital finance wonderland with a bare-bones website.

At this point, X.com had little to show for Musk's gargantuan promises. Partly, this resulted from Musk and Fricker's mid-1999 row, which had slowed down the company's product development by many weeks. Still, Musk didn't hesitate to broadcast his larger ambitions for X.com. He told the *Computer Business Review* that X.com would be "a combination of the Bank of America, Schwab, Vanguard, and Quicken." When asked about his business plan by *Mutual Fund Market News*, he emphasized X.com's "nonlinear" approach compared to existing financial services companies: "To have someone's entire financial wealth on a single statement sheet—loans, mortgages, insurance, bank accounts, mutual funds, stock holdings—is revolutionary." Musk declared that by year's end, X.com would have an S&P 500 mutual fund, a US aggregate bond fund, and a money market fund all up and running.

Musk believed that with the alchemy of the internet and his own boundless initiative, X.com could deliver these services cheaper, faster, and better than existing players could. "X.com had very high aspirations," observed an early employee, Chris Chen. "I think the online bank was just a core component of the product—but we wanted to be a financial supersite. So we wanted to offer insurance products. We wanted to offer investments."

These weren't wholly new ideas, of course, and industry analysts argued that incumbents would be able to sink X.com by simply building copycat products. But Musk had seen the big banks' unwillingness to innovate from within—he wasn't losing sleep over possible competition from the JP Morgans and Goldman Sachs of the world.

There was also a recent, powerful precedent for Musk's agglomerated approach to internet business. Jeff Bezos's similar put-it-all-in-one-place strategy was driving breakneck expansion for Amazon.com—and gaining notice. Bezos had pushed the company to sell CDs while it was still struggling to fulfill its customers' book orders.

Both Bezos and Musk knew that one site offering everything trumped five sites offering one thing apiece. This wasn't an especially ground-breaking insight—the concept of a general store was centuries old. But it took foresight to bring such a thing to life at internet scale, and to do so when customers were still taking their first, tentative steps toward online shopping and banking.

In one sense, Musk was attempting a higher dive with X.com than Bezos had with Amazon.com. Amazon.com wasn't barred by law from selling books and CDs side by side. But the government stood in the way of X.com simultaneously selling banking and brokerage products, at least until late 1999 when Congress repealed much of the 1933 Glass-Steagall Act. Outside of those specific rules, each of X.com's finance offerings was heavily regulated—and to a regulator, Musk's financial superstore sounded like a nightmare.

To Musk, money merely represented "[entries] in a database." X.com was just uniting the world's "entries" into one database—and cutting out the profit-seeking intermediaries. "My vision for [X.com]," Musk proclaimed, "was essentially the global center for all money."

■ ■ ■

Based on that vision, Musk rapidly expanded the team. Tim Wenzel, a freelance recruiter, consulted for X.com in the early days. "At this point, the Valley was on fire. It was really hard to hire people. Everyone had multiple offers if they were good," he observed. "But I knew very quickly that there was something special about X.com, because almost every candidate wanted to work there. Almost everyone was willing to pass on their other opportunities to go there."

Eventually, Wenzel faced this choice himself. He was paid on a fee-per-hire basis, but X.com told him that the bills were growing too steep. He'd have to join the company full-time and recruit exclusively for X.com—or part ways with them. "I was not hesitant at all. I was like, 'I'm in,'" Wenzel said.

Several early X.com employees observed the marked contrast between Confinity's mostly male, twenty-something initial hires and X.com's far more varied roster, which included parents, women, and experienced hires with decades in the financial services trenches. Deborah Bezona had seen her share of companies as a benefits consultant, and when she signed X.com on as a client, she remarked that it "was the most diverse company I had ever worked with. That was notable to me."

During the height of the dot-com boom, Bezona advised many startups on their health care and retirement administration, and, even within that fast-moving set, X.com and its CEO stood apart. Musk gave employees ample freedom—"the room to be everything they could be"—but set palpably high expectations for performance. "I have never worked so hard and fast in all my life," she said.

Bezona enacted Musk's preferences around salaries, benefits, H1B visas, and severance packages, and she found X.com "very generous in its benefit packages"—and its CEO gracious even when individuals exited.

"If somebody couldn't cut it—if somebody wasn't doing their job—Elon always let them go with dignity and grace." Bezona recalled severance packages being given to departing employees regardless of rank.

X.com also drew talent from recruiting and staffing firms. One firm, Kelly Services, helped to bring aboard temps, including Elizabeth Alejo, hired as a new accounts manager. For her, X.com's online offerings represented a pivot in a career that included stints as a retail bank teller and bank manager. Her time in retail banking proved an asset. She examined new X.com accounts and matched the information submitted against bills and other verifying documents, which she had seen plenty of during her brick-and-mortar banking days.

Alejo was also among the first to see the full spectrum of fraud, including people falsifying utility bills to open X.com accounts. Dialing up fraudulent customers, she recalled the patient process of sniffing out malfeasance. "We would let them talk, and you know, let them *blah blah blah*—and then go in for the kill . . . then there'd be silence, or they'd hang up," Alejo said.

Alejo was hired full-time soon after joining as a temp. During this period, Musk also hired John Story as X.com's executive vice president. Story had a decades-long career, including senior-level roles at Alliance Capital and Montgomery Asset Management, and his arrival generated some stories in the financial trades, burnishing the narrative that X.com was knitting together the old guard with the new. "A company with zero assets under management and no branch offices plans to eat your lunch," wrote Ignites.com. "What gives its claim credibility is its leaders."

Another finance veteran joined shortly thereafter. Mark Sullivan left his job as a vice president at First Data Investor Services Group in Boston to join X.com as vice president of operations. "My career had always been bricks-and-mortar," he said, "and I hadn't dipped my toe into the dot-com world." Sullivan agreed to fly to Palo Alto and have lunch with Musk and Story. Musk quickly made his move. "We finished lunch, and [Musk] said, 'So when can you get out here?'" Sullivan remembered. "Jesus, I wasn't prepared for that!" Sullivan gave notice and moved to

Palo Alto within weeks. Only in his late thirties, Sullivan became one of X.com's "adults." "I was the gray hair," Sullivan joked.

Another of the "gray hairs" who joined shortly after was Sandeep Lal. He came by way of Singapore and Citibank, where he earned financial services expertise. His interview with Musk was memorable. "I remember that I used the words 'change management.' And he said, 'Stop using bullshit words,'" Lal recalled. To check Lal's competence, Musk offered a test. "He said, 'Okay, if I were to do a funds transfer from Singapore to the United States, how would it work?'" Lal carefully outlined each step—and Musk made him an offer on the spot.

■ ■ ■

One of the team's most consequential hires during this period was a business development manager named Amy Rowe Klement. Klement had begun her career at JP Morgan—where she found her work not as fulfilling as she'd hoped. "I always wanted to have a broader impact on the world," she explained. After leaving the bank, she came west and worked in corporate strategy and business development at Gap, but still she yearned for something more.

While applying to business schools, Klement talked to a banking contact, John Story, who told her about the exciting financial services start-up he had just joined. Initially, Klement was reluctant, but Story insisted that she come down and meet Musk. She found the interview— and Musk's pitch—"really interesting." "Why *does* it cost so much money to move bits and bytes within the financial system?" she wondered after hearing Musk's industry critique.

Klement joined X.com as a business development manager but soon found herself working on use cases for the product. "My job became . . . the intermediary between the developers and humanity," she joked. At X.com, Klement came to realize what David Sacks had experienced just blocks away: it took discipline and strategy to wring products from code. By multiple accounts, Klement translated from "developer to humanity" with aplomb, and not just in managing X.com's nascent products. More than one employee cited Klement as the person they turned to in a crisis—whether regarding products or colleagues. Several people referred to her as a vital "buffer," an ace diplomat who defused tense contests of personality and kept a hothouse organization on an even keel.

Klement had interviewed with X.com on a lark, mid-application to graduate school. But joining the company changed her life. She joked that her product role evolved to become a mix of "therapist, historian, and operator." "The therapist was just that, you know, things were difficult, and there was some buffering that needed to go on," she remembered. "The historian was that it was really hard to come in there and build product if you didn't understand the codebase or how it would trip up a certain localization challenge."

And finally, Klement the operator. "I really care a lot about the *how*," she said. "I did a lot of sitting down and saying, *Okay, how are we going to work together across design, content management, engineering, QA, customer support?* I viewed that as a critical part of my job, which was making sure that things were flowing for everybody."

Klement remained at the company for seven years, from late 1999 through its IPO and eventual acquisition by eBay. In that time, she oversaw the product and design organization and became one of eBay's youngest executives. For many PayPal alumni, Klement became a guiding light. Musk himself called Klement "an unsung hero." Another colleague shared that she studied Klement's operating style as a model. "I always wanted to be just like Amy," she noted. "She was my idol."

■ ■ ■

X.com's engineer hiring moved swiftly as well. Colin Catlan received a phone call from a headhunter in September. Catlan had left a payments start-up called Billpoint, which had been acquired by eBay early in 1999. It was his first Silicon Valley job, and with a team small enough to fit in a garage, each member played a vital role.

But Billpoint sold to eBay just months after launching, and Catlan soon felt sidelined by the corporate bureaucracy. His ideas—including the suggestion that Billpoint build a universal payment processing system—were met with a chilly reception. "I felt like I had unfinished business,"

Catlan said. "I had put all this effort into doing [payments] work. . . . If I couldn't do it [at Billpoint], I am going to do it somewhere." In his interview with Musk, he discussed building a payment network. According to Catlan, Musk was open to the idea, and Catlan joined X.com in early September as its director of engineering.

A Harvey Mudd College graduate named Nick Carroll arrived around the same time—just following X.com's executive exodus. Only two years out of school, he earned a battlefield promotion to senior-level engineer. Carroll recruited two other engineers from his days at Harvey Mudd, Jeff Gates and Tod Semple.

From Musk's network came another member of the engineering team: Branden Spikes. Spikes had worked at Zip2, where he had experienced all the ups and downs of start-up life. By his own admission, he was betting on the ups—and specifically betting on Musk himself, rather than X.com. "I was a little worried actually that doing an online bank would become boring," Spikes said, laughing. Branden Spikes was given a director title and a coveted email address: b@x.com.

■ ■ ■

The growing team began to shape the product. They introduced a placeholder website. Visitors to X.com were told to "Register your email address here to be notified of our launch!" The site also featured a statement of what it was poised to become:

> The Internet has made traditional ways of managing money nearly obsolete. Already, thousands of people enjoy the benefits of low-cost online trading, thousands more save money through online insurance rate research and financial planning—but millions of people still pay brick-and-mortar banks for expensive branches and tellers, when they are more intimate with the corner ATM.
>
> X.com's mission, as a purely Internet-based company with no branches and no old, expensive-to-maintain computer infrastructure, is to put those banking fees and hidden charges back into the pockets of our customers, while also providing low-cost solutions

for personal investing, insurance, and financial planning. X.com will be the seamless solution for personal finance management.

In a nod to Musk's first company, the site included directions to X.com's office "courtesy of Zip2 Corp."

X.com also continued its use of third-party vendors to speed up its development efforts. One such vendor, Envision Financial Systems, built software for asset managers and financial firms. Satnam Gambhir, an Envision cofounder, was accustomed to dealing with big banks and financial institutions—not typically fast movers. "Our sales cycle usually is six months to two years, in terms of when we first meet a client to when we close a deal and we implement," Gambhir explained. By contrast, Envision and X.com signed paperwork within two weeks of an initial visit, and Envision gave X.com access to its code shortly thereafter. "And then within ten weeks, [the X.com team] had built the integration and they were live," Gambhir said, marveling at the turnaround.

In September, X.com announced a deal with Barclays that would allow X.com customers to invest in its mutual funds. A deal with a community bank—First Western National Bank in La Jara, Colorado—followed quickly. This agreement would allow X.com to purchase First Western National Bank if regulators approved, and it allowed X.com to call itself "bank-chartered" and "FDIC-insured." Importantly, X.com could now create its own branded debit cards and distribute checks.

These developments earned X.com coverage from CNBC, the *Wall Street Journal*, and *Fortune* magazine, among others. Musk used these press hits to broadcast his bold pronouncements. Even while X.com remained under construction, he forecast its dazzling future feature set. The user application process would take a scant two minutes, he claimed. He promised no fees and no redemption penalties. He highlighted the—not one, but two—security firms carefully monitoring the site and said that the company's focus was "customer advocacy."

Musk also took the opportunity to contrast X.com with its competition. He maligned two online banking competitors—Wingspan Bank and Telebanc Financial Corp—as weak on the technology side. Then he set his sights on a storied industry player: the Vanguard Group. Asked how X.com's investment pricing would compete with the famously price-efficient Vanguard funds, Musk replied, "We will not be undercut by anyone, period."

Narratives like Musk's played well in the media, successfully tapping the public's perennial interest in underdog stories. But Musk also had a special knack for capturing the press's attention. He discovered that his willingness to veer into exaggeration often did the trick; X.com wasn't even in existence yet, and it was already earning breathless press mentions. So was Musk himself. In August of 1999—weeks after his company hemorrhaged half its team—Salon.com wrote that Musk was "poised to become Silicon Valley's Next Big Thing."

■ ■ ■

As September turned to October, Musk leaned on the X.com team to launch the site. Like at Confinity, X.com's engineering team had to endure the discomfort of asking a demanding CEO for more time. "Elon was ready to go, as soon as we had the architecture ready in September," Catlan said, "and to hold him off until October was hard." The team was concerned that *i*'s needed dotting and *t*'s needed crossing for a would-be financial company; Musk was concerned that if nothing launched soon, X.com would slide into irrelevance.

Musk's focus intensified in the run-up to launch. "The way he conducted himself around the office was almost frenetic. He's running from person to person—developer to finance to operations. He wanted answers. He wanted answers now. You had to be on your toes when he came around. You didn't want to say *I'll get back to you*," Sullivan said. No detail escaped Musk's notice, and more than one employee described the stress of working under his watchful eye.

That said, Musk demanded as much of himself as he did of his team. "We slept under desks," Catlan said. "Even Elon slept under his desk. He didn't pull himself away from that sort of thing." The engineers recall their CEO working elbow-to-elbow with them through knotty technical challenges. "Most CEOs are not very transparent with their staff," Spikes said. "Elon was like, 'We're in the trenches together. Let's do this' . . . It was powerful to work with him because of that."

For corporate veterans, X.com was a taste of scrappy start-up culture. "I didn't really have an office or a desk," Mark Sullivan—the big finance transplant—said. "I had a chair and a milk crate." Wensday Donahoo, who joined the company in an administrative position, recalled the office's decorated cubicles, young workforce, and casual clothing, including the company CEO arriving at the office in a T-shirt and shorts.

On one occasion, investors were set to visit with Musk and other X.com leaders, and Donahoo overheard someone urge Musk to change into a suit and tie. "I remember him saying, 'If they don't like the way I dress . . . they're not going to like my product—and it's the product that's going to get them to invest, not the way I look.'" The moment stayed with her. "If you've got something that's important, people are going to want it—it doesn't matter what you look like."

Nick Carroll, who joined X.com by way of aerospace giant Lockheed Martin, learned fast that he wasn't at Lockheed anymore. At one point, Carroll recommended hiring a database developer to create X.com's database. "Elon says, 'We don't need a database person. Setting one up in SQL server is easy. Let me show you,'" Carroll remembered. "At a start-up," Carroll said, "you have to wear every hat. The new experience for me was that there's no backstop, no calling anybody else."

Musk spared no expense if something helped get X.com to market quickly. While desks, for example, wouldn't speed up the release of a website, a better server might. Carroll recalled that Musk told the team to spec a Dell server capable of dealing with a flood of incoming web traffic. "We configured the most expensive, most powerful server that we could literally buy," Carroll said. The price tag arrived in the tens of thousands of dollars, but Musk approved the purchase. (Later, Branden Spikes encased the server in bulletproof glass. "It was a bank, so I thought I should take security seriously," he said.)

Speed forced improvisation. Even such consequential decisions as the look and feel of X.com's site were made on the fly. Carroll remembered wondering, *"What's our front-end design going to look like? Are we going to hire a designer?* And Elon goes, 'I want it to look like Schwab.' Because I guess that's what he used at the time? So we pull up Schwab. And X.com's original color scheme ends up blue. Why? Because Schwab's color scheme is blue."

The entire team felt the weight of the work. "For me, with only six years of experience as a software engineer," Alexander said, "it was like this tremendous responsibility to be in charge of figuring out, from a blank piece of paper, how to make the mutual fund system operational." Dealing with money and customers' finances, the engineers pushed themselves to write airtight code. "We believed in writing clean code, very well-written code," Alexander said. But code quality existed in an uneasy balance with speed. "I remember thinking, *I am so glad I'm not an executive right now—because I wrote this code, and it is not going to survive*," Carroll said.

For all the chaos of this period, the team thrilled at watching the X.com website and product suite come to life. "There was so much to do," recalled Mark Sullivan. "And you were so exhausted. But you didn't mind doing it because you knew you were building this crazy thing and every day you left, something new was developed or built or some new idea was generated."

■ ■ ■

In many ways, X.com was a prototypical Palo Alto start-up, but X.com did break with Silicon Valley orthodoxy in one critical respect: it used Microsoft products as the backbone of its technical architecture rather than building atop an open-source operating system like Linux.

For its proponents, the Microsoft platform offered a stable, professional platform backed by a multibillion-dollar public company. For its critics, it was a closed, vaguely amateurish system that stripped the artistry out of programming. The Linux platform, by contrast, was often thought to be the technical architecture "of the people." Capable of being rewritten from scratch, it was as open and flexible as the early internet aspired to be. On internet forums, this Microsoft-versus-Linux debate sometimes took on the character of a religious conflict.

X.com's use of Microsoft technology would later become a flash-point, but early on, its engineers believed Microsoft to be the obvious choice. "We had done some research and concluded the only framework that was really commercially viable—one that could handle an enterprise system—was Microsoft's framework," engineer Scott Alexander said. "And that was blasphemy in Silicon Valley."

Speed mattered to the team, and unlike Linux, Microsoft offered a set of plug-and-play frameworks available to simplify the engineering workload. "At X.com we had this philosophy: frameworks are good," remembered Alexander. "Today, everybody uses frameworks. But back then, X.com said, instead of writing everything yourself, we should use frameworks. You can get a lot more done in little time." Musk supported the decision because it swapped flexibility for efficiency. "If you fast forward like ten or twelve years, now Linux has a lot of tools," Musk said. "But not then." With Microsoft's prewritten software libraries, he noted, three X.com engineers could do the work of dozens.

Musk announced that the site would launch by late November 1999, and as the Thanksgiving holiday came into view, the team pushed as hard as ever. "At the time, they turned the traffic lights off at midnight in downtown Palo Alto. They all went to blinking red," recalled Carroll. "And I know this because we walked to our cars at like one or two a.m. to go home."

The launch was set for Thanksgiving weekend, which troubled some on the team. "I had previously been at JP Morgan and the Gap, and this is my first start-up experience," recalled Amy Rowe Klement, who was just weeks into her X.com tenure, "and it was like, 'You have Thanksgiving off, right? It's the biggest holiday in the country?'" The night before Thanksgiving, a handful of engineers, including Nhon Tran and Musk, worked through the night. Musk called Scott Alexander the next day—Thanksgiving morning—at around 11:00 a.m. "I still remember the exact words he used. He said, 'Nhon's been here all night, and he's not running on full thrusters anymore. So can you come in and just make sure everything's okay?'" Others recalled a livid, company-wide email from Musk excoriating those not at the office over the holiday.

X.com's services went live to the world over Thanksgiving 1999. Soon after the launch, the team left the office as a group and stopped at a nearby ATM. Musk inserted an X.com debit card, punched in his PIN, and requested cash. When the machine whirred and issued bills, the entire team celebrated. "Elon was very, very happy with that," Sullivan recalled.

■ ■ ■

In the summer of 1999, X.com's banking heavyweights had tried to oust Musk as CEO, then fled. Following their departures, the company's head count numbered in the low single digits. At that point, 394 University Avenue was better known for its first-floor bakery than its second-floor bank. The "company" was, essentially, a mysterious URL, some loyal holdouts, Musk's dwindling capital, and an idea.

Four months later, that episode was ancient history. In the intervening period, X.com earned funding from a top-flight venture firm, built a functional product, grew its engineering and management benches, and signed agreements with banks at home and abroad. As ever, Musk wanted faster, more thoroughly dazzling results—but at least he and his team could look back with relief and look forward with resolve. X.com was real.

PART 2
BAD BISHOP

8

IF YOU BUILD IT

Despite each team's outsized ambitions, neither X.com nor Confinity was truly prepared for the customer growth they would soon see. Musk had forecast rapid scale, but his team dismissed it as Muskian hyperbole. Now, though, his predictions were coming true. The first few days after launch, users came in drips—then, in a deluge. "The first day, we had ten people. The next day, we had twenty people. The day after that, we had fifty people," Colin Catlan said. Five weeks later, X.com's user base numbered in the thousands.

Once it began, X.com employee Julie Anderson remembers "wildfire" growth. After its frenetic launch, the X.com team enjoyed no postdeployment reprieve. "There was a time when we were hoping things would slow down," Catlan said, recalling concern over the company's limited server capacity. "We were worried the servers would overload and stop." The exhausted team kept building out the site, pushing updates with little time for rigorous testing.

Ken Miller had just joined X.com during this period of fast growth. Brought on to help combat fraud issues, he was shocked by the daily new account reporting. "It's like, 'Oh, cool. First Name: Mick. Middle initial: E. Last name: Mouse. Perfect. Oh, and they sent a transaction for $2,700. Perfect. *And* we gave them a line of credit,'" Miller said. Miller soon took the heat from X.com's partner bank, First Western, which was aghast at the Disney character customers.

Musk had promised every new user a physical checkbook and a debit card, each of which had to be mailed out by hand. "I can't tell you how many checkbooks we printed to first name 'asdf' last name 'jkl' . . . and all of them got printed," Steve Armstrong remembered. On top of it all, X.com's phone line exploded with customer complaints. One news article pointed to X.com's call volume as evidence of early traction, but for its team members fielding calls in a makeshift back-office call center (dubbed "the cave"), angry customers were a perpetual source of anxiety.

Everyone, it seems, was a critic. In late January 2000, X.com's CEO's mother, Maye Musk, wrote to her son with product guidance. "A friend and I don't use our titanium credit card much as we cannot get frequent flyer miles. We also cannot pay accounts from X.com. When are you going to make using X.com more attractive? Love M."

Security problems also dogged X.com's expansion. "There were a ton of bugs we were trying to fix, and a ton of people trying to hack the system and do SQL code injections and all sorts of things," said Musk, who had all but moved into the office during this period.

Despite now having real users, X.com still functioned as a messy start-up, to perhaps a greater extent than its customers—who were entrusting the team with their money—would have appreciated. One morning, Branden Spikes discovered a homeless person asleep on the office couch. "He was the nicest guy," Spikes remembered. "He was just looking for a place to sleep."

■ ■ ■

Some growing pains spilled violently into public view. On the morning of January 28, 2000, X.com awoke to a devastating *New York Times* headline: "Security Flaw Discovered at Online Bank." The article detailed a vulnerability in X.com's payment process that allowed customers to transfer funds using only a bank routing number and checking account number—both easily obtainable from any voided or canceled check. "In what may prove to be a cautionary tale about the headlong rush into electronic commerce," the *Times* wrote, "a new online bank permitted customers for almost a month to transfer funds from any other account in the nation's banking system."

The story picked up steam, earning follow-up coverage from the *Washington Post* and *American Banker*. X.com soon found itself in the midst of a destructive media storm. "They ought to go out of business," one security analyst told the *Washington Post*. "Frankly, I don't know how long they'll be able to survive as a business anyway." Yet another critic told *U.S. Banker Magazine*, "The name X.com is forever poisoned. They need to . . . relaunch as Y.com or something else."

Senior team members tried to contain the damage. They explained that there had been only a handful of unauthorized transactions totaling less than $25,000 and that the company had already taken measures to close the loophole. Users would now have to submit a voided check, a signature card, and a copy of their driver's license before moving money out of an external account.

The team's defense—that this wasn't a "security breach" but instead a "policy issue," related to lax transfer regulations—was technically correct. But the negative press fit people's concerns about online banking, and the mood inside the company was pure panic. Anderson, whose responsibilities still included public relations, feared for her job. "That whole thing was mortifying," she remembered of the crisis. "It had huge potential consequences." Anderson remembered Musk's concern that the coverage would act like quick-drying cement—irreparably harming the company's reputation and dissuading new customers.

In the end, Anderson kept her job. And by mid-February, X.com's rapid user growth drew media attention away from the uncomfortable fact that, for a moment, the company had built a digital bank robber's dream. An X.com employee from that era also pointed out a lesson the team learned from the security crisis that had nothing to do with breaches and bank safety: the extensive coverage left X.com with more sign-ups than before the negative headlines.

■ ■ ■

Just down University Avenue, Confinity's PayPal was experiencing growing pains of its own. Following a friends and family launch in late October, PayPal expanded more slowly than its X.com counterpart, but by mid-November, it had registered more than one thousand users. By late winter, thousands more were signing up—and the company was consumed with work.

"People were working twenty hours and sleeping for four," Confinity engineer David Gausebeck recalled. Levchin had moved a sleeping bag into the office and occupied it nightly. Other life concerns had to be put on hold. During this period, Gausebeck had driven his car over a large piece of wood left in the road, ruining two tires and denting a wheel. "I put the spare on, and the other had a slow leak," he said. Without a free moment to fix it, he drove on the spare tire for the next three days.

The PayPal product had launched with core questions unresolved. For instance, what if someone misspelled an email address—sending money to "Macks@Confinity.com" instead of "Max@Confinity.com"? Would Confinity force the money into a phantom account? Or hold it to see if an account was opened? The team's on-the-fly solution—debiting sender accounts and holding the money in escrow—solved one problem but caused another. Years later, the team discovered hundreds of thousands of dollars in escrow, all unclaimed.

As the site grew, Confinity struggled with bugs, errors, and frequent outages. One telling crisis occurred early in 2000. The team left the office for an off-site—a chance to duck the day-to-day grind and discuss strategy. "Every single person in our twenty-person-ish crew went to this place," Levchin remembered, "which had no cell phone or pager reception. The site went down and was dead for an hour."

Ideas that seemed promising at launch became problematic live. Confinity users could retrieve money by check, for instance. But as customers mushroomed, so did demands for mailed payments—a cumbersome process. The team had to download the day's transactions by way of a dial-up modem, and the company's CFO, David Jaques, loaded the office's sole printer with blank checks, signed them by hand, and stuffed envelopes by the hundreds alongside his teammates.

David Wallace oversaw customer service—and felt a "sense of dread" throughout this period. Users jammed the Confinity phone lines to the point that "people couldn't call outbound on their desk phones." Existing users could scarcely be helped, he and others remembered, before the newest arrivals lodged complaints. "This is the moment the company's been waiting for," Wallace said, "but customer service is not prepared for."

For both teams, the explosion of interest was exhausting yet energizing. "Every day, we'd all come in and group around like little chipmunks, just to see how many people signed up," X.com's Colin Catlan remembered. At Confinity, the so-called "World Domination Index" tracked user growth. The program provided reliable dopamine hits for the team—until they realized it was also dominating the company's scarce server capacity. The World Domination Index had to be disabled until further notice.

Confinity celebrated its growth with confections: when the PayPal service hit 10,000 users, the company hosted a party with five cakes—one shaped like the number "1" and four others shaped like zeros. When the site hit 100,000 users, they reprised the party—with an added sixth "0" cake.

■ ■ ■

But what explained the sudden interest? Neither X.com nor Confinity could claim to have invented online banking or email payments. Around the same time, users could make digital payments using CyberCoin, ClickShare, or Millicent, among countless others. Need a mobile wallet? Try 1ClickCharge's "super-thin" wallet, or QPass's micro-payment system, or Trintech's NetWallet. Keen to bank online? Sign up for Security First Network Bank, NetBank, Wingspan, or CompuBank.

Even companies not in the payments space had a tough time ignoring the sector's lure. Ryan Donahue, who became Confinity's second designer, was working at a struggling digital invite website called mambo .com. In late 1999, Mambo's leaders told Donahue and others that the company would pivot into payments and try to compete with, among others, PayPal. That was enough for Donahue to reach out to David Sacks, whom he had met at a bar. "I just wrote to David [Sacks] and said, 'You know, I think I'd like to come work for you rather than, you know, try to beat you,'" Donahue admitted.

Even Musk, for all his boasts, was clear that X.com and Confinity represented evolutions, rather than revolutions, on the era's payment technology. "It wasn't even that we invented money transfer. We just made it useful," Musk said. "Other companies had the idea of doing payments before Confinity or X.com, they just didn't do it right." He pointed to Accept.com and Billpoint as two sites rendering similar services.

One way in which X.com and Confinity did it right was by choosing email as the backbone of their platforms—riding a surging wave of adoption. In 1999, Americans sent more email messages than the Postal Service delivered packages. Email had even gone Hollywood. In 1998, Tom Hanks and Meg Ryan starred in the romantic comedy *You've Got Mail* (named after the well-known email notification of the popular internet service provider AOL), whose plot revolved around an email-based romance. Confinity hopped on the bandwagon, riffing on the film title in PayPal's referral emails. "You've Got Cash," their subject lines read.*

Of course, neither team had set out to build the world's foremost email payments system. For X.com, like Confinity, the feature emerged as an afterthought. In the fall of 1999, Musk and another X.com engineer discussed the concept of emailing money from one user to another, and they determined that an email address could function as a unique identifier, not unlike the digits of a checking account number. Nick Carroll, the engineer, recalled that the program took only a few days to build, "if even that." Musk concurred: "It's trivial to do money transfer. It's literally, you have a SQL database with one number, decrement that, and move it to another row in the database. It's *super* dumb. My kid made one. He's twelve."

Carroll and Musk alike found the feature's success surprising. "It was totally an add-on," Carroll admitted. Amy Rowe Klement recalled that the X.com team thought of the person-to-person payment product as simply its "user acquisition engine . . . it wasn't the core business. That was the online financial superstore." Indeed, Musk was frustrated that X.com's other products didn't generate the same excitement. "We would show people

---

* In time, PayPal filed a trademark claim on "You've Got Cash" and "You've Got Money." AOL issued a legal challenge to PayPal's claim.

the hard part—the agglomeration of financial services—and nobody was interested. Then we'd show people the email payments—which was the easy part—and everybody was interested," Musk explained in a 2012 commencement speech at CalTech. "So I think it's important to take feedback from your environment. You want to be as closed-loop as possible."

Despite frustration, the team responded to the product's strong market feedback and shifted focus to the incipient email product. Musk insisted, for instance, that the original X.com sign-up email look and feel as though a real human being sent it. "It was very important that the email comes from the person, not from X," Musk said. "Some marketing email from a company carries no weight. Whereas an email from a friend carries high weight."

Given its early success, Musk wanted to broadcast the triumph of X.com's email product to the world. But Mike Moritz, his lead investor, advised otherwise. "He wanted me to keep talking about us being a bank as misdirection," Musk explained.

■ ■ ■

In the email money transfer battle, Confinity enjoyed a lead thanks, in part, to the insistence of a single team member: David Sacks. While many viewed Confinity's email program as an appendage of its main PalmPilot product, Sacks, Thiel's college friend and an ex-McKinsey consultant, thought otherwise. "I wanted to put a bullet in the PalmPilot thing," he recalled.

Meanwhile, Sacks boosted the email money transfer product and urged Levchin to give it a place of prominence on Confinity's inaugural website. With his red-hot focus on the company's product, Sacks fell into a role missing from Confinity's original org chart: Sacks became, in effect, Confinity's first head of product.

He soon discovered that product management was as much about avoiding distractions as producing breakthroughs. "As I took over product in the company," Sacks remembered, "I kind of became, like, 'Dr. No.' Because I'd always have to say no to everyone's stupid ideas . . . it was really important that we not squander our precious engineering bandwidth on ideas that didn't make sense for the long-term strategy of the company."

Sacks became a zealot for efficiency within Confinity—and simplicity without. When he saw, for instance, that an early iteration of the PayPal sign-up process forced new users through seven web pages and two PalmPilot syncs, he was horrified. On the office whiteboard, he outlined a new, single-page sign-up form, and after getting approval from Thiel and Levchin, Sacks "marched all the engineers in and said 'build this.'"

Sacks's pursuit of simplicity emerged as a rallying cry for the product team. "You would count the number of fields and the number of characters and, visually, the mind share of only doing what you must do on that page," Denise Aptekar recalled. "That's where a lot of my fundamental product instincts were formed."

Giacomo DiGrigoli, another product team member, remembered Sacks's frustration with one particular design. "[Sacks] was like, 'I do not understand why this is so complicated! This should be as easy as email!'" DiGrigoli recalled. Soon, a photo of David Sacks with the words "As Easy as Email!" graced the office walls.

Sacks's uncompromising stance often put him at odds with Confinity's engineering team. He pushed back forcefully against what he saw as extraneous technological creations with no practical application for users. It wasn't enough to build cutting-edge technology, which was the engineering team's focus; Sacks wanted to ensure that users could derive value from it.

This tension pushed the team in productive directions. The decision to focus on emailing money rather than beaming it, for example, proved prescient. "We always had a killer app," Sacks quipped to the *Wall Street Journal* years later. "It was just buried on our site."

By the end of 1999, just weeks after its launch, PayPal's PalmPilot product counted approximately 13,000 users. By the time it was officially nixed in late 2000—after a full year on the market—the product's user count had stagnated at roughly the same size. "When we were first told that we were going to [shut the PalmPilot product down], I just remember thinking, *This is kind of sad—for a very small number of people*," David Wallace said, chuckling.

■ ■ ■

While both X.com and Confinity blasted off thanks to email, another tactic helped them reach escape velocity: X.com and Confinity both paid new users cash bonuses to sign up.

In time, this bonus effort was hailed as one of the all-time great "viral marketing" programs, but starting out, there was something vaguely disreputable about it. If a firm had to pay users, did that imply an inability to earn them organically? Weren't users supposed to pay a business for services, not the other way around?

Luke Nosek—Confinity's head of marketing—had examined other digital finance players' efforts to court customers. Each new user of Beenz, Flooz, or DigiCash would receive a free, nominal sum of digital currency. By the same logic, Confinity decided to confer $10 on each new PayPal user. But Nosek wanted to go beyond the competition, so he began considering how free money could grow the payments network—not just lure individuals.

The seed was planted in Nosek's college years. In 1996, Hotmail had added the phrase "Get your FREE Web-based email . . ." with a sign-up link to the signature line of every email. That link pulled in hundreds of thousands of new users in record time. Two Hotmail investors, Tim Draper and Steve Jurvetson, wrote about the idea in a piece published on January 1, 1997, for a newsletter popular among early technology enthusiasts—including then-undergraduate Nosek.

"Attention is finite," Draper and Jurvetson wrote. "Rising above the noise of a thousand voices requires creativity. Shouting is not very creative. Just hanging up a web shingle and hoping for visitors is not very creative. Rather, new companies can structure their businesses in a way that allows them to grow like a virus and lock out the existing bricks and mortar competitors through innovative pricing and exploitation of these competitors' legacy distribution channel conflict."

The article's neologism—"viral marketing"—stuck with Nosek as he worked on PayPal. He saw an opportunity to leverage free money more effectively than Beenz, Flooz, and others. What if Confinity offered users not just money for signing up—but another $10 to give away to friends? And if those friends signed up for the service, what if the original gift giver received another $10? Suddenly, Confinity would incentivize person-to-person transmission, pushing the standard industry marketing play from merely infectious to full-on contagious.

From a financial perspective, though, the idea sounded ludicrous. To not only pay customers to give away the company's money—but then to *reward* them for doing so? It looked like a surefire path to bankruptcy. The caretaker of Confinity's accounting books, CFO David Jaques, was not exactly enthused by the bonus proposal. *You've got to be shitting me*, he remembered thinking. But as the Confinity team toyed with the concept, they began to recognize its power. Too many referral programs had failed because of one-sided incentive structures. Here, they saw an opportunity for a two-sided program with the power to turn customers into advocates.

The program struck a particular chord with prospects who saw $10 as a substantial sum. Jaques remembered his wife's muted reaction upon receiving her PayPal referral email. Then Jaques sent one to his college-aged niece. "*I love it! This is fantastic! This is beautiful!*" she told him. Other Confinity employees joked that the bonus program represented "the largest transfer of venture capital to college students in history."

As justification, the team compared its incentives to traditional banks' customer acquisition costs—which they estimated to be between $100 and $200 per customer. Confinity's proposed giveaways would cost it only $20 to $30 per customer. "So therefore, every time we added a user," David Sacks explained, laughing, "we weren't spending $20. We were making $180! This was dot-com thinking before the crash." Erik Klein recalled watching "rings of referrals" emerge in real time, as the graph of the PayPal network began to bloom and grow.

X.com had independently arrived at a similar conclusion about referrals and incentives. "Elon had the story of the bank who was giving away toasters to new customers," Nick Carroll remembered. "And he was like, 'Well, if we just give them cash, that's sufficient.'" At first, Musk suggested $5. The number eventually rose to $20. But the team soon discovered that a onetime bonus simply wasn't enough. "It was important to incent the referrer and the referee," Musk said. "Not just one or the other. You need to reward the initiation of it. And you need to reward the completion of it." In addition to its $20 bonus, the X.com team decided to give a $10 bonus to anyone who referred a new user.

The giveaway shocked some members of the X.com team. "You have to take your hat off to Elon for being willing to take his own money and basically give it away to build this new thing, when there is no way to know if it's going to work," Catlan said. "He was willing to take whatever he had left and put it on the line." Musk also doubled down on his financial commitment to the company by moving all of his personal bank accounts to X.com from Schwab. Musk's was not just one of X.com's earliest accounts—it was far and away its largest.

■■■

X.com and Confinity both tapped into the public's newfound embrace of email and the age-old thrill of free money—but those didn't entirely account for their rapid growth. The final ingredient arrived by way of internet auctions.

French-born, Iranian-American engineer Pierre Omidyar had not set out to build an online auction behemoth when he coded Auction-Web and posted it to his personal website, www.ebay.com, so named for his web consulting company, Echo Bay Technology Group. At first, AuctionWeb featured just Omidyar's discards, including a broken laser pointer, which he listed for $14.83. When someone actually purchased it, Omidyar was astonished—and realized that his side hustle might have a bright future.* Four years later, AuctionWeb was eBay—a billion-dollar publicly traded company and a defining dot-com brand.

The earliest account of a Confinity-eBay linkage came in April 1999.

---

* That someone was Mark Fraser. On the road doing presentations, he wanted a laser pointer, but was unable to afford a new one and suspected his boss would balk at buying one for him. As a professed "electronics geek," Fraser first tried to build his own, but it didn't perform as he'd hoped. "Somebody pointed me at a brand-new website, which turned out to be eBay, and I was amazed to discover a broken laser pointer that was listed," Fraser later shared in a video testimonial for eBay's twentieth anniversary. "And I thought, 'Hey, I could probably make that work.'"

On April 8, Thiel and his team met with Peter Davison and Graeme Linnett, two of Confinity's investors. In an email sent to Davison and Linnett, Thiel outlined the main takeaways from their discussion, including: "We will investigate further whether (and what kind) of collaboration with eBay might be possible—especially given the consumer-to-consumer disintermediation model that our two companies share."

However, the team shelved the idea for the rest of 1999. "eBay was such a sketchy company," Thiel later told a Stanford audience, "multi-level marketing people selling junk on the internet." Confinity, on the other hand, built cutting-edge mobile payment technology. Never the twain would meet.

When eBay acquired the payments start-up Billpoint in May of 1999, Confinity assumed that the purchase would turn Billpoint into eBay's default payments system.* *Phew, okay, we don't have to be on eBay*, Nosek remembered thinking.

But eBay soon experienced delays integrating Billpoint into its payment flow, and by late in the year, eBay's buyers and sellers were still sorting out auction payments on their own. Users alternately used cash, checks, money orders, wire transfers, and an emerging group of online payment services—including PayPal.

■ ■ ■

Sacks recalled the precise moment the team discovered PayPal's use on eBay. An eBay user had emailed Confinity customer service seeking permission to use the PayPal logo on her auction page. She also wanted the team's help resizing it. David Wallace forwarded the email on to the team, not thinking much of it amid thousands of more urgent complaints.

---

*eBay had responded, in part, to Amazon's acquisition of accept.com. eBay had been in talks with accept.com when Amazon's Jeff Bezos came in with a steep offer. Having lost their chance to acquire accept.com, eBay quickly purchased Billpoint, which had recently closed its Series A financing—with Sequoia Capital as the lead backer. Ironically, Billpoint's earliest ambitions mirrored some of Confinity's. Jason May, Billpoint's technical head, had pored through the literature on micropayments and explored the trajectories of digital currencies like Millicent and Flooz.

The team wondered if the user's logo-resizing ask was a one-off request—or if there might be more users like her. Luke Nosek, Chad Hurley, and David Sacks huddled together and searched www.ebay.com for the term "PayPal." Thousands of auction listings popped into view. "It was one of these holy shit moments," Sacks said. "Luke started spazzing."

How had this happened? The Confinity team wasn't entirely sure. David Sacks suspected that an eBay user had seen PayPal in the press, introduced it to the auction platform, and that it spread from there. eBay users were attuned to fresh internet developments and constantly comparing notes on software and services that improved the auction process. "In those days, you have to remember that anyone who was a Power-Seller on eBay was a little bit weird," Sacks explained.

Further searches by the team revealed that PayPal had become a hot topic on eBay's message boards—the backbone of its community, where eBay's sleuths shared their intelligence. "eBay was a very viral community because everyone watched what everyone else was doing," Sacks said. "So it started spreading organically."

However it happened, the sight of thousands of eBay auctions advertising Confinity's PayPal service was a welcome surprise for Sacks—proof that PayPal was solving a real problem. Given the team's distaste for eBay, however, his was not the dominant opinion. Levchin, for one, was horrified. "I had a fairly vague idea of what eBay was," Levchin recalled. "Oh isn't that the 'echo bay' thing that that guy Pierre Omidyar started? That seems like a whack idea."

Levchin even resisted helping the eBay user who had asked for assistance with the PayPal logo. "I definitely made some motions to prevent eBay growth," he said. He flirted with blocking the eBay URL from Confinity's servers outright.

Part of Levchin's reluctance stemmed from his attachment to Confinity's PalmPilot technology—which he thought should remain center stage. Now, instead, the afterthought email product was advancing rapidly, raising unanswered questions that he had little interest in addressing. "*Wait, what? They're using the demo? Will it even scale? What if it crashes our site?*" he remembered wondering.

eBay users had also adopted X.com's payments service, though the team discovered its use there later—a discovery met with similar surprise. Like Confinity, X.com hadn't set out to facilitate low-dollar, person-to-person auction payments via email. "We thought we would compete with Western Union—like if you had to send money to your son at college or to pay the landlord rent or something. It was going to replace big, clunky transactions that you would otherwise have to do at a bank," X.com engineer Doug Mak recalled. "It turns out people are sending ten or twenty bucks for little Beanie Babies." Leadership worried that small-dollar buyers and sellers on eBay couldn't be counted on to embrace X.com's checking and brokerage services—where the real profits would be made.

Despite doubts, eBay-driven growth was impossible to ignore. Queries in eBay's search bar for "X.com" or "PayPal" showed that eBay's users adopted and advertised Confinity's PayPal and X.com enthusiastically—and for good reason. If an eBay seller sold an item and signed up the buyer for PayPal through the seller's referral link, the seller earned an extra $10. As a result, inexpensive sales became profitable—the margins on Beanie Babies were suddenly 100 percent or 200 percent larger than before. And as often as not, the buyer's $10 PayPal bonus covered the cost of whatever they bought.

This corner of the internet—an auction website selling Beanie Babies and broken laser pointers—had become unexpectedly fertile soil for the companies' products. "On the product side, the eBay users defined our existence," noted Skye Lee, "It wasn't us saying, 'Oh my God, eBay! That's the genius idea!'" Technology thinkers frequently urged founders to build companies that solved problems in their own lives, but X.com's and Confinity's eBay-driven success offered a powerful counterpoint: solving *a* problem could be just valuable as solving *your* problem.

"I think there would be no PayPal today," Vivien Go concluded, "if [PayPal] didn't have the eBay platform to form their network."

■ ■ ■

In early 2000, Peter Thiel announced that one of the company's earliest board members, Reid Hoffman, would join Confinity as chief operating officer. Hoffman and Thiel had been friends for almost a decade after first meeting at Stanford.

Even before they met, each had heard rumors of another person on campus a lot like them—but with polar opposite political views. Then they signed up for the same philosophy class in winter term 1986. On Mondays, Wednesdays, and Fridays at 1:15 p.m., they attended Dr. Michael Bratman's Philosophy 80: Mind, Matter, and Meaning. "One aim of the course," the syllabus explained, "is to explore some of the issues and arguments currently debated in the philosophical literature."

With books like Gary Watson's *Free Will* and John Perry's *Personal Identity* as their backdrop, Hoffman and Thiel sparred over determinism, freedom, and the mind-body problem. They discovered divergent worldviews—but built a lasting friendship. "Peter and I still today have very different goals about what humanity should look like," Hoffman explained. "But on the value and fundamentals of being a public intellectual, speaking the truth, figuring out the truth, intense discourse . . . For me, part of the gift of Peter's friendship is that my thinking has gotten sharper."

In 1987, the two undergraduates ran for seats in Stanford's student government, the Associated Students of Stanford University (ASSU). Hoffman's and Thiel's respective platforms illustrated common values and starkly contrasting styles:

Hoffman: The ASSU has enormous potential for making positive
changes in this University. It is a very wealthy organization
with approximately $500,000 in reserves. Recently, the ASSU
Senate approved plans to renovate its own office space for
$80,000. While the ASSU needs repair, other student facilities,
like the Old Firehouse, seem to need the money more. I believe
the ASSU is suffering from an egocentrism inherent in many
bureaucratic organizations. It tends to serve its own needs
before the needs of the students. As a senator, I will attempt to
increase the ASSU's financial commitment to student activities.
Right now, the money is just sitting in the bank.

Thiel: I have no experience in the ASSU Senate. I have no
experience wasting $86,000 of student money on ASSU office
renovations, helping friends pack resumes with positions in
the ASSU bureaucracy, and giving them disproportionate
salaries on top. As an outsider looking at the current student
government, I am disgusted. As a member of several student
organizations that could not receive funding (supposedly
because of a "lack of funds"), I am furious about this waste of
our money; if elected, I will work to make the ASSU serve the
Stanford community rather than itself.

Both won seats. Incidentally, their future competitor Elon Musk also ran
for student government at the University of Pennsylvania. His platform
mixed idealism and insouciance. "If elected," Musk vowed, "I promise
1. To do my utmost to make the assembly responsible to student needs.
2. To do my utmost to ensure that the assembly is effective in its response. 3. That if this position ever appears on my resume, to stand on
[my] head and eat 50 copies of the offending document in a public place.
I'm running because I believe there is some good and some value in being
involved." Musk did not win his race.

■ ■ ■

After Stanford, Hoffman set off for Oxford on a Marshall Scholarship
with a plan to become a professor and public intellectual. But he pivoted, instead opting for a career in software development. He returned to
California, worked at Fujitsu and Apple, then launched his own start-up,
SocialNet.

An early social network, SocialNet struggled to take off. Hoffman
shared the trials of start-up life with Thiel on frequent walks around
Stanford Dish Loop Trail. "I literally would go 'And here's the things I
didn't know [on the] last walk,'" Hoffman said. "The cadence of learning at a start-up . . . *fucking intense* is an understatement. It's everything
from 'How do you hire people? How do you assemble it? How does the

capital game work? How does go-to-market strategy work? How does the thinking around innovation work?'"

By the time Thiel approached him to be COO in January 2000, Hoffman had been serving on Confinity's board and seen the product evolve from beaming money via PalmPilots—of which he was skeptical—to a quickly growing email payments platform. SocialNet, in contrast, was flailing, and Hoffman's board was moving in a strategic direction he thought unwise for the company. "This is what happens when venture capitalists who think they know what they're doing, but don't, get in control," he said of the strife.

When Hoffman confided to Thiel that he was leaving SocialNet to start a new company, Thiel pressed him to join Confinity instead. Hoffman remembered Thiel's pitch: "'Look, we're kind of running like a hot mess internally. We have no business model. We need to package this thing up for a sale.'" Hoffman wasn't immediately swayed by the offer of professionalizing a "hot mess," but Thiel assured him a brief Confinity tour of duty—and an exit that would burnish his technology resume.

To Confinity's investors, Hoffman was an unexpected choice for COO. "It seemed odd. He wasn't a COO type," Nokia Venture's Pete Buhl remembered thinking. "He was a community guy, a friendly guy. And we thought, *He's going to be your ball buster? That can't be right.*"

But Thiel was insistent. Confinity, he realized, needed more natural diplomats, and Hoffman, he knew, actually *enjoyed* dealing with fellow members of the species. Vivien Go interviewed with Hoffman in the winter of 1999—after finishing a summer internship at eBay. She was surprised when Hoffman didn't mine her for every scrap of intel; instead, he wanted to know who Go was and why she wanted to be at Confinity. "[Hoffman] sees people in a very three-dimensional way," she observed. "Some people put a formula or label to someone; Reid isn't like this. Reid is really *very* emotionally intelligent."

As the company grew, so did its intersections with external parties: users, executives at other businesses, competitors, and, critically, governments. Thiel saw Hoffman as an ideal fit for this kind of work. "If you don't believe in the government, it makes it kind of hard to work with the government," Nosek quipped. "And then you have Reid, who is a socialist."

Hoffman could play nice with others, but he was no pushover either. By his own admission, his childhood obsessions included strategy board games like RuneQuest, Dungeons & Dragons, and Avalon Hill's Tactics II. That game-playing honed his strategic savvy, which his PayPal colleagues saw on display. Dan Madden worked in business development and joined calls alongside Hoffman. "He'd sit, and I'd sit in the second chair, meaning taking notes. And he would go through, and he would constantly mute. And then he'd say, 'He's gonna say this. I'm gonna say this. Then he's gonna say this. Then I'm gonna say that.'" Hoffman unmuted the phone, Madden remembered, and the negotiation played out precisely as Hoffman predicted.

What was supposed to be Hoffman's months-long tour of duty stretched into several years. He would see PayPal through to its IPO, often serving as just the emissary Thiel had envisioned the company would need.

■ ■ ■

In December 1999, Confinity was approached with an acquisition offer. The company freely distributed thousands of dollars every day to strangers on the internet—such were acquisition targets in the "happy gas" era. Confinity had, however, solved a real problem—one that its prospective purchaser faced as well.

BeFree Inc. was a Boston-based affiliate marketing firm founded by brothers Tom and Sam Gerace. BeFree worked with traditional retailers to advertise products online. "We were working with about 400 merchants and 400,000 affiliates . . . and we were the platform that let basically retailers set up affiliate programs," Tom Gerace said. BeFree went public in November 1999, and its stock soared 700 percent in the next five months.

With BeFree's fast growth emerged a problem—paying the affiliates. "We'd send out physical checks to [them] . . . and we would get huge batches of checks back, and you'd pay a check return fee for each one that came back." As the site grew, so did the fees—and the associated administrative headaches. Upon discovering PayPal, Pat George, BeFree's head of business development, and Tom Gerace were both immediately struck by the product's potential.

"The virality . . . [was] just incredible," George said. "There's no way I'm not logging in and signing up for an account when I've got ten dollars sitting there." George also spied a solution to BeFree's payment problem. Instead of a check, the company could send its affiliates email.

BeFree asked to meet with Levchin and Thiel. At the meeting, Thiel trotted out a staple gimmick in the Confinity pitch: He'd pull a dollar from his wallet and declare it one of the most powerful viral propellants in existence. Confinity had linked that viral fuel to an unstoppable platform: email. "It made sense. It just clicked," George remembered of the pitch. "Why didn't I think of this?"

George and Gerace were convinced, but they still had to win over BeFree's board. BeFree had just gone public; this would be their first post-IPO transaction. The board was wary. "'What are we supposed to tell the investment community? . . . What do they have? What are we selling? It's not adding real revenue,'" George recalled them saying of Confinity.

The biggest sticking point, though, was price. Thiel sought a $100 million buyout for Confinity—which BeFree's board thought unacceptably high. "It was very hard for us to convince our board of directors to go up to what Peter's clearing price was," Gerace said. The board instead authorized a price less than half of Thiel's target.

George and Gerace planned a dinner with Thiel and Levchin to present the disappointing offer. The four met at a nondescript, strip-mall Chinese restaurant just outside of Boston. Rain pounded the windows. George and Gerace started by emphasizing their excitement about Confinity and the prospect of working together—then dropped the offer. "It was clear from Peter's expression that we were not going to get a deal done," Gerace said. "[Thiel and Levchin] were both looking at me," George recalled, "and all I remember is when I said the number, Max just closed his eyes and hung his head."

Looking back, Tom Gerace remembered the failed PayPal acquisition as "one of the great business errors of my life." As PayPal increased in size and value, Pat George would give his former leaders and colleagues at BeFree a good-natured ribbing about the acquisition that might have been.

In retrospect, Thiel and Levchin were less wistful. BeFree became one casualty of many when the internet bubble burst. Following a precipitous fall in stock price, BeFree was sold for $128 million to a competitor in 2002—a little more than three weeks after PayPal IPO-ed at a market cap of nearly $1 billion.

■■■

The failed deal revealed something about Thiel's position. Throughout the negotiation, George observed, Thiel had seemed eager to offload the business: "He seemed like he really wanted out of what he was in."

Thiel abhorred bureaucracies, and now that Confinity was growing, he risked being ensnared by the very things he had abandoned upon leaving law firm life—management, paperwork, meetings. "Peter is even less tolerant of bullshit than I am," the famously administrivia-averse Musk remarked. "My bullshit tolerance is low, but Peter is like zero."

Where Thiel had failed in relinquishing his CEO role, Musk had succeeded: By the first week of December 1999, Elon Musk had stepped down as CEO of X.com. "When Moritz invested, he was like, 'We should hire a CEO.' And I said, 'Great, I don't want to be CEO,'" Musk said. "I had no desire to be a CEO. It's really a lot of chores . . . Being CEO sucks." (Musk added that he had "tried hard not to be CEO of Tesla.")

With Musk's blessing, the company recruited Bill Harris, the former CEO of Intuit, to serve as its new president and CEO. Hailing from a well-to-do Boston family, Harris enjoyed a thriving career in magazine publishing, including stints at *Time* and *US News & World Report*. But he wanted a change. In 1990, while still living in New York, Harris was invited to join the board of San Diego–based ChipSoft, the makers of TurboTax, and was eventually asked to be its CEO. Upon accepting, Harris's Madison Avenue media bosses were nonplussed. Harris remembered them saying, "'San Diego? Is that even in the United States?'"

In 1993, ChipSoft merged with Intuit, where Harris spent the next six years, eventually rising to become Intuit's CEO. Since 1995, he had been "trying to push the company to the web," arguing that the company's products—Quicken, TurboTax, and QuickBooks—should live online as well as off. His was a rough-and-tumble tenure, and by his own admission, the job of running a large company didn't play to his strengths.

"I was a lousy CEO of a public company," he said. "It was not what I was interested in or, more importantly, good at." But the experience taught him the ins and outs of the internet.

Despite his turbulent record, when Harris left Intuit in September of 1999, he found himself a hot commodity. "They weren't saying, 'Hey, would you like to interview for this job?' They were saying, 'We'd like to give you this job,'" Harris remembered. "It was the peak and everyone was starting companies. And all the VCs needed someone with a name or credibility or something."

Amid the frenzy, X.com stood out to Harris. "I liked the idea. I liked Elon. And I liked Mike [Moritz]," Harris said. "It seemed like a powerful combination." Musk laid out his vision for a comprehensive internet-based financial services system, and Harris was sold. "The most amazing thing about Elon is his boldness," Harris said, reflecting on his audacious plan for X.com at a time when its team still numbered in the single digits.

Mike Moritz lobbied Musk to install Harris as CEO, but he wasn't the only one. Several of X.com's engineers also recalled pitching Harris with a late-night cold email. "The things you do at three a.m. when you've had too much caffeine," Colin Catlan admitted.

Musk had reservations. *Everything looks great, but my gut feel is uneasy*, he remembered thinking. Musk posed a question to Moritz in his kitchen: Moritz had seen start-up CEOs come and go, Musk said, so what rating would he give Harris on a scale of 1 to 10? Moritz replied: "A ten." Musk was astonished: "I was like, *Wow . . . Okay, I'll override my feelings of uneasiness and let's move forward, because you know how to hire CEOs*."

X.com's CEO announcement came the same week that it formally launched its products. A public relations bonanza ensued. With the former CEO of Intuit on board, Musk could plausibly argue that X.com had recruited the ideal person to bridge personal finance software and the internet. "X.com sounds like just the company Intuit would be if it were formed today," one industry analyst wrote shortly after the Harris announcement.

■ ■ ■

With the passage of time, Bill Harris has largely been written out of PayPal's history. In part, that's because of a tenuous tenure. Several long-term PayPal employees told me that they joined the company because of Harris; one executive cited Harris as the reason he left. Harris's exclusion from PayPal's history could also be chalked up to his five-month reign as CEO.

But from one angle, PayPal's future hung on that five-month stretch—and arguably on Harris himself. Because however brief and rocky, Bill Harris left a lasting imprint on both X.com and Confinity—as the linchpin in a hard-fought deal to fuse the two firms into one.

9

THE WIDGET WARS

X.com and Confinity spent the turn of the twenty-first century locked in a tense battle for customer growth. This contest consumed both companies from the end of 1999 through early 2000, driving employees and leaders alike to the brink and leaving lasting scars.

No one had expected this. The rival companies, after all, had been amicable enough neighbors just months before. While occupying adjacent Suites A and B at 394 University Avenue, members of the two teams commingled: taking smoke breaks together, buying coffee at the same downstairs shop, and even sharing a bathroom. The teams were friendly, and while each had a vague sense of the other's work, they didn't think much of it—each felt confident that the other was pursuing the wrong strategy.

That changed as both teams grew closer to an email payments strategy. In late summer 1999, Luke Nosek burst into the Confinity office with a worrying piece of intelligence: he had overheard an X.com employee talking about email payments on the phone. The team's concern over X.com escalated a few weeks later. X.com announced that it, too, would not only be entering the payments space, but joining the give-away-free-money and referral racket. Disconcertingly, X.com was promising $20 per user—double Confinity's rate—and the internet had noticed. Websites covering new developments on the internet began mentioning Confinity and X.com in the same breath—and pointing out the embarrassing incentive discrepancy.

Conspiracy theories blossomed. Had X.com stolen Confinity's viral marketing playbook? "They were paranoid," Confinity board member John Malloy recalled. "They got kind of crazy about it." Levchin recalls instructing Confinity employees, "Hey, if you're going near the old office, be careful what you say. The walls might have ears." X.com later shared rumors that Confinity personnel went dumpster diving for the shredded remains of X.com's business plan.

But the teams' paranoia wasn't entirely without foundation. David Wallace had a special view into the competition as head of Confinity customer service. In this capacity, he remembered a troubling sign in late 1999. "We were getting a lot of X.com people signing up here . . . *Hey guys, you might want to know there's something going on,*" Wallace recalled. Alarmed, he prompted the Confinity team to look into these suspicious sign-ups.

Meanwhile, at X.com, Musk also paid close attention to individual registrations—and several recent sign-ups had caught his eye. "I had a little window on my screen, and as people signed up, it would show me their name," Musk recalled, describing it as his "little dynamic fraud analysis"—a means of separating real users from phony ones. But shortly after X.com's launch, a new customer named "Peter Thiel" appeared on his screen. Thiel, he recalled, ran the money-beaming company that had formerly leased the office next door. This sign-up was worth looking into. He picked up his phone and gave Thiel a call.

■ ■ ■

By that December, Confinity was processing a growing number of eBay transactions. "We had an early lead," Confinity cofounder Ken Howery remembered. By launching first and reaping the rewards, Confinity proved Musk's intuition correct: in the era's overheated start-up environment, time to market was critical. And even more so for payments firms.

"Network effects trump everything else," Howery explained, alluding to the economics principle developed to explain the growth of the telephone in the early 1900s. Each new telephone added to the network increased the value of every other telephone on it and grew the incentives for non–telephone owners to buy one. By the end of the twentieth century, Confinity enjoyed the same fruits of scale the American Bell Telephone Company had enjoyed at the century's dawn. Every eBay auction seller accepting PayPal enticed more buyers to sign up, and each new buyer paying with PayPal drove sellers to adopt it.

Confinity took strategic steps to leverage and grow its eBay network. The team scraped eBay webpages and built tools specifically designed for auction buyers and sellers. Confinity's feature set now included a logo resizing tool, as well as a feature that auto-completed the eBay payment page (with PayPal preselected as the payment option). A feature dubbed "auto-link" made PayPal the default payment option for any eBay seller who had transacted with PayPal even once. "That increased the delta by an insane amount," Yu Pan said, referring to PayPal's adoption on eBay.

Pan was assigned to work exclusively on eBay tools—becoming one of a growing roster of Confinity's eBay anthropologists. Following Pan's lead, the team drove into eBay's message boards and other auction forums and studied eBay's "PowerSeller" community. David Sacks also told the members of the product team to purchase items on the eBay website. Confinity's newly minted eBay shoppers met to dissect every single step of the buying—and, specifically, the paying—experience. "We had to become the users," recalled Denise Aptekar, who purchased a landline phone, which, unfortunately, came "caked in cigarette smoke."

The team also became sellers themselves. "We got probably about a thousand of these desk grommets, and we would actually sell them," Oxana Wootton recalled. "Every once in a while somebody would actually buy them." Company employees would occasionally trek to the post office for eBay order fulfillment.

Though its users found the PayPal product useful, eBay's executives felt otherwise—seeing the budding payments service as a competitor to Billpoint, the payments firm they had recently acquired. Early on, eBay took steps to hamper Confinity's efforts, including blocking the scripts that Confinity engineers ran to scrape eBay pages—blocks that Confinity scrambled to overcome. "It was kind of adversarial," Confinity engineer David Gausebeck remembered.

On the eBay user side, meanwhile, the same early adopters who had spotted Confinity's PayPal had also taken notice of X.com. And because X.com was also distributing free money—and more of it—buyers and sellers embraced it with similar fervor.

Like Levchin, Musk hadn't wanted his company to become an email payments provider on eBay. But he couldn't ignore X.com's exploding use on the platform—nor could he ignore the fact that X.com was trailing on eBay. As Musk followed the Confinity team's machinations, he began to respect the team's ingenuity. "I thought, *Well, these guys are pretty smart,*" Musk recalled.

He concluded that X.com would have to do everything it could to win on eBay—a conflict for the future of online payments, he believed. To Musk, defeating Confinity on eBay would likely incapacitate it elsewhere. "They were the only competitor," he remembered. "What the banks were doing was hopeless."

■ ■ ■

Thus began one of the more ferocious and unusual battles in internet history: X.com and Confinity launched a weeks-long war to win customers on eBay. "It was kind of a race to see who could run out of money the fastest," Musk said wryly.

Both sides remembered the weeks that followed as a period of desperation, witheringly high stakes, and short nights spent in sleeping bags under desks. Both teams monitored their nemesis constantly and made moves accordingly. "I'd be like, *We gotta have a better widget!*" Musk remembered. "Then it's like, *Fuck it, now they've got a better widget!* It was like the widget wars."

The widget wars soon turned fierce—and fiercely personal. For Yu Pan's birthday celebration, the Confinity team brought out a cake with the words "DIE X.COM" written in frosting. During this period, Musk reportedly sent a memorable X.com-wide email with the innocuous subject line "A friendly note about our competitors." The message body contained a single line, which the recipients remembered roughly as, "KILL THEM DEAD. DIE. DIE. DIE." "Everyone knew he was kind of joking, but you know, he was staying up, making sure we were getting on the mark first, and signing up as many people as we could," X.com engineer Douglas Mak said.

Levchin hung a banner in the office reading "Memento Mori" with an X.com logo. "Memento Mori" is an ancient Latin philosophical maxim which translates to "Remember that you must die." Normally thought of as a reminder of life's great clarifier, for Levchin, the banner served to remind the Confinity team of the great clarifier just up the road: X.com. But some noted that the banner may have been unnecessary. "We didn't have any problem with memento-ing mori," Nosek said.

■ ■ ■

In Levchin and Thiel, Musk found something he rarely encountered: competitors as driven to win as he was. *It was a worthy adversary here with these PayPal people*, Musk remembered thinking. The speed of Levchin's PayPal code deployments, in particular, stood out. "I was really impressed," Musk recalled. "I'm pretty good at technology. So it's like, if somebody's keeping up with me, *Whoa. Respect.*"

Despite Levchin's speed, Musk remained confident that X.com would triumph in the end. His company had more funds than Confinity and could raise more if needed. Musk also benefited from a pedigreed team, including top talent lured away from established institutions. X.com had the backing of one of the world's top venture capital companies, the attention of the press, and in his view, a far superior name.

Musk's confidence generated a sense of self-assurance for his team. "I think generally we figured we could outlast them because, at the time, we had more money," recalled Julie Anderson. As a result, X.com didn't share the same level of paranoia over stolen ideas and pilfered plans. "We were very forthright in what we were doing," X.com engineer Colin Catlan remembered. "Elon is not a shrinking violet."

For its part, the Confinity team whipsawed between worry and confidence. "It's incredibly exciting—and it's incredibly scary," Thiel said. "We're all going to take over the world—and we're all going to die." Pan remembered that Confinity initially dismissed X.com for its lack of mobile technology. "We thought, *Well, they don't have a Palm solution!*" he remembered.

As the competition heated up, Levchin grew nervous. He didn't know Elon Musk well, but what he did know induced anxiety. He knew, for instance, that Musk had sold Zip2 for several hundred million dollars and that he drove a McLaren F1. Levchin, by contrast, still lived in an efficiency apartment and "couldn't afford AAA." "It was very much like, *Oooh, this guy is successful, and I don't really know what I'm doing*," he recalled. Confinity's team, too, felt the conflict asymmetrical. "Elon had already made a lot of money. [X.com was] backed by Sequoia . . . it was a different animal than Nokia. They had much deeper pockets and a lot more firepower than we did," Jack Selby remembered.

Earlier than many of his colleagues, Thiel saw X.com as an existential threat. "Peter likes to confront things. He likes to know if he's wrong," Nosek said. "He's actively looking for how things could break, how things could fail—constantly. Much more so, and much more proactively, than a lot of entrepreneurs I know." Thiel determined that X.com could simply spend Confinity out of existence. "Peter was good to recognize that they were a real threat," Malloy said.

And Thiel didn't like to lose. "Show me a good loser," Thiel once said to a Confinity employee, "and I'll show you a loser." Thiel's competitive instincts had been honed through chess. David Wallace had been housemates with Thiel briefly, and he remembered Thiel handicapping himself when they played—up to a point. "He would have to, like, take his queen off the board—and he'd still beat me. He'd take his queen and rook off the board—and he still beat me . . . ," Wallace remembered. "Then he took his queen and both rooks off the board, and I finally beat him. And we never played again."

Thiel's chess opponents remembered his aggressive style. "He was merciless," a fellow player, Ed Bogas, remembered. "There was no humor in the chess playing." Bogas had squared off against Thiel in some California tournaments—and what he witnessed on the boards led him to invest in Confinity's earliest fundraising round.

■ ■ ■

But that was chess, and this was business—here, it didn't always pay to let competitive instinct checkmate reason. Confinity was growing users, but the bonuses underwriting that growth accelerated its cash burn rate. Additionally, it's growing team had swelled its payroll. Confinity's spend-ing was unsustainable, and even the advantage its spending conferred—a marginally larger eBay user base—was a poor insurance policy. If eBay's executives awoke one morning and decided to ban third-party payment systems, X.com still had its investment and banking products to fall back on. Confinity, meanwhile, would be reduced to the questionable pros-pects of its PalmPilot application.

In addition to sparring on eBay, Confinity and X.com had also begun competing for business development deals. Confinity would offer to partner with established websites by providing payment services or pay-ing them for inbound traffic to PayPal.com. In approaching potential partners, the team often discovered that X.com had already been there—and was willing to pay more for deals. "We kept running against them," Howery recalled. "It started to make things a lot more difficult."

In late December, both X.com and Confinity opened discussions with Yahoo. What began as a business development negotiation quickly morphed into something more serious when Yahoo broached the idea of acquiring one of the companies. Here, too, Confinity was at risk. If Yahoo acquired X.com, then the portal could use its billions in market capital and its clout to finish Confinity off. It didn't help matters that X.com's lead investor, Mike Moritz, served on Yahoo's board.

And if all of that weren't enough, Thiel also foresaw market risks in the year ahead. Hype about the internet had hit a peak—newly public internet companies like Priceline.com were more valuable on paper than the entire airline industry combined, and so on. Confinity was a living ex-ample: It had no viable revenue model and was giving away money hand over fist, and yet was considered an internet success story.

"Let there be no doubt, that what we are witnessing is, indeed, history's greatest financial bubble," wrote an investor at the market's peak in 1999. "The indescribable financial excesses, the massive increase in debt, the monstrous use of leverage upon leverage, the collapse in private savings, the incredulous current account deficits, and the ballooning central bank assets all describe the very severe financial imbalances which no amount of statistical revision nor hype from CNBC can erase."

Thiel worried that Confinity might not survive the bursting of the internet bubble. He thought back on the "excruciating" process of raising money, during which he and the Confinity team had been turned down over one hundred times. If the market soured, raising capital would become even more excruciating.

Given a teetering market and a take-no-prisoners competitor, Thiel and others in the company began considering an alternative course. "A lot of us came to the conclusion that this would be a winner-take-all market, and that this should be a single company," Confinity cofounder Ken Howery said. "Or both of us would spend ourselves into oblivion."

The company's X.com tactics shifted subtly. Vince Sollitto, Confinity's communications director, had mastered his craft in the cut and thrust of politics. "My instinct was to try and find ways to poke holes at and discredit X.com," he said. But David Sacks told him to stand down. "I remember David pulled me aside and said, 'Look, you can do whatever you want PR-wise, but don't denigrate X.com,'" Sollitto said. The two companies, Sollitto realized, were in talks to become one.

■ ■ ■

Up the street at X.com, CEO Bill Harris wasn't resting easy. "We were both the same size, growing at the same speed," Harris remembered. "We would have destroyed ourselves competing." He saw the writing on the wall: two payment networks catering to the same market couldn't achieve scale simultaneously. "True networks are a naturally monopolistic business," Harris explained.

Harris felt the time had come. He requested a formal meeting between Confinity and X.com. Meeting at Evvia Estiatorio, a posh Palo Alto restaurant, Thiel and Levchin sat across from Harris and Musk. The mood was tense. "Bill had on his suit and tie, and you know, Elon had sold his company for three hundred million dollars," Levchin remembered. "They were trying to intimidate us." The conversation opened with pleasantries and shop talk—but with a probing undertone. "It was like, 'How many users do *you* have?'" Levchin said.

Then Harris broached the main subject: What if the two companies were to avert their path of mutual destruction and instead joined forces? Thiel asked Harris what terms they had in mind for such a deal. Musk presented an initial offer: X.com would acquire Confinity, with the Confinity team receiving 8 percent of the combined value of the companies.

The meager offer astonished Levchin. "I didn't know if I was supposed to speak up, but I was definitely not up for this," he recalled. Confinity's cofounders politely left the meeting—but smarted at the terms, which they considered lopsided. At a subsequent meeting at the restaurant Il Fornaio, Confinity's investors Pete Buhl and John Malloy attended—and balked at the lowball terms. "We walked out of the room and said, 'There's no way,'" Buhl recalled.

For Malloy, the low offers bolstered the case that Confinity ought to charge ahead on its own. "Eight percent. I was apoplectic," Malloy remembered, shaking his head. "If anything, *we* should be buying *them*, and we shouldn't even be buying them."

Malloy felt sure that Confinity was being undervalued. "Our value was so much better because of the team, but [the team themselves] didn't see it, because they didn't have the self-confidence," Malloy remembered. "I had faith in them that maybe they didn't have yet, which is ironic because they're all so damn smart."

Malloy likened Confinity's X.com obsession to a fighter pilot's "target fixation," a phenomenon in which pilots focus wholly on their target—and inadvertently collide with it or ignore a nearby threat. "They were too focused on X.com . . . immaturely focused on X.com. And every metric I could see I thought we were outperforming them . . . So why do we keep talking about these guys all the time?" Malloy recalled. "It had become an obsession."

Malloy lobbied hard against a merger—and was quick to point out that an acquisition by X.com would force Thiel and Levchin to concede to a banking-focused business model they had previously mocked. "Here you're telling me these guys are so well run, but you're going back to a business model you've already told me is bankrupt?" Malloy said. "I was trying to use that as an argument not to merge at all."

Despite Malloy's skepticism, over the coming weeks Thiel convinced him that merging was the only option. Confinity was quickly running out of funds, and it was likely to be outspent by X.com. So Malloy swallowed his doubts and set about trying to secure the best agreement possible.

By multiple accounts, Malloy drove a tough deal. "Mike [Moritz] is a hardball player," Malloy said of X.com's lead investor—and so was Malloy. During meetings, Malloy would feign distraction and disinterest. "I felt like they were trying to jam a deal through fast. I was like, 'That's not the way this is going to work, guys,'" Malloy recalled. "I thought they were trying to bum-rush some inexperienced people."

To secure leverage in its negotiations, Thiel instructed Luke Nosek to "push the gas pedal as far as [he could]" in acquiring new eBay users. As the days ticked by, the money in the two companies' coffers ran lower, and the pressure to reach a deal increased. But Confinity saw hope: as PayPal's user numbers kept growing, the percentage offers from X.com kept climbing.

■ ■ ■

Musk remained skeptical about any kind of merger. Though he had been impressed by Confinity's scrappiness, he maintained that X.com was a fundamentally different business—and, more importantly, a superior one. "My impression was these guys are really smart—but we can still defeat them," Musk recalled. Despite Confinity's lead on eBay, X.com had acquired more non-eBay accounts. "X was ahead—we did spend more—but we were ahead," Musk said.

Having lived through the failed merger of Citysearch and Zip2 early in his career, Musk came by his skepticism honestly. "Elon was a reluctant partner, and he said, 'These [mergers] rarely work, and we can win,'" Bill Harris remembered.

Harris pressed forward, nevertheless. The two pairs of executives began spending more time together. Levchin found Harris friendly and polished. He also grew to respect Musk. *I really like this Elon guy*, Levchin remembered thinking. "He's obviously completely crazy, but he's really, really smart. And I really like smart people."

Eventually, the two sides reached a hard-won provisional agreement. While Confinity would remain the junior partner, what had begun as a 92–8 acquisition had been hammered into a 55–45 one. Levchin was still "bummed" that the terms remained weighted against Confinity, but Thiel had convinced him that this was the right course—and better than an almost-certain death.

Others praised the deal—seeing the potential. "Mike Moritz came in to tell me that this was a merger for the ages," Levchin remembered, "that it was going to be the most important merger in the history of Silicon Valley." Moritz told Levchin that if the merger went through, he would never sell a single share of the combined company.

One key player didn't share in the excitement. Elon Musk saw the acquisition as a surrender in a winnable war. To put Confinity on par with his own company was bad enough, but especially so when he considered X.com's lead in non-eBay accounts. He wasn't overly worried about market trends, user growth, burn rate, or the competitive landscape—X.com could have won through will and skill.

At one inopportune moment, Levchin recalled, Musk's simmering frustration slipped out. Levchin was visiting the X.com office when Musk blurted out that Confinity was getting "a fucking deal." "My blood just boiled, and so I thought, *It's off*," Levchin remembered. "If it's a partnership, it's a partnership. If you think I'm getting a steal, it's not going to work." Levchin called Thiel, saying the deal was off. He didn't want to be treated as a charity case or as a junior partner.

When word of the breakdown got to Bill Harris, he switched into deal-maker mode. Harris called Levchin and told him that they should meet to talk terms. "Bill, I don't think we're going to do anything here," Levchin responded. Harris asked him where he was, and Levchin replied that he was at home doing laundry. Harris told him to stay there. "I'll help you fold," he promised.

Harris arrived at Levchin's apartment at 469 Grant Avenue, and standing in the laundry room, Levchin told him what he had told Thiel. "I don't think this works if you guys think of us as somebody who is walking away with your equity," Levchin recalled. "It can't add up to a good partnership in the long term."

"What if it were fifty-fifty?" Harris said. "What if we were equal partners?"

"Then it would be hard to claim afterward that anybody got a steal," Levchin admitted.

"If that works for you, I'll make it work," Harris replied. Levchin told Harris that he would support a 50–50 partnership but asked what Musk would say, given his lack of enthusiasm about even the 55–45 split. Harris told him not to worry about it—he would stitch the deal back together.

■ ■ ■

To this day, Harris is circumspect in speaking about what happened next. Musk is not: "I was like, 'Fuck you. We're just going to kill [Confinity].'" If Confinity wasn't going to accept a junior partnership, that was their problem as far as he was concerned. "It's like, *Okay, back to hack-and-slash on account growth*," Musk said.

Harris responded by dropping the bomb: he told Musk that absent a deal between the two companies, he would resign as X.com's CEO. Musk remembers saying, "'Bill, we need to raise a round. And you're basically putting a gun to my head. And saying that if we do not do this deal, then basically the CEO of the company is departing. And we are literally raising a round right now. That's a very difficult situation. Like this could kill the company.'"

Harris stood firm—leaving Musk no choice but to concede. "The reason I agreed to the fifty-fifty is because Bill Harris said he would resign if I didn't," Musk said. "Otherwise, I was going to pass on the deal."

From Harris's perspective, there was simply no other option. "Would there have been a [single] winner? Yes," Harris remembers reasoning. "But it would have taken a lot longer and a huge amount of resources to get there. And it's not at all clear which side would have won."

To Harris, the merger wasn't just defensive—it was a strategic piece of offense. He cited Metcalfe's Law. Devised in the 1980s by Robert Metcalfe, the inventor of Ethernet, the basic idea was simple: The value of a network grows by the square of the size of the network. If a computer network contains five machines, the total network has a value of 25—5 squared; if it has a thousand machines, the network has a value of 1,000,000—1,000 squared. Per Metcalfe, the bigger network has 200 times more machines—but its value is 40,000 times bigger.

True for telephones, faxes, and the world wide web, Metcalfe's law also applied to payments. "Volume wins," Harris explained. "Nobody wants to be on a payment system where there's no one to pay. And no one wants to be a recipient on a payment system where there's no one paying. And so it's all about getting size." Despite Musk's protestations, Harris felt merging was the only answer—even if it took an ultimatum to get it done.

■ ■ ■

Anyone looking at the merger of X.com and Confinity could have been forgiven for forecasting doom. X.com's founder, Elon Musk, was opposed to it. Confinity's lead investor, John Malloy, was skeptical of it. Confinity CTO Max Levchin had called it off once before. And X.com CEO Bill Harris had put himself permanently on the outs with Musk in order to make the merger happen. "It was always an uneasy truce," Malloy said.

The shotgun wedding gave rise to a popular PayPal parlor game: What might have been? Who would have won the eBay wars? Would Confinity have gone bankrupt without X.com? But counterfactuals would come later. For now, the executives and their respective teams had the unwelcome task of wedding the two start-ups. Though Harris and Levchin had shaken hands over still-warm laundry, neither had sorted out the salient details.

What followed taught them all valuable lessons about mergers—what makes them work and what makes them fail. "A merger isn't two companies joining together," Luke Nosek remarked. "It's actually closer to hiring fifty people, sight unseen."

10

CRASH

In early 2000, Thiel and Musk were set to meet with Mike Moritz at Sequoia's office at 2800 Sand Hill Road in Menlo Park to discuss the merger. Musk offered Thiel a lift from Palo Alto.

The year before, Musk had purchased a Magnesium Silver McLaren F1, Chassis #067, from Gerd Petrik, a German pharmaceutical executive. A $1 million sports car complete with gull-wing doors and an engine bay encased in gold foil, Musk dubbed the automobile a "work of art" and "a really beautiful piece of engineering." Even among McLarens, #067 was distinctive—one of only seven McLaren F1s legal to drive in the United States at the time.

McLaren modeled the vehicle's architecture on Formula 1 racers, and it set the lofty ambition of building the world's best car. When it debuted, the McLaren earned universal acclaim. "The F1 will be remembered as one of the great events in the history of the car," wrote one review, ". . . very possibly the fastest production road car the world will ever see, a walking, talking piece of history."

The car had a low weight, but boasted an output of over 600 horsepower. "Just imagine a car that weighs as much as a Miata," said Erik Reynolds, one the world's great McLaren aficionados, "but with four times as much power." As a result of its low weight-to-power ratio, the car was capable of reaching speeds of over 200 miles per hour.

That power, though, also made it dangerous for inexperienced drivers. One owner, British actor Rowan Atkinson, famously crashed his

McLaren twice. Around the moment Musk completed his F1 purchase, a young British entrepreneur fresh off a start-up exit was killed along with two passengers when he drove his McLaren into a tree. "The McLaren forces restraint," warned *Car and Driver* in its otherwise gushing review, "because there is no way to drive it legally . . . and even begin to probe the full extent of its power and speed."

When Musk took delivery of his F1, CNN was there to cover it. "Just three years ago I was showering at the Y and sleeping on the office floor," he told the camera sheepishly, "and now obviously, I've got a million-dollar car . . . it's just a moment in my life." While other McLaren F1 owners around the world—the sultan of Brunei, Wyclef Jean, and Jay Leno, among others—could comfortably afford it, Musk's purchase had put a sizable dent in his bank account. And unlike other owners, Musk drove the car to work—and declined to insure it.

As Musk drove Thiel up Sand Hill Road in the F1, the car was the subject of their chat. "It was like this Hitchcock movie," Thiel remembered, "where we're talking about the car for fifteen minutes. We're supposed to be preparing for the meeting—and we're talking about the car."

During their ride, Thiel looked at Musk and reportedly asked, "So, what can this thing do?"

"Watch this," Musk replied, flooring the accelerator and simultaneously initiating a lane change on Sand Hill Road.

In retrospect, Musk admitted that he was outmatched by the F1. "I didn't really know how to drive the car," he recalled. "There's no stability systems. No traction control. And the car gets so much power that you can break the wheels free at even fifty miles an hour."

Thiel recalls the car in front of them coming fast into view—then Musk swerving to avoid it. The McLaren hit an embankment, was tossed into the air—"like a discus," Musk remembered——then slammed violently into the ground. "The people that saw it happen thought we were going to die," he recalled.

Thiel had not worn a seat belt, but astonishingly, neither he nor Musk were hurt. Musk's "work of art" had not fared as well, having now taken a distinctly cubist turn. Post-near-death experience, Thiel dusted himself off on the side of the road and hitchhiked to the Sequoia offices, where he was joined by Musk a short while later.

X.com's CEO, Bill Harris, was also waiting at the Sequoia office, and he recalled that both Thiel and Musk were late but offered no explanation for their delay. "They never told me," Harris said. "We just had the meeting."

Reflecting on it, Musk found humor in the experience: "I think it's safe to say Peter wouldn't be driving with me again." Thiel wrung some levity out of the moment, too. "I'd achieved lift-off with Elon," he joked, "but not in a rocket."*

■ ■ ■

Driving together, no—but Thiel and Musk were now riding together for the time being professionally as X.com colleagues.

On paper and in the press, X.com appeared to have much going for it: a team of talented technologists, a fast-growing base of nearly half a million users, and leadership that included the former CEO of Intuit and an entrepreneur boasting a nine-figure exit from his last start-up. Thanks to its merger, the companies could make a powerful pitch: in neutralizing their former foremost competitor, wedding together their user bases, and leveraging network effects, the combined company could capture the entire online payments market. Even as merger terms were being finalized, Bill Harris instructed Levchin to tell Yahoo that its deal-making

---

*Musk held on to the McLaren for several years. The car had a complicated—though ultimately redeeming—post-Musk life as well. As reported by one of the organizers of a McLaren F1 Owners Club 25th Anniversary Tour: "The third owner bought the car in 2007 and kept the car in good hands and drove it for a couple of months. However, he hit major trouble when the car caught fire due to a catalytic problem in Santa Rosa, USA, in 2009. It was badly damaged and was sent to MSO (McLaren Special Operations) for a complete rebuild. MSO and McLaren managed to rebuild the car and fortunately it [retained] its original carbon fiber chassis. The repair work took a year to complete and the car was returned to its owner who actually still has the car. He kindly brought it to the McLaren F1 Owners Club 25th Anniversary Tour in the South of France in 2017."

with both companies was now off. "The biggest thing was the creation of a unified front," Levchin explained to a Stanford audience years later.

As news of the merger leaked, a new PayPal customer wrote to X.com's Julie Anderson and Confinity's head of public relations, Vince Sollitto, sharing her positive impressions of the merger, which she called a "win-win":

> The last thing I want to see on Ebay (where I sell AND buy) is a BETA/VHS style Jihad over PayPal versus X.COM. Taking payment from a buyer immediately via PayPal is infinitely better than waiting for a check, then waiting for it to clear. . . . Anyone in the computer biz knows that "Standards Matter," and if you folks become the de facto standard it will make a lot of people's lives easier. The flip side is that if you are the standard you have an enormous responsibility to your users, more so than if there are many alternatives to your product.

Not all reactions were so positive. eBay's users may have been pleased with the merger of X.com and Confinity, but eBay corporate sensed a threat. They also had a response in the works. Just after the merger announcement, eBay announced a partnership with Wells Fargo to manage its payment platform Billpoint. It also introduced a partnership with Visa, promising three months of free payment service for its users.

This was welcome news to many eBay users. "The primary objection that sellers have had to the Billpoint system has been its cost," said Rodrigo Sales, the cofounder of AuctionWatch, one of the internet's hubs for auction news. "That's why companies that offer free payment services, like PayPal and X.com, have been well-received by the eBay community." Indeed, eBay's partnerships with Visa and Wells Fargo seemed designed for a sole purpose: reclaiming ground from X.com and Confinity's PayPal.

X.com's and Confinity's rapid user growth had also bred copycats. In March 2000, one of the nation's largest banks, Chicago-based Bank One, had launched eMoneyMail. The same month, Yahoo acquired dotBank, another person-to-person payments platform. Even one of Confinity's own investors, IdeaLab Capital Partners, funded a competing product called PayMe.com.

■ ■ ■

To make matters worse, X.com's ace in the hole—the explosive growth in customers—was both blessing and curse. Still more users meant still more user complaints. eBay and other auction message boards lit up with gripes when X.com or PayPal.com went down, or when bonuses didn't materialize, or when a payment went awry.

Soon, the companies faced the additional scrutiny of government regulators. The user complaint backlog spurred an inquiry from the Federal Trade Commission, and the US Secret Service grew concerned over PayPal's use in illegal transactions. Through it all, customers at both companies poured in by the hundreds per hour, a growth rate that stymied efforts to bring order to chaos.

The merger itself hardly fostered calm. With the exception of former Intuit CEO Bill Harris, the two teams had minimal management experience to fall back on, let alone experience with mergers. X.com and Confinity had discrete user bases and distinct websites, and they had built their services on different development platforms—X.com's on Microsoft Windows, and Confinity's on Linux.

If that weren't enough, the merger had to conclude quickly. Once X.com and Confinity had reached an accord, neither Thiel nor Harris wanted to risk a disruption of the fragile agreement—a concern driven in part by fundraising. Both companies had been trying to raise funding before the negotiations; the faster they could seal the deal, the sooner they could raise jointly.

Candidates extended offers to join one company during this period were told they would instead be joining a new, larger company. One candidate recalled Levchin urging him to accept his Confinity offer quickly to benefit from the pre-merger equity distribution. Basic questions—like what to call the company's core product—remained unanswered. "I remember *hours* of debate about the logo," Amy Rowe Klement said. "Like how do we want to present the combined logo?" Both sides had agreed that X.com would be the official corporate name for the post-merger entity, and that Confinity would be retired—but what would become of PayPal?

One proposal was to call the product "X-PayPal"—a prefix that spoke to Musk's vision of X.com as a hub for financial products and services of all kinds. A March 18, 2000, email from Bill Harris outlined the potential for an X-brand family—including X-Fund, X-Click, X-Card, X-Check, and X-Account. But for the Confinity contingent, the hyphen separating X and "PayPal" perpetuated fears of being relegated to a junior partner position.

The merger's due diligence process revealed red flags on both sides. According to several senior executives, on the day the merger closed, X.com had to provide an immediate cash infusion into Confinity's coffers. Though Confinity had raised another round of funding in early 2000, its pedal-to-the-floor growth had chewed through much of that funding.

X.com had issues of its own. To grow its customer base, X.com had been giving out lines of credit to prospective customers, part of its plan for a full suite of financial services products. But with X.com expanding as fast as it had, appropriate underwriting had taken a back seat. "We would be issuing lines of credit to people that either weren't real people, or had stolen someone else's identity," Ken Miller explained. "And then kind of secondarily, we were giving lines of credit or too much credit to people who were the real people but didn't deserve it."

Both companies ultimately accepted downsides like these as the cost of doing a crucial deal that would theoretically leave them stronger together than apart. But the merger hadn't solved a fundamental problem: the new entity's combined burn rate. The joint company was on track to spend almost $25 million that quarter alone, with salaries, bonus payments, credit card fees, and fraud tearing through its balance sheet. "If we were standing on the roof of our building throwing wads of hundred-dollar bills over the side of the building," remarked Reid Hoffman, "we'd be spending money less [quickly]."

Musk remembered the myriad crises colliding at the point of the merger: "If the fraud thing is not solved, we're gonna die. If customer service is not solved, we're gonna die. . . . If we didn't have a revenue model—if our business consists of only costs and no revenue—we were obviously dying."

■ ■ ■

The two teams had been primed to fight an epic battle for supremacy, complete with morbid cakes, dark banners, and lacerating emails. Now, just weeks later, the teams were expected to unify as one fast-growing, happy family. Many felt nervous at the prospect.

In late February, word of the merger trickled down from the top brass to the rank-and-file—and for many, it came as a surprise. "At the time I think [Confinity] thought they were working hard against us. And we thought, *Hey we're ahead, and we'll still crush anyone that's near us,*" X.com engineer Colin Catlan remembered. "And so the people at X.com were a bit shocked that they had to integrate."

The story of the merger differed depending on whether Team Confinity or Team X.com was telling the tale. "Internally, it was positioned to us that we are a much superior offering," Confinity engineer David Gausebeck remembered. "X.com is offering credit and has a horrible default rate and they're bleeding money and they have all these issues—and we're in great position relative to them. But because we're not the only one in the market, that hurts us in terms of investor perception."

In his memoir, Eric Jackson, a member of Confinity's marketing team, recalled Luke Nosek, his manager, soothing his concerns about the integration:

> Look, this isn't a bad deal for us. For one thing, [X.com] actually [has] almost two hundred thousand users, about as many as we do! . . . Also with all the financial services like money markets, index funds, and debit cards that they offer, each of their accounts is probably worth a lot more than ours. . . . And since we were beginning to burn through cash pretty quickly and will have to do some more

financing soon, merging with our top competitor will help us raise a lot more funds.

X.com employees, on the other hand, were sold an opposing narrative: that they were "bailing out" Confinity—that Confinity had grown faster on eBay but blown through its cash as a result. Additionally, X.com told its employees that its experienced leaders would bring much-needed expertise and regulatory know-how to Confinity's more junior team.

Throughout March, groups of employees began to travel back and forth from Confinity's office at 165 University to X.com's at 394 University—Confinity's own former office building. "It was ironic because we had [sublet] this office space to X.com—and next thing you know, we merge our companies, and move right back into our former office," Confinity's Ken Howery recalled.

Not all interactions during this period were as easy as moving back into a familiar space. One engineer, Erik Klein, remembered a frosty engineering meeting at the Creole restaurant Nola in Palo Alto. "It ended up being hours of just arguing and debating and yelling at each other in front of Nola," Klein offered. "We did not mesh at all . . . it was like oil and water."

Other employees, though, felt relieved. "Nobody wanted fifty percent dilution," X.com's Todd Pearson said, referring to employees' reduced post-merger equity stakes, "but now at least we're not going to kill each other." X.com's Julie Anderson saw the merger as the natural next step. "It wasn't a big shock given the financial situation," she said. Both companies had grown their customer bases, but together, she observed, they would have a better chance of turning their user base into a viable business. "We all thought it would be nice to move to that next stage," she recalled.

That next stage required a new, larger home: in March, the company leased office space at 1840 Embarcadero Road in Palo Alto, the former home of Intuit—and Bill Harris. The 21,874-square-foot space would cost the company $102,807.80 per month for the first year. Lee Hower, who joined X.com fresh out of the University of Pennsylvania, recalled the move to 1840 Embarcadero as a challenge. "It can sound mundane, but in the context of mashing two organizations together, rapidly growing, rapidly hiring and doing everything else," Hower remembered, "it was just one more element of chaos."

The unfinished Embarcadero Road space hosted one of the first combined team meetings. Harris, Musk, and Thiel spoke, each offering reassurances that the joint entity was on the right trajectory. Attendees recalled Thiel wearing Confinity's Sistine Chapel T-shirt with shorts—a marked contrast to Harris's suit jacket and pressed slacks. They also remembered Thiel calculating the conversion ratio between Confinity and X.com shares in his head, on stage.

On March 30, 2000, X.com's head of human resources, Sal Giambanco, sent a single company-wide email to both all@paypal.com and all@x.com with the subject line "It's Official." "As of today, X.com and Confinity are now one," he wrote. "Congratulations to Everyone!!!!!"

■ ■ ■

X.com and Confinity had another cause to celebrate: on the same day they formally broadcast the merger to the press, X.com's and Confinity's leadership also announced a $100 million Series C round of financing. "We've had a tremendous response," Thiel said in the company press release. "Our financing round was substantially oversubscribed, as we've seen a great deal of enthusiasm about participating in X.com's unique and exponentially growing financial platform." Added Musk: "The magnitude of this round highlights the value of X.com's position as the leader in Web-based payments."

The fundraising process had been frenzied. Jack Selby, a member of the finance team, had lived out of his suitcase for several weeks, traveling "literally nonstop" to finish the round. Thiel wanted to close commitments quickly—arising from his belief that the US economy sat on the brink. "I give the credit to Peter," Selby said. "He made the macro call, and said, 'We have to close on this . . . because the end is near.'"

But for all its fear of economic unsteadiness, the team had no problem drawing investor interest. "I wouldn't call it raising money when it's like, *Okay, of all the various people trying to smash the door down and give us money, who should we accept?*" Musk recalled. "We were getting fire-hosed with cash." Thiel remembered being cornered seemingly everywhere he went. Once, he was followed in a hotel lobby by a prospective investor; Thiel wasn't there to meet with him, but the investor simply pulled up a chair to hear Thiel pitch another group of investors.

On a trip to Korea, Thiel's corporate credit card was declined as he tried to purchase a return ticket home. The investors he had met with were only too happy to furnish a first-class plane ticket—which they did on the spot. "They were excited beyond belief," Thiel remembered. "The next day, they called up our law firm and asked, 'What's the bank account we need to send the money to?'"

The crazed nature of it all confirmed Thiel's suspicions about the market. "I remember thinking to myself that it felt like things couldn't get much crazier, and that we really had to close the money quickly because the window might not last forever," he said.

The final $100 million figure actually disappointed some on the team. Confinity and X.com had secured verbal commitments for double that amount, and some on the team had wanted to hold out for the remaining funding or push for a billion-dollar valuation.

Thiel disagreed, urging Selby and others on the financing team to turn handshakes into actual checks, to get term sheets signed, and have deposits confirmed. "Peter kicked everyone's asses to get that funding round done," David Sacks remembered. Many Confinity employees— who had seen Thiel at his toughest—rarely remember him this insistent. "If we don't get this money raised," Howery recalled Thiel saying, "the whole company could blow up."

Musk, too, anticipated an impending downturn. In mid-1999, he warned an interviewer from the University of Pennsylvania alumni magazine about a coming collapse. "Any change this profound is bound to set off speculative frenzy," he said of the internet bubble, "and people need to do their homework, and not blindly buy into companies that aren't well put together. There are a lot of Potemkin villages out there built on flimsy foundations, and many, many will fail."

Musk predicted a reckoning. "This is the longest peacetime expansion in history," Musk said, "and for young people who've never really seen a serious recession—and anyone who's studied history knows they happen—a downturn will be a rough experience." This prediction contrasted with his usual bombastic optimism—if Musk preached caution, it meant something.

Musk also had the sense to know that X.com's $500 million valuation was "ridiculous." When his earlier company, Zip2, sold for $300 million, it had paying clients and millions in revenue. X.com was now valued at almost double that, even though its principal achievement was trading investors' money for email addresses.

■ ■ ■

Fittingly, the team chose a lead investor for the round who was insulated from dot-com hype: Madison Dearborn Partners (MDP), a Chicago-based private equity firm. MDP dipped its toes into venture capital, with a series of small bets on start-ups in technology, media, and telecommunications.

Tim Hurd, the MDP partner leading the Confinity/X.com round, had followed the growth and expansion of internet businesses, and when the pitch deck for the Confinity/X.com offering came his way, it piqued his interest. "I knew a bit about payments, and I said, 'Hmm, this is pretty interesting,'" he said. X.com and Confinity had managed to grow users fast, which Hurd knew was tough in the payments world. "Once you have a network effect, it becomes much harder for someone else to have one," Hurd said.

Hurd had no previous allegiance to either X.com or Confinity; it was, as he put it, "dollar one for me." And while those dollars were substantial, MDP wasn't investing a make-or-break sum—its $30 million stake represented a small fraction of its assets under management. "[PayPal] was a one-off thing for me," Hurd recalled.

With MDP leading the round, Selby, Thiel, and the X.com finance team set about raising the remaining $70 million from what they described as "a phalanx of leading investors." Other investors joined MDP, including three investment firms in Singapore, two in Japan, and one in Taiwan. Closer to home, the team locked down LabMorgan, JPMorgan's e-finance unit, Capital Research and Management Company, Digital Century Capital, and Bayview 2000.

The timing was auspicious: just days after X.com closed its round, US public markets entered a downward slide that would ultimately wipe out $2.5 trillion in market capitalization and sour the mood on technology stocks. "Months of greed that fueled one of the greatest bull markets in history," reported CNN in April 2000, "turned to fear on changing sentiment that the highest flying technology stocks rose too far, too fast." By the end of the year, Nasdaq stocks had lost half their value. On the eve of 2001, CNN asked a portfolio manager for stock picks. "I would sit on the sidelines for six months," he replied, "and let the angel of death gather up the corpses."

Later, Thiel would call the cataclysm clarifying. "Perhaps the peak of insanity was also the peak of clarity," he recalled, "where in some sense you saw very clearly what the distant future was going to be, even though it turned out that a lot of specific things went very wrong."

Suddenly, Silicon Valley's excess curdled into austerity. "All the other companies in Silicon Valley that had waited to close their funding rounds, for whatever reason, the money just dried up—instantly," Sacks remembered, snapping his fingers. Members of the team remembered the shock of seeing once-busy Palo Alto storefronts now boarded up.

Even high-profile support didn't count for much once the correction began. Sequoia's Mike Moritz had invested in one of the dot-com boom's highest flyers: the pet supply site Pets.com. In January 2000, Pets.com purchased a pricey thirty-second Super Bowl advertising spot titled "If you leave me now." On November 7, 2000, just 282 darkly ironic days after the ad's debut, Pets.com shut down and its assets were liquidated—turning "Pets.com" into a synonym for the dangers of dot-com speculation.

During the bust, fuckedcompany.com—a snarky twist on the technology magazine *Fast Company*—became popular with the tech crowd. As its name suggested, Fucked Company logged the era's many misadventures.

Several X.com employees remembered browsing Fucked Company daily during this period—not out of schadenfreude, but out of fear that they might be next.

That Confinity and X.com didn't end up in the Valley's discard bin was attributable to a number of factors, not least that it had enough runway to ride out a rocky year. "Back then, there were probably five to seven other little piddling online money moving services . . . that just got starved of oxygen over time. And they all died out by the fall," said Vince Sollitto.

Former employees point to the $100 million round's timing as a watershed for PayPal. "I don't think people know how precarious it was," Amy Rowe Klement offered. "If we hadn't raised that $100 million round, there would be no PayPal." Mark Woolway extended the counterfactual: "If the team hadn't closed that one hundred million," Woolway said, "there would be no SpaceX, no LinkedIn, and no Tesla."

Reflecting on it all, David Wallace drew on theology. "There was this feeling of, you know, if we just keep working as hard as we can, we seem to be living a charmed life," he observed. "We did come to a merger, *just* in time to get our funding closed before the whole thing crashed. . . . [in] Christian theology, there's this sense of human effort versus predestination, and sometimes they get opposed to each other. But the only way that theology really works is when you see it as the two things in conjunction with each other. Things that are predestined *include* the works."

■ ■ ■

Thiel's doomsday predictions also prompted an unusual request. In preparation for a summer 2000 board meeting, Thiel had asked Musk if he could present a proposal. Musk agreed. "Uh, Peter's got an agenda item he'd like to talk about," Musk said, handing the reins to Thiel.

Thiel began. The markets, he said, weren't done driving into the red. He prophesied just how dire things would get—for both the company and for the world. Many had seen the bust as a mere short-term correction, but Thiel was convinced the optimists were wrong. In his view, the bubble was bigger than anyone had thought and hadn't even begun to really burst yet.

From X.com's perspective, the implications of Thiel's prediction were dire. Its high burn rate meant that it would need to continue fundraising. But if—no, when—the bubble truly burst, the markets would tighten further, and funding would dry up—even for X.com. The company balance sheet could drop to zero with no options left to raise money.

Thiel presented a solution: the company should take the $100 million closed in March and transfer it to his hedge fund, Thiel Capital. He would then use that money to short the public markets. "It was beautiful logic," board member Tim Hurd of MDP remembered. "One of the elements of PayPal was that they were untethered from how people did stuff in the real world."

The board was uniformly aghast. Members Moritz, Malloy, and Hurd all pushed back. "Peter, I totally get it," Hurd replied. "But we raised money from investors on a business plan. And they have that in their files. And it said, 'use of proceeds would be for general corporate purposes.' And to grow the business and so forth. It wasn't to go speculate on indices. History may prove that you're right, and it will have been brilliant, but if you're wrong, we'll all be sued." Mike Moritz's reaction proved particularly memorable. With his theatricality on full display, Moritz "just lost his mind," a board member remembered, berating Thiel: "Peter, this is really simple: If this board approves that idea, I'm resigning!"

"The pure drama of Mike Moritz's reaction was one of the best moments of the whole thing," remembered board member Malloy. Thiel was angry with the board's refusal and skipped its next few meetings in protest. The board, he felt, was being shortsighted in the face of a historic market collapse in the making—one that, if approached properly, could yield a windfall. "The tide was changing and Peter is always pessimistic, but he recognizes it is changing, and he was definitely right," Malloy said. "We would have made more money [investing] than anything we did at PayPal."

11

THE NUT HOUSE COUP

eBay message boards, June 2000:

> PayPal has worked for me. I may try bidpay too. I'm QUITTING
> Billpoint! I say ebay Sellers should stand together and BOYCOTT
> Billpoint!
>
> PayPal is an awesome service for buyers and sellers! And free to
> both! I love it! . . . I can't see why ANYONE on ebay would choose
> Billpoint instead!
>
> I've been using PayPal for about the past 2 months and it's just
> wonderful. About half of my buyers use it now . . . and our
> transactions go like greased lightning.

Feedback like this buoyed the PayPal team through its early tumult. "The users loved us," X.com engineer Colin Catlan remembered. "We would get hundreds of emails a day from people letting us know that we had changed their life." Entrepreneurs who had long dreamed of operating their own businesses now could—buying and selling on eBay using X.com's tech. "We actually built something that was solving a real problem," said Jim Kellas, Levchin's high school friend and now a QA engineer at the company.

But with all the love came more than a few complaints. Early on at X.com and Confinity, addressing these problems had been an afterthought. When it first launched PayPal in October 1999, Confinity team members could simply hop on the phone to talk through users' specific issues. As the company grew through the winter, a sole hire, David Wallace, managed the entirety of Confinity's customer service.

But by early 2000, the status quo was failing. Over a five-day stretch in February, X.com received a staggering 26,405 customer service calls—or roughly seven calls every minute. Confinity experienced a similar tidal wave. "Twenty-four hours a day," Reid Hoffman recalled, "you could pick up literally any extension and talk to an angry customer."

Both companies coped by ignoring emails, unhooking office phone lines, and even disabling and replacing team members' cell phones. "[Wallace] pokes his head out and says his email backlog is one hundred thousand," remembered David Sacks of this moment. "And we're like, 'Wait, what? Maybe you should have told us this sooner?'"

■ ■ ■

For users entrusting Confinity and X.com with their financial lives, platform glitches had serious implications. One early X.com user had flown to San Diego for a weekend away with his girlfriend. "I checked my X.com checking account balance at approximately 5:30 PM PST, shortly before we left for the airport, and saw that it was $746.14," he wrote in a detailed email to the entire X.com executive team. Upon landing, his X.com check card was declined at the car rental counter, failed at a nearby ATM, then was rejected at his hotel. He called the X.com service number from his hotel, but after an endless hold, he gave up.

"It is worth noting at this point that, had I been traveling by myself," he continued in his email, "I would have been sleeping on a bench at the airport with no car, no hotel, and no money, and your 'customer service' department unable to even answer the phone, much less do anything to assist me . . . I have deep reservations about continuing my relationship with your company."

X.com's own employees struggled with the company's products, too. In April 2000, an employee's debit card failed twice on a $59.22 charge at Starbucks. "I was just declined twice on my debit card and was told by [our customer service representative] that this was due to day-end processing," the employee wrote in a stinging email to his colleagues. "This is not good at all." The Starbucks patron was X.com chairman and founder Elon Musk.

One customer charged an overdraft fee by X.com took to the online review site Epinions to share his displeasure, promising to "be in touch with the FDIC and the Attorney General's Office." Frustrated customers contacted the press, the Better Business Bureau, as well as the Federal Trade Commission.

Vivien Go had to deal with the Better Business Bureau complaints. "I would get served these, like, court orders," she remembered. "As somebody who is not American . . . I was so scared . . . I got a lot of heat from the San Jose Better Business Bureau lady. She was a *tough* lady. It's so difficult to think 'Today I have to go meet with this person.'"

Some customers took matters into their own hands. "People thought we were keeping their money hostage," Skye Lee recalled. "So there was somebody who drove, with a gun, and came to the PayPal offices demanding his money. So security was something we had to really think about back then."

Dionne McCray, a quality assurance manager, remembered leaving her house wearing a PayPal T-shirt. "Someone started yelling at me because they couldn't get some PayPal thing done," McCray said. "It's a very surreal experience, because they think because you work there, somehow you can help them with whatever or you can get their account unfrozen or you can explain whatever." McCray, who remained in tech for the rest of her career, drew a lifelong lesson: "To this day, I do not wear company logos on clothes outside my house."

Admittedly, some of the issues weren't entirely the company's fault. To get an X.com ATM card to work at a rental car counter or at a Starbucks required a complex sequence of steps, any one of which could prove a point of failure. When they looked into the San Diego–bound IT specialist's situation, for instance, X.com's leaders discovered that his troubles were due to server maintenance on a third-party debit card processing system.

But deficient customer service left users in the lurch, unable to distinguish between a company glitch and a third-party service goof. If something went wrong, users reasoned, it must be X.com's fault. Customer service, company leadership decided, must be made a priority.

■ ■ ■

At first, X.com tried the typical approach: outsourcing calls and complaints. X.com contracted with California-based firms, including staffing a call center in Burbank. But these solutions were expensive and often incapable of solving user problems. "They charged us tons of money, and they were terrible," Musk said.

X.com's Julie Anderson set out to find a solution. Anderson scouted other customer service firms around the country, including one promising location in Boise, Idaho. Then came an idea. "I don't know why or where [it] came from," she recalled. "But I just thought, *Well, I can go teach all my extended family how to do customer service from home*, because I have a great big family."

Specifically, Anderson thought of her sister, Jill Harriman, who lived in Nebraska and whose Midwest patience she believed would offer a strong antidote to simmering user frustration. Musk saw promise. "Just go hog wild," he remembers telling her. "Get a building and just go. We need a hundred people in thirty days." So Anderson flew to Ceresco, Nebraska, and trained her sister—who in turn trained fourteen of her local friends.

This venture represented X.com's first step into greater Omaha—a presence that would grow over time. The initial group of customer service specialists proved more effective than their California predecessors—faster, less expensive, and with fewer language barriers. "They were great—the best we had. Reliable. Responsible. Hardworking. You name it," remembered Anderson.

Because of the outpost's early success, X.com leadership gave the go ahead to briskly expand the Nebraska operation, which grew from a couple dozen customer service reps on April 17 to 161 reps by May 12. In a mere matter of weeks, the Nebraska call center had more employees than the company's Palo Alto headquarters, and the group's results were dramatic. By May 12, 2000, X.com could proudly announce in a companywide email that "the email backlog is nearly gone." The company also closed the expensive Burbank customer service operation.

That summer and in the years that followed, X.com employees made regular pilgrimages to Omaha—product team members in order to understand the tools needed by reps, company executives to establish relationships with the Omaha senior managers, and more. Anderson herself moved to Omaha for a period to help build the team and craft the customer service process.

Omaha employees also became the connective tissue between Palo Alto headquarters and the company's customers. Michelle Bonet, an early PayPal Omaha employee, remembered being impressed by the company's speed in responding to customer issues with the website. "We would find a glitch in the system, and we would notify [Palo Alto] . . . and the next day it would be fixed." As the face of the company to its customers, Bonet also recalled the difficulties of dealing with irate customers. "We had bomb threats. We had a *lot* of threats—both written and verbal," she recalled.

Amy Rowe Klement remembered that Omaha's success created something of a Palo Alto blind spot. "Looking back, after I grew, I realized that dang, I was not in service enough to customer support," Klement shared, "because it was sort of like Omaha's deal, right? Once I grew a little bit and realized, *Oh, I need to be on a plane, and I need to be in Omaha, because that's my job. If there's issues in Omaha, it's because my team didn't do their job well. And so we have to be more integrated.*"

Musk had high praise for the Omaha call center employees. "They crushed it, and they were awesome!" Musk remembered. "It cost way less and the customer happiness level was way higher." On Friday, June 2, Musk himself traveled to Omaha for the ribbon-cutting of the company's first Nebraska office. He was joined by some fellow Palo Alto employees, Omaha Mayor Hal Daub, and X.com's Omaha team, including a customer service rep named Andre Duhan III, who marked the occasion by shaving the X.com logo into his hair and dying it blue. The stunt raised money for the Child Saving Institute, a local charity.

In choosing Omaha, X.com benefited not just from Anderson's chance family connection, but also the US military's presence in the area. Protected by half a continent on either side, Nebraska hosted the Strategic Air Command headquarters—the military command controlling much of the country's nuclear stockpile. During the Cold War, Nebraska's Offutt Air Force Base planned the country's "mutually assured destruction" response to a Soviet nuclear attack. Private sector interests, including X.com, took advantage of the military's investments in the area's telecommunications systems. In the early 1990s, the region featured one of the country's first fiber-optic cable networks.

That left Omaha remarkably well suited for the far-flung call center of a West Coast payments start-up. PayPal's international customer service operation would later grow out of Omaha as well. Omaha-based reps would travel the world, training new reps and opening sister customer service sites in India, Dublin, and Shanghai. Over time, Omaha's seed group would expand to thousands, and scale to many times the staff of X.com's Palo Alto headquarters. To this day, PayPal remains one of the region's largest employers.

■ ■ ■

Years later, Anderson reflected on her scrappy approach to solving customer service for the company: "I never stopped and thought, *Will this work?* That question was completely foreign to those years. It was, *What can we do? And how fast can we do it?*"

Speed had a cost—but one the company was willing to cover. Designer Ryan Donahue remembered that he once broke a key site function on a Friday afternoon, during a moment of heavy payment volume. He alerted the company's CTO, Levchin, who went off and diagnosed the issue. "He came back . . . and he's like, 'Congratulations. You single-handedly broke the ability to send money and cost the company $1.5 million.'" Donahue panicked. "I've never made such an expensive mistake before," he said. "It was okay. He was laughing about it. And I was like, 'This place is awesome.'"

Musk and other senior leaders tolerated failures as a side effect of iteration. "I remember once Elon saying one thing which was like, 'If you can't tell me the four ways you fucked something up . . . before you got it right, you probably weren't the person who worked on it,'" Giacomo DiGrigoli recalled.

Musk echoed this sentiment. "If there were two paths where we had to choose one thing or the other, and one wasn't obviously better than the other," he explained in a 2003 public talk at Stanford, "then rather than spend a lot of time trying to figure out which one was slightly better, we would just pick one and do it. And sometimes we'd be wrong. . . . But oftentimes it's better to just pick a path and do it rather than just vacillate endlessly on the choice."

■ ■ ■

On the other side of the merger, however, employees and executives alike began to notice more vacillating and less path-picking. Even basic issues appeared irresolvable. The company's corporate email systems took months to merge. Fewer products were released, less code deployed. "I sort of showed up and clocked in," one employee shared, "but I didn't know what I was supposed to be doing or who I reported to."

The delays compounded the fresh threats on the horizon: eBay's payments gambits, new competitors, and clever fraudsters. "Two or three months of not getting anything done was an eternity in this company," remembered Sacks, "given that in the two or three months before that, we had launched, beaten competitors, merged, and raised this funding round."

Those in or near the executive ranks had grown accustomed to small, informal meetings, particularly at Confinity. But at the new X.com, lengthy meetings became a fact of life. "We would attend these exec meetings where you've got twenty-plus people in a room!" remembered an exasperated Sacks.

CEO Bill Harris bore the brunt of the blame for the slowdown. "He never solved the 2x problem," one executive recalled, alluding to the talent duplication following mergers. By way of example, some pointed to the fact that both companies had senior leaders who oversaw finance—both of whom were named David (Jaques and Johnson).

Harris faced not just the operational complexities of a newly combined business but a newly combined team of mammoth personalities. Of the four executives at the top—Levchin, Musk, Thiel, and himself—Harris would say, with a laugh, "Four guys, not a single one of us [had] an ego that would fit in a large gymnasium." Harris was also a decidedly nontechnical CEO. By his own admission, this presented challenges at engineering-focused X.com.

Many X.com executives were upset by one Harris decision in particular: his push to end X.com's sign-up bonus programs and to reduce the Confinity incentive from $10 to $5. He directed the company to issue a customer-wide announcement letting users know that, as of March 15, the program would be ending for former X.com users, while grandfathering in Confinity's old PayPal customers—but at half the prior incentive rate. If customers asked why one program was being scuttled as the other survived, the official line was: "It only makes sense to have one referral program in operation as the companies combine."

Harris's decision to cut incentives arose from his concern over the company's cost curve. *Let's staunch the bleeding*, Harris remembered thinking. "I thought we'd won," he said, referencing X.com's post-merger domination of the payments market, "and that what we had to do was stop spending."

Others believed this confidence to be premature—recklessly pumping the brakes on growth in what remained a precarious time for the company. Because eBay users still represented the majority of its customer base and payments volume, X.com remained at the mercy of the auction giant. A single eBay decision could decimate X.com's business—a nightmare scenario it had experienced firsthand. As a part of a spring 2000 promotion for Billpoint, eBay had announced that sellers could list auction items for free if they included Billpoint as a payment option. After a single "free listing day," Billpoint went from being listed as a payment option on 1 percent of all auctions to 10 percent. Achieving that kind of market share, wrote Eric Jackson, "took PayPal a month to reach."

This, many on the team believed, was why bonuses mattered so much. X.com had limited arrows in its quiver to attract eBay customers.

Other than a few superfans, auction sellers were overwhelmingly brand agnostic—payment services were utilities. While sellers appreciated the convenience of X.com and Confinity's PayPal, they had advertised the two services because X.com and Confinity had paid them to do so. Ending the bonuses, many on the team felt, would amount to laying off this motivated and exceptionally effective sales force.

Even two decades removed, the decision to end incentives irks members of the team, including Luke Nosek, among the architects of Confinity's referral program. "It was a mistake," he declared flatly. Despite PayPal's later success, Nosek maintained that the service may have grown further and faster had bonuses been kept as-is.

■ ■ ■

One late evening at the office, Bill Harris noticed an engineer going home earlier than his counterparts. The engineer mentioned that he wanted to catch a favorite television show and then return to the office. "But if I had a TiVo, Bill," the engineer joked, referring to the then-hot, new product allowing viewers to record television programs, "I could just set it and then stay here." A few days later, the engineer arrived at his desk to find a brand-new TiVo, compliments of Bill Harris.

In this instance, as in others, Harris's openness as a leader provided a welcome contrast to X.com's other officers. Harris also created a provisional org chart and tried to bring order to the engineering backlog during this period. He accelerated the pace of business development deals and helped to close a deal with a site called AllAdvantage—a site that paid its users while they surfed the web—to grow X.com's user base.

Other X.com employees felt that Harris's focus on such deals was not a success but rather a symptom of a broader issue. X.com, they felt, needed a revenue strategy, not a new growth strategy. The service was already growing virally—by tens of thousands of users a day—thanks to the bonus program Harris wanted to end. Development deals helped, but the central problem remained the company's ill-defined path to making money.

At X.com, the original plan had been to upsell people into an expansive set of nonpayment banking services—which would in turn generate revenue. At Confinity, meanwhile, the team had intended to earn interest on PayPal account balances—a strategy dubbed "making money on the float." In both cases, the plans hit hard reality: X.com's other banking offerings didn't attract many users, and Confinity's earnings from "the float" turned out to be negligible.

To make financial matters worse, X.com also had to pay hefty transaction fees. Most X.com accounts were linked to customer credit cards, requiring X.com to pay fees to credit card companies like Visa, Mastercard, and American Express with each customer transaction. "The more transactions we did," Amy Rowe Klement observed, "the more money we lost."

Harris wasn't blind to the soaring costs and lack of revenue, so he proposed that the company charge a flat fee to money senders as a solution—similar to the fees paid for sending a money order or a wire transfer through a bank. Thiel believed this idea would be disastrous. Part of the reason Confinity's PayPal service had taken off—he felt—was that it had promised free transfer services that competitors charged for. Many eBay buyers and sellers, in particular, used PayPal to avoid the fees and hassle of Western Union. Instituting payer fees risked losing market share to eBay's Billpoint, especially at a time when eBay was making serious moves to win back users.

By charging for its services, X.com and Confinity also risked more angry customers. Their respective email products had entered the world as avowedly free. Confinity's website bore the words "ALWAYS FREE," and Musk had loudly proclaimed X.com's war on extraneous fees of all kinds. Both sides believed that once the company had successfully wooed enough customers, revenue could be sorted out.

For these reasons, the idea of charging users was quashed at the time. Heated discussions at the top of the company revealed strongly held differences between Harris and other senior managers over the company's costs and revenue strategy. More fundamentally, the X.com team sensed that even if it could crack the code on either issue, the organization had become too chaotic and slow-moving to make any solution work. As costs continued to rise, the pressure mounted—threatening a rupture.

■ ■ ■

Peter Thiel spent some good measure of his life pondering human freedom. At Stanford, the question emerged as a philosophical exploration; later in his life, it would take a political turn. But during his time at X.com, the question was distinctly personal.

Just after noon on Friday, May 5, 2000, Thiel arrived at an answer and sent a company-wide email bearing the subject line "Resignation as Executive Vice President":

> All,
>
> Effective today, I am resigning as Executive Vice President of X.com. There are three main reasons motivating my decision:
>
> (1) We've scaled from 4 people (on the PayPal side) to over 300, built a customer base of 1.5 million users, and grown into one of the leading efinance sites in the world. It's been an exhilirating [*sic*] ramp up, but after seventeen months of working literally day and night, I am simply exhausted.
>
> (2) In the process, we've gone from the early planning stages to a business that's implementing our plans for world domination. The basic vision is to build the financial operating system for the world, and thereby provide the underpinnings for global commerce. I'm more of a visionary and less of a manager. And precisely because the initial vision has gained so much traction, it has become all the more critical to transition to a team that will manage and scale X.com's operations.
>
> (3) The recent $100 million financing round (at a pre-money valuation of $500 million) represented a resounding affirmation by the investor community in the prospects for X.com. This seemed like a natural point of closure for my day-to-day involvement, and like a good point to transition to those who will lead X.com's IPO.

I intend to remain actively involved as a strategic advisor to X.com. You should always feel free to contact me, with any questions or concerns you may have.

On a personal note, I've grown and learned more than in any other year of my life (with the possible exception of going from age 2 to age 3). Even more importantly, I've formed some great relationships and friendships with the tremendous individuals we've assembled at X.com. And I'm certain those will continue in the months and years ahead.

Thanks for everything,
Peter Thiel

Whatever rationale Thiel may have offered, those close to Thiel understood the subtext: He had grown frustrated with Bill Harris. Thiel had objected to Harris's proposal for a fee on PayPal users and to Harris's decision to use company money to pay for lobbyists to deal with regulatory issues—which he thought wasteful. Relations between the two didn't improve over time.

Thiel's objections to life at X.com weren't limited to the CEO. The company had grown from a handful of people to hundreds, and Thiel detested the demands of the larger operation. After the merger, he was named X.com's "Executive Vice President of Finance" and reported up to both Harris and Musk. In this structure, he was given five direct reports—David Jaques, the CFO; Mark Woolway, Ken Howery, and Jack Selby, who comprised the financing team; and the company's still-to-be-hired general counsel. From Thiel's perspective, this counted as five subordinates and two bosses too many.

Between the end of February and the end of March, Thiel had finished the financing round, and now that X.com had the funds it needed to survive, he felt no need to stick around. The company would be fine without him in an operational role—and more importantly, he would be better off without the encumbrances of executive life.

■ ■ ■

Thiel's departure deeply concerned many Confinity alums. "I was very unhappy about Peter leaving," remembered Sacks, whom Thiel had hired over the objections of his colleagues.

For Musk, Thiel's departure was one more troubling signal about his CEO. Of course, Musk's concerns about Harris predated Thiel's exit. He had never forgiven Harris for ransoming the company's future to complete the merger. "I was pretty unhappy that he had held a gun to my head over that," Musk remembered. "That was a dick move."

The company's present state compounded Musk's frustration. He had observed the product development slowdown with displeasure and took exception to Harris's re-prioritization of its technology road map. An April 7 document outlining X.com's engineering goals listed additional auction payment features ahead of features such as "brokerage," "credit cards," and "mutual funds." Musk still firmly believed that auction payments were but a launching pad, and he concluded that by de-prioritizing this vision, Harris wanted "to take the company in strategic directions that [made] no sense."

Musk also blanched at the CEO's desire to hire more business and finance heavies. "He was going to 'tame us young whippersnappers' with these, like, seasoned financial executives or whatever," Musk remembered. "And we're like, 'Uh, these are the same seasoned executives at these banks who can't do jack, who can't compete with us? Doesn't make sense.'" Musk believed that 'whippersnappers' like Thiel—whose loss troubled Musk—stood the best chance of innovating and winning.

■ ■ ■

By this point, Musk had also gotten to know and like David Sacks. Both were immigrants from South Africa, and both brought an intensity and energy to their work that the other could appreciate. "David and I got along really well," Musk recalled.

The week following Thiel's departure, Sacks, Musk, and Mark Woolway met at a nearby bar called Antonio's Nut House for a drink. The bar was a Palo Alto melting pot, best known for its bottomless free peanuts—and for the cracking of discarded shells under patrons' feet.

Musk and Sacks talked about their respective visions for the X.com product. "It was a real good spitballing session," Musk remembered. Sacks pitched some incipient ideas, including his belief that the company could ultimately run payments not just on eBay, but everywhere transactions occurred online. As e-commerce expanded, he predicted, other websites would face the problem that X.com had solved on eBay: enabling cheap and easy payments.

The conversation soon veered to X.com's CEO. Musk opened up about his deep reservations about Harris, including his lingering distaste for his scorched-earth merger tactics. For Sacks, this was a revelation. Until that point, many Confinity alums had assumed Harris and Musk were united.

Sacks shared Musk's view that post-merger growth and development had slowed to a rate that risked the operation's future. Harris's imposition of additional meetings, formality, and process, he believed, came at the expense of releasing new features. Sacks also disagreed with the decision to reduce customer incentives, doubting that bonus spending was as unsustainable as Harris believed. The bigger risk, in his view, was X.com losing the eBay payments war. Besides, Sacks felt, boosting revenue should take priority over cutting bonus costs. Musk agreed.

The Nut House meeting revealed overlap between Sacks and Musk where they had expected to be at odds. The unexpected unity prompted immediate action. Sacks and Musk placed a few calls to other X.com employees, including Levchin, who soon arrived at Antonio's to hear the news—and make plans.

"By the time we left the Nut House that night, we realized everybody was on the same page about this," one participant said. "That it wasn't working." That night, the assembled employees began plotting a putsch against their CEO.

■ ■ ■

The plan was simple—and, given Harris's approach during the merger talks, fitting. The rebels planned to go to the company's board and present an ultimatum. If Harris wasn't removed as CEO, they—meaning Musk, Sacks, Levchin, as well as their rank-and-file supporters—would resign.

The mutineers felt confident about their odds. Two of them—Levchin and Musk—sat on the board. Thiel, also a board member, clearly shared their views, and they anticipated John Malloy would side with Thiel and Levchin. That left two holdouts: Mike Moritz and Tim Hurd—but even without their assent, the challengers had the necessary votes.

That night, the organizers called board member Tim Hurd. "He was shocked," a coup participant recalled. The organizers had hoped that Harris would simply resign in the face of revolt. But Harris wasn't ready to go quietly. He had been tipped off and had prepared a counteroffensive—a presentation to the board convincing them he had a winning plan for the company's future.

At an emergency meeting of the board, "[Harris] tried to make the case . . . that we didn't know what we were doing," Musk remembered, "and that seasoned leadership was necessary for the good of the company." The board reportedly didn't allow Harris to get very far. With the votes breaking as expected, they told him it wasn't working out and that he would need to step down.

Given the numbers, Harris never stood a real chance. Rather than talk about his plan, the board opted instead to discuss his resignation, and the next steps proceeded quickly from there. Precisely one week and twenty minutes after Thiel had sent his resignation letter, Musk sent the following company-wide note:

Hi folks,

As a company, X has truly entered its most exciting period:

- We're the #1 financial site on the web in terms of user traffic. It's pretty amazing to think that we have significantly more people using our site on a daily basis than any bank, brokerage, or other financial site on the planet.

- We've successfully built out a 500 person customer service center in Omaha in record time
- We now have over 1.7 million users and a 30%+ market share on EBay
- The Red Herring recognizes us as one of the top 50 most important private companies in the world, and Fortune Magazine has placed us as one of the top 25 small businesses in America
- We've closed our second round of funding, raising $100M at a half billion dollar valuation

However, our rapid growth requires increased attention, focus and rapid decision-making to respond to the ever changing market conditions of the internet economy. As many of you are aware, Bill Harris and I have shared the role of Chief Executive Officer. We jointly believe that X is now at that junction where it is important to have singly clear direction, vision and purpose. Our Board of Directors concurs with this assessment.

Therefore, effective immediately, our Board of Directors has asked me to solely assume the role of Chief Executive Officer.

I want to thank Bill for the service and leadership he has provided to X over the course of the past six months and wish him the best of success in his future endeavors.

This will be an incredible time for X as we continue to build out our business model and extend our product offerings towards the goal of becoming the financial operating system of the internet. I look forward to working with all of you to make this happen and really change the world.

Feel free to stop me in the hallway or send an email if you have any questions.

Thanks,
Elon

■■■

To some, Harris's departure came as a surprise. For Sandeep Lal, it was "a shock." "It was a shock because it exposed me to [a] way, which I thought—and I still think—are not the best ethics of Silicon Valley," Lal said. Lal felt a pang of guilt about the fact that Harris had hosted a company-wide celebratory party for the merger and the closing of the $100 million round—even as the moves against him were in the works.

For many, boardroom politics were an afterthought entirely. "The bottom line here is that whatever *mishegoss* was going on between X.com and Bill Harris, Peter, and Elon and all that, I would come in every day and enjoy myself every day working. And I think that that is probably a testament to those people that that stuff was not trickling down on me. I could just do my job," Denise Aptekar said. "Whatever was going on, I would usually hear about it when it was all over. *Oh, we have a new CEO. Okay, I go back to work.*"

A few members of Harris's favored team, business development, were upset. "Goddamnit . . . you all pulled this Nut House coup!" one business development executive yelled to Sacks and the others, frustrated at the prospect of his team's diminution in the wake of Harris's departure. His taunt immortalized the insurrection as the "Nut House Coup."

■■■

Harris was gracious upon his departure, thanking employees for their work as he left the office. He recalled feeling "disappointed" at the outcome, but not embittered. In his view, he, the CEO, and Musk, the chairman and cofounder of the company, differed over strategic direction. "I think we had a legitimate business disagreement," Harris said. "If that's going to be the driver, then that's the right kind of thing to drive this kind of decision."

Despite the short length of his tenure, Harris notched some achievements. His arrival to X.com propelled the brand's public stature. He also served as a magnet for talent, inspiring employees to stick with the company through the aftermath of a messy merger.

Harris also did his best to provide a professional mien to the operation. He recalled a moment when X.com had neglected to dispose of customer documents and then had to hustle to do so before a regulator's visit, with the CEO himself carting shredded pieces of paper to the dumpster. "We were still functioning as a frat house, not as a financial services company," Harris remembered of his early days at X.com. Among other steps forward, Harris opened channels to important government bodies—relationships that served the company down the line.

Harris's lasting contribution, however, would be the merger of X.com and Confinity. Had he not, by hook and crook, brought Levchin and Musk to the table, it's entirely possible that Confinity would have run out of money, or that X.com would have lost the race on eBay—or both. Without that deal, PayPal may not exist today.

Ironically, sealing this legendary deal also sealed Harris's fate as CEO. Once he served his ultimatum to Musk, the two were never going to work well together, even if they agreed over the substantive business issues in question. Musk also hovered in the wings as chairman through the post-merger period, an unusually active presence for the head of the board. "We had many people who at one point or another were either CEO or felt like they were CEO," said Harris, smiling.

Harris's style—deliberative and consensus oriented—might have been a plus elsewhere but hurt his reputation at X.com. "According to insiders," *Fortune* magazine reported in late 2000, "[Harris] created lots of structure and held endless meetings, virtually none of which yielded any resolutions. Decision making slowed to a crawl." His critics blamed him for the post-merger listlessness, and some felt that Harris had lost faith in the company altogether.

The more nuanced of his critics said that he was simply "overwhelmed" by the chaos, the growth, the burn rate, the intense personalities, and the blending of two hypercompetitive teams—chaos that might have overwhelmed whomever took over the still-combining entities. In their telling, blame could fairly be cast on all sides, not least on the mutineers. "They put him in charge of the kids. But that isn't going to work with this crowd," said John Malloy.

■ ■ ■

Right or wrong, this episode cemented the team's allergy to "executive experience."

This belief would emerge as a start-up truism later, but at the time, the team's sense defied received wisdom. Standard operating procedure saw boards installing a seasoned CEO to steer dot-coms once they found their footing: eBay's Meg Whitman, Yahoo's Tim Koogle, and Google's Eric Schmidt stood as but a few high-profile examples. Even at Amazon, under the vise grip of Jeff Bezos, there had been a brief flirtation with a COO named Joseph Galli in 1999, who was supposed to step in as "adult supervision." Galli lasted a grand total of thirteen months, and Amazon hasn't had a COO since.

X.com's leaders took Bill Harris's rocky tenure as evidence that such "supervision" was not only unnecessary, but counterproductive. For every Schmidt-like success, there seemed to be a John Sculley waiting in the wings. Sculley, the former CEO of PepsiCo, had been installed to lead Apple following the ouster of Steve Jobs—with mixed results. "We saw what had happened at Apple when they brought in the Pepsi executive," David Sacks recalled. "We saw what had happened at Netscape when they brought in Jim Barksdale. And we saw that we were on a similar trajectory."

Musk, too, was skeptical that a wizened adult figure was needed to whip young companies into shape:

> The founder may be bizarre and erratic but this is a creative force, and they should run the company. . . . If someone's the creative force, or one of the creative forces, behind a company, at least they understand which direction to go. Maybe they don't run the ship perfectly. The ship may be a little erratic, and the morale may be mixed. And some parts of the ship aren't working that well. But it's going in the actual right direction. Or you can have a ship that has everything buttoned down. The sails are full. Morale is great. Everyone's cheering. And it's heading straight for the reef.

Musk admired Steve Jobs and studied the period of his departure from Apple. "That ship was sailing really well," Musk observed of the interregnum between Jobs's departure and return, " . . . towards the reef."

David Sacks remembered this as "a period of time when Silicon Valley didn't have self-confidence in its own executives," he said, arguing this approach resulted in disaster. "This might have been the moment at which Silicon Valley flipped . . . away from the 'Sculley model' to the 'Zuckerberg model,' which is, you grow with your entrepreneurs, you let them keep running the company."

It could all sound a bit self-serving to critics: *of course* a group of young founders would excoriate "adult supervision." And, just as several high-profile adult supervisors flopped, the opposite approach—backing neophyte founders to the nines—counted just as many disastrous examples for each successful one. Over the course of 2000, after all, scores of fresh-out-of-college founder-CEOs crashed dot-com companies into the ground.

But at the time, Musk, Sacks, Thiel, and their cohort weren't interested in comprehensive case studies. They had seen at X.com a CEO they felt hadn't grown up with the company, wasn't moving fast enough, and whom they didn't have faith in. "I think we just lost trust in him," Musk concluded.

■ ■ ■

In May 2000, just shy of his twenty-ninth birthday, Elon Musk retook the title of X.com CEO. "Kind of by process of elimination, it was me," Musk recalled. "I wasn't planning to be CEO. It was kind of like, 'If I don't do it, then who is? And okay, Peter's not here. So, I guess I'll be CEO.'"

It was a fine—if perhaps understated—account of his own role in the decision. Musk didn't become CEO by accident or default. Thiel had departed post-merger; Musk continued to grind away at X.com's problems. And when he felt those problems weren't being addressed well, he led an overthrow of his CEO.

The ship was now his, as was the accompanying work of steering

X.com away from various reefs. Many of those involved, including Musk, would remember the months that followed as among the most trying periods of their lives. "It wasn't quite a mid-life crisis, because we were twenty-five," said Confinity cofounder Luke Nosek. "But we were pretty depressed."

12

BUTTONED-UP

As newly reinstated CEO, Musk instituted changes swiftly. "He refocused the company in a lot of ways," Mark Woolway recalled.

On June 1, 2000—nineteen days into his tenure—Musk introduced a reworked executive structure. He would now count seven direct reports: David Jaques, CFO; David Johnson, senior VP of finance; Sandeep Lal, VP of customer service and operations; David Sacks, senior VP of product; Reid Hoffman, now senior VP of business development and international; Jamie Templeton, former Confinity VP of engineering, would once again lead the engineering team; and Levchin would remain as CTO, with no direct reports up to him. Notably, the reorganization left no place for a COO or president.

Another Musk dispatch dropped a week later. "I'm glad to announce that Peter Thiel has been appointed chairman of the X.com board of directors," he wrote in an all-company email. "He will also be helping Jack [Selby], Mark [Woolway] and Kenny [Howery] on the Series D round and acting as a strategic advisor to the company." After his abrupt departure, Thiel had taken a break. His return as chairman sent a comforting signal for those X.com employees who started at Confinity.

Many others in the rank and file, though, met internal changes like these with indifference. By this point, the company had weathered intense pre-merger chaos, a turbulent merger itself, and extensive confusion afterward. For Confinity employees, Musk was their third CEO in as many months. Changes at the top had become routine, and there was simply too much work to be done to stress about who was in charge.

Several junior- and mid-level employees also described an environment in which leaders insulated them from the company's C-level discord. "I felt like I was fairly sheltered . . . ," an early Confinity engineer, James Hogan, remembered about executive turnover. "I had the luxury of naïveté."

■ ■ ■

For those reporting to David Sacks, the reorganization—and his elevation—proved consequential.

Musk's reorganization included an important change: engineering leads would now work with product managers as discrete, semi-independent teams. Prior to this, engineers functioned more like free agents, tossed at problems by dint of their ability, interest, and company need. But that could cause confusion and disorganization.

The change toward semi-independent teams, Sacks and Musk hoped, would lead to more rapid iteration. Both had observed an irksome start-up paradox: as X.com had grown in size, it began to accomplish less work of substance. They were far from the first to identify this paradox. In 1975, decades before the commercialization of the internet, Dr. Frederick P. Brooks, an IBM engineer and later founder of the Department of Computer Science at the University of North Carolina at Chapel Hill, explored this conundrum in his software engineering bible, *The Mythical Man-Month*.

"[W]hen schedule slippage is recognized," Brooks wrote, "the natural (and traditional) response is to add manpower. Like dousing a fire with gasoline, this makes matters worse, much worse. More fire requires more gasoline, and thus begins a regenerative cycle which ends in disaster." More programmers assigned to a given project, Brooks explained, multiplied the number of communication channels. This time spent talking— whether keeping team members up to speed or building interpersonal relationships—was time not spent coding. Two heads, in other words, weren't necessarily better than one.

Various solutions to this problem would later become popularized, often under the banner of "agile software development," which prioritized rapid iteration and small teams. But in the summer of 2000, such literature was limited, and X.com had to improvise. Sacks built small, self-contained units, pairing, for example, X.com producer Paul Martin with a designer and an engineer: Chad Hurley and Yu Pan, respectively. As a group, they focused on all things auction-related. Sacks and Musk believed small units freed innovators from the entanglements of bureaucracy.

The big changes to team structure paired with smaller, atmospheric changes. For instance, the team opted to call the product role—whose work involved a mix of strategy, analytics, and operations—"producers" instead of the more traditional "product managers." "The word *manager* had acquired this negative connotation," explained Sacks. "To call them 'product managers' would imply that their job was just to 'manage things' as opposed to 'make things happen.'"

To encourage ownership, X.com gave even new arrivals substantive and sensitive assignments. Janet He left a job at a bigger financial firm and joined X.com as a quantitative marketing analyst. Within days of joining, Sacks assigned her a research question: Determine PayPal's share of eBay auctions. She was surprised at the outreach: not only had Sacks, a senior leader, approached her, a days-old employee, directly for the analysis (without getting her manager's assent), but he was comfortable with a spreadsheet rather than a polished PowerPoint.

"When I joined PayPal, it's like no one tells me how to do things," He remarked. "They just throw me questions. Question after question. And I just figured out how to answer the question. The whole company was . . . no nonsense."

In that same no-nonsense spirit, Sacks and Musk outlawed big meetings, which Sacks called "a deliberate tactic to break with this banking culture and to re-institute the original, start-up-y culture at PayPal." One employee remembered Sacks glaring pointedly through a conference room window where too many people had congregated, his message unmistakable.

■ ■ ■

In the view of X.com's leaders, growing organizations often made a crucial mistake: employee happiness became a bigger concern than output.
Its leaders feared X.com would fall into the same trap, and to avoid it,
company leaders set a cultural tone of impatience. They sacrificed solidarity for speed and made decisions by fiat when necessary. "It wasn't an
open democracy of ideas," recalled early X.com engineer and later Yelp
cofounder Jeremy Stoppelman.

Progress required shipping code and launching products, aggressively and all the time. This approach, X.com leadership believed, was
how they would win. But it also meant employees worked nonstop. "I
remember in my interview coming in and seeing sleeping bags under
people's desks and saying, *Oh, I'm never going to sleep under my desk*," remembered Kim-Elisha Proctor. "And yet, there I was, during one of my
first releases, when I was moving us to a new credit card processor. I think
I did a thirty-six-hour stint . . . I actually slept in one of the conference
rooms."

X.com's caffeine consumption was legendary. One engineer, Doug
Ihde, was famous for his prowess as a software engineer—and for the
mountainous collection of empty Diet Coke cans that populated his office. Levchin, too, guzzled coffee. Later in his life, during an interview
for NerdTV, a short-lived PBS program, he'd expound on the virtues of
late nights. The interviewer, Robert X. Cringely, had arrived at Levchin's
office before ten in the morning. Levchin had been there all night.

"You've just been up all night. Why?" Cringely asked.

"I'm having fun, and that's what you do when you have fun, you just
don't want to stop," Levchin replied, matter-of-factly. Then Levchin offers a lengthy meditation on the wonders of the wee hours.

> I think there's something very special about the all-nighter ethic . . .
> There's definitely something about the nocturnal lifestyle for en-
> gineers specifically that really opens up the chakras of creativity or
> code-writing. People get slightly sillier, but also maybe a little more

creative. They get tired, and some spirit and camaraderie wakes up in those hours. And you get more done because you're not afraid to tell people to "shove it" when they're doing something wrong, and the interactions become more interesting.

But I also think there's this massive value that you harness when you're doing an all-nighter when you've gone for presumably seven or eight hours of work, and you're really getting up to a point when something's about to be born—and then you go for eight more hours! And instead of stopping to go to sleep and letting these ideas dissipate, you actually focus on the findings you've made in the last few hours, and you just go crazy and do some more of that.

The tone was set from the top. Engineer William Wu remembered that Musk expected employees who worked late on a Friday night to return by Saturday morning. (Later, Wu purchased shares early in Tesla, just after its IPO, based on this experience. "[Workaholism] does no good for me as an employee, but then I feel like, if Elon does that at Tesla, then Tesla's going to succeed no matter what. It's painful to work with him as an employee—but as an investor in his company, it's a wise decision.")

Dionne McCray, who worked in quality assurance, recalled both the peer pressure and the bonds built from that duress. "You'd get to work at . . . nine thirty or ten [in the morning]. And we'd stay until who knows how late—maybe ten o'clock, well over ten hours easily," she shared. "There was this weird peer pressure. If you left, people were like, 'You're leaving already? You've only been here for like fourteen hours? Are you tired?' So there was that, but there was also a lot of bonding."

The company coalesced around idiosyncratic, middle-of-the-night rituals. Blaring Salt-N-Pepa's song "Push It" during code pushes. Vaporizing potatoes against the outside wall with high-speed PVC guns. Even simple endurance exercises, like battling to see who could sit atop a basketball the longest without falling off.

Many employees described the magnetic pull of the company's chaos. "You get sucked into it. Unless you leave the company, you can't *not* be in it," recalled Oxana Wootton. "We would have a meeting, for example, and there would be some new goal and everyone just *completely* immersed themselves into accomplishing that goal."

■ ■ ■

Other elements of PayPal's culture wore employees down. Personal hygiene standards, for example, varied widely. A quality assurance analyst recalled one engineer putting his bare feet up on his work desk—and removing toenail gunk in full view. "You grew thick skin because you had to rise above that," she recalled.

The unforgiving intensity strained marriages and families. One employee remembered having to bring his eight-month-old daughter into the office on both a Saturday and a Sunday. "I remember everybody looking, like, *What the hell is that?* I'm carrying my daughter around the hallways of X.com," he remembered. "It was stressful." Many of the firm's top leaders were childless—and scheduled weekend meetings with abandon. Several X.com parents suffered in silence.

Though the passage of time has dulled negative memories, many still viscerally recalled X.com's everyday workplace hostility. For all their talk of common foes and outward focus, the company was riven by rivalries fierce enough to make George R. R. Martin blush. Employees regularly called each other out in email threads, and even technical debates evinced an unusual ferocity.

In one back-and-forth—a debate about the company's sixty-day approval for debit cards—team members exchanged heated email volleys. One employee offered that the sixty-day requirement was "critical," to which another fired back: "We understand that you think the 60-day requirement is critical. I think what people are looking for is a convincing explanation why." Another threw a jab right back: "If you care to attend some of these meetings, you will get a convincing reason why."

And so on. Bitter fights like this roiled the organization, with behind-the-scenes politicking and backbiting to boot. For all X.com's strengths, it was also a workplace in which a colleague concluded a thought on the sterile subject of ACH transmissions, international sending limits, and card issuance with a biting: "Do you understand the difference??!!"

■ ■ ■

The PayPal product known to the world today took shape through the spring and summer of 2000. During these months, X.com released several of PayPal's fundamental distinguishing features—features that would take it from viral product to viable business.

Two weeks after the restructuring announcement, X.com launched a redesigned PayPal website, for which Sacks sent a company-wide email, praising "a number of individuals who worked very long hours to get us here within a relatively tight timeframe." Among its new features, the website included an update designed to outflank big credit card companies, like Visa, Mastercard, and American Express.

Since its launch, X.com had maintained what amounted to a frenemy relationship with credit card companies. For small-dollar sellers, becoming an approved credit card merchant was a cumbersome, paperwork-laden process—and X.com capitalized on those difficulties. It stepped in as a virtual credit card clearinghouse for auction sellers—effectively declaring them reputable businesses and enabling thousands to accept credit card payments through PayPal instead of receiving payment by check, cash, or money order. "What PayPal was, at its heart, was [a system to enable] high-risk and low-dollar amount merchants to accept credit cards online," Vince Sollitto said.

But playing the de facto "eBay master merchant," in credit card vernacular, introduced another vulnerability into X.com's core business: Visa and Mastercard serviced X.com's transactions *and* competed with it directly. "They should have killed us when they could have. We were so competitive, and we were so abusing their system," remembered Todd Pearson, one of the caretakers of X.com's credit card relationships. "It's hard to feel sorry for them—these giant companies that are monopolies . . . But they should have shut us down."

X.com's reliance on credit card companies, combined with those companies' high transaction fees, generated an uneasy alliance. It also forced several team members into years of tense diplomacy with the card associations and card-issuing banks. More than one PayPal alumnus credited employees Todd Pearson, Alyssa Cuthright, and their teams for "saving the company"—simply by preventing Visa and Mastercard and their ilk from bringing the hammer down.

The credit card issue drove also a strategic imperative: the company had to encourage users to connect their PayPal accounts to banks instead of credit cards. The issue rose to the highest levels of the company, including the board of directors. "I called it the 'war on credit card funding,'" said board member Tim Hurd. "I was obsessed with it."

■ ■ ■

Musk's grand vision of building a financial services empire offered one solution. If enough customers kept money in their X.com accounts, the team realized, then the company could transfer dollars between users at no cost. "The internal transaction . . . costs like a millicent," Musk explained. "Basically zero. And this is why you want to maintain balances."

To that end, Musk pursued X.com's broader "X-Finance" product portfolio, including its savings and brokerage accounts. To compel users to move money onto the platform, the company set a 5 percent interest rate on its savings accounts, among the highest in the nation. "We gave back one hundred percent [of our profits on savings accounts]," Sacks noted. "We weren't trying to make money. . . . We were trying to incentivize people to keep money in their accounts."

This process also produced some counterintuitive insights. For example, the company found that the simpler it was to remove money from their accounts, the more money users put in. Thus, Musk insisted that the company continue distributing debit cards and even checks. "If you're forced, in order to conduct your life, to move money out of PayPal," he observed, "you'll move money out of PayPal. So if you have to write checks—and PayPal won't let you write checks from your PayPal account . . . you must move your money to a checking account." (Commenting on the modern PayPal's lack of checks, Musk became impassioned about the subject anew. "So give them goddamned checks! Sweet baby Jesus, what is wrong with you people!")

Musk saw the company's North Star as the accumulation of total user dollars—not just the total transactions. "Whoever can keep the most money in the system wins," Musk explained. "Fill the system, and eventually, PayPal will just be where all the money is because why would you bother moving it anywhere else?" Musk walked the talk, of course, keeping millions of his own fortune on the platform.

But the average user wasn't about to follow his lead, and this proved a stumbling block. X.com users already had checking and savings accounts with offline banks. To most, the hassle of consolidating those funds at X.com wasn't worth a few-percent interest rate bump.

The next best option would be for X.com to shift its transaction base from credit card–funded transactions to bank account–funded ones. Each credit card payment cost the company 2 percent or more; the equivalent transaction through a user's bank account cost only a few cents. If more users linked their bank accounts to PayPal, X.com would save millions—and get a powerful leg up on Visa, Mastercard, and others.

To do this, X.com would have to use a piece of banking infrastructure called the Automated Clearing House (ACH). ACH was a decades-old system which digitized repeat, predictable payments like paychecks and bills. Without the costs of paper and postage, ACH payments were half as expensive to manage as mailing checks. By mid-1994, one-third of Americans received their paychecks electronically through ACH payments.

If X.com could do this with PayPal payments—linking its transactions to the ACH system—the company could reduce its costly credit card dependency. But gaining access to bank accounts carried its own hazards, including some X.com had already experienced—its January 2000 negative press barrage resulted from a lax approach to bank account security.

In order to make ACH the secure backbone of X.com's payments, the company would need to authenticate bank account ownership, which promised to be cumbersome. "The problem was, how do you authenticate a bank account without having some sort of signature card?" Musk explained. "Basically, without an in-person verification, which would be very expensive, we'd grow like a snail, super slow. Unless there's some way to authenticate bank accounts, we were screwed."

■ ■ ■

The X.com authentication process proved to be one of the company's lasting contributions to the machinery of digital finance. It came by way of a book, a walk for coffee, and an X.com team member's breakthrough insight on signals and noise.

Sanjay Bhargava came to X.com by way of Citibank's international payments division, where he had been for over a decade. Early in his time at Citibank, he concluded that an email address could be a powerful, lightweight way to send money abroad—a kind of universal financial passport.

When he pitched the cross-border email payments business, his Citibank bosses had a tepid response. "They kind of liked it," he recalled. "But then there was this moment of saying, *'Why should we be the innovators? It will cannibalize our business.'*" Citibank was making a killing on traditional funds transfers. Email payments would threaten those margins.

Bhargava left Citibank to pursue the concept on his own. At the beginning of 1999, he cofounded a company called ZipPay. Then Bhargava was forced out. When it happened, Bhargava was forty-two, and he planned on simply returning to his successful banking life.

But Bhargava's ZipPay pitches had put him in front of various venture capitalists, including Sequoia's Mike Moritz—who had other plans for him. It was August 1999, just after the exodus of X.com's executive team. Musk was in recruiting mode and, on Moritz's prompting, called Bhargava to request a meeting. "I said, 'Okay, next time I'm in the Valley, we'll meet,'" Bhargava remembered. "And [Musk] said, 'No, no, I'm buying you a ticket, you've got to come down right now.'"

Their planned ten-minute meeting turned into dinner at a nearby burger joint called Taxi's Hamburgers. "We met at around eight o'clock, and we talked 'til about four in the morning," Bhargava remembered. "And then Elon told me to come in at seven that morning and collect your offer."

■ ■ ■

Of those early X.com days, Bhargava recalled hundred-hour-weeks and a culture where speed beat planning. "Colin, Elon, and I would just sketch out stuff until two or three o'clock in the morning," he said. "I remember saying to Colin once, 'Oh, I've got to write this thing down,' and he said, 'No, we'll talk, I'll build, and that's how we'll get this thing done.'"

He found X.com a welcome change from big banking, though not without its own frustrations. When the team began linking bank accounts with X.com user accounts, Bhargava argued for strong security and verification—challenging the X.com approach of launching a product and fixing issues later. "You can't do this," Bhargava argued, "because people will put someone else's account information in." Musk overruled Bhargava, arguing that an elaborate security process would hobble account growth. "Elon had this view that generally people are honest," Bhargava remembered.

Musk's decision pushed the limits of Bhargava's (usually ample) patience. "I actually blew my top on that particular thing," he remembered. "Then I thought: *Okay, why am I overreacting like this?*" If he was correct in his assessment, the company would be defrauded quickly. If not, then everyone could move on. "Sure enough, within ten days, we had those articles," Bhargava said, referencing the first reporting on unauthorized account activity.

After the bank account controversy, X.com raced to install clunky, traditional verification methods—users would have to mail in voided checks to confirm bank account ownership. Later, X.com made it possible to fax these checks instead, without much success. "Sometimes you could barely read these faxed checks," Bhargava remembered.

The experience left Bhargava pondering security and identity verification within complex systems. Early in 2000, Bhargava read *Secrets & Lies: Digital Security in a Networked World* by computer security architect Bruce Schneier—a bestselling IT book featuring readable and lucid explanations of cryptography, hacking, and, notably for Bhargava, the concept of signal and noise.

Signals were the meaningful bits of information that a sender hoped to get to a recipient—a song on the radio, for instance. Noise was anything that interfered with the information's arrival—i.e., static that distorts the song. X.com needed, Bhargava realized, a cleaner, quicker signal than voided checks or inscrutable faxes to confirm bank account ownership.

Banks used such signals already: A four-digit ATM PIN confirmed debit card ownership. X.com needed something like that—a signal as simple as an ATM code.

Then, Bhargava had a thought: What if X.com generated its own onetime equivalent? Specifically, the company could manufacture four-digit passcodes by sending two random deposits of under $1 to a user's bank account. If a user received $.35 and $.07, for example, they could now enter the code "3507" on the PayPal website. Entered successfully, the onetime code confirmed bank account access—and without grainy faxes or snail-mailed checks.

Bhargava filed the idea away and went to bed. The next morning, he and his colleague Todd Pearson went out for coffee, as they often did. The pair shared a lot: They had both joined X.com pre-merger, were skeptical financial industry veterans, and were fathers, a rarity on the young X.com team.

As they strolled, Bhargava explained his notion of using two random deposits to authenticate bank account ownership. Pearson's reaction was immediate: "This is amazing. You're a genius!" Bhargava's proposal struck a chord with the rest of the team, too, and work to make it a reality began briskly.

With random deposit and the company's other gambits to connect bank accounts, the product team had challenging work to do. For many users in those early e-commerce days, even entering credit card numbers was asking a lot. The company now had to help users input bank routing and checking account account numbers—more digits and twice the fields.

"All the check layouts are different, too," Skye Lee recalled, "So we had to create that for the user experience and figure out, 'How can we explain this complicated thing to users when there isn't something like this out there?'" The company's designers took screenshots of checks, drew circles atop the relevant numbers, and displayed them on the website as a visual aid. The image innovation stood the test of time: Designer Ryan Donahue remembered the company's original check images floating throughout the internet for years, with the same dummy account numbers visible on other websites.

X.com tied the launch of Sanjay Bhargava's random deposit confirmation feature to its bonuses. Now, in order for a new user to receive their sign-up bonus, they would have to connect their bank account with PayPal and confirm the two deposits. The change, combined with other products, paid off mightily. By late June, one-third of new users were registering bank accounts with X.com.

In time, X.com took several more steps to encourage bank account linking, including a $10,000 sweepstakes it ran in July 2000 as well as features reserved specifically for bank-account-backed customers. Once it had more bank accounts verified, the company also employed its familiar tactics of shifting defaults to its benefit: At one point, the company automatically switched PayPal users who linked both credit cards and bank accounts to bank-funded payments—a risky changeover but a critical one to bend the company's cost curve.

These moves helped wean X.com off Visa- and Mastercard-backed payments, driving down onerous transaction fees and reducing the associated business risks—and leaving a lasting mark on the industry. Sanjay Bhargava's innovation, for instance, endures: today, random deposit is common within banking.

Musk was unreserved in his praise for random deposit: "That was a *fundamental* breakthrough." David Sacks captured the idea's elegant simplicity in his launch announcement, calling it "an idea that, like Velcro, you wish you had thought of."

■ ■ ■

Designed to fight deceit, the new authentication system revealed a suprising degree of user honesty. As the mechanism rolled out, some users felt obligated to return the company's random deposits via traditional mail.

This deluge of envelopes stuffed with loose change created an administrative headache. "As a legal financial institution, we were required to deposit those funds into their account," Daniel Chan, the young recruit charged with opening the envelopes, said. "So I would manually credit their account. . . . And then I would drive the money to Silicon Valley Bank to make the physical bank deposit."

Outside of work, Chan had been training as a magician, performing at children's events and doing tricks in the office for his colleagues. "I was making more doing kids' birthday parties in Silicon Valley than I was at PayPal," he admitted. Once he had deposited all the X.com customer coins he could take, Chan quit—and went on to a successful life as a professional magician. His body of work included, of course, coins vanishing before his audience's eyes.

■■■

Random deposit authentication mitigated some risks, but another still loomed large over X.com: eBay.

In one sense, X.com's dominance on eBay represented a triumph—X.com effectively ran a portion of the cash registers at someone else's store. But it was also a hazard: By mid-June, the overwhelming majority of X.com's transactions originated on eBay, and the store, X.com leaders feared, could commandeer its registers at any time. The company needed to reduce eBay's influence, and fast.

When Confinity had first spotted eBay users' enthusiasm for its products, designer Ryan Donahue worked with David Sacks to improve the auction payment mechanism. An early incarnation consisted of two steps: First, the user would press the PayPal button; next, they'd enter the dollar value of the transaction and click Pay. It occurred to Donahue to simply fold the second step into the first: if users entered the dollar amount and pressed the button, the next page could pre-populate the total and confirm payment.

The change seemed quaint, obvious, even trivial—but it shaved precious seconds from transactions. And in the view of David Sacks, every moment of friction was fat to be cut. Small, time-saving improvements, he believed, led to stickier products—and instant gratification won over impatient users.

Those improvements to the payment design produced a corollary insight: What if buttons were the core product? What if these slices of pixels could help PayPal become the web's default payment system? The team began to brainstorm a "whole suite of embeddable buttons that, if someone was on your website, they could click to pay you," explained Sacks.

Buttons? The idea sounded laughable, but its implications were significant. Strategically, a focus on buttons catapulted the company into a space with few rivals. Sure, copycats could marry money to email. They could lavish bonuses on would-be users. And they could fight for auction territory. But it would be a while before they obsessed over buttons.

The one-button-to-beat-them-all approach also solved a genuine problem for web merchants. E-commerce grew rapidly from the late 1990s through the early 2000s, and a new crop of smaller online merchants faced familiar questions about how to get money from point A to point B quickly and securely.

Ironically, X.com first spotted the growth of an independent set of e-commerce players on eBay itself. PowerSellers—eBay's marquee users and the purveyors of most of their auctions—were beginning to move off eBay. "Any eBay seller that got to a sufficient level of advancement would create their own e-commerce site, and they would sell on that site," Sacks recalled. The team also spotted a market signal: Those newly independent sellers frequently used PayPal.

X.com nurtured this rebellion—to eBay's chagrin. "One of the things [eBay was] very worried about with PayPal was that we were enabling their sellers to go off eBay," Sacks said. X.com even took certain core eBay features and replicated them for these rogue sellers, copying, for example, eBay's reputation system and incorporating it into PayPal. Button development could feed this insurrection further. This also hearkened back to the company's roots: button resizing had led an eBay user to reach out to Confinity, alerting them to PayPal's use within auctions.

Buttons had been the breakthrough then—and Sacks and others believed they could power the company's future growth. Donahue remembered the team's modest early ambitions for its button suite. "It was like, 'Oh man, you know, there's all these bands out there that probably want to be able to sell their T-shirts and their CDs.' I was excited about targeting people who were doing ten- and twenty-dollar transactions," he said. "It just seemed so cool and punk rock to me that any nontechnical person could just turn a web page into a payment-enabled thing."

■■■

Even before the merger in late 1999, David Sacks had put pen to paper on an early vision for a button product. Over time, that product spec incorporated countless ideas from team members and captured many of the concepts that propelled PayPal to internet ubiquity. In many ways, the document represents the ur-text of modern PayPal.

In deference to Musk's passion for the "X-" branding, the team initially called the button product X-Click, though later renamed it Web Accept. Its closest precursor was a PayPal feature called Money Request, which allowed users to send a personal request for money by email. That email contained a link to a PayPal page. X-Click would take this function and make it omnipresent, "by allowing PayPal users to paste the Money Request link on their own websites, personal home pages, auction listings, or other URLs . . . The result is a single-click payment system for the entire web."

The product spec made a business case for X-Click, too. It would fuel PayPal's virality, bringing its products to websites everywhere, and dial up PayPal's network effects. Other "tightly integrated payment competitors like eBay/Billpoint, Yahoo/dotBank, and Amazon 1-Click/zShops" would remain so focused on home turf payments that they'd miss PayPal's spread across the web.

The document pushed a familiar refrain about time to market. "Speed is of the essence for three reasons," the spec noted:

1. The product's inherent network effects meant the first mover will have a tremendous advantage. Every day we have the market to ourselves is an irreplaceable chance to build an insuperable lead.

2. The company needs to demonstrate a revenue track record going back at least 6 months for the IPO. X-Click could provide immediate revenues.

3. Competitors such as Yahoo, eBay, and Amazon are hot on our heels in terms of matching basic P2P functionality. X-Click is needed to counter their superior distribution and ability to integrate.

The team aimed for a June 1 pilot product, the development of which would be personally driven by Sacks. The work on X-Click in early 2000 hinted at a PayPal future separate and apart from eBay—which gave the team a new horizon to pursue. "It painted a vision for how PayPal could really proliferate the web," Amy Rowe Klement observed.

■ ■ ■

X.com's reorganization, its development of X-Click, and its random deposit breakthrough all coincided with another pivotal evolution: in the summer of 2000, the company instituted its first fees.

X.com knew fees were inevitable. Deep debates emerged over the correct course of action. Should the company charge senders or recipients? How would X.com transition users away from its "always free" promise? And if X.com charged for its services, wouldn't eBay's Billpoint undercut it? "This is *it*," Lal said. "*This* will determine if our customers stay with us." Musk himself captured the company's conundrum: "We had to have a means of generating revenue that didn't destroy our user growth."

The right answers lived at the fuzzy intersection of user behavior and financial modeling. The team learned from user behavior on X.com's products and on competitors' systems, including its eBay rival, Billpoint, whose fee structure—a flat fee *and* a percentage of the payment—angered eBay users.

Admittedly, some of that grousing had to go with eBay's origins. "eBay's roots were in a very scrappy community of sellers that had to figure out payments for themselves because eBay didn't offer that," an eBay attorney from that era, Robert Chestnut, admitted. "So I think the idea of a payments company—that by the way, eBay would make money from, because [Billpoint] charged money—wasn't universally embraced. Because sellers don't want to pay another fee. They're already paying eBay a fee."

X.com also realized that across-the-board fees for money senders would be a death knell. No one wanted to pay money to send money—users would simply migrate to cheaper options that charged the recipient, not the sender. By contrast, a carefully chosen, narrow fee structure could work, especially when tied to something worth paying for and targeted at the right audience.

Thus, the team settled on starting to charge by creating a category of premium products, which offered more features than the standard free accounts. These would be called "Business" or "Premier" accounts, depending on whether the user was a company or an individual. Crucially, users had the choice to pay for premium features, or stay with the free services as they were.

In its announcement of its paid accounts, the company touted three modest features: (1) the ability for businesses to register under a corporate or group name (for "business" accounts); (2) a dedicated twenty-four-hour customer service hotline; and (3) an automatic sweep of the account balance into a bank account each day. It wasn't much, but the company promised more benefits to come.

X.com would initially charge 1.9 percent on payments received, with no additional flat fee—a bargain relative to its primary competitor. The announcement bragged that its pricing was "less than half of what you'd pay with other payment services (for instance, Billpoint starts at 3.5 percent plus $0.35 per transaction)." X.com knew its audience: explicitly undercutting Billpoint's rates appealed to price-sensitive eBay PowerSellers.

At one meeting during this period, Musk acknowledged the peril of charging for a previously free product. "In that meeting, [Musk] said, 'We will charge. We will price. This is like throwing the dice. This is a gamble, but this is what it's all about. This is like gambling'—I remember the word he used—'one hundred million smackeroos,'" Lal recalled.

The company was explicit about optionality. "**No one will be forced to upgrade to a Business/Premier account,**" the product's announcement declared in bold print. If you liked your free PayPal account, in other words, you could keep it.

But if users could keep free accounts, would anyone sign up for the optional offering with its limited benefits? By 5:00 p.m. on the first day of release, the team had their answer: Despite only sending the announcement to a subset of users, 1,300 accounts were opened. On the strength of that success, the paid products were broadcast to the full user base. One week later, on June 19, the company had amassed 9,000 premium customers. That day, paying users brought in $1,000 in fees; the following day, the number more than doubled, to $2,680.

"Once we got [fee-bearing accounts] going, there at least became kind of a revenue *option*—it became *possible* for someone to pay us," recalled David Wallace. "There were people that were benefiting from some sort of advanced features. And the main thing there was, any new advanced features that we built now had a place to go that would draw people into paying for it . . . Conceptually, it shifted us from just being focused on the 'free people' to getting 'paid people' in."

Given the summer's frenzy of activity, the launch of fee-bearing accounts didn't culminate in company-wide celebration nor capture the world's attention. But with its premium accounts taking root, the company had achieved what many of its digital contemporaries could not: its website was earning money, not just giving it away.

■ ■ ■

When he reclaimed the CEO title, Musk delivered a version of his May 2000 board presentation to the entire company, including a slide titled "Major Actions" that surveyed the most urgent to-dos. "If we make these items happen," he wrote in a follow-up note to the full team, "I'm confident we will be unstoppable."

Musk had good reason for confidence. By late summer 2000, the company was shipping new products again. Six weeks after David Sacks's note about website changes, Julie Anderson announced that X-Click was officially live—and that for the first time, non-eBay sites featured X.com services. X.com had also unified its branding: "Users typing www.PayPal.com into their browser will be redirected to www.X.com," the company announced.

As X.com made these important changes, the wider world took notice. X.com won a "People's Voice Award" in the Webby competition—the Oscars of the internet—and was named a top 100 digital company by the tech publication *Red Herring*. For four consecutive weeks, X.com was the most-visited finance website on the internet, as measured by PC Data Online. As icing on the cake, *Fortune* magazine named X.com one of the hottest new businesses in the country.

Industry players began paying attention to the upstart in their midst. The American Bankers Association organized a roundtable discussion of community bankers, at which the subject of X.com arose:

Andrew Trainor: X.com recently merged with PayPal, an online
   email-based payment service. The combined companies use
   a whole different style of marketing. Instead of using a lot of
   dollars to market their bank, they paid each customer $20 to
   open an account. Then they would pay every customer for
   every referral up to a given ceiling. At this point they have a
   million and a half customers.
      The reason they did that is this. The CEO [Elon Musk],
   he's 27, from Palo Alto, California, and he said they are going
   to acquire customers and then develop them like a land
   developer, through fee income, through loans, whatever else.
Henry Radix: To a certain extent, banks have already done that.
   We've already brought in our customers and now we need to

mine those relationships. We didn't have to pay $20 apiece. Or maybe we did, we just don't know that we did.

David Beito: That X.com model is a serious threat. You can send money to anyone that has an email address with their PayPal service. I have a bunch of friends that work on the online auctions and every one of them has signed up with PayPal.

They're taking the payment system away from us. They're going to get people hooked on that, and pretty soon they're going to be able to charge for it. Is it worth, say, six bucks a month to be able to do that? Bankers used to wonder about getting $25 for an overdraft, but we all charge it, and people pay it.

On top of all that, the company's user base was expanding, with over 10,000 new accounts still being opened daily. "X.com crossed the TWO MILLION account mark yesterday," wrote Eric Jackson in an update to the team on June 1, "as the number of PayPal accounts hit 1,738,989 and the number of X-Finance accounts topped 267,621."

As ever, the company's "viral" strategy drove the growth. That virus first infected eBay, and it showed no signs of letting up there. In April, X.com estimated that its services appeared on 20 percent of all auctions on eBay; by late June, that number was 40 percent, with 2 million auction listings featuring X.com products. By contrast, Billpoint, eBay's in-house payments platform, was servicing just 9 percent of auctions. "The torrid growth of X.com in the auction world bodes ill for postal carriers everywhere," the *Weekly eXpert* bragged. "Personal checks are becoming an endangered species."

Importantly, user growth was no longer in conflict with customer service. The Omaha team had fully eliminated the complaint backlog, and websites that tracked public sentiment consistently ranked PayPal.com and X.com high on customer service—a far cry from just two months before.

Even the US government had come to appreciate X.com. The

company's Account Review Department had helped the FBI in an operation against a multimillion-dollar organized crime ring in Chicago, and the company was now in regular contact with the Secret Service, investigators from the Postal Service, and local law enforcement.

■ ■ ■

Internally, the team took steps to integrate as well. In June 2000, X.com officially moved into its new 1840 Embarcadero office space. "Moving from the haphazard world of University Avenue, with its crowded cubes, radiation, strange smells, and temperamental air-conditioning, to the clean, organized, and huge world of 1840 (fully equipped with free vending machines and video games) is a bit of a shock," the company newsletter noted.

That summer even brought some levity and camaraderie. The company booked a screening of the new X-Men movie at Century Cinema 16 in Mountain View on July 14. X.com's Tameca Carr organized the outing and "was even able to fend off the clutches of Steve Jobs who had made an offer for our showing at double the rate," observed the company newsletter. Having already signed its contract with X.com, the theater turned Jobs down, handing the Apple cofounder a rare negotiating defeat. Team members arrived at the theater in X.com T-shirts.

In addition to the movie night, X.com hosted a Summer Solstice Celebration—reportedly wild. "Our Chairman, Peter Thiel, was able to make it out onto the dance floor but wasn't able to compete with Max Levchin's flying splits," jibed the company newsletter. The team surprised CEO Elon Musk with a party for his twenty-ninth birthday. Musk was "led by his wife, Justine, to the local hangout, Fanny & Alexander, ostensibly to meet some friends for dinner. However, as he arrived at F&A's patio, he was welcomed by over forty employees ready to drink the night away with him. . . . Elon was even talked into downing some tequila shots . . ." Some weeks later, the company hosted a barbecue for Levchin's twenty-fifth birthday—with a rousing game of basketball knockout included.

These slice-of-life updates came via the *Weekly eXpert*—a newsletter that chronicled company ephemera, celebrated employee birthdays, and introduced new arrivals. The mere existence of such a document was a sign of maturity. By this point, X.com's ranks had swelled to hundreds— no longer would ad-hoc updates in the downstairs bakery suffice. That August, a full X.com team meeting even had to be split into two gatherings—last names began with A through Kn attending a 10:00 a.m. session; and Ko through Z attending at 11:00 a.m. "Yes," the newsletter exclaimed, "we've gotten that big!"

■ ■ ■

Musk looked at the landscape over those months and saw clear sailing— but others in the company spied warning signs. For all its growing revenue and reduced costs, the company was hemorrhaging money in fraud and fees. For all the displays of office unity, the executive team was divided on everything from branding to technological architecture to the company's mission. And for all of Musk's focus, there were some—particularly Confinity veterans—who believed he was steering the ship onto a reef.

The conflict bubbled under the surface, but in late summer 2000, it burst into view in a sequence of events that reshaped Musk's life and the company's future. Musk had unknowingly foreshadowed it all in a note that accompanied the revised org chart. "Naturally, given that we are a very rapidly growing start-up with over 400 employees and counting," he wrote, "the org chart will change and adapt with time." Change it did, more rapidly than he—or anyone else—anticipated.

13

THE SWORD

If he glanced up, the list would be there as a constant reminder, just as Roelof Botha, X.com's future CFO, had designed it.

Tacked to the wall in front of his desk, the list detailed young Botha's goals. If his eyes were to drift away from his homework, the list reminded him of his aims and forced his focus. If he tried to leave his bedroom, he'd find a duplicate list taped to the back of his door, admonishing him to sit down.

The dual lists worked like a charm. He crossed off his ambitious academic target—*rank in the top ten of all South African students*—with aplomb. Not only did he rank in South Africa's top ten students, but he earned the distinction of being number one, notching the highest-ever marks in what was considered the country's most competitive field: actuarial sciences.

Roelof Botha was the scion of a powerful political family in South Africa. But he wanted to make a name for himself, rather than simply coast on his surname. With that in mind, he left South Africa to earn an MBA at Stanford.

After his first year, he interned at Goldman Sachs in London, where he worked on web company IPOs, including one for the financial services site egg.com. Botha left the Goldman internship with two conclusions: investment banking wasn't that interesting, but internet consumer finance was.

At Stanford, Botha roomed across the hall from Jeremy Liew. Liew had worked at Citysearch where he had crossed paths with a competitor (and fellow South African entrepreneur) named Elon Musk. Liew figured Botha and Musk would have much to talk about, so he put them in touch.

When they met in fall 1999, Musk pitched Botha on joining X.com with signature urgency. Botha declined—he was in the US on a student visa with no work authorization and didn't want to skirt immigration rules. Besides, he wasn't about to drop out of Stanford to join a start-up. Some months passed, and Musk tried Botha again. Botha, yet again, said no. Still, Musk left an impression. "There are people you meet, and then two weeks later, you can't remember anything about them," said Botha. "Elon lingers."

The idea of X.com lingered, too. Botha turned his assignments at Stanford into opportunities to explore X.com's business, its competitors, and consumer finance. "I just used every excuse to think about PayPal as a business. . . . I was trying to think about, *What's the business model for the payments business? How's the banking side of it, the deposit taking, the issuing of credit lines?*" Botha remembered.

From this critical distance, Botha judged X.com to be far from a sure bet. "It didn't have a natural advantage," Botha said of the company's late-1999 outlook. "There's no network effect. The cost of customer acquisition was high. It was unclear if the unit economics were great." But Botha saw potential in X.com's email payments product—specifically how its virality could drive scale.

Botha's confidence in the company grew at the same time a personal crisis unfolded. In late 1999 and early 2000, a financial downturn in South Africa decimated Botha's savings account. He had to make rent somehow, and he hadn't come all this way to fall back on his family's largesse. In need of funds, Botha asked Musk if he could work part-time at X.com.

■ ■ ■

Botha's February 2000 message to Musk arrived as X.com and Confinity were finalizing their merger. Since Botha would be joining the new, unified entity, Musk asked Peter Thiel to interview him. When they met, Thiel lobbed a brain teaser Botha's way:

There's a perfectly round table of indeterminate length, and you don't know the length in advance. Two players have a bag of quarters of infinite depth. Each player can place a coin in the table, and they can touch but not overlap. The last person who puts a coin down on the table and fills it up wins the game. Is there a way to guarantee victory in advance, and does that involve going first or second?*

Botha answered correctly and received his offer letter on the same day X.com and Confinity announced their merger.

Shortly after he started working, one of Botha's Stanford business classes welcomed a guest lecturer: Meg Whitman, CEO of eBay. As Botha sat watching, Whitman was asked about PayPal's emergence on eBay. Would this third-party company, a student wondered, be permitted to nest within eBay's auction ecosystem? Botha remembered her answer: *We're going to crush them.*

Botha was stunned. "It was like, *Don't tell me that!*" he remembered. This precariousness haunted him and many others for the duration of their time at the company. "David [Sacks] said that we had the sword of Damocles hanging over our head the whole time," Botha recalled. "And that was my first exposure to the sword."

■ ■ ■

Botha began working nights and afternoons after class, borrowing a cubicle next to Musk. His inaugural assignment was to rebuild X.com's financial model from scratch.

While X.com had raised millions, Botha felt its financial modeling was "super simplistic." He began building a more robust one using a wider set of metrics. What portion of existing accounts are active? How

---

*Answer: Yes, and go first. Place your coin in the center. The other player will place their coin somewhere on the table. Now you can place your coin on the same line of diameter as the other player, and an equal distance away from the border. Keep repeating that step, and your opponent will run out of space before you do.

much exactly does the company pay in credit card fees? What happens if the fraud rate goes up, or down? What about eliminating bonuses? Botha's spreadsheet enabled the team to toggle assumptions and forecast outcomes—providing a holistic, predictive picture of the business's health.

Over time, Botha's spreadsheet took on oracular significance—one had to consult "the model" before big decisions. On the strength of this work, Botha was invited to join the company full-time after graduating and attend a board meeting in June 2000—which proved memorable. "[Mike] Moritz arrived at the June board meeting and said, 'Look, you guys have seven months of runway left,'" Botha recalled. "'You're not going to raise money again. The market is gone!'" Moritz's comment was bracing but clarifying. "It was really helpful because he just drummed into us that we should not assume we could raise any more money," Botha said.

The board meeting stuck with him for another reason. In haste, he had presented the company's cash flow incorrectly—the final line in an otherwise impeccable spreadsheet. Mike Moritz spotted the error. Botha, a perfectionist, turned red with embarrassment. Once the meeting dispersed, Botha returned to his desk and wept. Levchin, a fellow perfectionist, came over to console him.

■ ■ ■

Botha's dive into the weeds of X.com's finances led him to an obsession with the business's losses. To build an accurate model, he had to study individual loss types, understand their origins—whether fees, chargebacks, or fraud—and tally them line by line. His number-crunching revealed a troubling discrepancy: X.com's current losses were lower than his model's future projections. Botha went on alert, "digging, digging to understand what's the nature of this thing."

Eventually he found it: X.com hadn't accounted for the time delay in disputed and fraudulent credit card transactions. If a customer won a credit card dispute, the card company issued them a chargeback. But the chargeback process didn't begin until the bill was sent, the customer complained, and the issue was investigated—a process that could take a month or more, and well after X.com had paid the merchant. "The chargebacks we were seeing in May were related to transactions from February or March," Botha remembered.

X.com's forecasting had failed to take this delay into account—leaving it unprepared for an approaching tidal wave. "It was around June that I started to realize we have a massive, looming problem," Botha recalled.

Botha understood looming problems better than most: his actuarial training included techniques like "chain ladder analysis," which insurance companies use to estimate reserves needed for future claims. When Botha applied his actuarial chops to X.com's books, he discovered a grim reality: the company didn't have anywhere near the reserves it needed.

If we don't fix this, Botha remembered thinking, *we're going to die*. To make matters worse, Botha sensed that X.com's CEO didn't share his fear of extinction. Musk, it seemed, was far more concerned about X.com's continued expansion.

■ ■ ■

Botha gave Levchin a crash course in chain ladder analysis—and used it to paint him a dire picture of the company's reserves. Even before this warning, Levchin was on edge about the future. He had been closely examining the company's fraud profile—and what he found shook him.

Luke Nosek vividly recalled his pager vibrating after midnight one evening that summer. It was Levchin—he wanted Nosek to call. "Luke, I think we're dead," Levchin began, before explaining to him how fraudsters were fleecing the company for millions.

If that weren't enough, Levchin found himself caught in the middle of a power struggle. Despite Levchin's CTO title, Musk, his boss, had commandeered the company's technology. The tussle came at a critical juncture for the company's system architecture.

"The site was growing, doubling every week, or every two weeks, whatever it was," recalled Ken Brownfield, one of the company's database engineers. As a result of the site's rapid growth, it became unstable, with users facing weekly, hours-long outages. "And so that was one hundred percent of my life," Brownfield remembered. "Those were some of the darker days, when we're just heads down, keeping the site up, making sure we survive Monday."

Part of the challenge was how the website was built. With each exchange of funds, observed Brownfield, "you have to, like, stop the world, make sure this person gets the money, make sure that's written into this transaction, make sure this person loses the money. And that all has to happen with nothing else touching it. And so there's a lot of contention over data in this database." Stopping the world challenged server capacity. "We would hit these barriers that we [couldn't] really foresee," Brownfield remembered.

To be fair, these issues weren't exclusive to X.com. Many websites of that pre-cloud computing era struggled with capacity and outages, including eBay, which suffered legendary blackouts, including a gut-churning, almost-24-hour-long interruption in June 1999. But eBay's monopoly on online auctions carried it through the crisis, and its users returned in droves. X.com couldn't bank on loyalty if its service failed to perform—users had plenty of other payment options.

The merger magnified the technical hiccups. "We still had two websites that were operating independently," engineer David Gausebeck recalled. Two websites—and two engineering teams: the Confinity team, recruited by Levchin; and the X.com team, recruited by Musk. The fissure only got worse as the summer went on, as did the mounting capacity issues.

Musk proposed a solution: rewriting the PayPal.com codebase. He thought the original codebase—built by the Confinity engineers on a Linux foundation—ought to be reconstructed from scratch on a Microsoft platform, like X.com's original site. Musk believed this would yield stability and efficiency. He dubbed the effort "PayPal 2.0," and it became known within the company as V2.

■ ■ ■

Arcane as it might seem, the Linux versus Microsoft question was more than a mere technical debate within X.com. The company was but one theater of a wider war being waged between technologist camps.

By 1999, Microsoft had become the world's dominant software company. That success had come, in part, through simplification. Microsoft Windows had supplanted the mercurial interfaces of yesteryear—black screens with blinking cursors, requiring commands like "c:\photos" or "del *.*" to open photos and delete files. Microsoft Windows—with its simple, polished icons, buttons, and cursors—elevated the experience of computing from inscrutable to inviting.

Microsoft's simplified features also earned it fierce opponents, particularly those who had come of age computing the hard way. Programmers were especially vocal critics. Microsoft's software cost money and was copyrighted. Hackers saw Microsoft products as simplistic, inelegant, and workmanlike—the computing equivalent of a minivan.

From such critiques grew a series of open-source and freely distributed operating systems, frequently built on a platform called Unix. Linux, the most famous of these operating systems, was created by a college student named Linus Torvalds in 1991. Its proponents liked that Linux was everything Microsoft was not: flexible, responsive, and free. Linux's users could make alterations to the core of the operating system to fit their needs.

But its flexibility came at the price of usability. Even a task as simple as installing a modem on a Linux machine could produce so-called geek fatigue—a version of which afflicted PayPal.com. Levchin—true to his hacker roots—had built PayPal.com on Linux. He hired engineers who, like him, had all trained on Linux. But PayPal's Linux foundation led to a lengthier and more cumbersome codebase. "It was like ten years of software development had somehow failed to make landfall at PayPal," one engineer joked.

Musk wanted to do away with Levchin's Linux foundation, and switch over to Microsoft. Given their familiarity with the Microsoft platform, this change would put the three engineers who had built X.com's initial products—Jeff Gates, Tod Semple, and Nick Carroll—in charge of re-creating the entire PayPal.com website. It would also leave the Confinity engineers who had originally built the PayPal.com website out in the cold.

■ ■ ■

Musk explained the switch from a Unix-based system to a Microsoft-based one as a matter of efficient resource allocation. He estimated that Microsoft's off-the-shelf solutions would allow fewer engineers to accomplish more work. "The evidence for this, by the way, is that we had maybe forty or fifty engineers working on the Linux system," Musk said, referring to the Confinity contingent working on the original PayPal.com codebase. "And [X.com] had four engineers replicate all of that functionality in three months on Microsoft C++ . . . Four people versus forty."

An avid video game player and once video game engineer, Musk also pointed to Microsoft's use in the most advanced gaming code as evidence of its superiority. "The stuff that was being done in video games was way more advanced than any other field," Musk explained. "The best programmers are in video games." He observed that feature-rich video games were technically complex—far more so, in some ways, than websites of that era.

Musk also considered the recruiting advantages of a Microsoft codebase. At the time, "Linux was weird and unusual," Musk said, and in switching the company's architecture, X.com could draw from a broader talent pool. "Linux in 2019 was not Linux in 2000," Musk said. "Linux in 2000 was very primitive. It didn't have much support . . . So why the fuck are we using Linux?"

Strategically, Musk saw V2 as step one toward the comprehensive, global-center-of-all-money X.com. "That required a lot more software than what PayPal had," Musk recalled. "So therefore it made sense, in my view, to use the most powerful development system in the world"—Microsoft.

In July 2000, the X.com team traveled to Redmond and met with Microsoft's top brass, including CEO Steve Ballmer. The company's weekly newsletter reported on the meeting with enthusiasm:

Our engineering team recently had a meeting with some very senior members of Microsoft—so senior that some of them report directly to Bill Gates [then-chairman of the board]! What does Microsoft want with us? Our advice! The Version 2.0 X.com/PayPal sites are currently being integrated onto a Microsoft 2000 platform, and that news set Microsoft to seek us out. The meeting was held to find out exactly how they can improve or modify their tools to cater to us and help us work on their platform.

Musk spoke of X.com as a company for the ages—not unlike the Seattle giant. That ambition demanded an architectural overhaul. "He would say that if you're building a company that is going to last for decades, you want to build it on top of a foundation that you know would be around decades from now," Luke Nosek remembered.

■ ■ ■

Musk's Microsoft rebuild, perhaps unsurprisingly, earned intense displeasure from senior engineers on the team, Levchin first and foremost.

The principal issue: PayPal ran on single, monolithic database. From the Confinity engineers' perspective, the simplest and cheapest way to expand that database was by adding server boxes built by Sun Microsystems.

By contrast, these engineers felt that Microsoft's technology was both more expensive *and* not built for PayPal's scale and needs. "Microsoft Database Server was meant to be an enterprise product," noted Brownfield—a Linux partisan. "[Microsoft] was set up to run your enterprise and have ten thousand records of people. It was not meant to be this high-performance online processing, run-for-years sort of system."

Another engineer knocked Microsoft as having been "written because it solved an existing problem. . . . If you have these off-the-shelf tools that will just work for you, then you're not doing something that's new and interesting and unseen." PayPal faced nothing but new and unseen problems—which, some Linux partisans argued, made Microsoft's services a poor fit.

Operationally, Linux- and Microsoft-based systems differed in some respects. One example: responses to process requests. Microsoft kept processes running, even after the requests were complete. "The problem is that if you have a process serving requests that's always alive, then it just gets slower and slower and slower and slower," Jawed Karim observed. "[T]he Linux server didn't have that problem. The reason is, the way the Linux web server works, every time there's a request, it starts a new process."

Case in point: early V2 iterations struggled with "memory leaks." The ad infinitum processes taxed the systems and demanded frequent server reboots. "For a technical purist, rebooting machines is kind of an embarrassing solution," noted Jawed Karim. "It's like if you're into cars, and I say, 'Hey, this is a great race car—but you have to turn off the engine every five minutes.'"

Others predicted this issue would worsen with time—which it did. "We were doing load testing, and we basically were like resetting the servers every day," said engineer David Kang. Indeed, a July 10 communication from one V2 engineer testified to the issues. Asked how a million new accounts would impact the V2 system, the engineer replied, "Right now, the business logic isn't quite in a state to handle creation of a million accounts directly due to memory leaks (we're down to about 20k/sec under maximum load—leading to approx 2.5 hours of operation, and thus 225K accounts before a restart of the business logic is needed)." Eventually, another engineer recalled, the servers needed rebooting "every thirteen seconds."

As work on V2 progressed, the team's doubts deepened. Testing an early V2 iteration, the site's Send Money button—arguably the most vital one of all—failed to function. "As we kept going with the development process, it felt pretty clear to developers, I think, that this is just not on a good track," one engineer recalled. "And that while we had a lot of stuff built, the distance to get it all the way there was not small and was not shrinking quickly."

■ ■ ■

Even some X.com partisans acknowledged that a Microsoft-based architecture may not have been ideal. Sugu Sougoumarane had interviewed with X.com before the merger—and was rejected. "I come back home and I get an email from the recruiter saying, 'Elon has passed on you.' So then I send an email back to the recruiter, saying 'Give me Elon's email. I'm going to send him an email.'"

Sougoumarane wrote an effusive note to the X.com CEO that led Musk to give him a call. Once on the phone, Sougoumarane "told him that [X.com] is going to change the internet, basically. And I said, 'I don't care what you give me. I'll work there if I have to sweep the floor.'" Musk hired Sougoumarane—and forwarded his email to the entire X.com team.

By the time Sougoumarane joined the company, X.com and Confinity had begun their merger, and the Linux-versus-Microsoft war was just brewing. Sougoumarane had spent his career building database development tools, and from his perspective, "the [Linux-based] system was going to take us much further than the [Microsoft] SQL server was going to . . . I don't know how well it [Microsoft SQL servers] could have scaled."

Doug Mak, an early X.com engineer, saw merits to both. On one hand, a Unix-based system was easier for engineers and could handle multiple programmers working on it at one time. It also lent itself to a site that had multiple users on it at any given time. "It's a more friendly environment to write things in Unix, because Unix has always been, since day one, a multi-user platform. Windows was grown up as a desktop PC OS [operating system]. It was never meant for multi-user, concurrent transactions," Mak explained.

On the other hand, Microsoft's off-the-shelf tools made some tasks simpler. "Business logic is easy to write in Windows," recalled Mak. "You have to do quite a bit in Unix to make that happen." Microsoft simplified basic tasks like standing up a barebones website, he recalled. And if you ran into issues, customer support was but a phone call away.

Ultimately, though, Doug Mak and many others on the team concluded that while the V2 effort had led to some modest improvements, the juice wasn't worth the squeeze. "We wrote and rewrote and rewrote things that didn't have to be rewritten. And we wasted a lot of engineering time when we could have launched a product six months ago, and PayPal would have been even more successful then," Mak said.

The opportunity cost of that time was significant. During those several months, the company lost millions to fraud. "If you're spending that time fixing memory leaks," one QA analyst remarked, "you're not solving the problem that's causing $30 million in loss."

■ ■ ■

Several engineers—including some who were loyal to Levchin and the original PayPal.com codebase—offered that the Microsoft rewrite could have been made to work. With enough time and effort, they could have rebuilt the entire site, retrained the engineers, and reorganized on a Microsoft-based PayPal.com. But the question hovering in their minds: Why? The problems Musk hoped to solve, they argued, could be fixed without a gut renovation.

The web's information technology forums spoke to this Microsoft-versus-Linux schism—and illustrated the debate's faintly religious character. "Fan boys on both sides argue to the death that their ~~religion~~ operating system is the best and safest to use," wrote one IT expert in a preamble to a which-is-more-secure post. "I prefer the Linux way," wrote one engineer in response. "As like life, it is harder to get into but once you get over that initial learning curve, it's highly beneficial in the long run. (It's like learning anything else in life, be patient and persistent)."

With the benefit of maturity and hindsight, the engineers acknowledged that part of their aversion to V2 was a symptom of a broader dislike for Microsoft products. For Confinity's engineers, the "Linux way" *was* the way. "For me, my life at that time was all about Linux," said Brownfield, speaking for many Confinity alums. "I didn't want to touch Windows with a ten-foot pole." With its open-source codebase and hacker roots, Linux reflected personal preference as much as architectural choice—and made it hard to swallow a changeover to a closed-source system built by a massive, multibillion-dollar corporation.

"A lot of people were really frustrated," Karim admitted. He recalled running into a Confinity engineer in the parking lot who was leaving the office unexpectedly early. When Karim asked him where he was going, he replied, "I'm just going sailing. This V2 shit's never gonna work. Fuck that."

Engineer William Wu had joined X.com in late 1999, while moonlighting as a master's student in computer science and commuting from San Francisco to Palo Alto for work. When X.com and Confinity merged, he added "write code in two platforms" to his already packed-to-do list.

"When I was coding the PayPal debit card," Wu recalled, "I actually wrote two versions of the code. One was the Windows version, in case, you know, Elon got his way. But I also had to write a whole separate version in Unix, on the PayPal platform, just in case PayPal eventually got the upper hand. So I had to spend so many hours just coding: writing two separate versions of the code, and also testing on two separate platforms." Wu freely admitted that the exercise was one of self-preservation. "I kind of, like, planned it that way to make sure I could survive after, one way or the other," he said. "It was pretty much the hardest time in my life."

V2 damaged morale in the engineering ranks. "It was a really weird time. There should have been a lot of urgency, because it's a very risky time and we have no idea if we're going to succeed. And yet, from a developer's perspective—I shouldn't be admitting this—there were days I went to the movies at three p.m.," engineer David Kang said.

■ ■ ■

Musk understood that the V2 decision wasn't universally popular. But the alternative to V2 as he saw it—slow progressions on the product, two websites, near-weekly downtime—seemed worse.

Musk tried to reward (and accelerate) the team's efforts, launching an incentive program in August: "To make timing of the V2.0 & V2.1 launches interesting, the following bonus plan will be in effect: $5,000 for pushing V2.0 to production by midnight September 15, declining by $500 for each day of slippage, e.g. if site goes live on September 20, then everyone gets $2,500." The end result "must meet the scalability requirements as defined by Max, and any problems that ensue from going live with V2 must not be significant (i.e. reach the press)."

"Work like hell," Musk signed off. But the deadlines came and went—without a finished product. Even non-engineers began to worry. "I knew this engineering thing was a major problem," Todd Pearson, a non-engineer, said, "[Finishing the rebuild] was three weeks away, then three weeks turned into three months."

Almost a month after Musk's incentive email, the company's weekly newsletter tried to put a positive gloss on the delay:

Wondering when V2.0 is going to roll out? It's easy to understand why such a huge project can have a few delays. The design folks need to create an entirely new website designed on a new platform. The project group is constantly trying to upgrade our services and keep our competitors in the dust, while making sure consistent changes are made across our site. Our back-end group is working endlessly to create a new, upgraded version of Admin Tools on the new platform. Our engineers are tearing their hair out trying to get the multitude of programming done, while new requests are still coming in for changes to the site! The QA team is working ceaselessly to make sure all the bugs in the entire system have been found and fixed. The PIGs [product integration group] are working to make sure all those little details are covered during the change. And all this is happening while maintaining the current site, and making constant improvements, like a new phone system in Omaha, working on an Upsell Campaign, dealing with our customers, and much more. So now we know why so many of us work into the wee hours of the morning and drink so much coffee! We're all working hard to make our product the very best it can be, and we're working double time, because we're creating a mirror site on a new platform! It's a lot of hard work team, but it'll all be worthwhile in the end when you're relaxing in the Mediterranean one day with a cocktail in your hand, and sand between your toes . . .

To speed things up, Musk ordered a halt to all non-PayPal 2.0 development and code deployment—which, given the large number of PayPal 1.0

customers, worried many on the team. Then came another red flag: Musk announced that he planned to push PayPal 2.0 to the world without a rigorous rollback plan.

"We have a really limited window and not a lot of money, so we need to do this fast," Hoffman remembered Musk arguing. "We don't have time to build a rollback plan. We just need to build a new system and transfer entirely over to it."

Engineer Santosh Janardhan noted that this approach wasn't necessarily as risky as it seemed. "There was this phrase thrown around a lot in the early 2000s, which was 'fix it forward,'" he explained. "Which is, *We are committed. We are going out, even if we have to stay all night.* It was better to spend the night fixing it than spend the week before having a rollback."

Still, the move caused concern. By this point, millions of dollars' worth of transactions coursed through PayPal.com each day. If something went wrong with V2, the outcome could be disastrous.

■ ■ ■

V2 was one dividing line—but it wasn't the only one. Since the time of the merger, the company's name had remained a flashpoint.

At this point, typing in "www.paypal.com" took users to the www.x.com website—a Musk decision. Many Confinity veterans privately groused about it. The numbers, they felt, spoke for themselves: by July 2000, there were millions of total PayPal transactions and only several hundred thousand X.com ones. Users had coalesced around the PayPal brand—linking to it on their eBay auctions, and displaying it in email signatures. Musk, they felt, risked squandering that hard-won trust.

Musk decreed that PayPal be referred to as "X-PayPal" and that all stand-alone references to PayPal be scrubbed. X would prefix the entire ecosystem—including products like X-PayPal and X-Finance. "If you want to just be a niche payment system, PayPal is better. If you want to, say, *Let's, like, basically take over the world's financial system*, then X is the better name, because PayPal is a feature, not the thing itself," Musk said. To him, naming the company PayPal "would be like Apple naming itself the Mac."

That summer, the issue came to a head. Focus groups rated the Pay-
Pal name more highly than X.com. Vivien Go, who helped spearhead the
market research, remembered "again and again, the theme of *Oh God, I
wouldn't trust this website. It's an adult website.*"

Go admitted that user opinion had its limits—"You know, people
used to think 'Apple' was a funny name, too"—but she was hearing concerns directly. "It's kind of hard to refute when people say over and over,
almost in the same words, *I just wouldn't trust that. That sounds really mysterious.*"

Rena Fischer, who came to X.com by way of the buttoned-up accounting firm KPMG, recalled her own and other employees' experience
of receiving "so many terrible, horrible emails" because of the salacious-
sounding name. "Our product *was* PayPal. PayPal was, to me, an easy way
to explain what the goal of the company was," she said.

Amy Rowe Klement had originally joined X.com because she had
been persuaded by the expansive vision. "X was the core, and it was going
to be a house of brands," she observed. But by this point, she could see
that the company's breakthrough was lightweight email-based payments.
"PayPal grew faster, partly because X.com accounts were bank accounts,
so they were much more expensive and time-intensive to run," she observed, "So ultimately, if we weren't able to quickly upsell them to a variety of other products that were significantly profitable, it didn't make
much sense to be doing the X.com platform."

Musk was steadfast—the name would have to change. His reaction
to the focus group research bred resentment. "PayPal" partisans felt that
Musk was letting his personal opinion—rather than user preference—
drive the decision.

But the naming skirmish was just a visible manifestation of a deeper
division. "If that had been the only issue, it might have been more sur-
mountable," Hoffman admitted. To Musk, "PayPal" was a fine name—
for a stand-alone payments service. But "X.com" was (or at least, would
be) the world's financial nerve center. "There's a decision," Musk argued.
"Do you want to go for the grand prize, or do you *not* want to go for the
grand prize?"

Musk's colleagues acknowledged—even admired—the vastness of his vision. "I think the thing I would give Elon tremendous credit for was that he had sort of the biggest, most ambitious vision for PayPal and for what the business could be—of any of us," Thiel said. "It was not just a payments company." In the right context, this big thinking was Musk's ace in the hole. "He's the kind of entrepreneur who has a vision, where he's absolutely sure that that vision will play out," Hoffman noted.

But at the time, company officers and board members, including Thiel and Hoffman, weren't sold. To them, this wasn't about vision—it was about math. "We had about $65 million dollars left in the bank in September," Thiel recalled, "and I believe the burn rate was $12 million in September of 2000. There was sort of a sense that we had to try to dial things back—super fast."

Personal circumstances played a role here, too. Musk set a big goal because he sought a big win—bigger than Zip2. "I built a company four years out of college that sold for three hundred million dollars. So an outcome like that would have been, like, *I already did that*," Musk admitted.

But other executives—including Levchin, Sacks, Hoffman, and Nosek—hadn't. X.com's senior leaders weren't about to seek a grand prize—and risk a Fucked Company consolation prize.

■ ■ ■

Code could become surprisingly personal. The original PayPal.com codebase, for example, was quintessential Levchin, with templating conventions even referred to as "Max code." Musk's V2 changes would scrap Max code altogether—and, some engineers feared, scrap its namesake as well.

Indeed, Levchin debated quitting the company entirely. He had enjoyed the start-up's gestational period, when the future was unknown and his imprint unmistakable. Now, as just one of dozens of employees, and with his underlying work being unwound by his boss, he spoke about leaving it all behind and launching something new. *I'm just going to leave*, Levchin remembered thinking. *This V2 thing is just destroying my will to live.*

Like Musk and Thiel, Levchin was allergic to office politics. But also like them, he was intensely competitive. By this point, he knew that X.com's CEO wouldn't give in—not on the Microsoft decision, not on naming, and definitely not on strategy. But as he talked about it with others, X.com's CTO was persuaded not to give up either.

In the late summer and early fall of 2000, Levchin found sympathizers in other X.com executives. All had participated in the mutiny against a prior CEO. What worked once, they thought, could work again. So began the clandestine effort to cut Musk—X.com's cofounder, CEO, and biggest individual shareholder—out of the company.

14

AMBITION'S DEBT

In January 2000, Musk married his longtime girlfriend, Justine Wilson. But their planned honeymoon was canceled due to what Musk termed "company drama." He hoped to make up for it with a mid-September trip to the 2000 Summer Olympics in Sydney, Australia. The still relatively newlyweds' itinerary would take them around the world, with stops in Singapore and London.

With work never far from his mind, Musk also planned several fundraising meetings and check-ins with X.com employees based abroad. "It was meant to be a belated honeymoon *and* fundraising trip," Musk explained.

As they departed, Musk sensed a shift within the company. "I just got increasingly weird interactions," Musk recalled. Ordinary phone calls struck him as "unusual." "They were extremely concerned and upset and they said, 'We don't want to do these things.' And I said, 'Nope, you've got to do these things.' And I think that's basically the turning point," Musk remembered.

Musk didn't realize that a move was being made against him—and had precipitated the pushback. His executive team had hatched a coup. After failing to get Musk to abandon V2 and cease the X-PayPal name change, they planned to deliver an ultimatum to the X.com board demanding his ouster under the threat of a mass resignation. They had drafted a "vote of no confidence" document and quietly collected signatures from sympathetic employees.

Some employees signed—though without the coup organizers' depth of conviction. "Talk about ignorance being bliss," joked Giacomo DiGrigoli, a junior member of the product team. He remembered a tense meeting, with team members forecasting that the very future of the company was at stake—and would rest on the board's reaction to the Vote of No Confidence they just signed. "And of course, at twenty-three, I was like, 'I guess this is business? This happens when you're business-ing?' And of course, I knew absolutely nothing about it," he chuckled.

Just another Tuesday, one employee remembered thinking as the mutineers furtively moved against Musk.

■ ■ ■

The plan took shape in the weeks before Musk's departure. Luke Nosek, Peter Thiel, Max Levchin, and early board member Scott Banister attended the same technology conference in August. While there, they aired frustrations about the company's direction.

That weekend and in subsequent meetings, the group also discussed Musk. Their CEO, they believed, stood in the way of X.com's success and would need to be removed. Taking Musk down would be harder—and carry greater risk—than the "Nut House Coup." Bill Harris had a short tenure and shallow company ties; Musk was a cofounder with many loyalists and a big supporter on the board in Mike Moritz. More than that, he had technical chops and a forceful personality. To oust him as chief executive, they would have to move strategically—and stealthily.

Musk's honeymoon trip presented the perfect opportunity to act. One coup ringleader observed that while the timing seemed cruel, it was also necessary. Founders like Musk, he argued, brought such charisma into boardroom battles that persuasion could trump facts. In his view, a fair trial required Musk's absence.

With hindsight, Musk could appreciate the need for stealthiness. "Maybe they thought I would come back and convince the board of my original strategy and then just fire them," Musk said. "I think that's probably what they were concerned about happening." By this point in his life, he was also self-aware about his effect on people. "I think they were all so scared that I would come back and just obliterate them," Musk said, chuckling. "People are just, like, scared. I don't know. I'm not going to murder them."

Hindsight even allowed for Muskian humor. "Sneaky backstabbing bastards," he joked. "Too scared to stab me in the front. . . . All of you guys, you still want to stab me in the back? C'mon! Come at me from the front! There's twelve of you."

■ ■ ■

Board member John Malloy was abroad when Levchin called—"in the lobby of a big Chinese investment firm," Malloy remembered. Levchin informed him that several leaders in the company had decided to make a move against Musk. "And I thought, *Oh man, I gotta get this done and get back,*" Malloy recalled.

Musk's flight lifted off on Tuesday, September 19, 2000. With Musk safely in the air, Thiel, Levchin, Botha, Hoffman, and Sacks caravanned to the Sequoia offices to convince X.com board member Mike Moritz—a crucial vote. If Moritz—Musk's strongest ally on the board—sided with Musk and convinced board member Tim Hurd to do the same, the board would be deadlocked at 3–3, with Thiel, Levchin, and Malloy on one side and Hurd, Musk, and Moritz on the other.

The group arrived at Sequoia bearing the No Confidence signatures of all the employees who had promised to resign if Musk remained CEO. Moritz listened, unfazed as the group laid out their case, and he asked several clarifying questions. In addition to letting Malloy and Moritz know, Thiel was tasked with calling Tim Hurd to secure an emergency meeting of the board.

With Musk abroad, Hurd in Chicago, and Malloy hustling back from Asia, much of the next several days' discussion took place over the phone. The conspirators huddled together in person, alternating between Levchin's and Nosek's apartments at 469 Grant Avenue in Palo Alto. As board members, Thiel and Levchin joined board phone calls in one apartment, then returned to the other apartment to report back to the group.

Max Levchin immigrated to the Chicagoland area from the Ukraine. He took an active role in the Stephen Tyng Mather High School Computer Club, whose 1993 members are pictured here. Levchin (back row, center) stands alongside future PayPal engineer Erik Klein (back row, left). Recruiting at a moment of peak demand for tech talent, many of PayPal's earliest employees came through high school and college contacts. *Courtesy of Max Levchin*

Among the earliest team photos of Confinity, the company cofounded by Peter Thiel and Max Levchin that launched PayPal. Pictured (back row) is Max Levchin, Jamie Templeton, David Wallace; (middle row) is David Terrell, Peter Thiel, Tom Pytel, Russel Simmons, Luke Nosek; (front row) is Yu Pan, Lauri Schultheis, Ken Howery, Matt Bogumill, and David Jaques. *Courtesy of Russel Simmons*

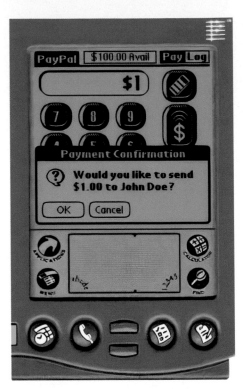

At Buck's Restaurant in Woodside, Confinity launched its inaugural product: a service to beam money between the infrared ports on PalmPilots. The product helped them secure venture funding from Nokia Ventures in mid-1999 and put the company on the path to creating PayPal—an email-based money exchange service. *Courtesy of Russel Simmons*

Fresh off the sale of his first start-up, Zip2, Elon Musk waded into online finance with a robust financial services offering he called X.com. Team members recalled his joy when the X.com debit card successfully spit out money at an ATM close to the company's Palo Alto office. *Courtesy of Seshu Kanuri*

In 1999, Musk purchased the rare sports car pictured in the advertisement above: the McLaren F1, Chassis #067. In early 2000, Musk picked up Thiel, and they drove together to Sand Hill Road. The car was violently totaled when Musk attempted to demonstrate its power and speed. *Courtesy of duPont REGISTRY™*

Elon Musk took over as CEO of X.com just shy of his twenty-ninth birthday. As the company grew, it began to attract press attention, and here, Thiel and Musk show off the company's website as well as its debit cards. The "X-PayPal" branding featured on the computer screen bothered many Confinity veterans, who felt PayPal was the more successful and appropriate brand. *Associated Press*

Sisters Jill Harriman (left) and Julie Anderson (center) helped inaugurate PayPal's customer service operation in Omaha, Nebraska, widely credited with helping to solve the company's mounting customer service troubles and becoming one of the company's most important outposts. "The story that doesn't get told is that there were three hundred people in Omaha who did a *huge* amount of work to ensure PayPal's success," described Sarah Imbach, an executive who helped steer the Nebraska presence. *Courtesy of Steve Kudlacek*

Underlying PayPal was a complex fraud-fighting operation, which Levchin and other engineers helped bring to life. The technology won Levchin the 2002 "MIT Innovator of the Year" award, and here, he is pictured with the trophy. *Getty Images*

PayPal's culture was a metrics-focused one, and video screens throughout the office displayed live data. On the right is a cardboard cutout of Star Trek's "Scotty" character, the remnants of a failed "Beam Me Up, Scotty!" marketing campaign, devised when the company was promoting its PalmPilot money-beaming technology. *Courtesy of Russel Simmons*

PayPal could be an unforgivingly intense place to work, and employees sought sleep when and where they could. One engineer was so sleep deprived, he totaled two vehicles driving home from the office. *Courtesy of Russel Simmons*

Life at PayPal proved a curious mix of gravity and levity. Office pranks were common, and here, one PayPal employee, Karen Seto, is pictured in a cube packed with balloons—a surprise for her birthday. *Courtesy of Russel Simmons*

PayPal's was a game-playing and puzzle-solving culture, and virtually everything that could become a competition was turned into one. *Courtesy of Max Levchin*

From its modest origins, PayPal debuted on the Nasdaq as a public company on February 15, 2002. Many employees who had been with the company for years felt their hard work vindicated as their once-small start-up joined the public stock exchange.
Courtesy of Russel Simmons

For most employees, the IPO day's most poignant memory was witnessing Peter Thiel (right) play ten simultaneous games of speed chess. Astonished onlookers wondered how Thiel managed it. Thiel's only loss during speed chess was to David Sacks (left), the company's COO. *Courtesy of Russel Simmons*

PayPal invaded an eBay live event and distributed thousands of T-shirts to attendees. The PayPal T-shirt made it onto the cover of *USA Today*'s "Money" section, where a user wore it while standing next to eBay's CEO, Meg Whitman. PayPal's successful commandeering of the event set the stage for a renewal of eBay's acquisition negotiations. *Courtesy of Oliver Kurlander*

On PayPal's final day as an independent company, its executives donned inflated sumo suits and wrestled in an oversized ring.
Courtesy of Russel Simmons

The "PayPal Mafia" moniker was created in earnest in 2007, when several of its alumni were featured in a photo on the cover of *Fortune* magazine. The photo was controversial, as it excluded any number of key participants in PayPal's creation. That said, the image inspired others, including two young prisoners in a maximum-security prison facility near Jessup, Maryland. They studied the PayPal founders and their achievements and shared those stories with fellow inmates. *Robyn Twomey/Redux*

Each side presented its arguments. Thiel and Levchin focused, mainly, on the concerning changeover of the website's technology. It was the board's first time hearing about it. The other members were shocked to learn that such a consequential change wasn't run by the board first, and about the lack of a rollback plan. "That should have been vetted by the board," one board member said. "I couldn't believe that it wasn't. . . . [It] was appalling to me that you'd take that kind of risk."

Hurd analogized the situation to piloting a 747. "It's got four engines. You're flying over the Himalayas in a storm, in a bad storm. Two of your engines go out. And there's no mechanics on board, but you're going to change the other two engines midflight." Board members Hurd, Malloy, and Moritz weren't engineers, but were persuaded by Levchin's case nonetheless.

Thiel and Levchin brought other issues to light as well. In its earliest incarnation, X.com had offered lines of credit to its customers. But in its haste to launch quickly, the company hadn't conducted sufficiently rigorous screening of loan applicants. As a result, X.com had given out shaky loans that would, eventually, have to be recorded as losses. In early 2000, Musk had announced the program's closure. But much to the surprise of the board, the company's books still showed the loans as interest-generating assets—with the expectation of repayment.

Others disputed this characterization, citing Musk's earlier ending of the unsecured credit lines program. The issue, some of his supporters believed, was Musk's desire to keep pieces of the X.com business going for longer than some in the company wanted—a sign to his opposition that he was running unnecessary risks. "[Musk] realized the [broader X.com] business had to go. We had to close. We had to take hits," Sandeep Lal recalled. "His thing was he was committed to the customers, because he felt he had started a product. And he didn't want to yank it out under their feet. So he was taking a lot longer than some of the other folks in the company were comfortable with."

Lal concluded for his part that "he wanted to close it down . . . the delta was on the speed." Part of the delay, per Lal, was the influence of the original deal X.com had made with First Western National Bank. A

First Western National Bank representative seconded to X.com had cited regulations that slowed the closing of X.com's banking and loan products.

Underlying the specific claims, the board saw for the first time the depth of the X.com-vs.-Confinity fault lines. "There was such tumult between the two companies," Malloy remembered. "I don't believe they had briefed the board on the level of discord. And the extent of problems underneath the surface wasn't apparent."

■ ■ ■

The coup rested mainly on the risk of an employee mass resignation. The participation of David Sacks and Roelof Botha carried particular weight: Sacks had been promoted by Musk; Botha had been hired by him. Both felt an affinity for him, but neither could see a way out of the company's current dilemmas with him staying on as CEO. Particularly for Botha, threatening to resign meant potentially giving up his job—and his immigration status—if Musk prevailed. He didn't make the choice lightly.

"The board met—absent me," Musk said. The back and forth between the company's executives and the board lasted several days. Musk would be the second X.com CEO removed in a single year; it would no doubt make waves in the press. But to the board, the risk to the company's internal dynamic outweighed the risk of external noise. Musk would remain a significant shareholder in the company, even if no longer CEO. How would the boardroom function? How would Musk continue to work with Thiel and Levchin?

During this time, the board also heard from employees. One wrote a lengthy, impassioned email to Hurd. He cc'd Musk and included colleagues he believed had misgivings about the coup. "I was presented with a letter that described a Vote of No Confidence for our current CEO, Elon Musk. I did not sign this letter and I do not agree with the content that I read," the author began. He then outlined what he saw as Musk's strengths as a CEO:

In my professional opinion, Elon is a very good CEO. He is easy to communicate with because he reads every piece of email that is sent to him. In the meetings that I have been in with Elon (Intuit, Microsoft and many others), he was very impressive and did an excellent job in presenting our company. Elon is a very tough negotiator and because of this, we have struck an excellent deal with Intuit and we have outstanding deals with many of our vendors (like First Data and MasterCard). We should soon have a deal with Microsoft and I believe that we have a good chance to connect with an AOL deal by the end of the year.

He concluded by encouraging Hurd to solicit an array of opinions before the board made its decision.

Musk replied to the group, removing board member Hurd from his response: "Thanks folks. This whole thing is making me so sad that words fail me. I have given every last ounce of effort, almost all my cash from Zip2 and put my marriage on the rocks, and yet I stand accused of bad deeds to which I have not even been given an opportunity to respond— I'm not even sure what they are supposed to be."

From the middle of that week through Sunday evening, the board deliberated. But in the end, Musk simply didn't have the votes to hang on. "It was a done deal by the time I got back," Musk remembered. "It was a fait accompli," Lal said. "He was not there when it happened. He was overseas, coming back on a plane . . . he did not have an opportunity to fight back in time. And when he came in, it was already too late."

■ ■ ■

On the evening of Sunday, September 24, Peter Thiel sent a company-wide email:

All,

As you know, Elon Musk agreed to reassume the position of Chief Executive Officer of X.com in May during a period of instability following the unexpected departure of the former CEO. By demonstrating an unbelievable work ethic and entrepreneurial leadership, he quickly re-established stability within the company and with investors. Through his efforts enormous progress has been made by the company across wide areas: X-Finance and PayPal have nearly 4 million users, the payment volume is approaching $2 billion/year, and by some measures X.com has become the largest efinance company on the Internet. We are poised for a major jump upwards in terms of organizational size, complexity, and strategic partnerships.

As a result of this successful growth, Elon and the Board have decided to form a search committee to recruit a veteran CEO to lead the company to the next level. Elon will remain active on the Board as a Director and major shareholder. I have agreed to function as Chairman with operational responsibility until the new CEO is named. Reporting to me will be Reid Hoffman, Dave Johnson, Sandeep Lal, Max Levchin, David Sacks, and Jamie Templeton.

Peter Thiel
Chairman, X.com

Five hours later, Musk sent a follow-up, with the subject line "Taking X.com to the next level":

Hey everyone,

X.com has grown very rapidly to the point where less than two years later, we have over 500 employees. So, having given this a lot of thought, I've decided that the time has come to bring in a seasoned CEO, with the large company experience to take X.com to the next level. As an entrepreneur, my interests lie much more in the foundation and creation of something new and less in the day to day management of a large (but great) company.

I'll be driving hard to find a really great CEO for X.com and do some PR, where it makes sense for the company. After that search is done, my plan is to take a sabbatical for about three to four months, think through a few ideas and then start a new company early next year.

Peter Thiel, who has been involved with the company from the beginning and is an exceptionally smart guy with a strong knowledge of the issues we face, will be assuming operational responsibility for the interim, allowing me to focus on the CEO search. Please give Peter and the company your full support over the coming months as we have a huge amount to accomplish and will face some tough competition. At the end of it all, I have not the slightest doubt that X.com will be an enormously valuable company and represent, in creating a new global payments system, one of the greatest advances made possible by the Internet.

Been great working with everyone (although I'm not gone yet). You are like my family.

Elon

■■■

Musk *did* see the X.com team as family—if only because he often spent more time with them at the office than he did with his actual family at home. But it wasn't his "having given this a lot of thought" that had led to his exit—that was simply a bit of standard-issue face-saving.

Still, the message was surprisingly gracious, as even his critics would admit. His public praise of Thiel—just hours after Thiel had pushed Musk aside—showed self-restraint.

Indeed, Musk didn't seek retribution. Jeremy Stoppelman—an early Musk X.com recruit—reached out to Musk in the immediate aftermath to ask if he and others should show their support by threatening to resign en masse. Musk instructed him to stand down. Even Musk's longest-serving allies within the company were thrown off by his moderation. "It was very odd to me how graciously he was taking it," Branden Spikes said. "If it were me, I'd be pissed."

Musk's position was born of realism. "While I didn't agree with their conclusion," Musk explained years later, "I understood why they took the action they did." The board had made its decision, and, from his remarkably pragmatic perspective, a fight would have been unproductive. "I could have fought it hard, but I said at this critical time, best to concede," Musk remembered. He added, "Peter and Max and David and the other guys are smart people, with generally good motivations, and they did what they thought was right for the right reasons. Except that the reasons weren't valid, in my opinion.

"It's easy to be bitter and hate them forever," he went on. "But the best course of action is to turn the other cheek and make the relationship good. And I put a lot of effort into making things good." Others saw this effort and, in spite of their misgivings about Musk as CEO, praised him for his restraint. "He behaved for the better of the company," Malloy recalled. "He does not hold grudges," Levchin observed. "He's been remarkably gracious with a bunch of people who basically ousted him as CEO while he was on his honeymoon."

When pressed about his concession, Musk referenced the biblical story of the Judgment of Solomon. In it, King Solomon must adjudicate two womens' claims for maternity of a baby boy. The king proposes to split the baby in half—which leads the first woman to immediately relinquish her claim for the sake of the child's life. "Give the first woman the living child, and by no means kill him," King Solomon decrees, "she is his mother."

"I did view the company as at least partly my baby," Musk said, his voice tinged with emotion. "If I attack the company and the people there, it's like . . . it would be attacking my baby. I don't want to do that."

This was Musk's second experience of being pushed aside at a company he founded, and it pained him. Jawed Karim recalled a moment in the cafeteria late one evening during the period in which Musk's fate was being decided. Musk walked in and silently made his way over to a full-sized Street Fighter arcade game. "He looked really, really distraught," Karim said, " . . . and he was playing Street Fighter on the arcade by himself. And then I said, 'Hey, hey, Elon, how's it going?' And he says, 'Eh, alright.'. . . And then two days later they announced that he got fired by the board."

■ ■ ■

It was one thing, the conspirators in Shakespeare's *Julius Caesar* discovered, to execute a coup; it was entirely another to explain away regicide. Blood still warm on his knife, Marcus Brutus addresses a gathering crowd of confused, angry Romans. "Fly not; stand stiff," Brutus tells them. "Ambition's debt is paid." The crowd doesn't buy it, drives the conspirators out of Rome, and a civil war follows.

Thiel, Levchin, Sacks, and other coup plotters now faced a parallel task: uniting a fractured team of revolutionaries and loyalists. *Nobody's happy when you're done with a civil war*, engineer Erik Klein remembered thinking.

The mood in the office was tense, and certain post-coup moments highlighted the divisions within the company. A pair of engineers partial to the Linux-based system celebrated V2's demise by destroying copies of *VBScript in a Nutshell* and *Inside COM+: Base Services*—two reference guides for programming in a Microsoft-based environment.

Even those who supported the decision to remove Musk found themselves caught in awkward situations. Mark Woolway, a finance team member, was abroad in Asia when the coup happened, but the organizers had given him a heads-up about it. When Musk called him to say "Hey, I just got fired," Woolway had to feign shock.

The divisions in the company went beyond moments of awkwardness and immature insensitivity. For all the No Confidence signatories, X.com also had its fair share of Musk supporters. "I remember to this day that I saw people crying. Like sobbing. Some of the engineers had invested so much effort into V2," Jawed Karim recalled.

Amy Rowe Klement called the coup "a mini-crisis for me." She had joined X.com in late 1999, but her aversion to the coup wasn't born of deep loyalty to Musk. She was disturbed by the behind-the-back manner of the mutiny. "The way that it went about—as far as asking people to sign this petition—it just goes to morals and values that I found troubling," she said.

Klement had been commuting in from San Francisco and often

arrived at the office at dawn to beat traffic. She recalled more than once walking in on Musk sleeping in the office after a full night of work. "We've all worked so hard, given so much of our life and energy, and we can't attempt to work things out in sort of a productive, mature way?" she said.

Jeremy Stoppelman, another X.com engineer, was livid. "We all loved Elon. He's kind of the pied piper for engineers," Stoppelman said. About the overthrow, Stoppelman didn't mince words: "I was super pissed. I was furious." Stoppelman, then twenty-five, let loose at Thiel and Levchin. "I was very candid. I remember telling them that I thought what happened was really shitty." Stoppelman especially objected to the process by which Musk was removed. "I think I understand the rationale . . . but the idea of him getting on a plane and not being able to defend himself just felt very shitty."

Thiel and Levchin heard Stoppelman out and took the time to explain themselves—winning him over in the process. "They didn't just say, 'Oh we don't care about you. You're just some junior engineer,'" Stoppelman remembered. "They made me feel the love and it definitely defanged me."

Sandeep Lal had made his views about the issues underlying Musk's departure well known, and he thought it might poison his relationship with Thiel, the incoming CEO. But it did not. When Thiel asked Lal what the most pressing company issue was and Lal offered his thoughts, Thiel organized a meeting the next day, set a team to work on it, and demanded a fix within twenty-four hours. "To this day, I'm amazed at the amount of trust he put in me without knowing me," Lal said.

Reid Hoffman, another coup organizer, defaulted to diplomacy following Musk's removal. He sent out a series of messages to disaffected players on the team, attempting to reassure them and roughly outlining what the future might bring. Still, diplomacy could only go so far. The members of the formerly separate teams—Confinity and X.com—still went out to their respective favorite bars separately.

Personal history was a large part of the division. The coup organizers hadn't even brought the letter of no confidence to many original X.com employees—who they assumed would be unsympathetic. Thus, many were left in the dark about the machinations. "When the coup happened," Sandeep Lal remembered, "and I was in Nebraska, and Reid sent me a note saying . . . 'Where do you stand on the coup?' And I said, 'Coup? What coup?' I just came from Citibank! We have no coups there."

Levchin and Thiel refrained from all-out purity tests, and many Musk hires thrived in his absence. Among several others, Julie Anderson, Sandeep Lal, Roelof Botha, Jeremy Stoppelman, Lee Hower, and Amy Rowe Klement all stayed on with the company and rose in its ranks. To this day, Musk takes pride in recruiting these talents.

But for others, the fault lines proved too much to bear. Once Musk was out, they were either shunted aside or put into positions that made working at X.com deeply uncomfortable. "They were polite about it. . . . But it was not a fun place to work if you were an Elon fan," Spikes remembered. In the coup's aftermath, the Harvey Mudd trio of engineers—X.com's earliest developers and lead engineers on PayPal 2.0—quit, almost simultaneously. It was a move driven by both solidarity and the supposition that their useful days at the company as Microsoft experts would be numbered. With Levchin driving the company's technology, PayPal 2.0 would be no more.

But the departure of the Harvey Mudd contingent spooked Thiel and Levchin. Would other engineers follow in a huff, hollowing out PayPal's engineering team? In fact, most didn't go as far as the trio had, in part because they could sense the company's potential. "I could tell that something magical was happening with the business, so if we could keep it going, it would be a good outcome," Stoppelman said. "I wasn't eager to throw it all away." In time, even many coup objectors would acknowledge that X.com needed a strategic shift. "The challenges the company was facing were apparent to all," Lee Hower said.

■ ■ ■

Two decades later, the coup organizers speak carefully about this moment. Many remain on good terms with Musk, communicate with him regularly, and count him as a friend. The group also admires his achievements in the intervening years; several have invested in his post-X.com ventures. A few choose to remain mum because of genuine misgivings about how the ouster took place; still others simply believe that long-buried hatchets should remain so.

Despite their reticence, they do not doubt their decision. In their view, the company was undeniably headed in the wrong direction and correcting course necessitated Musk's removal. One coup organizer maintains that the company would not have survived for six more months had Musk remained CEO. Others echoed that sentiment, arguing that the combination of the high fraud rate, the credit line debt crisis, the not-quite-closed X.com finance suite, and the stalled V2 process would have left the company in a precarious place—with money burning up, a tech team divided, and a website whose servers couldn't handle its still-rapid growth.

That said, the group also expresses misgivings over the unflattering portrait of Musk's PayPal tenure painted by some in the media. It was, they say, inaccurate. To them, there is no question of his contribution to the company—his outsized personal commitment, his financial backing, his board seat, and his founding vision. It was under his tenure that the company launched its first revenue-generating products, began to shift the underlying transaction funding mix, strengthened its product pipeline, elevated key people into leadership roles, and navigated the merger and the departure of Bill Harris. Even his deposers felt that media narratives unfairly excised Musk from the company's origin story.

■ ■ ■

Two decades later, Musk could muster a bit of grudging respect for the revolt. "It was a well-executed coup," Musk said, smiling. "It's slightly complimentary that they would only do it when I'm not there."

And with the benefit of time, Musk mined the moment for lessons. For one thing, he felt he had made a mistake by leaving on a personal trip abroad amid such complicated and controversial company transitions. "It was certainly not a good decision for me to . . . be away from the battle-front while there are all these extremely risky things happening," Musk said. "And I'm not there to steady their nerves."

Had he been there, he believed he could have persuaded his critics of his path—or at least cowed them into submission. "Some combination of reassurance and fear would not have resulted in a coup, I think," Musk said.

Despite his circumspection, Musk remained convinced that his vision was right for the company. He recognized his critics' concerns over PayPal 2.0 ("Do you really want to change the wheels on the bus when the bus is hurtling down the road?"). But he still believed it to be the right call. "From my standpoint, if we switch to the new architecture," he said, "we'd be able to evolve the system much faster. That was the trade from my standpoint. . . . So we should take this risk and do it."

Musk also reflected on the human dimension of the struggle. "I did not fully appreciate the emotional element of this," he admitted. "It's a little tough if you're thinking about getting rid of something called 'Max code.' Understandably, Max would be a little miffed about that." Musk also felt that he could have done a better job communicating his vision— particularly to Levchin. "I should have put a lot more effort into convincing Max in particular that this is the right technical move," he said.

Today, Musk can study his firing with the good humor of someone who has achieved a great deal in the time since. "It's hard to argue with the ultimate outcome, which was positive," Musk said. He has also largely buried the hatchet with his overthrowers—or, as he'd say, "I buried *their* hatchet." Still, obsessive to the end, Musk lamented what he saw as his biggest X.com failure: that it didn't become the epicenter of financial services he hoped it would, a potential "trillion-dollar company."

■ ■ ■

Employees from PayPal's earliest years spoke of the company's Dickensian highs and lows—that founding a payment services start-up amid the dot-com bust represented the technofied "spring of hope" and the "winter of despair."

Few experienced those fluctuations more viscerally than Elon Musk. From 1999 to 2002, Musk netted a fortune from the sale of his first start-up, launched another successful internet company, minted a second fortune when that company went public, and launched a third venture.

During those same years, he fought off one mutiny against him, nearly perished in a car crash, was ousted as CEO of the company he cofounded, almost died *again* due to a combination of malaria and meningitis, and lost an infant son to sudden infant death syndrome (SIDS).

Just after Musk's departure, an early X.com employee, Seshu Kanuri, wrote a note to him. "Elon," he wrote, "I am sorry to learn of the latest events concerning your position in our team. I would like to state that this is not something you should be disheartened about as I am sure you are destined to do greater things in technology." Kanuri recalled that Musk wrote back with appreciation.

Messy though it was, Musk's ouster from X.com gave him creative breathing room. Freed of X.com duties, he could return to his earliest passions: space exploration and electrical energy. "Steve Jobs made Pixar great because he was fired from Apple," observed early X.com engineer Scott Alexander. "Elon did SpaceX and made Tesla great because he was fired from X.com."

Those new ventures began briskly; for Musk, there was little time to lick wounds or nurse grievances. Just months after the coup, Mark Woolway took Musk out for drinks. "I asked him what he was going to do next, and he said, 'I'm going to colonize Mars,'" Woolway recalled. "We were at this little bar in Palo Alto called Fanny & Alexander, sitting outside. And he said, 'My mission in life is to make mankind a multi-planetary civilization.' And I'm like, 'Dude, you're bananas.'"

Less than two years later, on May 6, 2002, Elon Musk filed paperwork to incorporate a new business, Space Exploration Technologies Corporation. Seven days later, he registered its URL: www.spacex.com. On August 4, 2008, SpaceX announced that it had received $20 million in equity investment from Founders Fund, started by Thiel, Howery, and Nosek, with Nosek joining SpaceX's board.

On September 28, 2008—almost eight years to the day he was deposed as X.com's CEO—Elon Musk stood and watched SpaceX's Falcon 1 rocket rise to the skies above Omelek Island in the Kwajalein Atoll, southwest of Hawaii. Nine minutes and thirty-one seconds into launch, the Falcon 1 became "the first privately developed, liquid fuel rocket to orbit the Earth."

PART 3

DOUBLED ROOKS

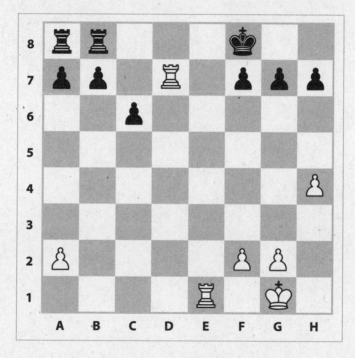

15

IGOR

When the board pushed Musk out, Mike Moritz had insisted on a stipulation. Thiel could be interim CEO, but PayPal would have to run a proper CEO search. To that end, the board hired a professional headhunting firm, Heidrick & Struggles, and asked Thiel and Levchin to put together a job description.

They returned with a pipe dream, one board member recalled. Thiel and Levchin's desired candidate would possess technological prowess, strategic savvy, a high IQ, have experience leading a company through an IPO, feel comfortable in a T-shirt-and-jeans start-up culture, and enjoy the cut and thrust of debate at PayPal. "It was the most laughable fucking thing," another board member said. "They were looking for the perfect human. . . . It was young naïveté."

The headhunters put forward a dozen candidates, but unsurprisingly, none passed muster. Some were rejected for "not being intellectually rigorous enough," per board member John Malloy's recollection of the PayPal executive team's feedback. Some candidates took themselves out of the running following a bruising screening process. Malloy recalled one particularly irate post-interview call from a candidate demanding to know what solving math puzzles had to do with running a company.

To be fair, Thiel wanted a new CEO as much as anyone. "Peter doesn't really want to work for people," explained Reid Hoffman. That included the people on PayPal's board. But other team members wanted Thiel to stay on and treated the search process as a farce. "We went through these fake job interviews," Sacks remembered. "We pretended to interview and just kept kicking the can down the road." Mark Woolway called the process a "façade."

■ ■ ■

One candidate made it through the farce. Only in his mid-thirties, David Solo had accumulated a lifetime of financial services experience. After earning electrical engineering and computer science degrees from MIT, Solo worked at O'Connor & Associates, a fintech firm that pioneered derivatives trading technology. He made partner by twenty-six and oversaw a merger between O'Connor and Swiss Bank in his early thirties. "He was a brilliant math guy, understood the whole thing, and he would have fit the spec," Thiel said.

Even before vying for the CEO job, Solo had crossed paths with X.com. In 1999, when Solo had just arrived on the West Coast, a venture capitalist friend introduced him to Musk. Solo remembered the X.com offices' large X logos, and recalled Musk explaining a still indefinite vision. They bandied about ideas, and while Musk impressed him, Solo was not convinced by X.com's business case.

A year later, Solo sat in a more expansive PayPal space. This time, Levchin and Thiel did the grilling. In a turn of fate (and tables), Thiel and Solo had met years before, when Solo had interviewed Thiel for a job at O'Connor & Associates.

Following the interview, Solo raved to his wife about PayPal's emphasis on merit—an echo of what he'd enjoyed at O'Connor. "When I was in my upper twenties, the managing partner of O'Connor said, 'David, we want to make you the global head of the fixed income and derivatives division of the bank,'" Solo recalled. "And I remember saying, ' . . . that's great, but don't you think you'd be better off hiring somebody from Salomon Brothers who actually knows all this stuff?' And [he] said, 'You know what, we might actually lose nine months or a year by not hiring the guy who has more experience, but in the end, we've always succeeded by betting on the people who we think have the talent and work ethic—and who we know.'"

Upon reflection, Solo felt the same logic applied at PayPal. "I remember going home and thinking, *You know what, this guy Peter's got it all*," Solo said. "If I'm honest to myself, he'd probably do a better job than I can, because he's been in this business from scratch. He knows the people. They clearly had huge respect for him, justifiably in my view." Solo took himself out of the running and told Mike Moritz: "If I were you, I would bet on Peter."

Board member Tim Hurd had come to this conclusion independently as well. "There's a very high probability that only Peter could have been successful as CEO, because people needed to respect him. Max needed to respect him. Reid, the others . . . people were there because Peter was," Hurd said. "Was Peter a good manager? Absolutely not. And he would tell you that. But no one else could have been successful at it."

By the time Solo interviewed, countless candidates had unsuccessfully run the PayPal gauntlet. Thiel had taken over in September 2000; the company was still meeting candidates in spring 2001. Solo would be the last of those interviewed, as the board dropped "interim" from Thiel's title. Thiel admitted that Solo's outside endorsement "played a big role in convincing the board to just go with me."

For Thiel, the mandated search process left a bitter aftertaste. One observer said Thiel felt "pretty unhappy" that some on the board had been trying to push him out. It created a rift between him and Sequoia's Mike Moritz, which never fully healed, and it reinforced PayPal's allergy toward "executive experience."

Thiel was both an example of and a proponent of putting talented neophytes in charge. Early on, Thiel appointed Reid Hoffman as COO—cutting against his board members' advice. He installed Sacks as VP of strategy—despite concerns about Sacks's collegiality. He promoted a fresh-out-of-business-school Roelof Botha to CFO and put a young attorney named Rebecca Eisenberg as the first legal chair on the IPO. Later, talk of Thiel's contrarianism would focus on his decisions in markets and politics. But during the PayPal years, his instinct to cut against the grain focused on human beings, as he placed unexpected bets on unconventional people.

Rebecca Eisenberg was a Harvard-trained lawyer and technology columnist who came to the company during the height of the dot-com bust—just weeks after being laid off. She reflected on her onboarding with passion and spoke of what it said about PayPal's culture. "The great thing about Peter and his group is that they really didn't care about the other stuff. That I was this outspoken columnist. That my face [was] on a bus before that. That I spoke my mind. That I was a woman—and known as a feminist. That I admitted a history of bisexuality," she said, "He didn't give a shit. He cared about smart people who worked hard."

■ ■ ■

Shortly after Musk's departure, Thiel called together a small group, including Botha, Sacks, and Levchin. They sat around a big wooden table in the apartment of Botha's girlfriend, and Levchin recalled the gravity of the moment: they had gotten what they wanted—with Musk out, the company was now theirs. But so were its crises. Thiel divided up responsibility for combating each of the existential threats.

A separate group had a get-together at the Gualala, California, home of Reid Hoffman's grandparents. They broke up the days as follows: day 1, diagnose the business's problems; day 2, propose solutions. One particular area of agreement: the company would abandon X-Finance, and it would focus on cementing its position as eBay's "master merchant." (On day 3, the assembled group also brainstormed next steps if the company collapsed. Hoffman floated an idea that he'd eventually bring to pass: a professional social network, which the world would later come to know as LinkedIn.)

In fall 2000, PayPal employees at every level felt agency and urgency. "At that time, at PayPal, every little thing you did, and every second, mattered. You—you!—could single-handedly be the bottleneck. And you felt it, and you understood it," Oxana Wootton recalled. "And that sense of urgency would drive you. You would skip your meals. You would skip going to the bathroom. And you would just get it done."

And PayPal had much to do. The threats from eBay, Visa, and Mastercard, and others still loomed large, and the company's coffers were growing ever tighter. By fall 2000, PayPal had mere months of runway left, with little hope of additional funding. Unless PayPal could turn itself around and show business health, wary investors didn't seem likely to throw good money after bad. "We thought we could very well go out of business," Mark Woolway recalled.

The board met the week after Musk's departure, and on September 28, Thiel outlined the strategic shift in an all-company email:

All,

Here's a quick update on the top priorities for X.com over the next month:

(1) Fraud prevention. Max Levchin will be leading this effort, and Sarah Imbach will be coordinating the requisite engineering, financial, and operational pieces of the company needed to make this happen. The good news is that the fraud crisis is readily containable and that we have a number of great front-end solutions (preventing fraudsters before they enter the system) and back-end solutions (detecting fraudsters once they enter the system).

(2) Product cycle/V1 platform. The product cycle is going to be accelerated as fast as possible, and therefore all engineering resources will be concentrated on the V1 platform . . .

(3) Branding. There will be no change in our dual branding: The product will be called PayPal (because that's what consumers are familiar with) and the company will be called X.com (because that's what investors are familiar with).

(4) X-Finance. We will close down X-Finance operations and start to consolidate everything onto PayPal. All of the people working on X-Finance will be shifted over to the PayPal product, because that one requires all of our focus at this point in time.

Thanks,
Peter

■ ■ ■

For a financial company that started out, as Levchin noted, "naïve about fraud," the fact that fraud now topped the list of its strategic priorities represented a seismic shift. Just days before Thiel's note, Thiel and the rest of the board had listened as Roelof Botha and Levchin outlined the severity of PayPal's fraud problem.

Botha's ongoing analysis of the business produced a critical insight: the fraud plaguing the site came in distinct forms. The first type: merchant fraud, perpetrated by buyers. Someone would buy an item, then falsely claim that it had arrived broken, or that it was the wrong item, or that it had never arrived at all. The buyer would demand a refund, and PayPal—the financial intermediary—stood liable for providing it. The company came to appreciate that this type of fraud vexed retailers big and small; it was table stakes. "Merchant fraud was sort of irritating," Botha remembered, "but it was a little bit of the cost of doing business."

The more concerning type of fraud involved credit cards, foreign drop-ship sites, and even shell companies. Some hackers opened PayPal accounts with stolen credit cards, bought and shipped goods overseas, then resold them. Other fraudsters devised shell companies and duped unsuspecting buyers into purchasing phony goods, then pocketed the money without sending anything. To cover their tracks, the fraudsters would siphon the money through an elaborate series of untraceable phantom accounts abroad.

This kind of professional criminality posed a more serious risk to the company. "You could have a couple smart criminals just continuously funnel millions of dollars out of your account and bankrupt you," Botha explained. "The unauthorized fraud had no brake on it."

The core challenge of fighting professional fraud was separating authorized and unauthorized charges, speedily and at scale. Early on, the company fought to be lenient—avoiding any extra steps to the transaction process in order to juice growth. But now, as PayPal was gaining recognition, its leniency was a liability. No longer was the company at war with bored college students opening fake accounts for beer money—now it was up against professional criminals bent on stealing millions of dollars.

Fraud, Botha concluded, presented more than a mere annoyance—if left unchecked, it could tank the business. Botha shared these insights with PayPal's board, who agreed with his dire assessment. "If we don't solve that problem," board member Tim Hurd concluded, "PayPal doesn't exist today."

■ ■ ■

In Levchin's favorite film, *Seven Samurai*, the leader of the samurai, Kambei Shimada, tells a fellow warrior to "go to the north," where the decisive battle will be fought. If Kambei knows where the battle is going to be, the warrior asks, then why not build a fence to keep out the enemy? "A good fort needs a gap," Kambei explains. "The enemy must be lured in. So we can attack them. If we only defend, we lose the war."

In its breakneck growth, PayPal had inadvertently built a fort with yawning gaps—and fraudsters took full advantage. But, as in *Seven Samurai*, the gaps in PayPal's armor served as critical lures. PayPal's close observation of the many fraudsters on its platform helped lead it to a series of cutting-edge fixes, including several that set an industry standard for deterrence. "[Fraud] saved us—on accident," Luke Nosek explained. "And it was cheaper than buying Super Bowl ads."

Before Musk's removal as CEO, the slow transition to PayPal 2.0 had left Levchin with free time. He used it to immerse himself in the fraudsters' chat rooms and online forums, surveilling the company's attackers on their own turf. "You would marvel at watching him solve these fraud problems," Todd Pearson remembered. "The creativity . . . like the fact that he'd go into the Russian hacking rooms and eavesdrop on them. I just thought, *Our poor competitors. They're so fucked.*" Board member Tim Hurd remembered Levchin calling up fraudsters on the phone and speaking to them in Ukrainian.

Levchin and his colleagues discovered varying levels of sophistication among the company's attackers. One mildly clever fraudster made a small fortune by creating the copycat site "PayPai.com"—exploiting the proximity of the "l" and "i" keys to lure users to a working replica of PayPal.com. But more sophisticated, and threatening, schemes emerged as well. From its earliest days, for instance, PayPal had faced assault from bots, bits of code written to open large numbers of new accounts in order to siphon off the company's $10 and $20 bonuses.

To fix the bot problem, the PayPal engineering team found itself grappling with a centuries-old philosophical question. In the 1600s, René Descartes pondered what human beings could do that robots—or "automata"—could not. "Automata" were nonexistent when Descartes wrote about them in his *Discourse on the Method*, but primitive versions were around in the 1950s, when the British computer scientist and mathematician Alan Turing took up Descartes's query. "I propose to consider the question 'Can machines think?'" Turing wrote.

Turing's answer was to subject computers to "an imitation game" in which a computer and a human are locked in separate rooms and tasked with responding to questions put to them by someone in a third room. If the questioner couldn't distinguish the machine's answers from the human's, then the computer passed the Turing test.

Driven by more utilitarian motives—thwarting fraudsters—PayPal's engineers joined the fray a few decades after Turing. "What is something that a computer couldn't do—but is brain-dead easy for a human?" Levchin queried his assembled team of engineers. Engineer David Gausebeck thought back to his college research on computers' ability to decipher images. Humans, he remembered, could read warped, hidden, or distorted letters—a much harder task for computers. He looked at Levchin and said, "OCR," referring to optical character recognition.

The concept wasn't new to Levchin. In the Usenet and other forums he frequented, hackers distorted words all the time to keep information from prying eyes. Thus *SWEET* would become $VV££+, and *HELLO* could be expressed as |-|3|_|_() or)-(3££0. Humans could read these codes; government computers could not.

"So I was thinking that night about, *What are problems that are easy for a human to solve and hard for a computer to solve?*" Gausebeck recalled. "And recognizing letters seems the archetypal example of that. I wrote an email to Max saying, 'Why don't we put images of characters and require a user to type them in? And that'll be hard to automate.'"

Gausebeck sent his email to Levchin late in the evening. By the time Gausebeck arrived at the office the next day, he found Levchin "halfway through building it." Levchin finished a rough product in a nonstop sprint that weekend. Once complete, he pushed the code live—then blasted Wagner's "The Ride of the Valkyries" over a cubicle-mounted speaker.

■ ■ ■

To perfect their creation, Levchin and his team studied the automated tools available at the time. Levchin trekked to a nearby computer store and bought armfuls of optical character recognition (OCR) software— programs (then still in their infancy) that extracted machine-legible text from images or handwriting. That research led to further refinements, including the use of a stencil font and the addition of thick, translucent lines over the text, both of which tripped up the store-bought OCR software.

The team predicted the "Gausebeck-Levchin test"—as they called it—would work well at first, then degrade over time. As with other PayPal creations, the team planned to research what failed, redeploy, and repeat. Clever though the initial solution was, Gausebeck expected fraudsters to be able to beat the system, if given enough time. *This is still a solvable problem*, Gausebeck remembered thinking.

The feature deployed, and the team waited for it to break. To their considerable surprise, it didn't. "It turns out the original version held up fine for years," Gausebeck remembered. "I guess the people who were motivated to try to defeat it weren't the same people who had the skills to do that. It's a very different set of skills than interacting with a web page."

The Gausebeck-Levchin test became the first commercial application of a Completely Automated Public Turing Test to Tell Computers and Humans Apart—or CAPTCHA. Today, CAPTCHA tests are common on the internet—to be online is to be subjected to a search for a specific image—a fire hydrant or bicycle or boat—from a lineup. But at the time, PayPal was the first company to force users to prove their humanity in this fashion. Gausebeck and Levchin didn't invent the

CAPTCHA—Carnegie Mellon researchers devised something similar in 1999—but the PayPal version was the first to scale, and among the first to solve the centuries-old challenge of separating human from machine.

■ ■ ■

"The world is run by robots," comedian John Mulaney would later joke about CAPTCHA tests. "And we spend most of our day telling them that we're not a robot just to log on and look at *our own* stuff!"

Some at PayPal foresaw this problem—that such tests might present a nuisance for real human users. When Levchin first approached David Sacks with a thick-line-over-mangled-text user test, Sacks remembers responding, "'Are you fucking kidding me? No one's going to understand this. This is going to deter everybody from signing up for our product. . . You want to do what to my sign-up page?!'" Skye Lee remembered a lengthy back-and-forth about creating images that worked for the CAPTCHA test—but that didn't hamper site use. "It can't take a long time to download that image," she said. "You want it to be fast—not just performative."

Ultimately, Sacks relented. But his resistance spoke to what would become a perennial balancing act at PayPal between the website's security, its usability, and its coffers. "Peter called it 'the dials,'" Sacks remembered. "It's easy to stop fraud if you're willing to kill usability. What's hard is maintaining a sufficient level of usability without letting fraud get out of control. So Max controlled the fraud dial. I controlled the usability dial. And we'd come together to agree on a compromise."

During this period, the company's leadership built what Sacks called "the tight, iterative loop between product and finance." Weekly weekend meetings became the norm, and the company watched each adjustment of the dials closely—to see, for instance, how a reduction in account growth affected its revenue, or how a change in bank account-funded transactions shifted its costs.

In time, PayPal's fine-tuning of these dials gave it a competitive advantage. "Where a lot of our competitors failed was they were starting to get their heads kicked in from fraud, and so they would immediately turn their sign-up page into, you know, four arrowed pages with one hundred questions," Ken Miller remembered. Despite losing millions of dollars to fraud, PayPal did not take such draconian steps. Instead, they made fine-grain tweaks, using a mix of product design, detailed analysis, and fraud-fighting tools to turn losses into breakthroughs.

■ ■ ■

The Gausebeck-Levchin test and Sanjay Bhargava's "random deposit" concept both stopped fraudsters at the door—but they didn't prevent *all* fraudsters from getting in. Many managed to make it past these safe-guards. In order to combat them, the company also had to figure out how to deploy back-end transaction monitoring; that is, keeping watch of users who had already established accounts.

In this space, PayPal would leave another pioneering mark on the industry—thanks, in part, to the contributions of an engineering intern. Bob Frezza arrived at PayPal circuitously. His father had attended a 1999 Cato Institute conference at which Peter Thiel spoke about the promise of internet businesses. Bill Frezza and Thiel exchanged email addresses, and when Frezza's son, then a Stanford undergrad, applied for summer internships, his father dropped a note to Thiel with his son's résumé.

Thiel wrote back promptly. "Thanks for referring Robert to us," Thiel replied. "We have about 14 Stanford graduates working at Con-finity already (including myself), and I make every effort to hire more people from Stanford, so I will definitely be giving him a call." Frezza was a burgeoning engineer, so Thiel forwarded the email to Levchin.

"At first, I thought, *Peter, what are you doing sending this intern my way?*" Levchin remembered. "I don't need anyone to get my coffee." Confinity didn't have interns in the traditional sense: Levchin preferred his teams small and his engineers self-reliant. He wasn't about to tutor a college student.

When some interns came in for interviews, Levchin pushed them toward full-time work. One early employee, Jawed Karim, was a junior in college when he interviewed with Levchin for what he assumed was a summer gig. "And then I said, 'Yeah, I'm just interested in, like, a summer internship thing.' And [Levchin] just ignored that—and just sent me a full-time offer." Karim accepted the offer, began his professional life at the age of twenty, and counted himself among several college dropouts on the company's roster. (Encouraged by its ability to best top-tier universities for talent, the company placed an advertisement in the *The Stanford Daily* pushing students to quit school and join up.)

Unlike Karim, Frezza was more explicit that he was only looking for summer employment, and Thiel urged Levchin to reach out and speak with him. "I had one conversation with [Frezza] at University Café in Palo Alto," Levchin recalled, "and realized that this was a special kid."

Frezza started his PayPal internship on June 20, around the time Levchin's attention began turning to fraud. One of Frezza's closest friends at the company was Bob McGrew, another Stanford intern. The rest of the team referred to the pair as "The interns Bob." "I think the joke evolved to where he was 'Bob the intern' and I was 'the intern Bob,'" McGrew recalled. "No one could remember which one was supposed to be which."

Without a formal internship program, the pioneering PayPal interns defaulted to performing the work of full-time employees—and were rewarded accordingly. Frezza was given a small amount of company equity, unusual for a temporary role. Bora Chung, who joined as a business intern during the summer of 2000, completed her summer work, stayed on part-time while she finished at Stanford Business School, and received stock options for that period—all before joining full-time in 2001. The company even granted stock options by the hour for certain consultants and contract employees.

Frezza, McGrew, and other short-term employees labored just as hard as their full-time counterparts and on projects of equal sensitivity. McGrew, for example, devised a way to improve the complexity of PayPal's master passwords. "Max thought about [my idea] for a while," McGrew recalled. "It was different from what he had done. And he said, 'That's a great idea. Let's go do it.' So then I rewrote the whole way we were managing passwords."

McGrew also recalled the latitude given to top performers—including his fellow "intern Bob." One day, Frezza showed up to work at 2:00 p.m., blowing off a scheduled meeting with his boss Levchin. When Levchin asked what had happened, Frezza explained that he had just gotten a computer steering wheel and had stayed up late playing a video game. "It was the kind of place where that kind of just happened," McGrew said, laughing.

■ ■ ■

John Kothanek, the company's senior security investigator, remembered that Frezza was fired up about the fraud problem—because he had been the victim of fraud himself, twice. Two sellers had sent Frezza empty boxes instead of the items he ordered. "He mentioned to me several times, 'I don't want this to happen to people. I don't want people getting ripped off. I want to help stop this stuff,'" Kothanek recalled.

Over the summer of 2000, Frezza joined Levchin in his hunt for fraud patterns. Fraudsters would leave clues, consistent sequences of behavior. Early on, those patterns yielded simple rules: a transaction's timing or size, for instance, could be used to detect fraudulent behavior. At one point, Levchin noticed that fraudulent accounts often contained a tell: the fraudster would fail to capitalize the first letter of the first name for their fake account profiles. The pattern could serve as a preventative test. An account with a lowercase *t* for *tom*, for example, would be flagged for extra attention by the team's human fraud analysts.

Fraudsters caught on to this kind of simple logic fast, though. "The bad guys . . . test if you use a simple collection of rules," Levchin told the industry publication *The American Banker*. If Levchin and his team set, say, a $10,000 threshold at which transactions were manually reviewed by a PayPal employee, thieves would notice and iterate. "Then they'd send ten $1,000 charges instead. Then maybe we set something like a review for any $10,000 charge total. Then they'd say, 'Okay, well, what if I create ten fake accounts and send $999 to each?'" McGrew said. "It's . . . quite hard to write rules for."

The bigger the company grew, the more sophisticated its fraudsters became. PayPal's real troubles began when international hackers started targeting the company. The boldest fraudsters entered into a cat-and-mouse game with Levchin and his engineering team. The fraudsters would find a loophole, the engineers would patch it, and the fraudsters would try again. "It became this arms race," Ken Miller said. "We would do something, and they would hit back just as hard with some new scheme."

One particularly persistent thief went by the nom de guerre "Igor." One of Igor's tricks was to create two accounts, both legitimate-looking enough to pass PayPal's initial screening process. Then, he would wait. After enough time had passed to avoid suspicion, he would use one account to purchase goods from the other using a stolen credit card number. The fake seller would then withdraw the money to a non-PayPal bank account.

To anyone watching, the transactions looked ordinary, no different than the countless buyer-and-seller exchanges PayPal facilitated every day. Igor's devious insight was in the creation of a facsimile of the kind of transaction PayPal wouldn't look twice at.

■ ■ ■

By the fall of 2000, the company was processing tens of thousands of transactions a day, and the dollar amounts and details could vary widely. Manually searching for wrongdoing was a nonstarter. So Levchin, Frezza, and others began studying more sophisticated patterns—suspicious zip codes, IP addresses, accounts hitting transaction limits, or other tells—that cut across varieties of PayPal's fraud landscape.

As Levchin, Frezza, and others dove into pattern recognition, they wondered if the activity on the PayPal systems could be depicted visually as opposed to numerically. So the team gave it a shot, building the equivalent of an echocardiogram for the company—a visual representation of money flows.

On a computer monitor, the picture showed a series of lines representing the flow of money, with the thickness of each line corresponding to the size of a given transaction. If an account had only ever appeared as thin-lined (small-dollar) transactions, a sudden thick line smack in the middle of its recent history might indicate trouble.

Illustrating financial fraud enhanced human intuition, and these digital tools gave teams of PayPal fraud analysts something to hunt for in the
maze of numbers. Before these tools, as Kothanek recalled, the team was
awash in voluminous paper records. "We were just printing out literally,
you know, boxes and boxes and boxes full of paperwork to be able to go
through it with a highlighter and putting stuff on the walls. I kind of see
it in the movies, but I've never seen it in any other place except at PayPal
in real life," Kothanek said.

Over time, a mix of product leads and engineers helped to iterate on
the original designs, building tools for fraud investigators to see concerning activity at scale. "Suddenly, with the click of a button, we could see a
web of forty-three hundred accounts that we believed were all related
and part of the same ring," said Ken Miller. "Whereas before, it would
have taken us weeks to draw that out."

The visuals also made it easier to compare categories of fraud. At
one point, Frezza suggested to McGrew that the team might try matching graph against graph. In theoretical computer science terms, he was
describing the subgraph isomorphism problem, a challenging compu-
tational task. Programmers had used this technique to compare, among
other things, the intricacies of chemical compounds.

Frezza and Levchin's efforts to apply this technique to patterns of
fraudulent activity yielded another breakthrough: now, PayPal could
match not just numbers to numbers but patterns to patterns. They augmented this with computer-generated rules that triggered an alert if one
pattern resembled an earlier fradulent one. If such a fraud pattern registered frequently enough, the team could write a blanket rule in the
system to prevent it from recurring again.

"A simple layman's explanation is that we started fighting patterns—
more than [fighting] fraudsters," observed engineer Santosh Janardhan.
"Patterns are mathematics. Some of the folks who ended up working on
this stuff were basically mathematics folks from Stanford that Max ended
up hiring, and they ended up creating models that detected changes and
anomalies in patterns, which was a very advanced way of looking at things
at that time."

Forced to use ever more complex forms of deception, PayPal fraudsters would often tire of the process. "[Our work] put the dumb fraudsters out of business," McGrew remembered. The extra effort also led to more fraudster error. "The more complex the scheme, the more likely it is that you leave some trace of yourself behind," McGrew explained. "You reuse an IP address that had previously been used in a suspicious transaction, and so that can set off a flag and that flag goes to a fraud analyst. The fraud analyst pulls up your new graph and suddenly they can recognize the pattern and see that you're trying to do something suspicious."

Frezza and Levchin's new fraud detection system was dubbed "IGOR"—in honor of the infamous PayPal fraudster. The human Igor hadn't just abused the PayPal systems, he had made things personal, too, taunting Levchin with mocking, incendiary emails. His immortalization in the program's name—which appeared in pitches to partners and even in SEC filings—added an ironic twist: IGOR helped end Igor's reign of terror.

■ ■ ■

Tools like IGOR offered PayPal a real-time, account-level view of fraud: if a certain account looked suspicious, its fraud team could watch the flow of money and suss out bad behavior on the spot. Still other innovations helped the team track fraud after it had been committed.

In this effort, the company used applied mathematics to compensate for inexperience. "The people who ended up working on this were not domain experts," engineer Santosh Janardhan observed. "And that, frankly, is good. They had no preconceived notions; they approached it with very fresh eyes. And converted [fraud] to a tractable, mathematical thing."

One such pair of fresh eyes belonged to Mike Greenfield, who had joined the company as a fraud analyst reporting to Levchin. "They effectively hired me to, like, throw a (hopefully) smart twenty-two-year-old at the problem and see what I could do," Greenfield remembered. "Honestly, the first six months I wasn't super useful." Greenfield built software to generate decision trees to predict fraud, but "[threw] too much data at it" for the software to be useful. The software turned out to be a strong fit, however, for identifying merchant fraud.

The algorithmic process underlying Greenfield's software is known as "random forests"—consisting of multiple decision trees aggregated together to improve predictions. The approach allowed PayPal to put transactions through the ringer. "After going down eighteen steps, we'd say, 'Okay, this transaction has a twenty percent chance of being bad. This other one has a 0.01 percent chance,'" explained Greenfield. "We would create one hundred of those."

PayPal's approach differed from that of traditional financial services firms: its models crunched hundreds of different variables at once, rather than the more limited variable regression models used by legacy banks. In 2000 and 2001, the industries that would spring from machine learning and big data were still far-off—but PayPal pioneered many of the techniques that defined those sectors. PayPal's use of random forests, for instance, was among the world's first applications of that learning method for a commercial purpose.

With these evolutions, PayPal effectively reinvented itself as one of the first big data security companies. "PayPal is actually a, more or less, commodity business," Levchin observed. "It sounds very cool and innovative . . . moving money on the internet. But the credit card interfaces have existed for twenty years. . . . All we really [did was] put a very pretty web front on it and let people use their email address instead of their account number." But beneath the surface, Levchin said, PayPal's core innovations sparkled:

> The submerged part of PayPal is this massive, and very, very numerically driven risk management system which allows us to instantaneously tell when you're moving money to someone else, with a very high degree of certainty whether the money you're moving is yours, or whether you got it illegally and we might be on the hook later on to help the authorities investigate or retrieve the money.

Even PayPal's millions of dollars in bad transactions could be justified for the extensive data set they generated. "Losing a lot of money to fraud was a necessary byproduct in gathering the data needed to understand the problem and build good predictive models," Greenfield later wrote on a personal blog. "With millions of transactions and tens of thousands of fraudulent transactions, our fraud analytics team could find subtler patterns and detect fraud more accurately."

Taken together, PayPal turned fraud from an existential threat to one of the company's defining triumphs. It also had the unexpected benefit of thinning out the competition. "As the Russian mobsters got better and better," Thiel said, "they got better and better at destroying all our competitors." Thieves forced to work ever harder to fleece PayPal customers moved on to easier prey. "We'd also find that fraudsters were kind of lazy, right? They want to do just the least amount of work . . . So we just kind of hoped to push them off onto [our competitors]," Miller observed.

■ ■ ■

On December 19, 2000, Roelof Botha sent a note to several executives: Fraud costs, he could now report, were down almost $2 million in the span of a month—from October to November. In time, PayPal would achieve one of the lowest fraud rates in the financial services industry, reducing its fraud rate by several orders of magnitude by the end of 2001.

Anecdotal signals also testified to the company's fraud-fighting progress. In late 2000 and early 2001, Levchin, Miller, and other employees perused various Internet Relay Chat (IRC) channels that fraudsters frequented and noticed that functioning PayPal accounts were now a collector's item. As the company shut down bad actors' accounts, the few that survived were sold like commodities. "You could see like the cost of acquiring a PayPal account is going up and up, which we took to be a really good thing," Miller said. In 2001, the company purchased stolen PayPal accounts outright, simply to reverse engineer the fraud and better understand their opponents.

The team's fraud-fighting success earned its members recognition. Levchin notched a place on the 2002 prestigious, peer-reviewed "Innovators Under 35" list, compiled annually by the *MIT Technology Review*. Other honorees over the years have included Facebook founder Mark Zuckerberg, Google cofounders Larry Page and Sergey Brin, and Linux founder Linus Torvalds. For Levchin and Frezza's efforts on IGOR, they earned US Patent US7249094B2: a "system and method for depicting on-line transactions."

Frezza was awarded the patent posthumously. On December 18, 2001, three days after his final exams and just three weeks shy of his twenty-second birthday, Robert Frezza passed away following heart failure. His obituary in the *Stanford Daily* featured Frezza's time at PayPal and his work on IGOR prominently. "IGOR is one of the two or three main reasons that PayPal is not a busted dot-com but instead is at the top of the pack," McGrew told the paper.

Frezza's death hit his coworkers hard. "There was a lot of grieving when he passed," noted the team's chief recruiter, Tim Wenzel, "because everyone just adored him." PayPal invited grief counselors to the office, and Levchin flew to Lawrenceville, Pennsylvania, for Frezza's December 22 memorial service.

Sal Giambanco also suggested that the team compile a PayPal memory book for Frezza's parents and brother, and Levchin sent a company-wide request for anything "interesting, personal, funny, silly, whatever, that pertains to your work with Bobster."

Levchin delivered the book to them at the funeral, and the family was deeply touched. "I can say without exaggeration that no single thought, no single word, deed, or gesture has meant as much to us as the memory book put together by you all at PayPal," Bill Frezza wrote to the team. He noted that his late son had relished his PayPal tenure and "the challenge of proving himself to his talented, skeptical, and demanding colleagues."

"I knew Bob had achieved that state of grace known to the engineer operating at the peak of his capabilities," Frezza wrote. "Knowing that he experienced this profound joy in his very short life will forever be a comfort to me." A few weeks later, the Frezza family visited the PayPal office. Some years later, Levchin stood before an audience of start-up founders and referenced Frezza to make the case that inexperience was no barrier to impact.

16

USE THE FORCE

Just prior to Musk's departure, the product team launched a second effort to grow the company's revenue. Through a campaign called "the upsell," PayPal would encourage users—gently but firmly—to admit if they used PayPal for a business purpose. If they answered yes, the website would prompt them to upgrade to Business or Premier accounts.

The task of uniting the engineering, design, and business elements of the upsell fell primarily to two producers: Paul Martin and Eric Jackson. Jackson, another Thiel-recruited Stanford alum, had joined the company in late 1999. Originally assigned to work on marketing with Luke Nosek, Jackson later became a David Sacks disciple on the product team.

Paul Martin had been a Stanford track athlete and history major who had connected with Thiel through the *Stanford Review*. On a visit to the Confinity office, Martin "saw a really cool group of people that . . . had this wonderful . . . us-against-the-world mentality." Soon, Martin dropped out of Stanford to join Confinity as a marketing associate making $35,000 per year.

With the May launch of its original Business and Premier accounts, PayPal had abandoned its "always free" philosophy, but because it didn't force upgrades, the company faced limited backlash—and proved that it could generate revenue. "We succeeded where so many other companies failed, in what was considered to be the most difficult tasks in Silicon Valley at the time, which was getting people to pay for what was a previously free service," Martin said.

Now came the upsell, which would push these account upgrades further. The product team turned its collective attention to this campaign—and buckled in for a maelstrom of user fury. Martin understood better than most the vehemence of online auction users. In his role working on auction products, he had joined the various auction-related message boards and become a visible presence. "PayPal Paul," as he was known on eBay's Feedback Forum, AuctionWatch, and the Online Traders Web Alliance (OTWA), was also one of several PayPal employees savaged whenever PayPal.com experienced hiccups—perceived or otherwise.

He wasn't alone in this. eBay had also struggled with its users' outspokenness. When one of eBay's first employees, Mary Lou Song, designed new auction categories, she innocently lumped the "buttons" section in with "sewing collectibles." The designation seemed logical enough, but the auction boards seethed with rage. Journalist Adam Cohen captured the button affair in *The Perfect Store*, an early history of eBay's creation:

> Button collectors, a group whose existence had escaped her until now, excoriated her for being so ignorant about buttons. "Did you know there are vintage buttons, antique buttons, and modern buttons?" one irate button-seller lectured her. "That buttons don't belong in Sewing Collectibles? That they belong in their own button category? Did you know that you can have plastic buttons, or metal buttons? Did you mean pin-back buttons or did you mean four-hole buttons?"

Song conceded defeat and created a new category for buttons. *If McDonald's unveils a new sandwich*, Song told Cohen, *people just decide to buy it or not. They don't say, "Why didn't you talk to me?"* Both Song and Martin had come to recognize that, whether they liked it or not, the online auction community felt a peculiar sense of ownership over platforms and tools.

■ ■ ■

With the upsell, PayPal doubled down on its "always free" flip-flop, and the team knew they had to walk a tightrope with users. The company would pitch the upsell as a slight tweak to procedures—asking users who were already utilizing PayPal for a business purpose to simply designate themselves as businesses on the site. "*This is not a new policy*," the team wrote in talking points shared with employees, "just a reminder of an old policy."

Of course, users were unlikely to see it that way. eBay sellers on PayPal didn't typically consider themselves businesses. Most had no storefronts, no inventory, and no employees; they thought of themselves as hosts of virtual garage sales more than budding entrepreneurs.

The team wrote and rigorously edited the page that users would see when they logged on to PayPal.com. It asked the user to "reaffirm" what category they were, and cited the service's "terms of use," which required PayPal users engaged in commerce to register for a business account. Users were given three options:

- Upgrade to Business: for companies that sell online.
- Upgrade to Premier: for individuals who sell online on a part-time or full-time basis, or who simply want all of our best features.
- I am not a Seller: for individuals who use PayPal for non-business purposes only and wish to remain a Personal Account.

At first, the team opted to show the page to only the most prolific eBay sellers—whose high payment volume businesses should have led them to choose options 1 or 2 already. Their reaction to the choices would serve as an important signal.

The days leading up to the upsell launch at PayPal had the feel of a city preparing for a siege. The all-hands effort included engineering, design, product, and customer service. Sacks wrote the draft copy for the interstitial page, and the entire company was forewarned about the coming customer outcry. Employees were told to refer all media inquiries to the head of PR, Vince Sollitto, and to punt all customer service inquiries to Omaha.

"Let the upsells begin, and Godspeed . . . ," Jackson wrote the full team on September 12, 2000, the night before launch.

■ ■ ■

And then: impact. Users raged, and the auction boards exploded with criticism. "When I signed up with PayPal, PayPal said it was free and would remain free," user "kellyb1" wrote. "What they have done is dirty and sneaky. They pulled everyone in with promises of free accounts— 'Don't worry folks, we get our money from the float time.'" On Honesty .com, a site that provided services for auction sellers and whose users relied on PayPal, one customer angrily wrote, "Is it up to PayPal to determine whether or not I am a business? It would seem that is between me and the government."

PayPal employee Damon Billian's full-time job was to immerse himself in customer discussions. Each day, he sent the company an overview of message board sentiment, along with select quotations, both positive and negative. In his report on launch day, Billian had nothing cheerful to relay. The top five phrases and feelings about PayPal:

1. Bait and switch
2. Float
3. Liars (saying we would never forceably [sic] upgrade)
4. Smaller sellers are worried about the fees.
5. Some may make a "NO PAYPAL" logo for their sites.

Most days, Billian made it a point to address message board queries individually. That day, he was simply overwhelmed. "There are well over five hundred different items within OTWA alone and more than that in AuctionWatch," Billian told the team. "I can't even read all of the posts, much less get to most of the inquiries at this point in time." The Omaha phone lines also lit up with complaints.

Billian warned that user dissatisfaction looked to be slipping the confines of the message boards. "As a result of the changes / clickthrough page," Billian wrote, "I have had 4 reports of users going to the media and several commenting on contacting regulatory agencies." Customers copied the interstitial page text and shared it with tech reporters. Sites like CNET jumped on the criticism and ran stories.

The flood of user protest and negative press made for a wearying few days. But over time, the power of the company's network effect began to shine through. "The early results," Jackson reported in a company-wide note, "are encouraging."

Of the roughly 30,000 people who had seen the upsell page thus far, almost 20 percent had converted to fee-bearing accounts, a rate that surpassed the team's most optimistic projections. Perhaps more importantly, only a handful of users jumped ship. "Despite the ruckus on the message boards," the weekly company newsletter reported at the end of the upsell campaign, "there were only 158 users who actually closed their accounts (only 0.004% of our user base!)."

As a part of its messaging, PayPal emphasized that its service would be still the cheapest payment option available. As the company wrote on its mass email to customers:

> X.com is committed to keeping its PayPal service free for personal use. To remain a strong and viable business, however, we need sellers to accept their fair share of the costs of accepting credit cards. Visa and Mastercard charge us for every transaction we process, and we need to pass this fee on to sellers to break even.
>
> Other companies charge twice as much—a $50 payment with X.com costs $1.20; with Billpoint the cost is $2.34; and BidPay charges $5.00. Don't be fooled by promotional offers from unproven services—no one else can offer instant, safe, and fraud-protected payments on a sustainable basis to online sellers at a cheaper price.

Users echoed the company's pricing message in public. One poster, who went by the name "waspstar," wrote, "So, the time has finally come . . . PayPal is no longer free for eBay sellers." Still, despite apparent misgivings about the switch, he admitted that he wasn't about to quit PayPal. "I'll still stick with them," he wrote. "Cheaper than others, I guess."

The September 2000 upsell yielded a powerful data point: "We found that the pricing was completely inelastic," explained Thiel. "As we increased prices, none of our customers could leave. People said, 'We refuse to pay,' and they left, and there is no other place they could get paid online so they came back." For the team, this episode offered a vital lesson in user behavior and switching costs. They realized that once embedded in users' lives, dislodging a product or service took meaningful effort. "Human beings are creatures of momentum," observed Amy Rowe Klement, "and finding ways to change the default (behaviors, thinking, narrative, etc.) can result in massive change."

■ ■ ■

The upsell campaign relied on forthrightness, rather than any enforcement mechanisms. "We ask sellers who currently have a Personal Account to play by the rules and upgrade to either a Premier or Business Account," the team wrote. "We count on your honesty when we give you the choice of an account type."

With no penalties attached, a PayPal user could still decide to flout the rules and opt to use the service just as they had before. The company told its employees that they had no plans for enforcement, but that they would reevaluate that position if users didn't upgrade to Premier and Business accounts rapidly enough.

By September 2000, that time had come. From May to September, over 200,000 PayPal customers had registered for Premier and Business Accounts—but that wasn't enough to cure the company's balance sheet woes. The collective account fees didn't cover fraud, overhead, or credit card payments and chargebacks—a still onerous cost category. Despite its efforts to transition users to bank account–funded transactions, by early September 2000, almost 70 percent of payments on PayPal were still backstopped by credit cards. "We were always eating away at the frankly fundamental flaws in the original business idea," Klement observed. "PayPal started off as a product with no use case. Then we had a use case but no business model. Then we had to build a sustainble business."

For now, PayPal remained a money-losing enterprise, with its paying users accounting for less than 10 percent of the company's total user base. The company would have to take a more forceful tack to both upgrade users to fee-bearing accounts *and* shift its transaction mix away from expensive credit card–funded payments. In other words, PayPal would no longer be able to nudge users to simply "play by the rules"—it would now have to step in as referee and enforce them.

The PayPal product had grown fast because of its permissiveness—in everything from distributing bonus money, to tolerating fraud, to underwriting small-dollar buyers and sellers by covering credit card fees. Now came the "forced upgrade"—a move that represented the riskiest change in the product to date.

The company would require that business users abide by its policies and upgrade their accounts, and it would simultaneously convert customers away from credit card–funded transactions to bank account–funded and internally funded ones. Some employees jokingly referred to the "forced upgrade" as the "FU"—a recognition that this was the most controversial shift in its relationship with customers and one that risked their wrath.

This move prompted a fresh round of worry within the company. "The forced upgrade was frickin' terrifying," Klement recalled, chuckling. "We didn't know what was going to happen." Would the almost 20,000 new users joining PayPal each day suddenly vanish? Or worse, would Billpoint and eBay—who had charged fees from the get-go—just undercut PayPal on price to win users? To the product and executive teams, the forced upgrade would either solve the fundamental business riddle—or reveal the limits of PayPal users' price insensitivity.

Much later, internet companies could turn to established bodies of research on "freemium" pricing models. Answers to the vexing questions of when to charge, how much to charge, and how to levy charges emerged through well-developed case studies and examples. But the word *freemium* didn't exist until 2006—and in this, as in much else, the team relied on instinct, improvisation, and iteration to find answers.

PayPal executives appreciated that a forced upgrade—more than any other decision so far—risked triggering an avalanche of user defections, so internal debates raged as the team wrestled with the mechanics of the change. A key insight developed during this period: PayPal had to time the upgrade process—something users didn't want to do—with something that users couldn't help doing. Thus, the team arrived at the concept that underpinned the forced upgrade: they would tie the upgrade to the receipt of money.

During the forced upgrade, Personal Account users would be restricted to a maximum of $500 in received payments via credit card over a six-month period. If a user exceeded that amount, they could still receive payments—but could only access the money in their accounts if they upgraded to Premier or Business accounts. "We figured no one ever wants to reject a payment from a customer," Martin explained during an appearance on *The Investor Show* podcast. "That was the beauty of it. We did not give anyone a choice of whether or not they wanted to be a business account. We made them choose whether or not they wanted to accept a payment."

PayPal also established a workaround: If the recipient of the money had hit the $500 limit but still wanted the payment, they could request that the sender reissue their funds—from a bank account or from their PayPal account. The company would then put money recipients in the position of forcing other users to make the change to bank account–funded and internal balance transactions.

With both outcomes, PayPal would win—either by forcing the recipient to upgrade to a fee-bearing account or by shifting the payer to a cheaper transaction type.

■ ■ ■

On October 3, 2000, the company sent a notice to its most active Personal Account users:

Starting two weeks from now, on Monday, October 16, X.com will introduce a new limit on PayPal Personal Accounts: a $500 limit on receiving credit card payments every six months. Following the implementation of the policy two weeks from now, Personal Accounts exceeding the $500 limit will no longer be able to accept credit card payments unless they choose to upgrade to a Premier or Business Account. Credit card payments sent to a Personal Account in excess of the limit will be held as "pending" until the recipient chooses either to accept the payment by upgrading or to return it to the sender by refusing the payment. (The sender can then resend the payment from either a bank account or existing PayPal balance.)

In its communications during this period, the company let users into its thinking—on the theory that candor would help quiet discontent.

We promised users that we would work to develop a policy that met several criteria: (1) it was generally fair and reasonable; (2) it was announced with two weeks' notice before it was implemented; (3) it did not force anyone to upgrade (though it could remove costly functionality, such as the ability to accept credit card payments, from Personal Accounts); and (4) it met PayPal's need to align the costs of credit card processing (and other expenses, such as customer service and fraud protection) with high-volume users who generate the bulk of our costs.

Still, the messaging contained a bit of rhetorical craftiness; the company effectively left users with no option but to upgrade. "The truth is it wasn't forced. You had a choice," David Sacks reiterated, not straying far from the script. "But if you wanted to keep using PayPal, you had to upgrade."

Predictably, the Omaha customer service lines and the message boards lit up once again with fiery complaints. "[PayPal] gave it away for free," one user wrote, "until they got us hooked and then started charging." "I'm very disappointed with this company," another grumbled. "To think I helped sell you, promote you, build you up, and then you do this to us? You should be ashamed."

Users fumed that the forced upgrade would cut into their revenue and that it ran blatantly afoul of the company's "always free" promise. "I am done with PayPal for good. Period. They have set their policy and I don't agree with it so my decision is to NOT use it," wrote one user. PayPal employees fretted as talk of boycotts and embargoes swept the message boards.

PayPal defenders emerged as well. "Protest all you want to, but I think you are going to be very lonely while doing it," one user argued. "I have spoke [*sic*] with so many people lately about all this, all eBay sellers, and most reasonable people agree that if this is what it takes to keep PayPal in business we are all for it. Of course people are not happy about the fees. By all means protest, I think you are cutting off your nose to spite your face."

Others could even see the company's perspective. "What on Earth is all the negativity around paypal about?" one user wrote. "They're fantastic. . . . My business has been boosted considerably, in both ease of accepting payments and deposits to my account. . . . What other service comes close? None I can think of." Another pointed out that because PayPal had better market penetration than rivals, using it led to higher bids on auctions. "Yes the new fees are crummy," a user wrote, "but it is true that bids are higher [when I accept PayPal] I figured they more than offset the fees. I will continue with PayPal and will continue to suggest it to fellow auctioneers."

Ethical questions nagged at the forced upgrade campaign. On the one hand, the company had reneged on an explicit promise. The about-face bothered users, particularly after the PowerSeller community had advanced PayPal's interests by advertising its service on their listings. The company had also designed its upgrade gate in such a way that a failure to upgrade could cost users money—the sender of a payment wouldn't necessarily know whether the recipient had upgraded or had hit the $500 limit.

On the other hand, PayPal was a company, not a charity. The shift in transaction mix away from credit cards was crucial to its survival, as was generating revenue on its core product. The company also hadn't opted to shut down the free tap all at once—the company had moved from optional upgrades, to gently encouraged ones, to forced changes, all phased in over the course of six months. What's more, had PayPal not taken these steps, the company risked having to shut down its payments product entirely—a disastrous outcome for all involved, not least auction buyers and sellers.

Over the years, these product design dilemmas dogged other companies that chose to wade into the choppy waters of freemium models. Such models enabled the proliferation of exciting new technologies—while earning unfuzzy feelings from users, who felt like frogs in a slow boil. A blogger captured this schizophrenia: "Freemium developers act just like cocaine dealers," he wrote. "They give the basic services for free and charge you when you ask for more." Then, mere paragraphs later, the writer acknowledged the model's adoption power: "The onset of the freemium model is probably the best thing that has ever happened to the world wide web."

Within a single month of the campaign's late October launch, 95 percent of targeted personal accounts had upgraded to either Business or Premier status. This proved a critical piece of PayPal's leap to a full-fledged business—and a stark end to the "always free" promise that had launched Confinity's PayPal into the world.

■ ■ ■

Besides the brief media flurry around the upsell campaign, the company's fall 2000 iterations were not widely covered in the press. The team preferred it that way, of course, assuming that the less was written about IGOR or the company's pricing strategy, the better.

But internally, the team understood the importance of the fall's iterations and improvements—particularly on the underlying transaction mix, a vexing problem baked into the PayPal model from the very start. Throughout late October and early November, Eric Jackson dutifully distributed line charts showing the blue line (bank and balance payments) rising and the red line (credit card payments) falling. On November 2, Jackson sent the graphs with a celebratory subject line: "It's finally happened—the lines have crossed!!!" Bank account and PayPal account–funded payments now matched credit card–funded ones.

Shortly thereafter, the company reached two other milestones. "On Friday, November 24, we processed our *$1 billionth dollar through the Pay-Pal system*," declared the writer of that week's *Weekly Pal*. "We're working with some huge numbers here, but we're not done yet. Of course we would never slow down until we reach the ultimate goal of World Domination!" And on December 8, 2000, PayPal inched closer to that goal, notching its five millionth registered account.

Coming at the tail end of a year's worth of internal turmoil and amid a steep stock market slide, these events gave employees confidence that PayPal might avoid the downdrafts claiming other dot-coms. Internal crises like website downtime began to feel less apocalyptic and more manageable. In November, when the PayPal site seized up for a lengthy period, the internal update testified to the team's growing self-belief:

> The bad news is the PayPal website has been suffering from really bad performance problems all morning today. You might even say we've been down for 7 hours.
>
> The good news is that this is a high-class problem that only the most successful websites can have. We're getting more users this morning than our network load balancing equipment can handle.

The outages still caused panicky all-nighters, but unlike in the early months, the company felt users were more forgiving. At this point, they needed PayPal as much as PayPal needed them.

PayPal also earned its share of public acclaim. In November 2000, *GQ* named PayPal its "website of the month," and *US News & World Report* included PayPal on its "best of the web" list. In October 2000, PayPal leadership attended the *Wired* magazine Rave Awards ceremony at the Regency Center in San Francisco. With red carpets and rotating spotlights, the event featured guest presenters like David Spade, Courtney

Love, Thomas Dolby, and San Francisco mayor Willie Brown, as well as a performance by the rock artist Beck.

PayPal had been nominated for *Wired*'s "Best Guerrilla Marketing Campaign," and while it lost to the music service Napster, the nomination itself spoke volumes. PayPal also ended up with the last laugh. "Napster ended up sweeping in all 3 categories they were nominated for," the company newsletter observed. "Speculations abound that [Napster] may have been receiving sympathy votes, as a Federal judge's recent ruling will likely put them out of business by year's end!" Following copyright-infringement suits from various recording industry groups, Napster indeed shut down operations in July 2001.

PayPal had now become a fixture in the digital firmament, allowing the perpetual stomach knots of its founders to loosen somewhat. The team celebrated accordingly. David Sacks took the product unit on a rafting retreat, which he had promised he would do if "the lines crossed"—referring to the blue and red payment mix indicators. Once-circumscribed luxuries began to appear: the office now had company-wide parties and enjoyed in-office massages and Jamba Juice smoothies.

On Halloween 2000, team members arrived at the office in costumes. "Our very own Peter Thiel was seen in an Obi-Wan Kenobi costume," the weekly newsletter reported. The newsletter expressed a touch of disappointment that Luke Nosek had not appeared dressed as Luke Skywalker, as he had apparently promised. Instead, the newsletter observed, Nosek attended the Halloween party dressed as a member of the mafia.

17

CRIME IN PROGRESS

Vasily Gorshkov and Alexey Ivanov went by the hacker code names "Kvakin" and "Subbsta," respectively. Living in Chelyabinsk, Russia, they had become adept at targeting US financial firms—stealing their customers' credit card and bank account information, then purchasing goods with them. The items were shipped to drop sites in nearby Kazakhstan, Georgia, and other former Soviet satellite states. The goods became virtually untraceable after traversing borders and time zones, and Gorshkov and Ivanov resold them for a profit.

The twenty-something hackers also ran a separate hustle, one they hoped would lead to a legitimate living in the tech industry. The two would hack into corporate computer systems, send the company evidence of the break-in, and offer their "security consulting services." Word of this side business had apparently gotten around, because in the summer of 2000, Gorshkov and Ivanov received an inquiry from a US-based company called Invita Security, which sought them out to reverse-engineer protections against hackers.

Invita offered to fly the pair to Seattle to talk things through in person. Gorshkov and Ivanov had heard stories of black-hat hackers becoming well-paid white-hat security experts, and a contract gig with Invita Security sounded promising. The trip from west-central Russia to Seattle took thirty hours, and the pair arrived in the US on November 10, 2000.

They were picked up and driven to the headquarters of Invita Security, a nearby office park. Driving from the airport, Ivanov was astonished that Americans obeyed traffic laws. "Why do you people drive so peace-fully?" he asked one of his hosts. "In Russia . . . we step on it the moment the light changes. . . . In Russia, it [is] common to see people drive on the sidewalk to get where they want."

Once they arrived at the Invita Security office, Ivanov remotely logged into his personal computer (left at home in Russia) and demon-strated the techniques he had used to break into US systems. His hosts were impressed. When asked for details about how the pair had accessed credit card information, Gorshkov seemed cagey. "This kind of question is better discussed in Russia," he said. When Invita executives asked them if they ever worried about the FBI, Gorshkov shrugged it off. "We don't think about the FBI at all," he said, "because they can't get us in Russia."

Once the demo was over, Gorshkov and Ivanov piled into a company van to go to their hotel for the night. As the van pulled into the hotel parking lot, the driver suddenly slammed on the brakes. The van door swung open, and a voice yelled out, "FBI! . . . Get out of the car with your hands behind your back!"

Gorshkov and Ivanov were surrounded by armed, windbreaker-clad federal agents. The two were hustled out of the van and cuffed while the agents read the pair their Miranda rights in English and handed them a piece of paper with the Russian translation.

■ ■ ■

To ensnare Gorshkov and Ivanov, the FBI sting—code-named "Opera-tion Flyhook"—used Invita Security, a phony company, staffed by "exec-utives" who were actually undercover FBI special agents Michael Schuler and Marty Prewett. The computer Gorshkov and Ivanov used to show off their hacking skills was equipped with a "sniffer" program that logged each keystroke, and audio-video equipment in the room recorded their every utterance and movement. Once Gorshkov signed into his com-puter in Russia, federal agents downloaded a multi-gigabyte treasure trove of his hacking exploits.

As documented in Steve Schroeder's *The Lure*, Gorshkov and Iva-nov were prolific. Together, they had compromised nearly forty US companies, including Western Union—from whose website they had stolen nearly 16,000 credit card numbers—and a website called CD Universe, from which they had taken another 350,000 numbers. The prosecutor assigned to their case observed that Gorshkov's "hacking skills were top notch." One forensics expert described the pair as "some of the best system integrators [he had] ever seen."

The archive also revealed what the prosecutors dubbed Gorshkov and Ivanov's "massive scheme" to defraud PayPal. The two generated hundreds of phony PayPal accounts and fake eBay accounts. Then they'd set up live auctions, pay for them with stolen credit cards, and move the money from account to account without sending any actual goods. What looked to PayPal like an ordinary transaction was, in fact, a complicated operation to convert stolen credit card numbers into cash.

They'd also use the stolen credit cards to bid on live auctions—with bots doing the bidding. "Ivanov's and Gorshkov's scheme was both elaborate and impressive: credit card numbers were stolen from PayPal accounts, acquired through well-crafted phishing attacks," Ray Pompon, a cybersecurity expert connected to the case, wrote. "Then, these credit card numbers were used by bots to purchase goods in eBay auctions. Goods purchased from eBay were shipped to Russia for resale." PayPal's losses totaled nearly $1.5 million.

Ivanov and Gorshkov defrauded non-eBay vendors who accepted PayPal as well. In one instance, they ordered various pieces of hardware from a computer parts seller. When the seller sent the invoice, Gorshkov and Ivanov paid for it using a stolen credit card routed through PayPal. The seller then shipped the goods to an address in Kazakhstan, where Gorshkov bribed customs agents to ferry the goods into Russia.

■■■

Special Agent Prewett called PayPal to relay what the FBI had found. On the other end of the call was John Kothanek, PayPal's senior security investigator. Kothanek had a unique background for a tech company: He started his career as a military intelligence officer in the Marine Corps.

"When I had gotten back from the Gulf War," Kothanek said, "I bought a computer. And I spent a gob of money on this 486 DX. And from the first 3.5-inch disc I put in there, I was addicted. It struck a chord in my head." For his budding nerdiness, Kothanek took some grief from his fellow Marines. "All my buddies were bagging on me. They were like, 'Jeez. Computers. That's never gonna go anywhere. Nobody cares about computers,'" he recalled.

After the Marines, Kothanek worked at Macy's as an internal investigator. He then received a tip from a friend at eBay that X.com and Confinity were joining forces—and might need someone who could liaise between the companies and law enforcement.

Soon after joining PayPal, Kothanek found himself facing a language barrier. Writing to the entire company, Kothanek searched for help: "Does anyone at X.com speak/read Russian? I am working an organized crime thing that has some Russian ties. In my search for clues I would like to have someone look at email addresses and tell me if they mean anything. DESPERATION!!!" Responses came back swiftly to the still-new-to-X.com Kothanek. "They were like, 'Max does. Don't you know that?!' And I was like, 'I have no idea who the hell Max is.' And so next thing I know, this guy with glasses comes into my cube," Kothanek recalled.

The odd couple of Levchin and Kothanek teamed up and corresponded with Russian fraudsters, with Kothanek guiding the tone and Levchin translating. "I'd say, 'Well, this is how I would reply to him. Let's just kick him in the nuts a little bit. Let's, you know, let's piss these guys off.' And Max was like, 'Okay,' and so he would, in my email address, type something out in Ukrainian and send it back to them. And then, sure enough, the next day, I'd get an email back." So began Kothanek and Levchin's "bizarre rapport" with PayPal's Russian fraudsters.

■ ■ ■

Kothanek had known about Ivanov and Gorshkov—though not by those names. Kothanek, Levchin, and others at PayPal knew them as "Greg Stivenson" and "Murat Nasirov." Kothanek's spreadsheet cataloging the pair's exploits against PayPal had grown to 10,796 transactions. After the

FBI contacted him, Kothanek emailed the agents: "I must say you guys definitely made my decade with that news yesterday. I have worked and obsessed over this group for the last 10 months."

Like Igor, "Greg Stivenson" had emerged as a particularly irksome PayPal nemesis. When first squaring off against him, Kothanek and the fraud team had simply shut down accounts with the "Stivenson" last name and wrote to the user's email address letting him know. The offender, Ivanov, wrote back to Kothanek: "You think you got me? Look at this." Thousands more fraudulent accounts were opened the same day.

In mid-October, Kothanek wrote to tell him that PayPal had caught him in the act:

> *Kothanek:* Hey buddy me again . . . Some of our customers say you have been emailing them asking for your shipments. Guess what they aren't coming. SO basically if you don't get a shipment it is because we stopped it Better luck next time.
>
> *Stivenson:* Are you here or this is NULL email address? Please reply i want talk with you about your security.
>
> *Kothanek:* how about let's talk about your fraud activity on our system.

Here, and throughout his correspondence, Stivenson fished for paid security work. "I can stop my activities with PayPal," he once told Kothanek. "I can sell this complete system to third parties." In one lengthy message to Levchin written in Russian, Stivenson again offered his security services, shared some of his tradecraft, and mocked the efforts to thwart him:

> Hello. You probably already understand that we have an entire system worked out here to pay for goods via PayPal.
>
> It may seem strange but more time is spent on the analysis and evaluation of the human factor (precisely because of it I can work via PayPal, so that, for example, nobody has been able to countermand human filth.) Your steps in defense of the company can be viewed as several steps forward.

In addition, we begin on the assumption that the basic mass of people are legal users and therefore after each and every change I simply try to act in such a way that your system also thinks that I'm a legal user.

With regard to your latest change, in the very near future such changes will take place on other Internet sites (stores, banks, etc.). A change like that will only win you some time (I think not more than 2 months.)

Now with regard to questions of security, I can help, but all security questions will be decided not by a mere "thank you," because a "thank you" does not put food in your mouth. Meanwhile everybody does their own thing . . . You yours, I my own. I hope you understand me well.

With best wishes.

The cat-and-mouse game persisted. PayPal would try to stop Stivenson, and Stivenson would find a way to break through the company's defenses. He'd also taunt them. "Screw you, American bastards," he once wrote to the team. "I'll be back."

"They were blatant," Kothanek told CNN. "They thought we couldn't touch them because they were in Russia." Levchin would later tell a journalist that he began to take Stivenson's jeers personally. "I am the impenetrable Russian," Levchin told the *San Francisco Chronicle*. "The rules of engagement are clear. They try to steal and I stop them." The team was able to stop him on occasion. Levchin and Kothanek remembered the pride they felt when they told Stivenson to try and break the Gausebeck-Levchin CAPTCHA—and he couldn't.

■ ■ ■

Not all thieves were in distant time zones. Once, the company discovered a talented fraudster living mere miles from its office. The team gathered a catalogue of his exploits and even allowed the fraud to continue so that law enforcement would have time to do its work. "We got all the evidence necessary to file a criminal conviction and gave it to the Secret

Service and the FBI. And they're like, 'Well, this is going to take figuring out which jurisdiction he's in,'" Musk remembered. "And it's like, 'For the love of God, he's stealing money right now! Here's his address! Here's what he looks like! Here's all the evidence!'. . . Crime in progress! . . . Finally, two or three months later, they went and arrested him. It took forever."

Though often frustrating and time-consuming, the company hoped to work with law enforcement to establish deterrent measures. "Getting the government to actually arrest somebody was important," explained Musk. "Because if nobody's actually getting arrested, then people just keep doing fraud, by one means or another. Word gets out real quick in the fraud community. 'Okay, PayPal's arresting people, so maybe think twice about it.'"

Melanie Cervantes, a fraud analyst, remembered reaching out to law enforcement in various states—and receiving confused responses. "We started out . . . like, 'Hey, this is PayPal, we've, you know, been a victim of financial crime of a guy who's in your jurisdiction.' And they would say, 'PayPal? What's that?'" Even when the team could pique law enforcement interest, Cervantes recalled, officials weren't sure how to classify digital crimes and whether they constituted money laundering, access device fraud, wire fraud, or money transmission errors. "We would reach US attorneys, and they would say, 'I think a crime has occurred, but no law exists to prosecute it,'" Cervantes remembered.

Thus, the FBI's efforts on the Ivanov and Gorshkov case represented a welcome change. Days after the FBI contacted the company about Operation Flyhook, a PayPal delegation—including Kothanek, Levchin, Erik Klein, and Sarah Imbach (PayPal's SVP for Customer Service Operations and Fraud)—sat at a conference table in Seattle with the FBI agents. The agents walked them through the details they had discovered in the sting.

The FBI and PayPal began collaborating on the case. "We were able to establish a link between their machine's IP address, the credit cards they were using in our system and the Perl scripts they were using to open accounts on our system," Kothanek recalled. The team discovered that Ivanov and Gorshkov were behind paypai.com—the PayPal impersonator website.

While PayPal was glad to have the government on the case, the media generated by the effort wasn't always welcome. When the prosecution filed its affidavit in federal court, a Seattle newspaper ran a story about the case. In it, they mistakenly claimed that PayPal's was among the credit card databases breached by Ivanov and Gorshkov. The two had used stolen credit cards *on* PayPal—not *from* PayPal—and to Levchin, the difference was night and day. The former, Levchin knew, was a problem the company could finesse; the latter risked eroding faith in PayPal's security.

Levchin was, by the prosecutor's account, "appropriately furious," and pressed the Department of Justice to correct the record. The prosecutor called the reporter, explained the error, and got a correction printed in the following day's paper.

■ ■ ■

The newspaper dustup spoke to one of Levchin's core tenets: no matter what else happened—the scuffles with eBay, the agonizing downtime, the volume of customer complaints—no hacker should ever be able to penetrate PayPal's systems and obtain personal information. "The development team was very in sync on values," David Gausebeck recalled. "About the standard we should build to, especially around security and guarantees of correctness, it was, 'Of course we have to make sure that this is bulletproof.'"

The "impenetrable Russian" had come to feel that the financial services industry didn't take information security seriously enough. Levchin and his team had closely studied the industry's cybersecurity standards and came away underwhelmed. If the PayPal system was to be truly secure, hitting those marks wouldn't be nearly enough. "There were standards already about how you're *supposed* to secure them, but they covered maybe one-tenth of the way that an adversary could attack your system," engineer Bob McGrew recalled. "The work at PayPal was unstructured, but it was actually really high quality. It was done by people who actually cared about achieving a truly secure system, rather than a team of people who cared about adhering to the protocol standard for securing credit cards safely."

Levchin also recognized that PayPal would be held to a higher standard. PayPal had no ATMs or public branches; the "PayPal brand" was its website. A hack of the site would be the equivalent of robbers hitting every local bank branch of a brick-and-mortar institution at the same time. "Wells Fargo had a competing bill payment system thing. But they weren't going to go away if they got hacked," McGrew explained. "At PayPal, any computer security issue was just absolutely an existential threat."

The team built internal safeguards in addition to external ones. "We had protections against fraud being done by our fraud analysts," McGrew recalled. Huey Lin helped to build the company's "permissioning" tools. In the company's early days, she recalled, "everybody and their cousin" had access to sensitive information. Over time, PayPal tightened these controls, so that even a C-level executive at the company could not access PayPal users' credit card information directly. The master password morphed into a shared, intricate system—any access attempts alerted all the other executives simultaneously and automatically. In the world of digital security, no one could be trusted—not even the company's founders and leaders.

Colin Corbett joined the team in 2001 as a network architect. He helped to revamp the PayPal data center. In that capacity, he constructed a three-tiered network architecture with an elaborate sequence of safeguards that became progressively more difficult as someone burrowed closer to the system's core, "to the point that, you know, the people administering the systems didn't like how it worked in some cases because it was so onerous."

In addition to the "logical segmentation" of the network, the company implemented "physical segmentation." Certain network boxes "would actually reside in separate physically locked cabinets," Corbett recalled. Access to the company's core infrastructure was only granted after a security engineer successfully passed through "five physical palm print readers." Once your handprint was verified five times over, Corbett noted, an engineer still needed "a unique eight-digit code to actually get into the cabinet."

In addition to formal safeguards, the company also had informal methods to secure information. An employee who made the mistake of leaving a laptop unattended would be subjected to a "burn." Another employee would hijack their machine and send a humiliating email to the entire company, posing as the laptop owner.

Over time, burns became legendary, with employees preparing them well in advance. "This was so elaborate," recalled Kim-Elisha Proctor, herself the occasional victim. "The engineers were really into this. They were constantly watching, and they would have emails ready. You leave your desk, and if [your computer] was unlocked, they'd email you the burn, run to your desk, take that burn, and then email it out to the list. And you're like, *Oh shit*."

Despite the company's emphasis on security, it wasn't immune to *oh shit* moments. On one such occasion, Levchin experienced the horror of accidentally deleting the company's master pay credential encryption key—all while trying to implement an elegant scheme to better protect it. "Without access to payment credentials," Levchin wrote on his personal blog, two decades after the incident, "PayPal doesn't really have a business per se, seeing how we are supposed to facilitate payments, and that's really hard to do if we no longer have access to the 100+ million credit card numbers our users added over the last year of insane growth."

This near-disaster stemmed from a catastrophic bug introduced into the PayPal codebase. Years earlier, Levchin had learned about a secret sharing scheme called Shamir Secret Sharing. Created by renowned Israeli cryptographer and computer scientist Adi Shamir, the basic concept was to split an important secret—like PayPal's credential encryption key—so it couldn't be known by one person but could be reconstructed if enough people combined their pieces, in the spirit of simultaneously turning keys to launch a missile.

Levchin decided Shamir's scheme was the perfect solution to add an extra level of security to PayPal's databases. The team would split the master encryption key into pieces—known as "shards"—and assign one to each of eight engineers, with any three required to reconstruct it. Each owner would encrypt their shard with a long, secure passphrase, the better to fortify the system. In testing, the improved security measures worked as designed, and the team briefly took the site down late one evening in order to implement the new-and-improved system. "We were finally going to close out the last vulnerability and be secure," Levchin recalled.

Except that, upon deployment, the system failed. It was three o'clock in the morning at PayPal headquarters when the head of database administration carefully entered his elaborate passphrase at his keyboard for the fifth time. The green-on-black console displayed: *"Sorry, one or more wrong passphrases. Can't reconstruct the key. Goodbye."*

"Minutes passed, confusion grew, tension rose rapidly," Levchin recalled. Engineer James Hogan jumped on a desk and half-jokingly implored everyone to start brute force hacking the key, testing every combination possible to crack it—a desperate strategy with almost no chance of success. To compound the crisis, Levchin realized with horror that the team had overwritten the original, real key during deployment. The PayPal master database was still running, but effectively useless without the proper master key to access its data.

At that moment, Levchin feared the end of PayPal. "After half a decade of trying to make something of myself (instead of just going to work for Microsoft or IBM after graduation)," he wrote, "I had just destroyed my first successful startup in the most spectacular fashion."

Levchin's own correct passphrase errored out, too. But then, per Levchin's recounting, came a slightly different result from one of the passphrases:

Finally, the last person . . . entered his passphrase. No error. The key still did not reconstruct correctly, I got the "Goodbye", but something worked. I turned to the engineer and said, "What did you just type in that worked?"

After a second of embarrassed mumbling, he admitted to choosing "a$$word" as his passphrase. The gall! I asked everyone entrusted with the grave task of relaunching crytposerv to pick really hard to

guess passphrases, and this guy . . . ?! Still, this was something—it
worked. But why?!

Levchin demanded the others' passphrases. All failed, but "a$$word"
succeeded. Then it dawned on Levchin: The encryption box ran on the
enterprise operating system Solaris, while his test computer used Linux.
At the time, Solaris automatically truncated passphrases over eight char-
acters, and thus, all the long, clever passphrases Levchin made everyone
pick had become useless stubs on the Solaris encryption box.

All except for "a$$word."

Panic gave way to progress. "The rest was an exercise in high-speed
coding and some entirely off-protocol file moving," Levchin wrote, "We
reconstructed the master key on my machine (all of our passphrases
worked fine), copied the file to the Solaris-running cryptoserv, re-split
it there (with very short passphrases), reconstructed it successfully, and
PayPal was up and running again like nothing ever happened."

As the office thrummed with activity in the early hours of the morning, Levchin dozed on his cubicle floor. His colleagues had no idea that
the company had narrowly escaped disaster thanks to luck, an anxious
all-nighter, and the resilience of "a$$word" against Solaris truncation.

■ ■ ■

As fraud grew, so did PayPal's fraud-fighting team. Before joining
the company, Cervantes had been working fraud cases for a Visa card
processor—a job she found stultifying. There, she began to notice a new
Palo Alto firm coming up repeatedly on her fraud reports. Cervantes
decided on a bold move. "If you're someone who investigates fraud for a
living, you need to go where the fraud is . . . So I reached out to [PayPal]
and I basically—I don't know where I got the cojones from—but I was
like, 'You guys have a lot of fraud. And I know that because I charge you
back all the time. So it seems like you need help.'"

Fraud fighters at PayPal witnessed some of humanity's worst actors.
Jeremy Roybal had come to Confinity by way of a temp agency. He
proved himself an ace customer service rep, but once customer service

migrated to Omaha, he needed a new role. "Kothanek pulled me off the scrap heap," Roybal recalled, "and said 'I want you to be a fraud analyst.'"

In that capacity, Roybal assembled catalogues of information to fulfill subpoena requests for law enforcement agencies—a bruising exposure to the dark side of PayPal's user base. He recalled compiling spreadsheets for child pornography purchases. "That hurt . . . [E]ach one of those lines is a sale or purchase of some horrible, horrible stuff," he remembered. Once, after testifying in court, Roybal returned to his hotel room and sobbed. "It would break you down," he said.

Despite their encounters with criminality and depravity, Cervantes, Kothanek, Roybal, and others on PayPal's fraud team cited the experience as a professional high point, in part because of their direct role in defending vulnerable people, but also because PayPal's inventive fraudsters pushed the fraud team to be forward-thinking. Given its advanced tools and techniques, PayPal was frequently able to identify malfeasance before banks or credit card companies. Digital crime-fighting "was very empowering and fulfilling," recalled Roybal. He and his colleagues felt like "modern-day superheroes."

Roybal and his colleagues were further buoyed by their fellow "superheroes"—including the law enforcement officials they met, who, over time, became important allies in bringing the online world's bad actors to justice. Roybal vividly remembered a call he placed to an officer in Arkansas. "'Sir, I believe there's someone scamming an elder person,' and it was so refreshing. He was like, 'Not in my county!' And boom, go get 'em."

Roybal stayed with the company for eight years; Cervantes for fourteen. "You know when you meet magnanimous, charismatic, genius people that you want to be around them?" Cervantes asked. "That's kind of how everybody felt in the office." John Kothanek, who now oversees global investigations for the cryptocurrency exchange Coinbase, echoed her sentiment. "I was just hooked," he admitted. "Wild horses could not have drug me out of that profession."

Even Levchin could look back on that which almost killed the company as a formative part of his PayPal experience. He recalled an infamous email he had written to Musk bearing the subject line: "Fraud is love," a sardonic inside joke. "In retrospect," he offered, "it was more than a joke. I've actually really gotten to like [fraud fighting.] It's the closest thing you can get to cloak and dagger. I'm a closeted, fanatic reader of spy novels, and this is the closest you can get to spy craft if you're a fintech nerd."

The fraud team also served as a reminder that for all of PayPal's advancements in algorithmic and automated fraud fighting, technology companies still needed flesh-and-blood human beings to deliver last-mile protection. "Fraud catching is a combination of people, machine learning, and automated rules," Cervantes noted. "People will always be a component of that. Always. Because there's an element of human behavior that bots just cannot quite emulate."

■ ■ ■

The FBI agents and prosecutors from the Ivanov-Gorshkov case paid regular visits to PayPal, and they made combatting "PayPal fraud" a federal priority. PayPal's collaboration with the FBI marked an ironic turning point in the company's history: When Confinity had originally launched, it flirted with starting a universal digital currency free from government shackles. Now, the same team sat elbow-to-elbow with FBI agents, helping them prosecute financial crimes.

"I think the big turning point was when we got to the point where we could call somebody up in a state, whether it's the FBI field offices or the Secret Service field office and say, 'Man, have I got a case for you,' and they would pick up the phone and they would listen to us," Kothanek recalled.

The road cut both ways. The FBI agents in the Ivanov and Gorshkov case requested that both Kothanek and Levchin testify at the trial, and Kothanek agreed to take the witness stand. He walked the court through Ivanov and Gorshkov's PayPal-based schemes, including their creation of paypai.com and the stolen credit card racket. The lead attorney in the case read Ivanov's lengthy "food in your mouth" email aloud to the jury.

Both Ivanov and Gorshkov were charged with multiple counts, including conspiracy, computer fraud, hacking, and extortion. Ivanov pleaded guilty and served an almost four-year prison term; Gorshkov stood trial and was sentenced to three years. These cases became landmark ones in the emerging field of cybersecurity litigation, and the FBI agents involved earned the prestigious Director's Award for excellence in investigation.

In retaliation, Russia sued the FBI, alleging that the bureau had illegally accessed Ivanov's and Gorshkov's computers, and in 2002, the Russian government opened a criminal case against Special Agent Schuler. The news splashed across the front page of the *Moscow Times*.

After Vasily "Kvakin" Gorshkov served out his sentence, he was deported back to Russia. While he was in prison, his then-girlfriend had given birth, and after his deportation, he reunited with his family in Russia. For his part, Alexey "Subbsta" Ivanov got his wish of white-collar, legitimate tech work. In an unorthodox take on the American Dream, Ivanov landed a job as an engineer in the United States.

18

GUERRILLAS

In the fall of 2000, eBay took a victory lap. Earlier that year, the company had topped $3 billion in market capitalization even as other tech companies tanked. By the third quarter of 2000, eBay boasted a 108 percent increase in net revenue, a 146 percent increase in registered users, and a staggering twelve-fold increase in net income over the previous year.

One analyst observed that eBay's third quarter results positioned it as "one of the few Internet stocks whose financial strength already rivals that of the best offline firms." Further, because eBay did not depend on advertising, the analyst wrote, its future appeared more secure than even AOL or Yahoo. According to some, eBay's auction model appeared poised to rewrite the rules of online commerce altogether. Fixed price retailing, they hypothesized, was dead—and eBay had killed it.

Which is why it meant something when PayPal's David Sacks wrote to a small clutch of PayPal executives and other leaders during this period, issuing a warning cry: "As you may know, ebay (in collusion with Visa) has declared war on us by making Visa free to sellers . . ."

■ ■ ■

Just miles from PayPal headquarters, the team at the eBay-owned-and-operated Billpoint payments service had been paying close attention to the changes at PayPal—particularly its introduction of fees and forced user upgrades. Billpoint spied a window of opportunity to regain lost ground and took steps in late 2000 to do exactly that.

On September 19, Billpoint criticized PayPal directly in an email to auction sellers. The email introduced new-and-improved pricing for Billpoint and announced the elimination of three-day holding periods for money. "Better yet, unlike PayPal, you need not make a special request every time you want access to your funds," the note said. Billpoint was "owned and endorsed by eBay," "endorsed by Wells Fargo Bank and Visa USA," and was the first to offer international payments, the company boasted.

Just weeks later, Billpoint made another move that sent shock waves through PayPal. From October 23 to the end of November, sellers who used Billpoint would not be charged fees on Visa transactions, and buyers who used a Visa credit card through Billpoint would receive $1 off every purchase. "No gimmicks. No nonsense," Billpoint told its sellers. "Just straight talk, reliability, and safety from names you can trust—eBay, Wells Fargo, and Visa."

With Visa transactions accounting for more than half of total credit card payment volume on eBay, PayPal leadership panicked. In sharing eBay's "declaration of war," Sacks observed that these encroachments arrived at a precarious time. "Unfortunately because of the forced upgrade scheduled to begin on Monday," he explained, "we are at our most vulnerable point. It is critical that we respond swiftly and creatively in the next week to give ourselves the maximum chance of success (survival?) over the next month."

Worryingly, this would be the first time in the Billpoint-PayPal saga in which Billpoint had undercut PayPal on price. ". . . this will be a critical test," Sacks wrote in his email to the group, which he dubbed "the Ebay [sic] Response Team." He included the company's top performers across a range of functions: its entire executive team, the producers of auction products, its head of PR, the stewards of its Visa/Mastercard relationships, its general counsel, data experts, and others he felt could help.

The eBay Response Team's first countermeasure: rebutting the Billpoint-vs-PayPal comparison email. They decided to write an email of their own to eBay PowerSellers to remind them of the many advantages PayPal offered that Billpoint didn't, like better customer service and fraud controls. The message also accused Billpoint of misrepresenting PayPal's new payment structure. "Billpoint uses a misleading chart comparing our straightforward Premier/Business account to their lowest fee account," the PayPal team explained.

PayPal used other volleys, too. David Sacks instructed Damon Billian to take to the message boards and correct "pricing disinformation," and asked Reid Hoffman to appeal to his eBay contacts to correct their messaging. Sacks floated other ideas as well. Was it time, Sacks wondered, to send a legal "nastygram" to eBay and a preliminary injunction for anti-competitive pricing? Could Vince Sollitto, head of PR, do anything to "win public opinion without appearing weak?" Could the customer service team create special designations for loyal PayPal users? "Suggestions are welcome from all," Sacks added. "We'll need lots of good ideas to beat eBay on variables other than price."

■ ■ ■

eBay's troubled relationship with payments long preceded its skirmish with PayPal. In the inaugural versions of eBay, founder Pierre Omidyar had simply trusted auction users to mail him their auction fees. eBay's first employees recalled thousands of envelopes arriving in the office, some with nickels and dimes taped to index cards.

Even as eBay grew, payments remained an afterthought. Reed Maltzman, an early eBay employee, recalled walking into a room of humming fax machines. When he asked what the fax machines were printing, he was told they were collecting credit card authorization receipts. The payments coated the office floor.

Omidyar knew that auction payments could be a lucrative revenue stream. He had witnessed rivals like Auction Universe introduce programs like BidSafe, which provided seller credit card processing for $19.95 per year. But then and later, eBay remained focused on growing and improving its core auction business, which meant sidelining many proposed bells and whistles. For that reason, eBay chose to remain remarkably hands-off with its users. In addition to letting users choose their preferred payment providers, eBay didn't offer shipping and handling, take auction photographs, or provide expansive customer service. Omidyar's laissez-faire approach was born of his libertarian sensibilities and his bedrock belief that "people are fundamentally good."

As eBay grew and matured, it shifted its position on payments slightly, acquiring Billpoint in spring 1999 to bring the last leg of the auction process in-house. But Billpoint's slow integration opened the door to third-party payment systems, including Confinity's and X.com's late-1999 offerings. "We hired executives from the banking industry to run Billpoint," Meg Whitman wrote years later, "and they took a bank's typical posture, namely, that you qualify everyone coming in the front door before you give them an account. But that more cumbersome process was off-putting to customers, including eBay sellers, whom PayPal welcomed with open arms, just a few clicks, and a cash spiff to boot."

In early- and mid-2000, eBay's Billpoint service had the misfortune of competing with PayPal's generous bonus program and no-fee promise. Jason May, a cofounder of Billpoint, remembered intense discussions at eBay about whether Billpoint ought to distribute bonus money or forgo fees. "We couldn't do much about [competing with bonuses and fees]. Because our pricing model was kind of controlled by our board owned by eBay and Wells [Fargo]. We did occasionally say, 'Well, maybe we go free for six months, or we do this thing to maneuver.' And this was where I feel like PayPal won . . . It was very explicit that our organization kept saying, 'We're not going to just go for broke,'" May recalled.

By late 2000, eBay users had thoroughly embraced PayPal, but that embrace created an operational catch-22 for eBay. On one hand, PayPal was skimming payment fees that could theoretically have gone to its own service, Billpoint; on the other hand, PayPal was helping eBay users complete transactions. "In a way," Ken Howery observed, "if a lot of people are using any payment service and [eBay] closes more transactions, they're making more money."

For eBay, a shift into payments represented small potatoes relative to its core auction service business. eBay's major revenue growth from 1999 to 2000 came from increasing users and expanding auction categories—not Billpoint's tangential services. "People probably looked at Billpoint and said, 'Oh this is just a few percentage points [of eBay's overall revenue],'" Howery said. "Whereas for [PayPal], that's all we had."

Despite that, eBay looked ready for a fight over payments market share. It made the next move in the battle, opting to more tightly integrate Billpoint into its auction platform. It started by changing the name "Billpoint" to "eBay Payments," a subtle shift meant to direct users to eBay's preferred payment system. eBay then quietly made a more consequential change, launching a feature called Buy It Now. Sellers would now be able to set a price—and if the buyer chose to pay it, the auction would close immediately.

At first, Buy It Now seemed no threat to PayPal. Whether a price was set by the seller or by an auction didn't matter to PayPal—as long as PayPal was used to settle up. But once the PayPal team dove into the Buy It Now button mechanics, they started to panic. In a traditional auction, an eBay bidder would place a bid, receive an email if they won, and then choose a payment system. Because auction buyers left eBay mid-auction, PayPal had a chance to worm itself into the payment process, by sending alerts when an auction was completed—and prompting the user to go to PayPal to complete the payment. A winning bidder could go from their email account to PayPal in order to pay a seller—thus completing the auction process without ever returning to eBay.com.

Buy It Now radically reconfigured this dynamic. If a buyer pressed the Buy It Now button, an eBay Payments form would now appear, allowing the buyer to complete their payment directly on eBay.com. This meant no email, and crucially, no window of time away from the eBay website. The buyer could still open a new web browsing window and navigate to www.paypal.com to pay if they chose, but the automatic eBay Payments page would significantly up the friction for buyers using PayPal. "It was easily the boldest move pulled by eBay up until that point," Eric Jackson wrote in his PayPal memoir.

■ ■ ■

eBay announced Buy It Now with flourish, waiving transaction fees on the feature to encourage its adoption. The company explained that it had surveyed 20,000 users and ran several focus groups to learn that "while members love eBay's selection . . . many buyers desire the ability to buy items faster and with more certainty, and many sellers want the ability to sell an item without having to wait for the listing to end."

Buy It Now launched—then quickly tanked. On October 23, just after its launch, eBay message boards lit up with criticism about an eBay Payments bug. Payment notifications were delayed, enraging users. "Took over a week to get the funds in my account after getting the thing fixed. What a giant pain," one user wrote. "Went back to PayPal and dumped Billpoint." Another commented: "I just received a letter from Billpoint telling me that a purchase was paid on the morning of the 17th. Duh. Today is the 21st. We ship priority. Now I'm late with this package. Thanks a lot Billpointless!"

Even by late November, Buy It Now remained broken. "I am a seller and I am trying to receive a payment," one user wrote. "My buyer paid with the Buy It Now Feature, and I have had no notification of payment from eBay. I signed up for Billpoint to try to receive payment to no avail. The Buy It Now Information page . . . is very unhelpful . . . The Buy It Now Feature has made this the most difficult transaction ever and I am going to remove the option from my auctions."

The press caught wind of eBay's troubles, and the publication *eWeek* ran a story—"'Buy It Now' Feature Flawed." The article pointed out that Buy It Now failed if the seller set an opening bid price equivalent to their Buy It Now price. In that instance, buyers who clicked Buy It Now would receive a "Problem with bid amount" error message. "We are working expediently to correct the problem and should have the bug fixed by early next week," eBay leadership said in an official announcement. In the meantime, eBay urged sellers to set their Buy It Now price one cent higher than the minimum bid price.

Buy It Now struggled, but eBay had time on its side. "This is a marathon. Not a sprint," Meg Whitman reportedly said of eBay's gambits to reclaim payments. By late November 2000, the PayPal team had real reason to worry about eBay's endurance. "Billpoint's market share has grown from approximately 9% to just under 15% over the past month," Eric

Jackson wrote in an update to the product team. The absolute numbers were concerning, too. By PayPal's estimates, Billpoint had gone from being listed on only 400,000 auctions in September to over 800,000 by early November—and outside observers, including the media, were beginning to notice the growth.

After eBay reported third-quarter earnings that beat Wall Street expectations, one reporter noted that eBay's "Billpoint online-payment system finally seems to be gaining traction after rival PayPal started charging some of its users."

■ ■ ■

eBay now stood a real chance of reclaiming payments and each change it made sent executives—particularly Thiel and Sacks—into paroxysms of anger. "David and Peter would get totally hysterical and say things like *They can't do this!* and *How dare they?*" an executive observed. "And we're like, 'It's their platform. They can do whatever they damn well want.'"

Anger and frustration aside, the feud led the two companies to build back channels. Reid Hoffman developed a relationship with Rob Chestnut, an eBay attorney, and together they helped to diffuse the tensions of 2000 and 2001.

Chestnut had been a federal prosecutor and was hired in early 1999 to oversee "trust and safety" at eBay, a role in which he'd adjudicate everything from minor fraud claims to deciding whether eBay users could auction off their own organs. It also put him in the position of dealing with third-party businesses like PayPal that had set up shop within eBay.

For Chestnut, PayPal was a trust and safety problem. eBay would have a harder time regulating its auction marketplace if someone else was controlling the flow of funds. "If you control the money, you can do a much better job controlling the fraud," he observed. "If a third-party payment system owns your marketplace, then they control the trust—but you can't control fraud."

Over time, Chestnut came to respect the PayPal team's aggressive growth efforts. "I'd say their competitors were probably going home at six or seven o'clock at night," he joked. "PayPal was just wheeling in dinner at that point . . . They were highly entrepreneurial, very aggressive. You've got to admire that." eBay's CEO, Meg Whitman, mirrored Chestnut's reflections. "PayPal was a company of extremely aggressive people with a real bias for action," she wrote in her business memoir, *The Power of Many*.

■ ■ ■

In their role as digital diplomats, Chestnut and Hoffman would have frequent engagement—"so many long, epic debates," Chestnut recalled. One especially tense flare-up was caused by PayPal's "verified by PayPal" logo. eBay sellers could earn it once they verified their bank accounts, and it signaled trustworthiness to eBay buyers. For PayPal, this was yet another strategy to wean users off credit card–based payments. For eBay, the logo was yet another frustrating piece of promotional PayPal flair graffitiing its site.

eBay opted to ban it outright, using the logo's size as a pretext for removal. Predictably, this caused fury at PayPal headquarters. But it also upset eBay sellers who had gone through the verification process. Hoffman was tasked with leaning on eBay's Chestnut to reinstate the logo. As tensions often ran too high for official visits, Hoffman's and Chestnut's various bilateral exchanges often had to take place surreptitiously at a Boston Market near the two companies' offices.

Hoffman managed to get Chestnut to reinstate the "verified by PayPal" logo, leaning on PayPal's trump card: eBay's users and their protests about the logo's removal. In other cases, however, Hoffman and Chestnut had to use more official diplomatic back and forth, notating each side's concession on a particular fight. Amid the Billpoint pricing skirmish, for instance, Hoffman laid out an item-by-item inventory of the issues to be resolved, in an email titled "agreements." Among the particulars:

3. We will fix our pricing page to reflect your pricing adequately. This will go out in our next push. [Commitment from X.]

4. You will correct your press and public announcements to reflect our chargeback and other status accurately. [Commitment from eBay.] We will send you a message with the definitive

information today, so you can get Janet Crane and others accurate. [Commitment from X.]

5. You will correct your websites and your eMail communication
    to being accurate on our pricing and chargeback facilities in
    roughly the same time frame that we correct (3-5 days at most)
    or best efforts. [Commitment from eBay.] We will provide you
    an eMail today on what needs to change. [Commitment from X.]

Over the course of two years, Hoffman and Chestnut dove into the weeds,
arguing over the minutiae of individual words and volleying screenshots
back and forth to prove their points. Their work on the finer details
achieved moments of détente.

■ ■ ■

As they developed a vital back channel, that effort also turned into something more. "We had our first official meeting with eBay today," Hoffman
wrote to the full company on November 10, 2000. The two companies
had begun a discussion about the possibility of formally linking their futures. From a modest revenue-sharing agreement to an all-out acquisition of PayPal, all options were on the table.

Hoffman cautioned the team that any potential deal remained far
off. Wells Fargo had taken an ownership stake in eBay's Billpoint, a con-
dition of which was that Billpoint remain the preferred eBay payments
provider. "Any payments deal with eBay will also involve Billpoint . . .
This will take time and has some obvious uncertainty," Hoffman wrote.

The details of the earliest PayPal-eBay talks were closely held. An
outside firm, First Annapolis Consulting, examined both parties' books.
For eBay's leaders, one concern rose above the rest: financial fraud. While
eBay had its share of fraudulent sellers, remarkably, the company maintained a fraud rate lower than most retail stores. Any deal with PayPal
that risked increasing fraud was a nonstarter.

As the two teams explored a deal, the First Annapolis team spent time
at PayPal headquarters, interviewed employees, and dove into its data to
understand the company's fraud profile. The team came away sanguine

on the business and communicated as much in their report to eBay: "If Billpoint's criteria for initiating conversations with PayPal is that PayPal must have adequate focus on risk management, we believe PayPal meets this criteria. The organization has invested heavily in risk management capability recently and has developed some innovative tools."

But First Annapolis noted PayPal's other, non-fraud risks: its tactics were new and untested, its growth was breakneck, and it had a bare-bones underwriting process. The assessment team questioned the "operational stability" of the business: Would employees flee in the aftermath of a potential eBay-PayPal deal? "All these concerns notwithstanding," First Annapolis wrote, "the key question in our minds is whether or not PayPal's business model will provide it adequate compensation for the risk it is taking."

At the time, the answer from the eBay-Billpoint side was no. eBay's leaders—including, most critically, Janet Crane, the CEO of Billpoint—looked at PayPal and saw a snake pit of fraud. For now, eBay concluded, they would use Billpoint to fight for payments, as opposed to making a quick and hasty deal. Though it did not lead to a deal, the pre-diligence effort of late 2000 opened the door to discussions, ones that the two companies would continue with varying levels of seriousness over the following two years.

■■■

Despite Buy It Now, the free Visa promotion, and other growth efforts, eBay's Billpoint gained only a marginal share of payments on the platform in late 2000 through early 2001. As Billpoint wound down its promotions, Billpoint's progress stalled and reversed. PayPal's numerous counteroffensives helped it stave off Billpoint's encroachments, and the two sides continued to fight for ground.

In one gambit, PayPal launched debit cards targeted at eBay PowerSellers—a feature Billpoint did not have. PayPal promised a cash-back incentive for sellers who used the card, and it prioritized distributing cards to those sellers who advertised PayPal as their exclusive payments provider. The team promoted the cards aggressively through their website, emails, and even phone calls. "We went through the database, we looked at the top 150,000 eBay sellers, and we just started sending them debit cards without them even asking for it," noted product team member Premal Shah.

In 2001 came the launch of PayPal Shops, a directory and service that featured non-eBay online stores and helped sellers build their own online businesses. PayPal Shops flowed from David Sacks's push to have PayPal offer payment services across the web—rather than just on eBay. For eBay sellers, PayPal Shops promised savings: if sellers could run their own online stores, they would no longer have to pay eBay fees. PayPal upped the stakes by building PayPal Shop–specific buttons and virtual shopping carts, and the effort presaged a "merchant services" division of PayPal, which helped extend its reach beyond auctions.

Internally, eBay referred to these off-eBay transactions as the "gray market," and did not cater to them with Billpoint. But eBay did respond in kind, with a June 2001 launch of "eBay Stores," a home for sellers who preferred fixed-price sales over auctions. Sellers on eBay Stores would have the choice between using a formal credit card merchant account or accepting Billpoint. eBay knew most sellers didn't qualify for merchant accounts, and hoped the tight integration of Billpoint would cut into PayPal's dominance.

The eBay Stores launch roiled PayPal leadership yet again. Hoffman was deputized to approach Rob Chestnut and demand a change. eBay made a minor modification, allowing PayPal's use on eBay Stores. PayPal also responded by providing detailed instructions for using PayPal on eBay Stores—and even recommending that eBay sellers list their stores in the PayPal Shops' directory.

Most eBay-PayPal moves and fights in 2000 and 2001 flew under the media radar—that is, until an early 2001 eBay salvo. eBay altered its "Sell Your Item" form so that when a seller used the form to create an auction listing, the payment field defaulted to Billpoint. "Had I rushed through this process to post my auction on eBay's site," Jackson wrote, "Billpoint would have appeared as a payment option, triggering all the Billpoint bells and whistles to encourage my winning bidder to use it to pay me."

The change was imperceptible to most users but carried massive consequences for PayPal. Virtually overnight, Billpoint's total share of the auction market soared by 5 percent. The PayPal team discovered that because high-volume sellers used automated tools to post hundreds or thousands of auctions, they rarely visited the "Sell Your Item" page. Thus, those sellers were unaware that Billpoint had been made their default auction payment mechanism.

PayPal sent a mass email to its user base, raising the alarm. "Unauthorized Billpoint logos can result in confused buyers using Billpoint to pay you, and this in turn can hurt your bottom line," the email read. "The only sure way to protect yourself from future unauthorized Billpoint logos is to close your Billpoint account." The team also included a phone number for eBay's customer service support center.

The conflict spilled out in the open, as sellers posted about the change on message boards. The press caught wind of the fracas, and the two companies traded public barbs. PayPal accused eBay of not playing fair; eBay accused PayPal of exaggerating the issue, calling PayPal's response "inflammatory" and dubbing its moves "deeply misguided."

Rosalinda Baldwin, the editor of an online auction publication called *The Auction Guild* and a critical voice in the online auction world, took PayPal's side in the spat. In a 1,356-word post titled "Billpoint's Unethical Tactics," Baldwin let loose about Billpoint. "We don't like the way they fail to protect sellers against unwarranted charge backs," she wrote. "We don't like how they defraud sellers on fraudulent charge card charge backs. We don't like how they sneak their logos into auctions when the seller does not select their service, and we don't trust them to protect user information."

Her choicest barbs were saved for the Sell Your Item shift. "eBay's Billpoint has used all kind of sleazy ways to sneak their logos into sellers' auctions," she wrote, but this change rose above the rest:

They set the Billpoint option to opt out rather than opt in, without announcing it. They automatically added their logos to relists even if it was not an option on the listing. ebaY [*sic*] is tricking new sellers into signing up for Billpoint, and are requiring bank information, not for site security as they claim, but to qualify sellers for Billpoint whether they want it or not. . . .

Baldwin ended with the haymaker: "Billpoint is not a good enough product on its own merits for sellers to want to use . . . the only way to avoid ebaYs [*sic*] sleaze tactics is to close your Billpoint account permanently." She then provided a link for sellers to do exactly that.

To be fair, some of Baldwin's accusations could just as fairly have been leveled against PayPal. On more than one occasion, PayPal had activated options without checking with sellers, and had shifted defaults to the benefit of PayPal user growth. One of the company's earliest moves—the "auto-link" feature, which posted PayPal logos on auctions for those sellers who had used it once—was essentially a carbon copy of eBay's Sell Your Item alteration.

Baldwin's commentary also spoke to a fiery independent streak within the eBay seller community. "There were some sellers that didn't like giving eBay as much power over their business as it had . . . [Using PayPal] was an opportunity to be a little more independent from eBay. 'eBay wants us to do A. Well, we're gonna do B.' There's definitely some of that in the community," eBay's Rob Chestnut said.

Ultimately, eBay's Sell Your Item adjustment may have been too little, too late in its effort to win back payment market share. Facing pressure from the traditional media, the "auction media," as well as its own sellers, eBay backtracked, reversing its Sell Your Item change. In the subsequent weeks, the payments gains eBay had made as a result of the change evaporated.

■ ■ ■

Throughout PayPal's first four years, Sacks, Thiel, and the rest of the leadership team felt that eBay could crush it on a whim. "One of the thought experiments I ran through was 'If I was running eBay Payments, what would I do to kill PayPal?' and I came up with lots of different things!" Sacks said. "I was always worried that one day they were gonna figure it out."

That fear drove contingency planning. At one point, they considered the threat of eBay blocking PayPal's corporate IP address—which would break PayPal's buttons. In preparation, PayPal registered hundreds of dial-up AOL internet accounts. If eBay turned off PayPal's ability to display its logo by blocking the company's IP address, PayPal's could route its service through those AOL connections.

As tensions mounted, the PayPal team worried that eBay would hit the limits of tolerance—and simply shut PayPal down, consequences be damned. Levchin, Hoffman, Thiel, and Nosek arrived at a radical solution: They would build their own online auction network, a plan they dubbed "Operation Overlord," the code name given to D-Day, the Allied invasion of Normandy during World War II. PayPal could use its reams of information about PowerSellers to lure them to a competing auction network. The idea was outside the realm of possibility, but its mere discussion illustrated PayPal's level of concern over eBay's power.

And while those fears never fully dissipated, they did begin to abate, driven in part by eBay's sellers supporting PayPal over eBay in moments like the Sell Your Item kerfuffle. "eBay had this whole history of whenever they'd introduce a change to their website, there would be an outcry from the users. It was a very ornery type of user base," Sacks said. "And they were legitimately afraid of that."

Per May, Billpoint's cofounder, the eBay executive team had flirted with the idea of a full PayPal shutdown—but opted against it. "[Shutting PayPal down] was definitely something that got thought about," May remembered. "But [eBay's executives] very explicitly decided not to be mean. It wasn't that they drifted along, not willing to consider these options."

By the time Baldwin's critique hit *The Auction Guild*, PayPal had achieved a ubiquity that had eluded Billpoint, and Baldwin's criticism reflected the community's overall sentiment. "We were really reluctant to do something that was against the community's wishes," eBay's Rob Chestnut remembered. "The community liked PayPal. The community was successful with PayPal. We didn't like it—but it was what our community wanted."

Perhaps no one understood the power of a loyal user base better than eBay founder Pierre Omidyar himself, who had fended off both Amazon's and Yahoo's attempts to take a piece of the auction business. "We had a big magnet, which was eBay, and all these little magnets came along and tried to pull people away," Omidyar explained to journalist Adam Cohen. "But eBay's magnet was so powerful it was hard for them to get started."

PayPal worked hard to strengthen its magnet, particularly with eBay PowerSellers. "We would get suggestions from our PowerSellers about a product they would like us to build," Paul Martin remembered, "and the next Monday, it would be available on the website for them." During this period, the team built several products to help sellers enhance auction listings. They released the Winning Bidder Notification, which automatically sent auction winners instructions for PayPal-based payments, as well as Smart Logos, which made the payment buttons change colors when an auction closed—an eye-catching update.

"These things sound simple," Martin would say of the team's efforts to ingratiate itself with the eBay PowerSeller community, "but you have to remember that all of these things were very difficult to build for us in terms of programming. Because we weren't building these things on our website. We were building things to work on someone else's website—who did not like us . . . it was almost like we were creating malware."

PayPal's off-eBay efforts paid dividends, too. Despite PayPal's early struggles with customer service, the success at Omaha endeared the company to sellers, who flocked to message boards to praise the twenty-four-hours-a-day service operation. The company's weekly newsletter captured the most powerful—not to mention unusual—signal that PayPal had won over eBay's own users. PayPal employee Damon Billian—aka "PayPal Damon" on the eBay message boards—had achieved "near rock-star status" and received everything from photos to marriage proposals from eBay sellers.

■ ■ ■

In May 1998, the US Department of Justice and twenty state attorneys general had sued Microsoft for anticompetitive, monopolistic behavior.

A multi-year legal struggle followed in which Microsoft was accused of, among other things, trying to "extinguish" its web browser rival Netscape. The government threatened to break Microsoft up.

The case sent a chill through the spines of technology leaders everywhere—including at eBay. PayPal's leaders fomented the fears. One of PayPal's newest team members, Keith Rabois, was tasked by Thiel to build an antitrust paper trail against eBay. PayPal also built a political action committee (PAC) to send contributions to members of Congress—then encouraged those members to pay careful attention to eBay's monopoly power.

In late spring of 2001, the company enlisted an outside counsel to issue a scathing, eleven-page, single-spaced note to eBay headquarters. Sent by both fax and FedEx to Meg Whitman, the letter was a shot across the bow. "eBay is abusing its market power over the online marketplace to distort and eliminate competition for online payment services. See, e.g., *United States v. Microsoft Corp.*, 87 F. Supp. 2d 30 (D.D.C. 2000). Like Microsoft, eBay is attempting to eliminate or limit competition in a second market (online payment services) in substantial part in order to enhance and protect its monopoly in its core business (online market-places)," the lawyer wrote. "The antitrust laws do not permit a firm with market power, like eBay, to extend its monopoly by eliminating down-stream competitors that, like PayPal, are providing beneficial competi-tion to consumers—i.e., better service at lower prices."

PayPal made sure to keep the eBay-as-monopolist threat ever pres-ent, leveraging it even in day-to-day communications. When Hoffman reached out to Chestnut about the Sell Your Item change, for instance, his message was clear: "Rob, if eBay has defaulted 'on' Billpoint, as some of the message boards suggest, please consider this my official regis-tering of concern about 'tying' products—e.g., tying your payment so-lution to your monopoly of auctions listing, and thereby creating an anti-competitive, anti-trust situation."

Vince Sollitto, PayPal's head of communications, justified the com-pany's use of these tactics: "[eBay's] view was 'We're going to buy you or we're going to kill you.' And as long as they weren't buying us, they were in the 'trying to kill us' category," he said. "And so in the [public relations] world and in the [government relations] world, it was scorched earth. It was anything I could do to screw them . . . I was basically running around Capitol Hill calling them an evil monopolist."

eBay's Chestnut saw his rival's fear as justifiable. "In fairness, their survival depended on us," he said. "I can understand that mentality." But Chestnut and eBay's leadership didn't sweat the antitrust threats as much as PayPal's executives might have hoped. "They weren't subtle," he said, smiling. "They really weren't. But look, I'm a lawyer. I'm a federal prose-cutor. People have threatened to shoot me before! You're really not going to intimidate me with antitrust stuff."

Far more intimidating to eBay than an antitrust case: the actual trust PayPal had built with eBay's own users. "What I really was worried about," Chestnut remembered, "was what would be the reaction of the seller community if we shut them down."

19

WORLD DOMINATION

When he took over as CEO, Thiel had named growth abroad as one of his strategic imperatives, but the idea predated his late 2000 message.

In its original pitch documents, Confinity cast Mobile Wallet as a means of liberating the masses from currency-manipulating governments and reserve banks. While those ideas eventually gave way to liberating eBay users from Billpoint, the team continued to plan for PayPal's global growth. When the team chose a product name, for instance, ease of international use was a key factor. Even the team's casual internal parlance—"The World Domination Index," for example, or the "New World Currency"—spoke to the aim of making PayPal a border-busting universal payments system.

X.com, too, had world conquest baked into its early DNA. One day, Musk hoped X.com would serve as the "global center for all money" and store the world's dollars, deutschmarks (soon to be euros), and yen in one place. To Musk, this trajectory wasn't revolutionary—it was obvious. Musk thought about currencies "from an information theory standpoint," a reference to the field founded by Dr. Claude Shannon in 1948. "Money is an information system," Musk explained. "Most people think money has power in and of itself. But actually, it's really just an information system, so that we don't have to engage in barter and that we can time-shift value in the form of loans and equity and stuff like that."

If the money stored in X.com's accounts was just another expression of information, as Musk saw it, then nationalized currencies were a pesky contrivance. A universal information network like the internet—which enabled bits to cross borders simply, rapidly, and cheaply—could eliminate the friction and fees of currency exchange. "X's ambitions were to basically be where all the money is," Musk explained. "It was supposed to *be* the global financial system."

By late 2000, PayPal was no longer trying to foment an international financial revolution—but it still spied opportunities abroad. As an individual country, the United States still led the world in total internet users, with 95 million Americans online. But continent-wide, Asia and Europe had roughly the same number of total internet users as North America, and foreign leaders once skeptical of the "world wide web" were now promoting it. In 1998, French president Jacques Chirac hosted a countrywide celebration of the internet—La Fête de l'Internet—and personally presided over an online discussion from the Élysée Palace. In 1996, Chirac had sheepishly admitted that he did not know that the point-and-click device that controlled a computer was called a mouse.

The internet's growth abroad piqued the interest of many American companies, including eBay, whose user base spanned ninety countries. In mid-1999, eBay purchased three-month-old German auction site, www.alando.de, with the intention of turning it into www.ebay.de, and later made similar acquisitions for France-based iBazar and South Korea–based Internet Auction Co. These sites allowed eBay to more carefully tailor services and languages and even take advantage of local laws; Alando auction sellers, for instance, could sell wine online to fellow Germans, whereas American sellers could not.*

As eBay expanded abroad, PayPal saw an opening for itself—auction sellers abroad needed payment services, too. "If you were a collector,"

---

*eBay's global acquisitions also helped it thwart the rise of foreign copycats. Alando's cofounders, for example, had made no bones about having borrowed liberally from the American auction giant. "We did a lot of trades on eBay," Alando cofounder Marc Samwer said to the *Wall Street Journal* early on. "We decided to copy what works and make it better. Why should we reinvent the wheel?" Mimicry earned Alando fifty thousand registered users in just weeks—and a $42 million acquisition offer from eBay months after launch.

noted Bora Chung, "you would not just look at the US. You would look at the UK, you would look at Germany, for collectors' items." The company began to see users sending money to foreign IP addresses. "David [Sacks] had sort of suspected and . . . was looking at the data and was like, 'People are hacking our system, because they just need to send money to Canada, or to the UK, or in English-speaking languages. We've just got to figure out how to make this happen,'" Giacomo Di-Grigoli recalled.

International customer interest dovetailed with another upside of going abroad: fundraising. Even after PayPal's $100 million haul in March 2000, the company needed more funds. But with the stock market still sliding, US investors had little appetite left for money-losing dot-coms. International investors, however, still felt tech's glow. "Silicon Valley was the center of all this innovation," Mark Woolway explained. "Paris wasn't. They saw that their access to this technology was from the US."

The team chose to use its international expansion to pursue two major goals: growth and fundraising. It began this effort as it had begun much else over the prior years: with little planning, quick action, and faith in itself to iterate its way to success.

■ ■ ■

Scott Braunstein was among those who helped with the early moves abroad. After finishing an MBA and JD at Stanford, he searched for a Silicon Valley company with a presence in London, where he hoped to settle down with his British fiancée.

Fortuitously, Braunstein's inquiries arrived as the company considered its international footprint. During what he called "the most long, drawn-out interview process ever," Braunstein watched chaos unfold. When he first started interviewing, Bill Harris had been the CEO; by the time he received his offer, Musk ran the company; and just weeks after he joined, Thiel replaced Musk at the helm. During this period, the Nasdaq also lost over a third of its value.

Shortly after joining, Braunstein was tasked with setting up PayPal's European operation in London—and given little direction beyond that.

"I hadn't set up a company in Europe," Braunstein remembered. "I'd never looked at lobbying or regulatory stuff either." Upon his arrival, he began to grasp the scale of the challenge. "European banking laws are arcane compared to US banking laws," Braunstein explained. Sandeep Lal, who eventually oversaw PayPal's international expansion, went one step further. "[US] regulators are actually quite good in terms of innovation," he said. "They keep a light touch . . . but that's not the case in Germany and all these [European] places."

It wasn't just foreign regulations—PayPal still hadn't figured out the precise technology needed to make currency conversion work. Throughout late 1999 and 2000, PayPal transactions took place entirely in dollars. One massive international market—Europe—had also just begun a 2.0 version of its native currencies with the introduction of the euro.

For Musk, Thiel, and other PayPal executives, urgency was the default posture on all things—including and especially its international expansion campaign. Braunstein had only just arrived in London when Musk dropped in for a speaking engagement. They agreed to meet at the small London office. "Within an hour, [Elon's] grilling me about the regulatory environment," Braunstein remembered. "And I said, 'Elon, I've literally been here for a week!'"

On the international front, PayPal felt behind from the outset. Visa and Mastercard were already in markets abroad; other start-ups were encroaching on the non-US payments business. In March 2000, Seattle-based eCash Technologies announced a German presence and pilot programs in several European cities and Australia. Then, on April 25, 2000, an old PayPal competitor, TeleBank, declared itself "the first US Internet-only bank to introduce its services globally."

PayPal puzzled over how to proceed. The company already faced enough difficulties managing its Palo Alto operations. Exporting that chaos abroad in the form of localized subsidiaries invited new problems, even at the level of the company's codebase. "In order to localize into any language," said one UX designer who worked on PayPal's expansion into Japan, "the first thing companies usually go through is to extract the localizable strings out of the code."

Because the expression of plurals and units can vary by language, developers have to create native-language conventions for local code-bases. In PayPal's case, this was a challenge. "When I went there, the first thing I noticed was that, like, all the localizable strings were embedded inside of the code—and it was written in 'Max code,'" the designer recalled.

Facing language issues, regulatory concerns, and even problems with currency symbols, the team realized PayPal couldn't just be ported over to foreign lands seamlessly and easily. Large portions of the website would have to be replicated piece by piece—and all while tending to the ever-urgent concerns and convulsions of the core US site.

■■■

Initially, the team settled on the simplest strategy available: PayPal would allow international users to transact with American customers on the platform in US dollars. Then it would extend that offering to some markets by linking overseas credit cards to PayPal. Finally, PayPal would pursue country-by-country joint ventures to provide locally denominated services—leveraging their help to navigate language barriers, currency conversion, and regulations.

As word spread about PayPal's partnerships, interest quickly emerged. "There's not a lot of innovation in the payments world. It's very slow moving," Braunstein explained. "When PayPal comes along, people are excited about it—and people are very nervous about it." European finance executives dreaded missing out on that innovation. If PayPal was the next big thing, they wanted in on the ground floor.

That enthusiasm wasn't limited to Europe. "When I'd land in Taipei, there would be people waiting for me with signs that said, 'Welcome Mr. Mark from PayPal!'" Woolway remembered. "The investors there just loved us . . . even after the downturn. . . . They loved the fact that someone from Silicon Valley would come out to Seoul or Taipei."

In late May 2000, PayPal was invited to participate in the first-ever Internet Finance Conference in Beijing—a powerful sign of approval. Cosponsored by Lehman Brothers and the China Development Bank, the conference featured the leading lights of Chinese finance. Jack Selby traveled to Beijing to represent PayPal, and once there, he reported his observations to his colleagues in what was, for him, a rare company-wide email:

> I arrived late Monday night after one missed connection and fourteen hours of flying. The conference kicked off the next morning, and all the 40+ US and Chinese delegates were all seated around a square equipped with headsets and microphones (it was like a U.N. session with every word being interpreted to/from English and Mandarin).
>
> After the morning session, I realized that the prime afternoon speaking-slot for the online bank had been granted to another group, Security First Network Bank—"the first online bank in the world." I cornered the Lehman head of the Beijing office and explained to him that 1) SFNB is really lame, and more importantly, 2) my talk would be the most exciting 15 minutes of the conference. It took some pleading, but eventually he conceded to cut the SFNB's CEO speech in half and let me speak for the rest of the allotted time. The SFNB fellow was very eloquent, but he had very little to say except that indeed SFNB was the first online bank in the world. However, X.com acquired more customers than SFNB in its first 4 weeks than SFNB has managed in nearly 5 years, and such tantalizing points certainly could not be left unmentioned.

At first, Selby wasn't sure if the audience was "in awe or didn't understand a word I said." But that evening he was seated next to the vice governor of the China Development Bank, who waxed poetic about China's need for a PayPal presence. Selby was introduced to other leaders in Chinese finance, and the next day, the vice governor peppered his own presentation with PayPal references, arguing that Chinese firms needed to model themselves on PayPal.

Selby observed that even casual American start-up culture went over well. "I was the only one at the conference over the three days that never wore a tie," he wrote. "They thought the no-tie was tremendous!"

■■■

PayPal's joint-venture model gave foreign banks and financial firms the opportunity to invest in exchange for a co-branded site. "We were essentially selling exclusivity for them to be our partner in the territory," Selby explained.

For the next several years, Jack Selby and his business development colleagues lived on the road. Thanks to their efforts, the company secured international partnerships with Crédit Agricole in France, ING in Holland, and Development Bank Singapore, among others. These firms were only too happy to pour money into PayPal's coffers—with the promise of a white-label PayPal offering.

Those white-label PayPals were slow to materialize, though, and in some cases never did. "The Crédit Agricole deal is a good example," Woolway explained. "They made a twenty-million-dollar investment . . . They wanted to roll out 'PayPal France,' but our main motivation was getting the money." Selby acknowledged the white-label delays—but also pointed out that the partner banks profited from their investments, if not from the release of a homegrown PayPal. "We were all rowing in the same direction, and as we succeeded, they would succeed, too," Selby said. "The timing was fungible."

Lal, Braunstein, Selby, and others had to stall—achieving enough work on international products to keep momentum up, while not distracting the team from its work on domestic PayPal. If an international partner's patience ran thin, Lal sometimes had to admit the hard reality: PayPal was still in a fight to win on eBay, and that domestic success was a precondition to building the international editions at all.

"One thing that was absolutely clear to all of us, including me," Lal said, "was that the top priority was winning domestically. If you didn't win domestically, there is no way anything international is going to last."

Despite the complexities of deal-making abroad, these partnerships helped keep regional PayPal copycats to a minimum and, more importantly, gave the company a source of cash at a critical time. These deals also enabled the company to nurture the domestic product without staffing up and launching fresh PayPal editions around the world.

However nascent, PayPal's moves abroad also served as an arrow in its quiver against Billpoint. The decision to enable US-dollar-based transactions for non-US customers, for instance, proved an important first step. eBay sellers abroad wanted to tap into the US market, but moving funds across borders carried hefty fees. "The only way they could receive money previously was through international remittances. That's twenty-five dollars on Western Union. Or you go to one of these banks, and you pay twenty-five dollars and huge foreign exchange fees [and] that just eliminates small-value commerce," Lal explained.

When PayPal began to allow foreign users to accept US dollars, it opened the floodgates for sellers abroad. Lal recalled an eBay gem seller based in Thailand—www.thaigem.com—who became the top PayPal merchant abroad for a period—and proved a case study in PayPal's off-eBay business. Calling it "an e-commerce success story," the *Weekly Pal* wrote that the company "started small, with five items on eBay, and has grown to be the major supplier of cut gemstones listed." PayPal was bringing in roughly $600,000 per month from Thaigem's transactions, but the real coup de grace was the gem seller's evolution: "They have migrated 95% of their business from Amazon and eBay to their own website."

Over time, the company found a way to launch localized products abroad as well. At first, Braunstein and Lal focused on Europe because of the continent's Electronic Money License program. "If you got this license," Lal recalled, "you could passport it to another country in Europe. So what you did was you applied in one country, you got the license, and it gave you the right to operate in every country by informing [their regulators]." The company worked hard to earn the license in the UK—which boasted, per Lal, "the most enlightened regulators"—and then parlayed it into other European jurisdictions.

As its currency conversion products began coming to life, the company returned to its ethic of rigorous simplicity. Giacomo DiGrigoli, who worked on international products, was eager to "empathize" with users and display as much information as possible about foreign exchange rates to put users at ease. "We built this, like, payments screen that was a fucking nightmare," he said, detailing a complex interface loaded with local exchange rates among reams of other relevant information.

Benjamin Listwon, the team's technical designer, also remembered the vigorous, weeks-long debate over multi-currency page design. "All tech companies," Listwon quipped, "seem to get caught up in the dumbest little quibbles while solving the world's biggest problems."

Giacomo DiGrigoli never forgot David Sacks's stark response. "David took one look at it and was like, 'No. It needs to be this simple. Like, a human being is trying to buy something on eBay. And they need to send that person eighty euros. You should have a drop down that says eighty and the number of the currency. And then on the permission screen, you can put all this other bullshit that needs to be here . . . Make it this simple, please.'"

On October 31, 2000—just one year after its US arrival—PayPal became available to customers in twenty-six countries. Those accounts were limited at first—denominated only in US dollars and allowing customers to send money only to people in their own countries and to the US. But they existed, and they generated revenue for the company, with a $0.30 levee and 2.6 percent on each payment.

By the end of 2001, international transactions accounted for almost 15 percent of the company's total revenue, and the team saw foreign user and transaction charts that moved up and to the right. As dollar-based transactions shifted into multi-currency ones, that growth accelerated, paving the way for a global expansion that led to PayPal operating in two hundred countries and twenty-five currencies.

■ ■ ■

Not all new market expansion was going to be traditional, and PayPal didn't march headlong into every potentially lucrative market. Reid Hoffman recalled one would-be merchant seeking PayPal services for a marijuana business. "I told him, 'Well, I have to go talk to our lawyers.'" His business was rejected.

Pornography proved ethically tricky as well. It was the largest source of internet traffic by far, but several PayPal employees wanted the company to steer clear. Thiel opened up dialogues with groups of employees. Kim-Elisha Proctor was a relatively new arrival at the company, but she valued the fact that the CEO "would listen to my concerns and talk me through the decision that we were making and why."

PayPal's executives compromised. "We wouldn't seek out that business," Sacks explained, "but there wouldn't also be some inquisition to [root them out] among this giant user base."

Some new market growth landed PayPal in regulatory hot water. On July 6, 2001, the company made the front page of the *New York Times*, with the PayPal logo pictured next to an article. In what should have been a reputational boon, the *Times* showed the logo atop a gambling website's homepage, with the headline "US Companies Profit from Surge in Internet Gambling."

As the internet took off in the late 1990s, the online casino market exploded along with it. Online gambling was illegal in most of the US, but Americans surfed over to overseas sites, often warehoused in Costa Rica or the Caribbean. As this sector raked in billions, a crop of US businesses emerged to support it, including gambling software designers and companies that placed casino billboards on US highways. Even reputable internet firms joined the mix: While Google and Yahoo rejected the advertising dollars of alcohol and tobacco companies, they embraced online gambling. "Gambling is not in the same class for us," a Google executive told the *New York Times* in 2001. "The laws are not conclusive on this."

Inconclusive though the laws may have been, the results of the online gambling proliferation were increasingly not. "You just keep clicking, and clicking, and clicking the button," one online gambler told a reporter. "It was a euphoria. It was like reality didn't exist." The gambler lost half her take-home pay for the year in the span of a single month, and considered driving herself into the Pacific Ocean in despair.

Digital casinos operated with murky regulatory oversight. "It's not just the fact that people with just a few clicks people can lose a lot of money," Woolway explained. "It's also not a Vegas casino where the slot machines get inspected by the Nevada Gaming Commission. . . . The problem with these online casinos is that you're playing against online slot machines from this Aruba-based company . . . how do you know what the real odds are there?"

Gamblers also reported shady interactions with companies running the casinos, particularly when retrieving winnings. If the gamblers lost, they observed, money was transferred from the gambler's account to the casino rapidly. But if they won, the casinos would often withhold payment for days, a means of enticing gamblers to keep gambling.

For that reason and others, many legacy American financial institutions avoided servicing offshore casinos. But that left an opening for a start-up needing to diversify its client base. "No one would process for them—and we stepped in and filled that void," Selby said. In 2001, the team experienced the darkness of the void, as several PayPal employees spent 2001 shuttling to casino operations on islands just off the US coast.

■ ■ ■

In 1998 and 1999, some who lost money through internet gambling filed suits against credit card companies. One woman in California sued Mastercard and Visa in district court after she accrued $70,000 in credit card debt. She won her case, and her debts were resolved. But as a result of that case and others like it, as well as the intensifying media scrutiny, Visa, Mastercard, and American Express put stricter prohibitions on offshore casino websites.

But as PayPal had learned from eBay, any market spurned by Visa, Mastercard, and American Express could be a gold mine. PayPal carefully considered the risks and rewards of servicing online gaming businesses, a debate that rose to the board level. As a Google and Yahoo board member, Mike Moritz understood the sector's upside and advocated for PayPal's involvement. So long as gambling's contribution to PayPal's revenue stayed low enough, he advised, PayPal wouldn't trip alarm bells.

PayPal's gambling entrée wasn't new either—another website had been servicing casino payments, and used PayPal to complete transactions. "[This company] listed all of the casinos they had on their site," Dan Madden, a member of the business development team tasked with executing the so-called Las Vegas strategy, remembered. "So I said, 'Well,

I can just go call all those casinos and say that they could work with us directly.'"

Both casinos and PayPal felt they were gaining something in the bargain: the casinos by having an increasingly reputable brand name as their payment provider; and PayPal by charging a steep premium for casino transactions. And so began a curious prospecting mission for Madden and the business development team, one that took them to the Dominican Republic, Costa Rica, Antigua, and Curaçao, the home bases of some of the world's offshore gaming enterprises.

The online gambling universe was subdivided in two worlds. There were, per Madden, legitimate bookmakers from Europe who wanted to expand their business into the Caribbean. Then there was the other, less savory element: New York– and Miami-based bookmakers who wanted to move their legally complicated US-based operations offshore. "It was uncomfortable," Madden said, recalling one memorable meeting with an offshore casino magnate. "Like, I was sitting in a meeting and the guy would have this pistol sitting on the desk with them."

Though gambling grew to represent only a small, single-digit fraction of PayPal's total payment volume, the profit margins ran as high as 20 percent and 30 percent—significantly higher than the margins the company earned on ordinary auction payments.

From the beginning, the company saw the risk of this business as a hedge against a far bigger risk: eBay. "We were always looking for ways off eBay," Woolway recalled. "Gaming was high-margin and growing quickly. And we were uniquely situated to be an obvious solution."

But as PayPal became enmeshed in online gaming, it came under greater scrutiny. PayPal was invoked in damaging Congressional testimony. Industry analysts and credit card association lobbyists pointed out that because PayPal was a payment intermediary—and not a credit card company—it gave casinos a convenient cover around credit card rules.

The expansion into this market, while lucrative, also exposed PayPal to the businesses that cropped up around gambling. "If you have a casino somewhere in a city near you," fraud investigator Melanie Cervantes explained, "it would not be unusual for you to see a bunch of crimes happening around the casino . . . Well, the same thing happens on the internet. When you have casinos, other frauds conglomerate around the casinos."

The sketchiness was hard to ignore. "Casinos are a great way to mask money movement . . . If Vladimir is making five-thousand-dollar payments to this guy in Malta, every third Wednesday, and it's pretty structured, he's probably layering," Cervantes noted, a reference to one stage of the money laundering process, during which criminals add "layers" between the source of ill-gotten funds and their destination. "Money laundering is illegal. It covers up some very egregious crimes in the real world," Cervantes said. As they explored the gambling web, they discovered links to everything from cocaine dealers to hit men to gun traffickers—a vast digital underworld which PayPal now had to navigate and police.

■ ■ ■

Despite the complications, PayPal considered making more serious moves into the gaming business, in the form of an acquisition. SureFire Commerce was the industry's leading payment processor, commanding 60 percent of online gambling transactions.

Internally, research on SureFire was given the code name "Project Sapphire," and PayPal spent several months running due diligence and assessing risks. PricewaterhouseCoopers was brought in to run a risk analysis, and executives from both SureFire and PayPal met for mutual grilling sessions on their respective business models.

As they dove more deeply into SureFire's business, PayPal executives found a red flag: SureFire was playing fast and loose with credit card association codes for online gambling transactions. In order to better monitor the space, the card associations had implemented a special code for such transactions—code 7995. If that code came up, those transactions would be given special oversight, and many would be declined outright.

Rather than use 7995, SureFire quietly opted to use other codes— including, for instance, code 5999: "Miscellaneous Internet Transactions."

That kept the business thrumming and attention from credit card companies limited. Such moves weren't illegal, but they were an unmistakable violation of the credit card associations' processing rules.

PayPal ultimately walked away from its negotiations with SureFire Commerce. The team did, however, leverage what they had learned to their advantage. In July and August of 2001, Visa and Mastercard began to enforce their rules more stringently, targeting payment processors who were fudging their coding classifications, including PayPal. Visa had noticed that some of the casino transactions from offshore gambling sites were improperly coded, and PayPal received a sternly worded letter of inquiry.

PayPal complied by changing its coding practices—and then went a step further, informing Visa and Mastercard that SureFire's violations were far more flagrant and deserved a close look. This took gumption. After all, both PayPal and SureFire were guilty of the same kind of misdirection. But the PayPal team sensed an opportunity: if SureFire's business took a hit, PayPal could win more casino market share—all while an old PayPal nemesis, Visa, did the dirty work.

In its flirtations with SureFire Commerce, its tussles with eBay, and its expansion abroad, the company showed itself at its most aggressive. What began with invention often had to survive through fierce opportunism: a TBD white-label product that never materialized; providing services to dubious offshore entities; building defaults on eBay and using the auction giant's own user protests to cement the changes.

In each case, the gamesmanship had a rationale, an ends-justify-the-means logic that reflected the reality of the low-margin payment business. Of course, the company didn't traverse all bright lines—it took care to avoid anything flatly unlawful, as in the case of the marijuana business, hewing to what Thiel reportedly dubbed the "no orange jumpsuits" rule. But when it came to skirting artificial rules—terms of service from Visa and Mastercard, for instance—the team showed little compunction.

Much of it came back to the grim data the company's leaders crunched for years: the majority of its payments still came from eBay—leaving the company on a perpetually shaky foundation. Thus, expanding into other markets became a pressing priority.

In a column for the company newsletter, David Sacks outlined his thinking about breaking into new payments markets. "As a practical matter, PayPal can only pursue a very limited number of markets, because payment products need to be specifically tailored to the needs of different kinds of customers," he wrote.

Sacks estimated that it took the company three months of pre-launch preparation and an aggressive post-launch sales and marketing effort to conquer a new market. Thus, whenever possible, PayPal would explore markets that "(1) are relatively proximate to our existing territory in terms of functionality and (2) have a strong need for our service because they are under-served by existing options."

That criteria led to a culling of possible expansion targets—as when Sacks rejected one employee's proposition that Pizza Hut or Amazon were ripe for the taking. For Sacks, offline retailers were "a revolutionary (rather than evolutionary) step from where [PayPal was] today, and it's also not clear that PayPal adds much over existing options." He also considered expansion to Amazon and similar sites a nonstarter: The team understood all too well the frustration and friction of burrowing into eBay's payment process. Established sites, he wrote, "are loathe to outsource their checkout line to PayPal."

The bottom line: PayPal would choose its conquests selectively. "World domination," Sacks concluded, "will not be achieved by indiscriminately parachuting into hostile lands."

20

BLINDSIDED

"We will have a thermonuclear IPO," declared Musk in the summer of 2000. Employees ranked it among his more memorable Musk-isms.

But a year past PayPal's founding, the markets had just survived a major blast of their own—and gone sour on technology IPOs. The Amazon-backed Pets.com was exhibit A. The much-hyped online pet food company IPO-ed in February 2000, opening at $11 per share and later reaching a peak of $14 per share. By November, the stock had cratered to 19 cents a share. Only months after its IPO, the company was forced into liquidation. It wasn't alone: in 2000, internet stocks collectively lost three-quarters of their value, wiping out a staggering $2 trillion in market capitalization.

Amid this wreckage, PayPal explored its options to go public. Thiel announced a new company-wide ambition: achieve profitability by August 2001. Profitability wasn't a prerequisite for joining the Nasdaq or the NYSE; in 2000, just 14 percent of companies achieved profitability prior to their IPOs. But given the market's bearish mood on tech stocks, Thiel thought profitability would persuade the skeptics.

Thiel and his team pursued this goal from every angle, including belt-tightening where it hurt the most: team snacks. In spring 2001, the company newsletter announced the unthinkable: fees for soda and vending machine snacks. The kitchen would continue to offer basics like peanut butter and milk for free, but subsidized company lunches would be scaled back to thrice-weekly sandwiches. "But in the end," the newsletter writers declared, their stomachs no doubt gurgling with hunger, "these small sacrifices will all be worthwhile."

The demise of free vending machine snacks inspired an act of rebellious innovation. "A couple of guys got together and said, 'Well, screw that. If we're gonna pay for it, let's at least get the stuff we want then,'" Jim Kellas remembered. "So they built a drawer, which had a bunch of candy and stuff inside of it. And then they created a scanner, [for the] barcode that you had on the back of your [company] badge. You scan it with the scanner, and it would automatically charge your PayPal account." George Ishii, one of the intrepid inside-the-company store's founders, reportedly called the store "Ishii Shou Ten"—Japanese for "Ishii Store."

To encourage the team to reach profitability, Thiel agreed to a wager. "A lot of people in our company are willing to give up a lot to help our company succeed," wrote the author of that week's *Weekly Pal*, in mid-April 2001. "We've given up sleep, free time, exercise, and sunshine. But now, our CEO, Peter Thiel, has agreed to make the ultimate sacrifice for the team. He has agreed that . . . if the month of August is profitable for us, he will dye his hair blue!!!"

■■■

Private companies apply to trade on public stock exchanges for several reasons. The first is financial: By selling some portion of their stock to the public, companies can raise capital from institutional investors, retail traders, and other buyers on public markets. For founders and early employees with equity, this process turns paper fortunes into real dollars. And for many, it serves as an opportunity to exit after the grinding work of building a company from scratch. An IPO also offers some determination of a business's fair market value, based on the price public shareholders are willing to pay per share. Finally, the press surrounding IPOs can serve as a branding boon—cementing a company name in the minds of the public.

PayPal had multiple reasons for going public, but the foremost was fundraising. The team had closed yet another round of financing for $90 million from international investors in March 2001, and the business was working toward profitability. But the additional funds raised through an IPO could provide insurance, particularly as the company carefully managed its eBay dependency, its fraud rate, and its tenuous credit card company relationships, among other risks.

Even in a booming market, the IPO process can be fraught and lengthy, spanning anywhere from three months to several years. The paperwork is voluminous and the lawyers numerous. During the pre-IPO period, a company undergoes scrutiny from investment banks, auditors, regulators, the media, and the investing public. Besides the time cost, an IPO can invite nuisance lawsuits and unwelcome press attention—both of which can do lasting damage. In exchange for the ability to raise funds through a sale of stock, a company also agrees to stringent reporting and regulatory requirements from the Securities and Exchange Commission (SEC). Even after the IPO gauntlet is done, employees must wait for a "lock-up period" before they can sell their equity.

By July 2001, Mark Woolway's job changed from raising money abroad to prepping the company for its IPO marathon. As a first step, he helped the company select an investment bank—a crucial decision. The bank would shepherd it through the perils of the IPO process and serve as its underwriter—the broker between the company offering shares and investors looking to buy them. Its bankers would verify listing requirements, share its story with investors, suss out demand for the stock, and price and time the IPO for maximum effect.

The team notched an early win when Morgan Stanley agreed to serve as its lead underwriter. The Morgan Stanley team, headlined by its star analyst Mary Meeker, had a strong reputation for tech IPOs, including the legendary 1995 Netscape IPO, seen as the starting gun for the dot-com boom. That same year, Meeker published the inaugural issue of "Internet Trends"—her "state of the union" for the digital world.

In-mid August 2001, PayPal began the IPO process by preparing its S-1, a multi-hundred-page document submitted to the SEC detailing a company's financials, operations, history, and legal issues. The Morgan Stanley team flew to Palo Alto to meet with the PayPal team over the last week of August, during which they committed to a late 2001 IPO.

On August 29, Thiel sent out lock-up agreements to all PayPal employees and shareholders, announcing that PayPal was starting its IPO process. The note contained a stern warning: employees should be careful what they share about the company from this point forward. The *Weekly Pal* reiterated his message, citing the famous World War II adage "Loose lips sink ships!"

■ ■ ■

An IPO would also help price the company—which, as multiple acquisition efforts had revealed, was difficult. "We needed to go public," Jack Selby said. "We can go public, let the Nasdaq tell you what we're worth, and then you can buy us."

More suitors emerged as the IPO process started. One—CheckFree, a company trying to digitize the paper billing process—was particularly drawn to PayPal's scale, its substantial payment volume, and the trust it had achieved while operating on a third-party platform. "Consumer brands are sticky," Pete Kight, the founder of CheckFree said, "and when you talk about moving money, trust is so difficult to build."

Kight was impressed that PayPal had managed to turn eBay's broken payment system into a full-blown business. "It isn't always that a solution finds the problem," Kight said of PayPal. "Sometimes the problem finds the solution."

Kight knew of PayPal's ambitions to go public, but Thiel had concerns about the IPO. "[Thiel] just kept saying, 'I don't want to run a public company. I [have] no desire to be a public CEO. I'd rather do other things. I don't want to go public,'" Kight recalled. "He convinced me. I didn't think it was any more complicated than that."

The two companies soon embarked on two attempts at a CheckFree acquisition, complete with due diligence. Despite their enthusiasm about PayPal, the CheckFree team was concerned about PayPal's eBay dependency—as well as some of the fiercely independent rhetoric its leaders used. "I went into it a bit like, 'I'm interested, but I have no interest in overthrowing the government,'" Kight said. Thiel tried to mitigate both those concerns in his talks with Kight.

CheckFree's overriding concern, however, was PayPal's dependence on the credit card associations' network. Kight was worried that a single change from Visa or Mastercard could wipe PayPal out. In that scenario, "we would just have bought a company that's not allowed to do what it does."

Ultimately, Kight decided that CheckFree couldn't go forward. Today, Kight is good-humored about the outcome. "When people talk about the history of CheckFree and people say, 'You're so smart,' I say, 'Well, if you think I'm so smart, how do you deal with the fact that I not only had the opportunity to buy PayPal, I had two opportunities to buy PayPal—and turned them both down?'"

■ ■ ■

On Friday, August 31, 2001, PayPal registered its ten-millionth customer. At PayPal's 1840 Embarcadero office, the team—already abuzz over the upcoming IPO—celebrated with after-work margaritas, and Thiel sent out an email reflecting on the milestone:

As of this week, PayPal has reached its 10,000,000th user. One suspects that too much importance is attached to round numbers. Still, it helps put things into some sort of context:

(1) November 18, 1999: 1,000 users. We're still not sure whether the product is going to take off, or whether the user numbers are just going to fizzle after an initial burst of interest.

(2) December 28, 1999: 10,000 users. PayPal is signing up about 500 users/day, and it's getting more and more difficult to mail (by hand) all the envelopes with people's identification numbers. Still, it's starting to look like the rate of growth is increasing from day to day.

(3) February 2, 2000: 100,000 users. It's definitely looking exponential. . . . But we have no idea what we're going to do with these users. We're starting to get nervous about the sign-up bonuses ($20 a person) and we know it can't go on forever. . . . Obviously, the spending is growing exponentially too. . . . A company down the street (X.com) has the

same bonuses, and we're scared that we're going to get bankrupted
in the race. [After the merger, it turns out they were kind of scared
too.]

(4) April 15, 2000: 1,000,000 users. We've just merged PayPal and
X.com, and raised $100 million as a result of the high growth rates.
Now it's up to us to create a business with the capital, employees,
and customer base. Robert Simon, the CEO of dotBank, an early
competitor acquired by Yahoo and morphed into PayDirect, suggests
that the online payments race will be won by the first company to get
to the 5,000,000-user number.

Good work everyone.

The "round numbers" made for great news copy. Vince Sollitto primed
reporters to cover the story, and PayPal distributed a press release.
August's successes did not, however, include Thiel dying his hair blue.
The company failed to achieve profitability on the timeline many had
hoped for.

■ ■ ■

Despite Thiel's reservations over being a public company CEO, he
wanted to move quickly with the IPO. To him and his executive team,
PayPal's business remained fraught with risk. In addition to other benefits, going public would put the company in the same league as eBay—
showing that PayPal wasn't just an annoying appendage that could be
dispensed with via a rule change.

That plan hit a snag one Monday afternoon in New York. The team
had met with Morgan Stanley and came away frustrated. Thiel reported
that the pair of analysts he met with seemed uninformed about PayPal's
business and hadn't even used the PayPal service prior to the meeting.
Thiel found their questions—"How do people get money out of Pay-
Pal?"; "How much does PayPal charge?"; "Does PayPal charge the
sender or the recipient?"—"perfunctory."

In the meeting, the Morgan Stanley team delivered bad news: a quick, late-2001 IPO would no longer be in the cards for PayPal. "The stated reasons," Thiel wrote in a recap email to board member Tim Hurd, "centered on the fact that their analysts felt uncertain about PayPal's projections and wanted to see at least two quarters of profitability before proceeding." Per Thiel, Morgan Stanley also told the PayPal team that they'd have to allow their analyst to track the company for at least half a year.

Thiel surmised that PayPal had gotten caught in an internal crossfire between Morgan Stanley's investment bankers and its equity analysts. The bankers, responsible for the deal-making that helps companies raise capital, had excitedly brought PayPal in, but the equity analysts, responsible for tracking stocks and providing research-based investment guidance, were more suspicious.

"For the analysts to assert their 'independence,' they had to resist the i-bankers," Thiel wrote to Hurd. "Ironically, this meant that the only 'independent' review of PayPal would result in the uninformed conclusion that PayPal is not fit to take public (since any other result of the review would have appeared insufficiently 'independent'). It's unfortunate that [Morgan Stanley] is such a broken institution that its internal fights end up hurting companies like our own.

"All of us were totally blindsided by this process," Thiel wrote. He had been assured that Morgan Stanley's equity analysts were supportive of PayPal's IPO, and he took the blame for "trusting them on that score." "As long as I remain CEO of this company," he concluded, "we will never use [Morgan Stanley] for any work again." The team would instead seek out a new lead underwriter, a process that would delay the IPO.

Throughout the IPO process, the team expressed frustrations with the finance industry in general. "I think he got frustrated with these investment bankers," observed Rebecca Eisenberg, one of the company's senior counselors and IPO stewards, "because they are low freaking integrity . . . [T]hey thought they knew how to translate PayPal to the SEC, but how do you translate what you don't even understand yourself? And Peter was right in trying to sideline them. The investment bankers just got in the way of PayPal's success."

In the meeting that day, Thiel reportedly looked at the bankers during one moment of pushback and said, "I hope we're not going to pretend that we don't have a vast difference of opinion about this company." At the meeting's dispiriting conclusion, Thiel, Botha, and Portnoy made their way to the airport, a trip made more difficult by bumper-to-bumper traffic on the way. "I just wanted to get out of the city so bad," Thiel said.

That was easier said than done, even once the team arrived at the airport. New York was hit hard by thunderstorms that evening, and the plane sat on the tarmac for hours, long enough that Jason Portnoy and Roelof Botha were able to watch a movie. Eventually, to their great relief, the flight took off.

The team returned west—on the night of September 10, 2001.

■ ■ ■

At 5:46 a.m. PST the following morning, American Airlines Flight 11 hit the north tower of the World Trade Center.

PayPal employees woke up to a nation in chaos. Engineer James Hogan recalled seeing the PayPal website's traffic drop. "There was a monitor that we had on the wall above the break room that was the real-time site usage graph," he remembered. "It always kind of had the same shape, like high during the day and then down at night, this kind of roller-coaster pattern. That day, it just tanked. It was an odd sort of visceral cue that stood out to me of how much the world was operating differently that day."

Mark Woolway's pre-IPO work came to a halt. The attacks had reduced more than one financial services firm to rubble and shut the markets down for days. At the office, employees watched the coverage in horror. Some were too shocked to continue working, and PayPal's leaders made clear that anyone wanting to return home was welcome to do so. Others, though, found their work a welcome distraction from the tragedy. "I was single, living alone, and my life was work," Hogan remembered. "My social life and my community effectively was my coworkers. It was nice to be with other people and process what was going on."

Giacomo DiGrigoli was a New Yorker who moved out west. For him, September 11 hit like a gut shot; he'd later learn that two friends from college and one from high school were killed in the attacks. Rebecca Eisenberg, one of PayPal's attorneys, had been on the East Coast with her husband and planned to fly back to the West Coast on September 11. They changed their plans and returned home one day earlier. Their original booking: flight 93 from Newark International Airport to San Francisco International Airport, the fateful plane that crashed in a Pennsylvania field when passengers fought back against the hijackers.

PayPal team members working abroad experienced the moment differently. Along with Scott Braunstein, Jack Selby was stationed in London, and they had planned a lunch at a nearby Italian restaurant, leaving their phones behind in the office.

As they returned to the office, Braunstein saw someone in hysterics on the sidewalk. "She's crossing the street saying, 'They've got the planes in the air! They've hijacked five planes!'" Braunstein remembered. Selby and Braunstein watched the news on a television inside a small room underneath their office building's staircase. "We were in total disbelief," Braunstein said.

When they returned to the office, Selby and Braunstein had dozens of phone calls and messages awaiting them. "I was having people saying 'I'm really sorry to hear,' as if I was representing America over there," Braunstein recalled. "I was getting a lot of super heartfelt messages coming in from business colleagues and friends. *We stand together with you. This is awful.* This sort of thing."

■ ■ ■

The *Weekly Pal* newsletter from September 14 turned into a catalogue of employee shock, grief, and anger. "I lost someone on one of the planes (wasn't a close friend, but it was my friend's best friend) and it's a spooky feeling," wrote one account manager. "I felt very, very violated and then very, very vulnerable," wrote another employee. "I'm a little paranoid. Like imagining an event as horrific happening right at me."

Peter Thiel sent an email reflection to the full company on Friday the 14th:

This last week has proven an incredibly rough one. Like people elsewhere in this country, the PayPal team has been frayed emotionally by the worst attack on American territory since the Civil War. We've tried to put up a brave face, saying that we're going to continue as we have before. Even so, we know that some things really have changed—in ways that we may not yet fully appreciate.

This was driven home to me at a meeting in downtown San Francisco on Thursday morning: I could not park my car in the building's garage (because the garage attendants weren't letting any people who didn't work there park cars); and when I finally found some other place to park and got to the building, people were streaming out. Somebody said there had been a bomb threat. Almost immediately, it turned out there was no threat at all, but that some people had started to panic and everything simply cascaded. In a similar vein, I've noticed in recent days that a number of employees in our Palo Alto office have been a bit more on edge; and I'd ask everyone here to show a little bit more sensitivity in the weeks ahead as we pull together through this crisis.

And what of the terrorists, who believe that the only path to liberation involves madness and murder? It may be a mistake to describe them as "Islamic," for the simple reason that they have no positive vision at all— rather, their identities are defined by a nihilistic negation of their enemies: globalization, capitalism, the modern world, the West in general, America in particular. Personally, I believe that the path out of this madness must involve an affirmation of what's best about the modern capitalist West—the belief in the dignity and worth of each human life (regardless of background or personal characteristics); and the related hope that a peaceful world community can be built around the free exchange of ideas, of services, and of goods.

For I believe that the terrorists were not only evil and insane, but also really stupid. One will not stop world trade by blowing up a big building, even if it happens to be called the "World Trade Center." To stop the modern capitalist West, one would have to destroy a great deal more—the global communications network and the whole infrastructure of global commerce. One would have to shut down the Internet and demolish PayPal and everything that this company is trying to build. That is why the attack on the World Trade Center in some sense was directed squarely at us—even if the terrorists had never even heard of PayPal.

On a more positive note, all of our employees are safe and accounted for—and it looks like all their immediate relatives are fine too. And we've done an awesome job in deploying some of our resources, however small, to help those who have been hurt: As of this writing, 22,238 members of the PayPal community have donated a total of $829,423 to the National Disaster Relief Fund of the American Red Cross.

Our thoughts and prayers are with the victims of senseless violence in New York and Washington, and throughout all the world.

■ ■ ■

Like many other companies, PayPal launched a relief effort in the aftermath of the attacks. "I get into the office," Vivien Go recalled, "and all anybody could think of was *Okay, how do we help?*"

Thiel emphasized urgency in standing up the relief operation. "Peter was super smart about it," Go said. "He knew that people would be charitable only with the initial shock. In the weeks thereafter, that shock is going to taper off . . . and they'll get fatigued with all the calls for help and charity, et cetera . . . [We] had to move as close as possible to the event." Denise Aptekar recalled that her colleague, Nora Grasham, dove into action that morning to spur the donation outreach effort.

The basic elements went live by the evening of September 11. The company moved quickly to set up relief@paypal.com, accepting email donations that PayPal would then contribute to the Red Cross. PayPal added a donatioin button to its website and built Web Accept donation buttons that users could embed on their own sites and auction pages. By the next day, 2,400 people had given a total of $110,000.

PayPal's effort mirrored those of Yahoo and Amazon, and all three companies received media coverage about the donation effort. Vince Sollitto called the company's response a "no-brainer" and pledged to keep the effort going for as long as needed. By September 15, donations to the Red Cross through PayPal topped $1 million. On November 13, 2001, at the Red Cross Bay Area headquarters, Thiel presented an oversized check for $2.35 million to Harold Brooks, the CEO of the American Red Cross Bay Area Chapter.

The team's instinct to do good was augmented by its instinct to win. One engineer noticed, for instance, that Amazon had built a click-through page that better explained their donation effort and suggested PayPal do the same. The team hustled to tweak and deploy changes, to keep up with rivals even as it raised funds for victims.

PayPal kept a wary eye on its old rival eBay's response to the disaster. The auction giant had struggled—auction sellers had been posting distasteful paraphernalia related to Osama bin Laden and the World Trade Center, including postcards, T-shirts, and newspapers. One seller posted what he claimed was a chunk of singed concrete from the buildings, and others tried to pawn home videos of the towers burning and falling. By September 12, eBay announced a ban on such auctions.

eBay mounted its own relief effort, which caused headaches. Responding to a direct appeal from New York governor George Pataki and New York mayor Rudy Giuliani, eBay launched the Auction for America, an ambitious effort to raise $100 million in 100 days through its community. Sellers posted items whose value would be donated to charity, and eBay would distribute the proceeds across seven different charitable funds.

The announcement made a splash, and eBay secured a number of high-profile partners and contributors. *Star Wars* creator George Lucas donated movie memorabilia for the effort, and late-night host Jay Leno donated a prized Harley-Davidson motorcycle. Every sitting member of

Congress signed a flag to be auctioned, and thirty-eight state governors donated items, including a quilt from the governor of West Virginia and an expenses-paid week in Hawaii from its governor.

eBay had launched the Auction for America with good intentions, but its community erupted in protest. Sellers were upset that eBay was hurting their sales by pitting charity auctions against traditional ones. Another point of contention: eBay had passed the shipping costs for charity auctions on to sellers—not buyers. "It sounds like we're ungrateful for not wanting to participate," one seller griped to CNET at the time. "It's not about not wanting to participate or not caring or not wanting to give, but eBay's kind of selling us down the river."

eBay's Auction for America also required users to pay for their auctions with Billpoint, squeezing PayPal out of the mix. eBay argued that the policy ensured proper accounting and the accurate transferring of charitable dollars. But sellers contended that eBay was using a charity effort as a cover to increase Billpoint registration. The press pounced, giving PayPal an opening to take a dig at eBay. "A PayPal representative told CNET News.com on Monday that the company would waive its fees if it were allowed to participate in the eBay auction," reported CNET.

Behind the scenes, PayPal went on the offensive. Reid Hoffman delivered a lengthy email to eBay attorney Rob Chestnut. "I write to formally express my disappointment that eBay has opted to exploit the recent tragic events to artificially boost the competitive posture of 'eBay Payments' (a.k.a. Billpoint)," Hoffman wrote. "By obliging all sellers who wish to participate in the Auction for America to register for eBay Payments accounts, you are depriving the victims of this assault significant relief."

Hoffman pointed out that most eBay sellers refused to accept Billpoint, and argued that eBay stood to lose relief dollars due to its "anti-competitive animus." "If your goal truly is to raise money for relief in this tragedy," Hoffman wrote, "you would be inviting PayPal to participate proactively and simply indicating to us how you would like us to support making this initiative successful. Instead, reasonable analysis suggests that you are simply continuing to exploit your market power through using false advertising and coercion to get the sellers to accept Billpoint."

Even as PayPal accused eBay of exploiting a national crisis for payments market share, PayPal itself added the dust-up to its growing antitrust dossier.

■ ■ ■

September 11 affected the company's operations directly. Nick DeNicholas had been brought in as a vice president of software development and was commuting from Los Angeles to the Bay Area. After 9/11, his colleagues recalled, he resigned, citing the strain caused by post-9/11 travel and the time away from family.

John Kothanek remembered a sudden interest in PayPal's work from various three-letter government agencies. "After 9/11 . . . The government—I'll just say 'the government'—came to us, and they said, 'We do not understand how money is moving around the world electronically.' Because they were still kind of number-two pencil people . . . And they were like, 'Can you help us?'"

Then there was the issue of PayPal going public. Public stock exchanges shut down from September 11 to September 17, their longest closure since 1933. When the markets reopened, they tumbled more than 7 percent; after five days of trading, over one trillion dollars in market capitalization vanished. Not a single company went public in September 2001—the first month without an IPO since the late 1970s.

Even before the attacks, PayPal's IPO had looked uncertain, coming as it did after a wave of dot-com failures. Several high-profile corporate accounting scandals also hung in the air. In 2000, Xerox had admitted to reporting $1.5 billion in income the company did not actually have. In October 2001, news broke that American energy and commodities company Enron had engaged in breathtaking fraud, including bribing foreign governments and manipulating the energy markets of at least two US states. That December, Martha Stewart became embroiled in her own securities fraud scandal. Each week seemed to bring malfeasance of the multimillion-dollar variety.

Into this maelstrom stepped PayPal. Despite the environment, the company continued to take tentative steps toward going public. After leaving Morgan Stanley, PayPal's executives chose Salomon Smith Barney to see the IPO through. The SSB bankers advised postponing the IPO until 2002, even as Thiel demanded it go forward sooner. "The longer it takes for us to go public, the worse it is for us," Selby explained.

The bankers' reluctance notwithstanding, Thiel had several reasons for filing PayPal's IPO with haste. For one thing, he understood that the IPO process was lengthy. "Who knows where the world is going to be in three months? So let's just get it started," he thought.

In college, Thiel had immersed himself in the work of a French literary theorist and philosopher of social sciences, René Girard, who was best known for a concept called "mimetic desire." "Man is the creature who does not know what to desire, and he turns to others in order to make up his mind," Girard wrote. "We desire what others desire because we imitate their desires." Girard postulated that such imitation could produce rivalries and conflict, and that one ought to be on guard for it.

Thiel's interest in Girard often led him to zig where others zagged—an instinct that informed the IPO filing. "If you're in a world where no one goes public," Thiel explained, "maybe paradoxically, that *is* the time to go public. Because, you know, it's a positive counterpoint to the chaos or something."

But the timing of PayPal's IPO wasn't solely a triumph of Girardian logic. Thiel admitted that rivalry, conflict, and emotion also played a powerful role. "The competitive thing in me was just, you know, if the bankers thought we weren't ready, then it was more important than ever. It was sort of like a Wall Street versus Silicon Valley thing," he said of his will to prevail, "and there was a part of my thinking where, emotionally, I felt like the Wall Street banks were especially negative because we were encroaching on their turf."

Thiel was reflecting many years after the IPO, and he acknowledged that such rationales benefitted from the distance of hindsight. The famous rationalist also caught himself laughing at the feelings involved. "I aspire not to be this competitive," he said, "but I'm not always successful.

I don't think it's emotionally healthy to be this competitive, but that's the honest part of what drove it."

■ ■ ■

On September 28, 2001, the financial press broke the news: PayPal had filed its S-1 registration documents and would go public under the ticker PYPL. "PayPal Inc. has filed with the Securities and Exchange Commission to raise as much as $80.5 million," wrote CNN, "making its plans for an initial public offering a rarity in an otherwise empty marketplace for IPOs."

The attention didn't earn PayPal a positive portrait. CNN pointed out that PayPal had no contractual relationship with the source of most of its users—eBay—and that eBay could "restrict use of PayPal advertising or compel sellers to use eBay Online Payments" at any time. Worse still, the article continued, "PayPal has yet to reach profitability."

Reuters dubbed PayPal "a popular but money-losing Internet payment service." The Associated Press noted only three other tech companies had gone public in 2001, and that the last to do so, Loudcloud Inc., opened trading at $6 per share—but by then was trading at a moribund $1.12. The *Wall Street Journal* dubbed the IPO market "frosty." A prominent aggregator of internet news, Scripting News, linked to commentary about the PayPal IPO from a writer named John Robb, simply quoting Robb's line, "Talk about a bad time to file an IPO."

Countervailing views cropped up, though even those supportive of PayPal conceded the harsh climate:

We usually find that most passive observers (i.e., the press) to be decidedly negative on [PayPal]. Indeed, this week, we were interviewed by a leading US publication and couldn't get a word in edgewise about Pal's demand-driven economies of scale and inherent value proposition; instead, being asked to opine about the GAAP losses and the likely involvement of PayPal in adult and gaming industries. In short, this is a company that the press and perhaps public may love to hate.

The writer, FinancialDNA.com's Gary Craft, ascribed the negative press in part to the fact that the company's "management team comes from without, not within" financial services.

One critique that especially irked Thiel was titled "Affairs of State—Earth to Palo Alto." "What would you do with a three-year-old company that has never turned an annual profit, is on track to lose a quarter billion dollars and whose recent SEC filings warn that its services might be used for money laundering and financial fraud?" the author asked. "If you were the managers and venture capitalists behind Palo Alto's PayPal, you'd take it public." The writer of the piece chalked PayPal's proposed IPO up to insufficient "adult supervision" and concluded that the world needed a PayPal IPO "as much as it does an anthrax epidemic."

Thiel raged about the media's coverage at the office. "It really pissed Peter off," engineer Russ Simmons remembered. "And he gave this speech in front of the whole company talking about how they were idiots and we were going to prove them wrong. That's one of the times when I've seen him most fired up."

21

OUTLAWS

Thiel had been spared a September of blue hair, but just barely: By the end of 2001, the company's profitability push had finally yielded fruit. Every month of the fourth quarter turned a profit—though only if the cost of stock distributions to employees and the "amortization of good-will" from the merger of Confinity and X.com were excluded.*

Whether such costs should count toward a company's profitability was a roaring debate in accounting circles, but examined one way at least, PayPal could now consider itself in the black.

Thiel explained the company's underlying financials in a team-wide note in September 2001. "We have high fixed costs, low variable costs, and high variable revenues. The more payments flow through the Pay-Pal network, the more profitable the company becomes," he wrote. "The challenge for all the people working in product, marketing, sales, and business development is to move PayPal in a direction where we can increase the volume further—if we can maintain our growth rates for even two more quarters, PayPal will be in spectacular shape."

Even the share of payments through eBay took an encouraging turn by late 2001. Thousands of small business websites had adopted PayPal,

---

*"Goodwill" in accounting refers to the attempt to quantify intangible assets—brand value, training, loyal employees, and the like. They matter especially in the context of a financial transaction—like the merger of Confinity and X.com—when those intangible assets must be priced for accounting purposes. In 2001, companies were required to "amortize" those costs over a period, which reduced profitability.

and a third of PayPal transactions now originated from non-eBay web-sites. That growth mitigated the eBay risk substantially—and pointed to a future of more balanced revenue.

Even the timing of the IPO—which puzzled some commentators and outside observers—ended up playing to the team's benefit. PayPal filed its S-1 with the SEC just seventeen days after September 11, as the stock market plunged to three-year lows. But by the time PayPal's IPO was in the offing, the stock market had rebounded almost 30 percent from its September lows. Because Thiel had insisted that PayPal push through and file just following a national catastrophe, PayPal was one of the only firms prepared to go public in early 2002, and the company earned a disproportionate share of media and investor interest.

Reflecting on it in 2004, Thiel admitted that such attention was a double-edged sword. "I thought [the IPO] would be a cool thing to do because no one else was doing it," Thiel said. "The unfortunate downside was that we got way more scrutiny than we otherwise would have." Indeed, that scrutiny would nearly scuttle PayPal's IPO altogether.

■ ■ ■

The team set a tentative date for its IPO—February 6, 2002—and continued preparations apace. With financial scandals in the headlines, PayPal's IPO would have to withstand even tighter examination than usual. Staff from the accounting firm PricewaterhouseCoopers camped out in a company conference room to run a rigorous, line-by-line examination of PayPal's books.

The company's operations also required tightening. In late 2001, for instance, the company had announced that employees' friends and family could register to purchase shares—not in and of itself unusual for a pre-IPO company. PayPal, though, sought a twist. The team decided to use the PayPal service to sell shares to friends and family, in hopes that the move might drum up media coverage.

But in early January 2002, the company was forced to reverse course. "Participants who moved money into PayPal solely for the purpose of paying for their allocations," the employees were told in an all-company email, "should move it back out again as soon as possible."

The closer the IPO date, the more guarded the company's atmosphere became. "I just remember the stress and pressure of, like, *We need to keep the site up. You know, no [code] pushes that introduce anything too new, or that break the site*," remembered Kim-Elisha Proctor. For some time, screens within the office had broadcast total users, active users, growth rates, and transaction volume, among other data. Now, the company limited that information to user statistics only. Similarly, the daily and weekly reports that Roelof Botha's team assembled and freely distributed were now locked down to just the executive team.

Mark Sullivan—who had now donned the title VP of Investor Relations—reiterated the need to remain mum about the company, even to close friends and family. "The questions may seem innocent enough," he emailed the team, "but they hold dire consequences to us as a company if we reveal anything that is not already in the public forum." The company had to protect itself both from inadvertent disclosure as well as insider trading claims.

Despite battening down the company's hatches, old habits died hard. Janet He had received her offer letter just before the IPO, and she recalled the team's recruiter, Tim Wenzel, urging her to accept and start work quickly, even if that meant forgoing the requisite two weeks' notice at her other job. "[Wenzel] said, 'You better get started next Monday. I don't mind you doing two jobs.'" Wenzel wanted He to benefit from the pre-IPO prices of her stock options. "He was really nice to give me that warning," she remembered, laughing.

■ ■ ■

In the months before a company's public offering, its underwriting bankers organize a so-called road show to drum up interest among institutional investors. For PayPal's IPO, Jack Selby was among the executives enlisted to travel far and wide to pitch the company's story.

Almost immediately, he faced the residue of the prior year's dot-com failures. "These guys across the table . . . are like, 'We've seen this before. We've got burned by this. And we're not buying into this nonsense again,'" Selby remembered. As a business, PayPal didn't slot neatly into investors' familiar categories. "These guys really hadn't seen our type of business before. . . . Do we go into the fintech bucket? Do we go in the tech bucket? Do we go into the services bucket? As a hybrid it was difficult to understand which bucket to go into, and these guys were very rigid," he recalled.

Another concern surrounded the team's relative youth. As a part of the S-1 filing, companies are required to document the names and ages of their executive teams. In PayPal's case, this rounded to an average executive age hovering in the late twenties. "[The underwriters] were like, 'You guys have to have more seasoned execs on here. We can't take this to our clients,'" Woolway remembered. "And we said, 'Nope. This is the team we have.'" Woolway understood the bankers' plight, though. "The underwriters' job is to push back on all that stuff," he said. "Their job is to sell the stock, so they're doing what they need to do to make it easier to sell the stock."

The months leading to an IPO are a vulnerable time for any company. Legal actions against soon-to-be-public firms require refiling SEC paperwork, which can be an expensive, cumbersome process, and invite unwelcome media scrutiny. Competitors and other actors often take advantage of this exposed pre-IPO period to launch lawsuits. "The IPO is a good time [to sue]," explained Thiel, "because it's very time-sensitive, so you're normally just willing to write them a check and make them go away."

On Monday, February 4, PayPal was hit with its first suit. The plaintiff, CertCo, a near-bankrupt, New York–based financial cryptography start-up, alleged that PayPal's "electronic payment and transaction system" infringed on CertCo-owned US Patent Number 6,029,150. CertCo demanded a jury trial and "unspecified damages."

No one at PayPal had ever heard of CertCo. The team didn't consider it a competitor, and had never, to their knowledge, stolen an idea or a piece of code from their products. Still, Levchin called technical advisor

Dan Boneh, and together the two stayed up all night going through the claim's details.

CertCo had filed the patent in question in 1996, two years before the creation of Fieldlink, the mobile security company that grew to become PayPal. Granted in February 2000, CertCo's patent outlined a payment system in which a group of customers send money to a merchant through "an agent." The customer has a channel of communication with the agent; the merchant does as well. The patent application identified how keys could be used to secure the information flows from customer to agent, agent to merchant, and back again.

Generously interpreted, the patent resembled a rough outline of what PayPal became. That said, CertCo's patent described a process no different than those of many other online payment systems, including several predating PayPal. Technically, Visa, Mastercard, most banks, and nearly every online payment or digital cash start-up also infringed on CertCo's patent.

The CertCo suit was emblematic of a wider problem: the US Patent and Trademark Office's penchant for approving overly broad patent applications that covered ideas instead of inventions. Criticism of this practice was especially fierce in technology circles. In one famous case in the late 1990s, Amazon was granted a patent for "one-click" ordering, which it used to sue a competitor, Barnes & Noble. The case remained in court for several years before it was settled in 2002.

Amazon's lawsuit and the one-click patent received widespread criticism, including from tech pioneer Tim O'Reilly, who popularized terms like *open source* and *Web 2.0*. "Patents such as yours," O'Reilly wrote in an open letter to Jeff Bezos, "are the first step in vitiating the web, in raising the barriers to entry not just for your competitors, but for the technological innovators who might otherwise come up with great new ideas that you could put to use in your own business." O'Reilly chalked up the Patent Office's decisions to its lack of knowledge about digital technology.

CertCo's suit against PayPal looked analogous to many—the exercise of an overly broad patent that should never have been granted. And

CertCo's timing, of course, suggested nefarious ends. At no point from late 1998 to 2001 had CertCo taken any legal action against PayPal or its predecessor entities. "Patent infringement is all about extortion," Levchin explained. "They just come in and say, 'Look, we have a patent. You have a product. You have a million dollars. We have no money. Hand it to us, or we'll take you to the cleaners in court.'" Board member Tim Hurd put the CertCo situation even more colorfully: "It was total bullshit."

PayPal's executive team was furious as well and opted not to settle with CertCo. "Peter goes, 'Absolutely not! We're not paying these people a penny!'" Hurd recalled. That was, in part, because CertCo had filed a suit—as opposed to floating the possibility of a lawsuit with the option to settle. Once the suit was filed, PayPal had no incentive to settle. Chris Ferro, a PayPal lawyer, remembered Thiel's acid remark: "It's like they shot the hostage—then sent the ransom note."

Jokes aside, the team hired a law firm to fight the suit, and by Monday, February 11, the company had filed its response. However, CertCo's damage to PayPal's IPO process was done—the lawsuit forced the company to refile its SEC paperwork, which delayed its IPO by a full week. Thiel was livid. "One of the most emotional meetings I've ever been in," Ferro recalled, "was a phone call with CertCo, just as the IPO was being delayed. Peter was out of his mind with anger, and he could barely keep it together. I was pissed off as well, but I realized, whoa, whatever this means to me, it means a lot more to the guy who's been working his ass off for the last four years on it."

On its original S-1 documents, a company is required to enumerate its business risks. PayPal had already included its auction-heavy payment volume, the fresh competitors springing up seemingly by the day, and its more than $200 million in losses from its founding to the end of 2001. Now the team had to add the CertCo lawsuit to the ledger.

The story of the CertCo suit and resulting IPO delay ricocheted through the press. "In this kind of depressed market [for technology stocks], delaying your offering puts a real taint on it," one market analyst told *Forbes*. "It's a real negative."

■■■

On February 7, PayPal became aware that they were the target of another suit. The plaintiff this time—Lew Payne Publishing, Inc. (LPPI)—was an online payment company for adult websites. It charged PayPal with breach of contract, misappropriation of trade secrets, and intentional misrepresentation. According to its suit, LPPI had approached PayPal with a partnership to marry PayPal's payment processing with its own recurring billing service.

By LPPI's contention, PayPal went back on the agreement and then went into the pornography market on its own, and LPPI sued for lost revenue and damages. But here, too, the timing suggested dubious intent: The lawsuit was first filed in September of 2001, just as PayPal announced its plans to IPO. And PayPal was not served with the lawsuit until February 7, 2002, as its IPO was imminent.

A third legal headache soon followed: Tumbleweed Communications accused PayPal of patent infringement. It claimed that the links used by PayPal in its emails to users infringed on Tumbleweed's existing patent for links within electronic messages. Of course, PayPal was just one of thousands of services placing links in emails—yet another example of the broken patent system.

With Tumbleweed, unlike the earlier two suits, PayPal found an out. The company had merely notified PayPal that it was preparing to sue; it had not officially filed suit. Without a lawsuit filed in court, PayPal was under no obligation to amend its SEC filing—so it decided to stall Tumbleweed until the IPO.

Thiel dispatched Hurd to deal with the crisis. Tumbleweed had hired a Boston-based law firm, and Hurd had already made plans to be in Boston for a funeral. If Tumbleweed failed to file suit by the end of the day, PayPal's IPO would be locked. Keeping the firm occupied until 5:00 p.m. would be Hurd's responsibility. "That was my only job," Hurd remembered. "Just go there and act like I was negotiating with him. Whatever I could come up with to keep the guy in the room for four hours."

Hurd left the offices at 5:15—he had done it.

■ ■ ■

With different intent than the plaintiffs who sought to sue and settle, the SEC had also been scrutinizing the PayPal IPO closely—and according to PayPal, perhaps a little too closely. "We had the bad luck of the draw. We drew a very short straw [with the SEC]," Thiel later told a Stanford audience. "We got the one [SEC examiner] who was ideologically opposed to companies. He thought all companies in the U.S. were run by crooks and it was his job as an SEC regulator to prevent companies from ever going public." Woolway concurred, remembering the reaction of the company's lawyers. "Right when we got our examiner, our attorneys said, 'Oh shit, we got a bad one,'" he remembered.

Difficult or not, PayPal had elected to go public in the aftermath of the dot-com collapse, the attacks of September 11, and a raft of financial impropriety. The SEC's heightened scrutiny was likely reflective of the environment rather than anything about PayPal in particular, although the agency would have been within its rights to lavish special attention on a dot-com whose cumulative losses exceeded $200 million.

The SEC came down on PayPal in one instance, alleging that the company had violated the IPO quiet period—the period that stretches from when underwriters file a company's IPO registration to several weeks after a stock starts trading. During that time, the company is prohibited from speaking to the press or releasing new information not already included in its registration documents. Quiet periods exist to prevent insider trading; they also make ordinary company business more cumbersome.

The SEC flagged the fact that PayPal had paid fees to a research firm called Gartner, which had released a report on February 4 showing that PayPal had become the most trusted person-to-person payment service on the internet. The press release emphasized PayPal's strengths: "33 percent of online consumers surveyed consider PayPal a highly trusted provider of payment services," the survey declared. "The next most trusted service, Billpoint, is considered highly trusted by only 21 percent of respondents."

The SEC took issue with the fact that PayPal was told about the pending results before they were released to the public. The SEC didn't say this *was* a violation—just that it *could be* a violation. But either way, PayPal was forced to add a line to the risks in its S-1 document. "If recent contacts by one of our employees with the author of a research note which was published by a third party were held to be in violation of the Securities Act of 1933," they wrote, "we could be required to repurchase securities sold in this offering."

Between PayPal's IPO filing date and the public offering itself, the company revised and resubmitted its prospectus to the SEC eight separate times—twice the revisions that eBay submitted before going public. The extra scrutiny was a sign of the times, but having never IPO-ed a company before, most of the executive team took it as par for the course. "The whole process was problematic and long," Woolway recalled. "But I had no frame of reference for how it should have gone."

■ ■ ■

Along with the SEC regulators, eBay was also paying careful attention to PayPal's IPO prospects. A PayPal public offering threatened eBay's position: a stock market ticker would confer on PayPal a measure of credibility, and an avenue to raise more funds. It would become increasingly challenging for eBay to paint PayPal as a disreputable nuisance: following an IPO, the payments start-up in its backyard would now be regulated by the SEC, just like eBay itself.

PayPal, for its part, felt concerned about eBay right back. "We're going public and all of these people are going to call eBay," Hoffman explained, "and eBay's going to say, 'Oh, we think PayPal is a house of cards. We're going to drive them off our platform as soon as possible.'" Public investors, Hoffman noted, had a reputation for risk aversion. If eBay poisoned the well with these investors, PayPal's stock issue could fail.

With the quiet period hovering over much of early 2002, PayPal could say little to defend itself publicly, so Hoffman and the executive team came up with another way of muzzling eBay. *If they're in negotiations to buy us*, Hoffman remembered thinking, *if they say anything to the public market, it's breaking fiduciary responsibility*. PayPal, the executive team and its board decided, would enter another round of acquisition negotiations with eBay—to silence it.

Hoffman, however, remained aware of the possibility of a future acquisition from eBay—and therefore didn't want to burn bridges. "I was pretty resolutely convinced they were going to buy us at some point," recalled Hoffman. "So we needed it to be a very clean process by which they don't feel like they're mistreated if it doesn't happen and allows us to go back for a third negotiation."

In January 2002, Hoffman and Thiel approached the PayPal board to set a cash price offer for the sale of the company, at a price point high enough to make a healthy return, but not so high that eBay executives would immediately balk. The PayPal board and its executives came up with $1 billion. PayPal expected its IPO to price the company somewhere between $700 and $900 million; the billion-dollar price tag included an expected premium from a would-be buyer.

Hoffman approached eBay with the offer. The eBay team came back with counteroffers, but Hoffman stood firm. "I have a mandate to sell the company for a billion dollars," he remembered saying. "I'm not trying to negotiate." And of course, every day of "not trying to negotiate" bought PayPal an additional day of eBay silence as its IPO marched to a close.

eBay recognized that an acquisition of PayPal before the IPO might prove wise financially and came back with a final offer of $850 million. "If what you're telling me is that your last offer is $850 million," Hoffman remembered telling eBay, "I can take it to the board. But just to be really clear, I have a mandate to sell the company for a billion dollars. If you gave me a billion-dollar offer, you'd own the company."

eBay's CEO Meg Whitman reportedly grew frustrated at PayPal's unwillingness to yield, complaining to Hoffman that eBay had shown good faith in increasing its offer, yet PayPal hadn't responded in kind. "I think she thought we were going to take the $850 million," Hoffman said. "She didn't realize that my principal goal was to keep them quiet, not sell the company."

Had Whitman offered $1 billion in the first months of 2002, Hoffman would have brought it to the board, and according to him, the board would likely have accepted. "Part of what I grilled the PayPal board on is 'No take backs.' If I come back with a billion dollars in cash equivalent, we're going to do it. Otherwise, they're going to fucking hate us," Hoffman recalled.

Hoffman drew out the negotiating period for as long as possible, rejecting eBay's offer just days before PayPal's IPO. At that point, Hoffman called Whitman to tell her that the PayPal board was unwilling to budge from its $1 billion price tag. Whitman asked what PayPal's response would be if she was willing to go to a billion. With the IPO just days away, Hoffman hedged, responding that they could revisit the matter following the public offering.

During early 2002, numerous articles ran about PayPal's impending IPO. The curiosity of a nearly public payment start-up nested within another company's platform earned eBay a mention in each piece. Yet eBay's top brass remained quiet about PayPal on the record.

■ ■ ■

On Thursday, February 7, 2002, another crisis emerged. The State of Louisiana informed PayPal that it would be barred from doing business there effective immediately.

PayPal had been operating in Louisiana and other states without a state money transmitter license—an authorization enabling banks to send money to other banks in the state. This was, in large part, because PayPal had always insisted that it was not a bank. "There is always this question of what a bank is," Thiel explained. "Fundamentally, a bank is an entity that engages in fractional lending that's backed up by the Federal Reserve System." Banking regulations—he pointed out—were designed to protect consumers from the risks of banks collapsing because of fractional lending. Because PayPal didn't engage in fractional lending, the company, in his estimation, was not a bank and should not be regulated like one.

Of course, such messaging was in PayPal's interest: to be a bank meant being regulated like a bank. PayPal's critics—including and especially the traditional banking behemoths—took issue with this self-styling. In their view, PayPal took deposits, issued debit cards, held money, and paid interest—and the law ought to treat it for being a bank in all but name, including requiring money transmitter licenses.

PayPal had managed to skate along because enforcement of money transmitter licenses varied widely by state. Louisiana hadn't bothered to take a look at PayPal's license status before the media attention leading up to its IPO. One journalist, *BusinessWeek*'s Robert Barker, contacted financial agencies in California, New York, Idaho, and Louisiana for quotes—outreach that, per Thiel, made its way to the SEC, who notified the state of Louisiana. "We do frown on anyone retaining funds for a customer," Gary Newport, general counsel in Louisiana's Office of Financial Institutions, told Barker. "Until we have resolved [our concerns], PayPal has been instructed that they may not do business." Authorities from California and New York also informed the company that PayPal's money transmitter licenses were a subject of inquiry. Once more, PayPal was required to refile its S-1 documents with the SEC.

Though Louisiana held only a small slice of PayPal's user base—roughly 100,000 users out of a base in the millions—the company feared that one loose thread could unravel the entire regulatory fabric. "Obviously, you don't want these kinds of negatives to come out in a panicky market like this," one analyst with IPO.com declared. "It's tough to say what will happen now. It's all going to depend on the fortitude of the investors that they had already lined up for the IPO."

Publicly, PayPal said it would reserve "the right to contest the [Louisiana] order through the appropriate administrative process." Privately, the team scoured the state for a sympathetic regulator, a process made more difficult because Louisiana's action against PayPal came amid the state's preparation for its annual Mardi Gras celebrations. Thiel and company managed to track down a state banking commissioner and plead their case.

The team pointed out that 100,000 Louisianians depended on PayPal, and if the state shut the service down, those constituents might blame state officials. "Did they really want to deal with all these people who, after all, vote in elections in Louisiana?" Thiel remembered saying.

"And [the commissioner] agreed that, yeah, maybe Louisiana didn't want to get a reputation as an unusually backward state," Thiel recalled. Soon thereafter, PayPal was back doing business in the Pelican State.

This move, according to others on the team, likely rescued the IPO. "Absent that . . . we would have had to postpone the filing," Selby said. "It was a pretty heroic, game-saving shot." As the team sorted out Louisiana, Thiel pressed them to contact officials in California, New York, and Idaho, to prevent other states from following Louisiana's example and complicating the IPO proceedings.

■ ■ ■

From the middle of January through early February, PayPal faced two lawsuits, the threat of a third, the Louisiana ban, license inquiries from California and New York, the Gartner survey flap, and skeptical investors. These stiff headwinds had delayed the IPO from February 6 to February 15, and some on the team began to wonder if the IPO would be pulled off at all. Thiel himself worried that any other shock would be one too many. "My sense is that this deal cannot withstand another surprise like this—the whole thing will just come apart," Thiel reportedly told his colleagues.

Thiel pushed the team and the underwriter to complete the public offering quickly, even if it meant pricing the shares lower than expected. Originally, PayPal's bankers anticipated that the 5.4 million shares the company was offering on the public markets would sell for between $12 and $15 each, raising $81 million on the high end. Now, Thiel told the bankers, he'd take less for completing the IPO quickly.

Uncertainty permeated the company. Rumors spread about another legal shoe dropping, and even about the IPO being called off altogether. Because friends and family had been invited to participate in the public offering, employees were now fielding the worries of old friends and concerned relatives as well. In New York, Ken Howery, Roelof Botha, Jack Selby, and others were trying to work with the bankers to update documents and soothe the anxieties of institutional investors. In Palo Alto, several employees pulled sequential late nights to address the patent litigation and fine-tune the IPO paperwork.

"We came that close to not getting the IPO done," Hurd said, pinching his fingers together.

■ ■ ■

On the evening of Thursday, February 14, 2002, the Associated Press first broke the news that PayPal had priced its initial public offering at $13 a share and would list on the Nasdaq exchange the next day.

Like its earlier IPO coverage, the night-before story wasn't exactly a glittering debut. "I can't help but think the company is asking for problems," said David Menlow, president of IPOFinancial.com, a site that covered public offerings. "Why would people get aggressive buying a stock like this when there's a day-to-day possibility that the service might be shut down?" Menlow had once counted PayPal among that quarter's most promising IPOs, but he had recently downgraded it to "risky" after the torrent of negative news. Another IPO analyst was "mystified" by PayPal's decision to go public. "Why would they want to price this offering," she asked, "when everyone is going to be waiting for the other shoe to drop?"

Employees recalled the foreboding of that sixteen-hour stretch and the sense of apprehension gripping the office. For PayPal employees in relationships, the evening of February 14 proved an especially uncomfortable Valentine's Day. Many were torn between long-planned dinners with significant others—and their colleagues assembling at the PayPal office, nervously finalizing IPO details.

■ ■ ■

After the Nasdaq opened on the morning of Friday, February 15, 2002, PayPal's 5.4 million shares went up for sale to public investors. Initially priced at $13 per share, the stock shot up to $18 within minutes. PYPL traded as high as $22.44 its first day, and closed at $20.09—a remarkable 55 percent increase, the best opening for an IPO so far that year.

"Bruised and battered by a week of bad news," wrote the *E-commerce Times*, "online payment company PayPal (Nasdaq: PYPL) finally staggered into the Wall Street spotlight, becoming the first Internet IPO in nearly a year." The positive coverage finally flooded in, and PayPal's head of PR, Vince Sollitto, did not restrain his relief. "I feel like a tank," Vince Sollitto admitted to a credit card trade publication at midday. "Everything's been thrown at us."

PayPal employees joyfully called family members, and as team members arrived at the Palo Alto office early that morning, the enthusiasm felt palpable. "The IPO was, at that point, the pinnacle of what you could do in a company. And we were a small enough company that doing this in the face of what had happened meant that you had arrived in some sense," remembered engineer Santosh Janardhan.

During eBay's and Amazon's IPOs, employees were admonished against obsessing over the stock price; in PayPal's case, the executives dispensed with that fiction and broadcasted the figure onto the screens that usually featured user data. "Everybody was checking the ticker every three minutes—or three seconds," Scott Braunstein remembered.

In the afternoon, the Barenaked Ladies song "If I Had a Million Dollars" coursed through the office—the signal that the party could begin. "I remember thinking, *Wait, we're not working the entire day? Is that possible?*" Amy Rowe Klement shared. "Gives you a sense of the soundtrack playing in my mind!"

For many of the earliest founders and employees whose once-small start-up was now a publicly traded company, this was a defining moment. "You have literally thousands of hours of work culminating in the rest of the world saying you're successful . . . ," Erik Klein observed. "You see your salary—but you don't see any tangible outcome from any of the work you've done for those years. Until that one point—in which case it's all dropped on you at once. It's toilet paper until that day." Several employees shed tears of happiness and relief throughout the day.

Early Confinity engineer James Hogan described the IPO day as "deeper than 'we did it!' It was deeper than a sense of shared accomplishment . . . it wasn't just that we were winning some David-versus-Goliath battle."

To him, it represented "a vindication of . . . the culture and values by which we were operating." After a long pause, Hogan remarked on "the sense of trust, which, in part, seemed based on this fact that everyone was kind of willing to evaluate ideas based on what's going to work. That we were able to find this value alignment that cut through a lot of bullshit. It was able to help us create good things in the world—and have the process of doing that, working together day-to-day, feel empowering and enlivening, rather than one-dimensionally stressful and soul-sucking."

John Kothanek remembered gazing across the crowd in the parking lot and seeing the parts that produced the whole. "We weren't a big company still," he said. "And you know, there's a couple hundred people standing out there at the most. And you could look at the people and you could say, 'I know what that guy did to get us to this moment. I know what that woman did to get us to this moment. I know what he and she, and her and him . . . did to get us here,' and I was, like, I was just so proud of everybody."

■ ■ ■

Max Levchin would later call it "the happiest day of my life," and colleagues recalled that their otherwise stoic CTO was caught up in emotions. He spent the day in revelry, captured in a photo in which he skewers a dollar-sign-shaped green piñata with an oversized plastic sword. "Considering I am doing this after consuming a full bottle of champagne," he wrote in a caption on his personal website, "it's pretty amazing I can aim so well."

Compared to the decadence of late-'90s dot-com parties, the PayPal IPO celebration was tame. Held in the parking lot of the 1840 Embarcadero office, there were no nationally recognized musical acts, elaborate ice sculptures, or pricey hors d'oeuvres. Instead, the team set up plastic folding tables and installed a handful of speakers for music. Kegs of beer, copious bottles of bargain champagne, and heaping piles of cheap food arrived. Some employees slinked away to Palo Alto Creamery, where they purchased the most expensive item on the menu: the "Bubbly Burger," a $150 hamburger accompanied by a bottle of chilled Dom Pérignon.

The team recalled their amazement at seeing both CEO Peter Thiel and general counsel John Muller performing keg stands. "People doing keg stands," Jeremy Roybal recalled, "who have *clearly* never done a keg stand before." After the stock market closed in the afternoon, Thiel and

Levchin sported paper crowns, and for the first time in a long while, only a few PayPal employees planned to work through the Friday night. "It was the one time we were allowed to just not worry about work," Klein observed.

The festivities had PayPal-ian quirks, of course, with celebration mixing with competition. The employees' most vivid memory of the day was Peter Thiel playing ten simultaneous games of speed chess in the parking lot. Each game included a cash bet, the bills tucked neatly under the sides of the chess boards. A large crowd huddled, as Thiel played each board and moved to the next in rapid succession.

During one stretch, Thiel won nine out of ten games. "Peter doesn't drink much . . . and we made him do a keg stand that day," Janardhan recalled. "And after that, he was half-drunk—and still beat nine out of ten people! It's crazy." David Sacks earned lifelong bragging rights for being the only player to beat Thiel during the simultaneous chess match. ("When Peter lost, he was pissed," one observer noted, "I just remember him getting up and clearly screwface—like livid.")

As the day wound down, Thiel gave a speech putting PayPal's success into context. "He said how PayPal's market cap was bigger than United, American, and Delta combined," Braunstein remembered. The team distributed PayPal windbreakers, which became known as the "IPO jackets" and signified early PayPal employee status. Dionne McCray crocheted the PayPal logo into a white beanie, which she wore for the occasion.

The company's celebrations lasted well into the night. "The IPO party was basically a massive blur in my mind," recalled Levchin. Oxana Wootton remembered the mix of "happiness, celebration, tears . . . kind of like a New Year's celebration . . . that kind of excitement."

Celebrations notwithstanding, some PayPal leaders understood that the IPO wasn't an end—it was a start. Amy Rowe Klement had joined the company in September 1999 as one of but a handful of X.com employees. She recalled her feelings of "disbelief and anticipation" that PayPal was now a public company. The disbelief was that "our hard work was coming to some level of fruition." But that feeling mixed with anticipation. "[It was] the recognition that the real work was ahead of us," she explained.

"In many ways, it was simply the beginning of a new chapter. We were now a grown-up company and had an even greater responsibility to our users and our investors."

■ ■ ■

The public markets had valued PayPal at just shy of $1 billion. Thiel, Musk, and others on the executive team had regularly lobbied the board for equity distributions to employees, and for many of those employees, the IPO provided a significant financial windfall. "This was the first liquidity event that any of us had, outside of Elon," Woolway remembered. Particularly for those who had joined early and stayed for several chaotic years, the IPO was vindication—a sign of success more tangible than user growth or transaction volume.

Post-IPO, Thiel, Levchin, and others at the executive level were, at least on paper, multimillionaires now, and Sequoia Capital, Nokia Ventures, Madison Dearborn Partners, and other investors all saw a healthy return on their investments.

Far and away the biggest personal windfall went to Elon Musk. Per public documents, Musk was historically the company's biggest individual shareholder and had acquired even more equity as time went on. By the time the company's ticker blinked on Nasdaq screens, Musk owned more PayPal stock than even institutional backers like Nokia Ventures and Sequoia Capital, and with his holdings, Musk's grub stake was now worth more than $100 million.

In the space of four years, Musk had expanded his fortune from eight figures to nine—and laid the foundation for his future efforts. "PayPal going public is what allowed me to have the capital to start SpaceX, because I could sell stock or borrow against the stock," Musk said. "Before that, I didn't really have meaningful cash."

22

AND ALL I GOT WAS A T-SHIRT

In the IPO aftermath, PayPal's employees undertook a new ritual: checking PYPL's stock price. Due to a lock-up period, most employees weren't allowed to sell their shares for several months, and even then, newer employees' shares would remain unvested—allocated but not officially distributed.

Estimating personal net worth would also prove therapeutic. Less than a week after PayPal's IPO, eBay announced that it would pay $43.5 million for Wells Fargo's 35 percent stake in Billpoint. This presented a problem for PayPal. To start, the price made PayPal's nearly billion-dollar valuation look inflated. If PayPal was dependent on eBay transactions, Wall Street analysts asked, then how could eBay's own payments platform be worth eight times less than PayPal? On the day the Wells Fargo deal was announced, PayPal stock tumbled 15 percent.

More troubling, though, was the prospect of eBay outright owning its payments arm. eBay would no longer be constrained by risk-averse bankers and could theoretically ramp up the product, make deals, or even spin Billpoint off as a stand-alone entity if it desired. The press covered the move as a threat to PayPal, and Billpoint CEO Janet Crane reinforced those concerns, promising that the buyout would allow "increased integration of Billpoint and eBay over time."

eBay also used the moment to gain leverage against PayPal. Out of the press's view, PayPal and eBay had resumed negotiating a possible deal. The Wells Fargo buyout looked to PayPal like a threat: if a deal wasn't reached, the auction giant would remain free to compete more aggressively for payments' share.

Beginning in late March 2002, PayPal's internal team prepared detailed reports about its business for their eBay counterparts. On March 21, 2002, eBay made an offer to purchase the company, at a valuation of $1.33 billion, with the merger agreement calling the two companies by code names: PayPal was referred to as "Orca," and eBay as "Ernie." (In a prior iteration of a merger agreement, PayPal had chosen a smaller marine animal for a code name. Before becoming a public company, PayPal was coded "Porpoise.")

At a morning board meeting on March 22, 2002, PayPal's directors discussed the deal. Thiel made the case, per board minutes, that "eBay executives expressed to [Thiel] a desire to put all of the speculation regarding a potential combination of the two companies behind them." He added that this was "a pivotal point for eBay, and they are making a strategic decision to either move forward on their own and 'fight' PayPal or to buy PayPal."

The board concluded that the two companies' fates were linked, for better or worse, and that an acquisition by eBay was better than another prolonged series of fights. The board "authorized Messrs. Moritz and Thiel to deliver their response to eBay and to continue discussions with eBay regarding the potential merger."

The board met frequently during this negotiating period, but by April 10, "Mr. Thiel reported that the likelihood that the merger will be accomplished has decreased since the previous board meeting." In the time between eBay's offer and April 10, PayPal had begun to prepare its first official quarterly update as a public company—and the announcement of its first profitable quarter ever. During the same period, eBay's stock price had stayed relatively flat, and eBay's executives had been "adamantly opposed to a floor or a collar on the stock price in the deal."

By April 11, the deal's fortunes had sunk. "The [PayPal] board determined that, in light of its pending announcement of a profitable first quarter, among other things, it was not prepared to proceed with the merger under the current terms." Thiel was authorized to present alternative terms, including "an increase in the exchange ratio" and "a price collar or floor on the value of eBay stock to be received in the merger." Neither, they suspected, would pass muster with eBay.

News of the negotiation leaked, and by the time PayPal's profitable first quarter was announced, the combination of a possible eBay acquisition and profitability sent PayPal's stock price over $26—rendering a deal even less likely. Some on the team suspected that the negotiations had been leaked to intentionally tank the deal.

Ultimately, the cause mattered less than the outcome: the deal was now off (again), and the two sides resumed their hostilities. Katherine Woo had joined the company just prior to the IPO, and she remembered a spring 2002 team meeting about eBay. "They called us all into this conference room . . . and gave us the speech—this intense speech!—about how eBay was trying to kill us. And like, eBay had hundreds of engineers working on Billpoint with the express purpose of trying to kill us," she said. ". . . And I was like, 'Shit. I'm going to be working *really* hard this summer.'"

■ ■ ■

In early 2002, eBay announced eBay Live, an in-person celebration of all things eBay scheduled to begin June 21 in Anaheim, California. The event would bring together eBay's universe of sellers, buyers, vendors, and hangers-on, and CEO Meg Whitman would keynote.

Vince Sollitto's wife had noticed the event in a newspaper. "She circled it and cut it out and gave it to me," Sollitto recalled. "And she says, 'You guys need to be there.' And so I gave it to David [Sacks] and David's like, 'You're right, we need to be there.'"

The company had already been making plans to attend and to do what other eBay vendors and third-party businesses had been invited to do: host a small booth staffed by employees. Sacks, however, thought the occasion merited a more dramatic appearance.

After brainstorming, Sacks and his team arrived at two ideas, both of which were designed to agitate eBay. First, PayPal would host a big event the night before eBay Live's opening. After PayPal sent the invitation, the Motley Fool reported, "PayPal's Crashing eBay's Party, Again."

Thunder successfully stolen, PayPal turned to its second idea. The marketing team had procured thousands of T-shirts featuring the PayPal logo on the front and the phrase "New World Currency" on the back. They'd distribute them at the event with an incentive: those seen sporting the shirts at eBay Live would be eligible for a $250 cash prize. The goal was to remind eBay senior leadership that PayPal was inextricably tied to its seller community. Even eBay's most vocal cheerleaders would wear PayPal swag.

As eBay Live opened its doors, PayPal logos were everywhere, with attendees wearing the shirts in the hopes of winning free cash. eBay took notice. It had ordered its own T-shirts for the event as well but had planned on charging for them. But with the proliferation of PayPal T-shirts, eBay changed course. "[eBay offered] people an eBay T-shirt if they traded in their PayPal T-shirt," Sacks recalled. "So people would just come and get a second free T-shirt from us and then trade it in for an eBay one."

As Meg Whitman took to the conference stage for her keynote, she was greeted by thousands of hushed eBay users—and a staggering number of PayPal T-shirts. For the PayPal team, the coup de grâce came when *USA Today* published a story on July 1, 2002, about eBay Live on the front page of its "Money" section. In the accompanying photo, Whitman is smiling and signing autographs. One autograph seeker is shown standing to her left—with the PayPal logo emblazoned across his chest.

■ ■ ■

Jeff Jordan, the head of eBay North America, was at eBay Live and saw all this firsthand. Of course, by that point, the eBay-PayPal conflict had been a fixture of his life for years. PayPal's tactics at eBay Live only deepened his distaste for the competition.

Jordan had come to eBay in 1999. Following business school and a stint in management consulting, he went to Disney, where Meg Whitman was a top executive. Jordan eventually became the CFO of Disney

Stores. From his perch in consumer retail, Jordan could see the internet freight train coming. He joined Reel.com, an online video rental and video-on-demand website, as its CFO. But Reel.com struggled, as its ideas were, per Jordan, "ten years too early," and he began searching for his next venture.*

In 1999, Meg Whitman, now at eBay, recruited Jordan to join her. Six months later, in early 2000, Jordan was promoted to running eBay's North American division, which included oversight of payments—and the exasperating PayPal problem. When eBay bought Billpoint to compete, Jordan was to oversee it, but the then-head of Billpoint, Janet Crane, petitioned Meg Whitman to run the business herself. "That was probably the best thing to ever happen to my career," Jordan admitted.

As Billpoint lost market share to PayPal, Jordan saw that PayPal had mastered the element of the payment business that bedeviled others: "PayPal leaned into risk," Jordan explained. By underwriting transactions between eBay buyers and sellers, PayPal earned small slices of payments revenue that grew as network effects kicked in. Over time, the

---

*That search led to a memorable job interview. Steve Jobs had been hunting for a CFO of Pixar and reached out to Jordan, who agreed to meet Jobs for breakfast at Il Fornaio in Palo Alto. "I show up in my suit jacket," Jordan recalled, "and [Jobs] walks in in Chacos and torn clothes, twenty minutes late." Jobs only had two interview questions for Jordan. Question one: "You went to Stanford Business School in the late '80s, and then you're in the center of the company creation universe in the most exciting time in the world . . . and you became a fucking management consultant?" Question two: "How could you work at Disney for eight years? Those guys are fucking bozos . . ." Jordan saw the questions for what they were: a Steve Jobs stress test. "I'll cop to the first one," Jordan said. "It took me ten years to find my way back here, but I'm back and I'm here to stay." On the question of Disney, he pushed back, hard. "You're wrong on Disney," he said. Then he explained that Disney stores had higher consumer ratings than the Disney theme parks. "And we sell stuff!" Jordan said. Jobs seemed satisfied and pitched Jordan on Pixar. Jordan demurred; he had just been a CFO, and he was looking for something different. Jobs proposed he join Apple instead to head a new division. "I have this vision for Apple stores," Jobs said, and proceeded to outline a reimagined shopping experience from the roots up. Jordan thought Jobs "delusional" and politely declined the offer. "Of course," Jordan said of Jobs's retail concept, "he nailed it."

team refined their risk models and reduced fraud—thereby turning raw scale into a real business.

Because he ran eBay's North American operations, Jordan had taken heat from eBay leadership for allowing PayPal to operate unbothered on the platform. But he felt that his hands were tied. He didn't run Billpoint (that was Crane's domain), and he couldn't block PayPal and make Billpoint eBay's default payments system. Like others in the industry, Jordan also had a healthy fear of antitrust issues. "We had all this hygiene going on," Jordan remembered, "like don't use the word *dominant* in any document." The PayPal team had intentionally stoked such fears. "It was very good posturing," Jordan said of Reid Hoffman's antitrust theatrics. "He'd come and meet with me and say, 'Boy, you know, if you guys tried to bundle Billpoint [with eBay], that would be a real antitrust concern, wouldn't it?'"

Jordan and his team were also highly attuned to the eBay community, where PayPal usage numbers spoke for themselves: millions of eBay users were actively choosing PayPal for their transactions. To kill PayPal, Jordan worried, eBay would be committing not just homicide, but suicide. "I was ambivalent on shooting PayPal," Jordan admitted, "because it made my business work."

Jordan and others on the eBay team recalled endless meetings about PayPal, and like his counterparts, he and his team gamed every possible plan for competing with, shutting down, or gumming up PayPal's efforts. But by 2002, it was deemed a lost cause: PayPal had become a publicly traded company with loyal users, and eBay would have to live with the indignity of its presence.

■ ■ ■

That presence had, by this time, graduated to interdependence. Nowhere was this clearer than at eBay Live. "They did a wonderful job of guerrilla marketing," Jordan recalled, chuckling.

For Jordan, the T-shirt gambit was a powerful reminder that the two companies should have been considered more symbiotic than competitive. Moreover, fighting over T-shirt convention market share illustrated the inanity of it all: users loved both eBay and PayPal, but the companies hated one another.

At the event, Jordan waved David Sacks over. "We basically struck up a conversation about how foolish this competition had become," Sacks said, "where we're now competing at the level of T-shirts."

Sacks had reached this conclusion long ago, as had others on his team. "So much of our volume came from eBay," Amy Rowe Klement emphasized. "We were completely dependent on our enemy." Few on the PayPal team saw that risk dissipating without a deal between the two companies, though. "Reid had a pithy means of describing the challenge: 'Just because someone shoots five bullets at you and misses . . . does not preclude the sixth one from killing you,'" Keith Rabois wrote on Quora years later.

Sure enough, eBay had a sixth bullet ready to go. In addition to buying back its stake in Billpoint from Wells Fargo, eBay had quietly entered discussions with Citibank. There was talk of selling Billpoint to the bank and eliminating all payment fees. The deal would solve eBay's payments problem and allow them to undercut PayPal on price; the bank would capture a brand-new set of customers. "If we did the Citibank deal, [PayPal] was done," Jordan hypothesized.

Still, Jordan saw more upside in acquiring and integrating PayPal into eBay than in selling Billpoint off to Citibank. eBay had, after all, just exited one bumpy relationship with a bank, and there was no guarantee Citibank could succeed where Wells Fargo had failed. And Jordan saw in PayPal a booming business in its own right—one that he believed could become bigger than eBay itself.

The PayPal team heard whisperings of the eBay-Citibank deal, igniting a fresh round of panic. Sacks and Levchin approached Hoffman to inquire about using the antitrust paper trail to stymie eBay's efforts. Hoffman explained that the antitrust paper trail had been, at best, a feint. There was nothing about the proposed eBay-Citibank deal that would cause antitrust authorities to take preventative action. Besides which, PayPal still functioned on eBay, alongside other services, which made the antitrust threat more bark than bite. "The gun looks very real. I can wave it at you. I can gesture it at you. I can point it at you," Hoffman explained. "If I pull the trigger, what comes out is a little flag that says 'Boom!' It's all psychological persuasion."

The Citibank negotiation may not have been enough to invite regulatory action, but it had another effect: the threat prompted David Sacks to renew the eBay-PayPal negotiation.

∎∎∎

When Thiel and Hoffman had to call off PayPal's pre-IPO negotiation with eBay, they had agreed that Thiel would deliver the message to Whitman—letting Hoffman take the fall for the deal's dissolution. Thiel would tell eBay leadership that Hoffman had taken things further than PayPal's executive team had wished. When he delivered the news, Meg Whitman grew furious and stood up from the table. "If it's war you want," she reportedly said to Thiel and other PayPal executives present, "it's war you'll get!"

These and previous negotiations had left a bitter taste. eBay leadership was justified in its frustrations: PayPal and eBay had now gone through four negotiations for acquisition, and the price eBay had offered had gone from $300 million to $500 million to $800 million to now over $1 billion. Each time, either the total value or the terms of the deal had torpedoed an accord.

Sacks and Jordan—the peacemakers this time around—recognized that they faced a microscope externally as well as internally. If the press got word of the negotiation, the news could doom the outcome, as it had in April.

The PayPal executive team agreed that, given the bad blood of the past, Thiel and Hoffman should recuse themselves from the talks. Coincidentally, Meg Whitman had scheduled a personal trip to Southern California, which pulled her out of the negotiations, too. "The only way we got the deal done at the end," Jordan admitted, "was that Meg and Peter were completely recused."

From July 3 to July 7, eBay's executives worked through the terms with David Sacks, John Malloy, and Roelof Botha. "We descended on

PayPal on a Saturday and started doing diligence," Jordan remembered. By the time the weekend was up, Jordan and his team had their presentation for the eBay board ready. "We went from term sheets to definitive merger agreement in four or five days," recalled Sacks.

The PayPal IPO had smoothed the way for these latest talks. "[The IPO] was incredibly helpful to the deal, because there was a mark," Jordan said, referring to the clarity offered by PayPal's stock price. "We had tried five times to buy it, but the first four times, we couldn't agree on the price. Once it was marked and it traded a little bit, it's worth $1.4 billion." Both Sacks and Jordan could present clear cases to their boards, and per PayPal board minutes, eBay had softened on a number of key merger provisions, including "lack of a collar on the price of eBay shares."

The PayPal board discussion on Saturday, July 6, 2002, was rigorous and covered "at length the current proposed transactions as well as the alternatives to the transaction and the risks of either doing the transaction or continuing as a stand-alone entity." Despite more favorable terms and a $1.4 billion offer, several board members still believed that PayPal's best days were ahead of it. Musk, for instance, believed that the figure still undervalued the company. "I'm like, you guys are out of your minds," Musk said. PayPal board members Tim Hurd and John Malloy voiced doubts as well. "I struggled with that one, because I knew that we were selling for less than what I believed the company would be worth," Malloy recalled.

The board minutes of that Saturday meeting documented PayPal's business risks—and detailed how an eBay-PayPal union might mitigate them:

- that a combination [of PayPal and eBay] would lessen the risks of the Company's strategic growth plan;
- the market check process conducted by the Company in 2001 indicated that eBay was the only realistic likely bidder for the Company;
- no other company has made a proposal to acquire or merge with PayPal or made an attractive proposal to enter into any other transaction with PayPal;

- the merger would minimize the risk of losing access to process payments on online auction sites;
- the potential to lessen the risks of changes to card association rules, risks from fraud and uncertainties regarding financial services and online gaming regulation;
- that the current consideration was the highest price per share that could be negotiated with eBay;
- the premium that the exchange ratio provides over the IPO price, the price of common stock sold in the secondary offering and the stock price as of July 5, 2002;
- the potential impact of the merger not being consummated, the potential inability to retain key employees.

Ultimately, the deciding factor for Malloy, Hurd, and Musk was the executive team's insistence that they and their direct reports were at the end of their tether. "They did ask us whether or not we wanted to be acquired by eBay," Skye Lee recalled. "And I was tired. I'm like, 'I'm ready. I can't do this anymore.'" Malloy knew Max Levchin could endure inhuman levels of work. "When he told me, 'It's time.' I knew we had to sell," Malloy recalled. "You can't force people to keep working if they've gotten to that point."

For many on the PayPal team, working at the company had become an exercise in perseverance—not production. "This repeated experience of almost dying is not something people can stand," Luke Nosek said. "You want out because of the exhaustion. It's better to have a financial exit than to have everyone so drained that maybe the next thing you need to do just won't come out."

Malloy also noted that once the idea of an eBay exit—and its associated financial rewards—hung in the air, it was hard to claw back. "It's very hard for normal people to put that genie back in the bottle," he said, although he saw Thiel as being less moved by post-exit riches than others. "He's more philosophical about it," Malloy said of Thiel. "He doesn't think about it at that mundane level. It's more like he's deferring risk."

On the morning of Sunday, July 7, 2002, the board met again for a final review of eBay's offer. Thiel called for a vote; Malloy seconded the call. "The directors were individually polled," per the minutes. "Each director present voted in the affirmative." PayPal would be sold to eBay.

■ ■ ■

At eBay, Jeff Jordan had convincing of his own to do, and he rehearsed familiar arguments: "I'm Amazon—without a cart," he remembered saying. "We should buy our cart."

Though eBay's executive team were supportive, one eBay board member, Starbucks CEO Howard Schultz, encouraged the team to reconsider. He pointed out that PayPal had only recently achieved profitability, and then just barely. eBay's $1.4 billion, he argued, could be better spent elsewhere.

Others saw the acquisition not as a short-term solving of a payments problem, but rather as a long-term play for the company. eBay board member Scott Cook, the founder and former CEO of Intuit, argued that PayPal would be additive to the eBay business—and that it could yield great returns over the long haul.

This was in keeping with Jordan's case. "In my pitch to the board, I said [PayPal] would be bigger than eBay—to some scoffing," Jordan said. "It was going to help eBay, but it was also going to be an enormous business built on eBay's back."

Though the majority of the eBay board ultimately voted to acquire PayPal, the vote had holdouts. "It was the first nonunanimous vote in eBay's history," Jordan said.

■ ■ ■

On Monday morning, July 8, 2002, the news broke: eBay would be purchasing PayPal. The two companies would continue operating independently, and the deal would be subject to "stockholder, government, and regulatory approvals." eBay Payments by Billpoint, the press release said, would be phased out.

At 4:30 a.m., Sal Giambanco sent an all-company message from Thiel making the acquisition announcement official. Minutes later, Giambanco followed up with a message about an all-hands meeting for those in the Mountain View office (which, later that morning, was divided into two meetings because of the team's size). As people rolled into the office on that Monday, the air was thick with rumor, chatter, and confusion. One employee likened the mood to soldiers learning of an armistice while still fighting on the field.

Rumor spread that Meg Whitman would address the PayPal employees at noon—confirmed when a podium appeared with the name "Meg Whitman" printed in the multicolored style of the eBay logo. As team members assembled in "Arctic Circle," the company's largest conference room (so named to honor a broken thermostat from the conference room of an earlier company office), Thiel took to the "Meg Whitman" podium—to some snickering from the crowd. "See what I have to put up with?" he joked. "This is why I'm selling the company."

As recounted in Eric Jackson's *The PayPal Wars*, he pitched the team on the sale. "They made us a pretty good offer—we get an eighteen percent premium over the current stock price of the company," he told the crowd. "There's always some question as to whether or not these kinds of deals make sense. But given that we got a good valuation and removed a huge risk from the company, I think it does."

No one's job would be at risk, he promised, and no positions would be eliminated—"Except for Billpoint." The room clapped and cheered. "It will probably take about six months for the deal to close and for the acquisition to be official," he said. "Until that time everything will stay the same; the two companies will continue to be run separately. After the sale is complete, PayPal is going to remain an independent unit within eBay with the current management team left intact."

After his brief remarks, employees filed out of the conference room. "I guess we won, didn't we? Although being bought, it just doesn't feel like it," one employee remarked to another.

Fraud analyst Mike Greenfield couldn't remember whether he heard the news about the eBay acquisition over the radio or over his company email. But he did remember his thoughts on his way to work. "While I was riding my bike to work, I was thinking *Maybe I should apply to grad school? I don't really need to stay here anymore.*"

■ ■ ■

Employees felt surprised, relieved, and anxious in equal measure. Their company had just been bought by the same entity it had spent years fighting and mocking. Despite Thiel's assurances, many wondered what this would mean for their roles and for PayPal's future.

David Sacks told his product team that it wasn't clear who the "victor" would have been if the two companies had continued fighting it out. "In these cases, if it's clear, then a deal usually cannot be struck," he explained to his team, per Eric Jackson's recounting. "Victors wouldn't want to be acquired because they'd know they were going to win, and losers wouldn't be able to convince anyone to acquire them." He also reassured them that he and Botha had driven the best bargain possible—reaching what he and the PayPal senior team felt was eBay's maximum buyout.

PayPal customers shared the team's apprehension. On the one hand, some noted on the message boards, the deal would put an end to confusion caused by eBay's multiple payment methods. But others argued that one of PayPal's strengths—quickly releasing "new features that are simple to understand and use," as one put it—might be put at risk under the new ownership.

Some in the press also looked askance at the deal. Wall Street analysts questioned whether PayPal had made the right move given the high expectations for the company. "Selling to eBay," one analyst archly noted, "may have just been the easy way out." Others saw rank self-interest in the deal. "Only a few people—namely early investors, management, and investment bankers—left richer," a CBS MarketWatch columnist wrote.

With the office abuzz, Meg Whitman arrived at noon, sporting a PayPal baseball cap. She took to her podium and offered warm greetings. She asked how many PayPal employees used eBay. A number of hands shot into the air. When she had asked a group of eBay employees that morning whether they had used PayPal, she confessed, almost every hand rose.

Whitman walked the PayPal team through eBay's business, providing a survey of its scale and growth. "You should be very proud of the company that you've built," she said in conclusion, "in spite of us sometimes putting up some roadblocks." She finished by thanking Sacks and Jordan for driving the agreement forward. After some Q and A, the PayPal employees exited Arctic Circle, and were handed eBay T-shirts on their way out in commemoration of the moment.

Whitman was trying to be gracious, but she faced a tough crowd—including many that were not immediately won over. One employee recalled her speech as "buzzword bingo." "Every third word was 'synergy.' And I looked around the room, and I could see she'd lost the room within the first five minutes," he said. "Because everybody's like 'This isn't the company we were. It was very, very corporate.'" In Whitman's defense, it's possible that nothing she said may have won hearts and minds in that moment. She was speaking before an audience that, in the heat of their competition against eBay's Billpoint, had once constructed a "Meg Whitman piñata."

Bob McGrew had arrived late that day and had not yet heard the news. Someone tossed him an eBay T-shirt, and when he asked why, someone else replied, "We just got bought by eBay."

"And I thought, *What is going on?*" McGrew remembered. "Slowly it sunk in that this was what was going to happen."

■ ■ ■

Coming after PayPal's IPO, the eBay acquisition felt anticlimactic—and controversial. For years, PayPal alumni would debate the merits of the decision, with strong partisans on all sides.

There were those who argued that the deal was essential and inevitable—after all, selling out was preferable to burning out. "We just kept, not running out of options, but running out of steam," Vivien Go remarked. "And a lot of effort and energy and resources were being spent on fighting eBay. It wasn't any more on value creation . . . A lot of people really felt that it would be better to get it over with . . . just so that all these resources that are being spent trying to destroy each other could be spent elsewhere, on actually growing the business."

Katherine Woo worked on non-eBay merchant service and she viewed the eBay-PayPal deal as the crucial intermediary step between PayPal's creation and its growth on non-eBay sites. "We needed footholds to get to where PayPal is today," she explained. "And eBay was a really important foothold. And so I think we needed to go through this period where we were bought by eBay to completely integrate, with no barriers, no war between us . . . We kind of needed that chapter to get big enough then to be taken seriously off eBay." By becoming the default payment provider on eBay, she noted, PayPal scaled rapidly, refined its fraud model more quickly, and more easily convinced non-eBay sites to adopt it.

Still, there were others who maintained that PayPal's true value was yet to be seen, and that selling to eBay curtailed the company's growth. And then there were those who felt the sale polluted PayPal's abiding mission—changing the financial system. "If this was the revolution, would you sell it for money?" Luke Nosek asked.

In the final analysis, the eBay sale was another in the company's rich history of risk-mitigation tactics. The list included merging, cutting bonus payments, fighting fraud, and even going public. From one angle, PayPal's success was an exercise in careful hedging as much as it was in innovating—and the sale to eBay was simply the latest hedge. "People don't understand the dynamics. They don't understand the competitive pressures from eBay and the lobbying pressures. It was much more com- plicated than it seemed on the surface," Jack Selby said.

■ ■ ■

As if to prove the point, one threat materialized the day following the deal's announcement. On July 9, PayPal received a subpoena from New York State Attorney General Eliot Spitzer. Spitzer had announced that he was investigating PayPal's links to offshore gambling.

By late 2001, PayPal's executives had begun to grow wary of the gaming business. The company's already tenuous relationship with Visa and Mastercard risked fraying further thanks to online gaming. They also believed that potential investors in the Middle East might balk if PayPal turned into the world's leading provider of gambling payment services. But perhaps the biggest risk arose from the world of politics. Congress was beginning to pay closer attention to offshore casinos, and Representative Jim Leach had introduced a bill in Congress to block US financial institutions from servicing them. State attorneys general were also beginning to crack down—chickens that came home to roost when the Spitzer subpoena arrived.

By this point, eBay and PayPal had announced their deal, but it was still subject to shareholder and regulatory approval. Spitzer's investigation, in other words, came at a sensitive time. One quirk of the investigation, however, turned out to be an unexpected gift. "Among the entertaining things is that they sent it snail mail," Hoffman recalled. "If they had sent it FedEx, it would have shown up before we closed the deal with eBay."

Chris Ferro, one of the team's lawyers, saw the subpoena risk as a live wire. "We were worried that eBay would take the position that the Spitzer subpoena was a 'material adverse change' and that they would try to get out of the deal. So my marching orders from Peter were, 'Don't let this become a material adverse change. We *need* to close this deal. Make sure that happens.'"

Of course, eBay wasn't blind to the millions in gambling revenue on PayPal's books, and the issue had been a point of contention during the negotiation. Sacks had wanted to keep the gambling business intact; Whitman wanted to jettison it, stat. eBay won the battle: PayPal agreed to abandon the gambling business, and the merger announcement stated as much. "It's critical to eBay that in the announcement of the deal, we're announcing that we are getting out of this," Hoffman remembered. "As it turns out, [that was] a godsend." (For Dan Madden, who landed in Curaçao just as the eBay deal was broadcast, the announcement was far from a godsend. His casino clients peppered him with questions about the fate of PayPal's gambling transaction administration. "It was an uncomfortable week," he said.)

The announced ending of PayPal's gambling business took some—though not all—of the teeth out of Spitzer's action. PayPal still had to address the subpoena. Hoffman appreciated that PayPal's past records weren't entirely innocent: it had, after all, been processing payments for offshore casinos, and while the company hadn't violated the law, there were gray areas that had ensnared other payment processors.

Hoffman and PayPal's lawyers settled on an unconventional approach: "I went to the PR department, and I said I want a booklet . . . that starts with every media mention that we've gotten out of gambling already. Start with all the most important national media. Then all the most important New York media. Then everything else. I want it all," Hoffman told them. "The booklet was also saying, 'That big press win you're hoping for? That's already gone. You're not going to get any wins by crucifying us.'"

Evidence against themselves compiled, the team requested a meeting with the New York AG's office. "We told them we wanted to meet at their first available convenience. 'You literally tell us the day, and I—a member of the exec team—and the general counsel and whoever else will come out at whatever hour you select,'" Hoffman described his strategy. "You're trying to steer into the 'We're adults and honest. We're collaborative. We're not trying to evade or delay.'"

Hoffman and PayPal's attorneys walked the attorney general's team through their own wrongdoing point by point, even admitting to what may have seemed the most egregious violation: a two-week stretch during which Visa had changed its gambling codes, and PayPal had processed payments incorrectly. "You could watch the change in their body language . . . they all leaned back, opened the folders, and said, 'Which dates did you say they were again?'" Hoffman remembered.

The company's ingratiating approach took the bite out of the prosecution's efforts, particularly once the team offered their help in finding other bad actors. The company would be let off the hook with a $200,000 fine.

■ ■ ■

In late July, the PayPal team gathered for its final off-site as an independent company. They chose a spot on the foothills of the Santa Cruz Mountains overlooking Silicon Valley. Thiel headlined the festivities with a speech reviewing the company's history, remarks captured in Eric Jackson's *The PayPal Wars*.

"Sometimes we've said it feels like the entire world is really against us . . . Well, it is!" Thiel began. "First, they thought the banks would put us out of business. And when that didn't happen they said our customers would stop using us. And when that didn't happen they called on the rest of the earth to join them."

Thiel then proceeded to quote two articles, one titled "Losing Faith in PayPal" and the other—an old favorite—"Earth to Palo Alto." He recited the latter's bracing words: "What would you do with a three-year-old company that has never turned an annual profit, is on track to lose a quarter billion dollars and whose recent SEC filings warn that its services might be used for money laundering and financial fraud?"

Thiel paused as the audience laughed, then switched gears:

"There are two major trends of the twenty-first century," he said. "First, the globalization of the economy. The economy is growing internationally and people from all over the world are becoming interconnected. One billion people now live in a country other than their place of birth. Second, the quest for security. In this globalized, decentralized world, violence and terrorism are widespread and hard to contain. Terrorism has contaminated all countries, and it's difficult to stop it. The challenge is finding a way to fight violence in the context of an open, global economy."

Thiel continued, explaining that in his trips to Washington, he had been disappointed by both sides—left and right—who seemed to him to misunderstand both the world's problems and possible solutions.

"Neither side is asking the right questions regarding the pressing needs of the day.

"In our own way, at PayPal this is what we've been doing all along. We've been creating a system that enables global commerce for everyone. And we've been fighting the people who would do us and our users harm. It's been a gradual, iterative process, and we've gotten plenty of stuff wrong along the way, but we've kept moving in the right direction to address these major issues while the rest of the world has been ignoring them.

"And so I'd like to send a message back to Planet Earth from Palo Alto. Life is good here in Palo Alto. We've been able to improve on many of the ways you do things. Come to Palo Alto for a visit sometime and learn something. I think you'll find it's a much better place than Earth."

While some recalled the insertion of politics into the celebratory IPO speech as an awkward moment, others reflected these sentiments back later, noting that PayPal's political subtext dovetailed with the company's belief in individual achievement. Vivien Go remarked that her time at PayPal "turned me into an American." "One of the mottos early on was to democratize payments," she remembered, "so some little seller in another part of the world who would never have had any options could, you know, do business and actually improve their life."

That paired, at least in her experience, with PayPal leadership's willingness to empower anyone at the company: "[PayPal's executives] were truly interested in changing the world, in celebrating the best that a human can be. So they celebrated each person's contribution. It didn't matter if you were just some rank and file. If you had something to say, they wanted to hear it . . . They really believed in individuals, as opposed to institutions."

■ ■ ■

On the penultimate day before acquisition, the team held another celebration in the parking lot of 1840 Embarcadero Road—the final hurrah before becoming employees of eBay Inc. The executive team donned inflated sumo suits and agreed to a mock wrestling match in an over-sized ring. The founders of PayPal—soon to be wholly owned by a competitor—slammed into one another as employees cheered for their particular boss from the sidelines. Even on the final day of PayPal's independence, friendly competition reigned.

CONCLUSION: THE FLOOR

Peter Thiel hadn't put a company-wide transition plan into place for the months following PayPal's acquisition. Instead, Thiel left for international travel in the wake of the announcement, leaving David Sacks in charge. Sacks had been serving as COO, and some anticipated that he may be promoted to CEO in PayPal's post-acquisition future.

Even as the deal was being finalized, the dispersion began. Thiel started planning his next move: a return to his global macro investment fund. Jack Selby, Ken Howery, and several other PayPal alums joined him and assisted in the preparations. "We were up trading by October," Selby said.

Thiel sent a brief departure note to the full company on Thursday, October 3, 2002:

All:

Effective at the close of markets today, eBay completed its acquisition of PayPal. After some careful reflection over the last few weeks, I have concluded that this is the right time for me to move on to new challenges, and therefore this will be my last day with the company.

For all of us on the PayPal team, it has been an incredible and unforgettable few years. I have always known that people are the most valuable part of any business, and today I'm more certain than ever that this is the case. As long as we stay focused on that reality, the future for the eBay-PayPal combination will be bright indeed.

In founding PayPal, Max and I started by hiring a number of our friends. Over time, we also hired our friends' friends, and so on, moving out in concentric circles. I consider it a lasting testimony to our success that the existing friendships have grown stronger, and many new ones have been formed. I know that we'll keep in touch.

Cheers,

Peter

■ ■ ■

In the months between the acquisition announcement and its commencement, it became clear that neither the eBay nor the PayPal executives had fully prepared for the reality of integrating the two teams. PayPal executives weren't all that keen on becoming eBay employees. "We all had to play the game of going and talking to the eBay folks about wanting to stay," Woolway remembered. "But it was very obvious that no one at eBay wanted anyone at PayPal to stay . . . and no one [from PayPal] had any ambitions to stick around at the combined company."

Both sides anticipated cultural hiccups, and early meetings confirmed the teams' stark differences of approach. "It would take like a day to schedule a meeting," one PayPal board member remembered, "because [eBay was] so bureaucratic." At one point, the PayPal team trekked to eBay—only to be subjected to a 100-plus-slide PowerPoint presentation. "Well, I guess we're going to need to hire a PowerPoint person for ourselves," one PayPal executive joked after the meeting concluded.

eBay's goal had been to buy and integrate PayPal's technology and users—not recruit talent. "The vast majority of the skill set we brought as a leadership team was redundant," Selby explained. Meg Whitman appointed a homegrown eBay executive—Matt Bannick—as overseer of payments and, it was assumed, the future president of PayPal. Sacks would not be getting the top job.

eBay took pains to keep certain individuals on board, including several team members in key positions. Todd Pearson, for instance, had been responsible for maintaining the company's relationship with Visa and

Mastercard over the years. His skills and relationships had kept PayPal functioning. "If he were to walk out the door," Selby said, "they would have been screwed."

Several who stayed at eBay found big company life stultifying. "We're changing from our jeans-wearing mentality to a culture of wearing khakis," David Wallace said. But Wallace saw no value in fighting the tide of cultural change, as eBay had "decided what it was going to do . . . [PayPal] was no longer a giant version of a family business."

Former PayPal employees noted a disturbing increase in office politics, meetings, and reports to file. While some of this was the natural side effect of being a wholly owned subsidiary of a bigger company, PayPal employees accustomed to independence and speed felt at wit's end. Janardhan recalled that his new eBay boss didn't understand his job, going so far as to ask him for a spreadsheet that detailed what Janardhan did and how he spent his time, "so that I can appropriately allocate resources." Janardhan was nonplussed. "What are you talking about? This is, like, out of *Office Space*."

PayPal employees admitted that they did not make the integration of the two companies easy. "There were three to six months that were living hell—and we made it living hell on eBay," remembered Kim-Elisha Proctor.

PayPal alumni did not hide their displeasure. One memorable display came when eBay distributed plush mongooses tied to a company-wide emphasis on setting smart goals. In the PayPal area of the company's offices, former PayPal employees massacred their mongooses. One was strangled with an ethernet cable and left hanging from a ceiling. Another was stuck against the wall with a knife through its sternum. Yet another was crucified while wearing a miniature crown of thorns. The mutilated mongooses did little to endear PayPal employees to their new eBay brethren. "I found the behaviors of some of my colleagues embarrassing and downright inappropriate," admitted Amy Rowe Klement. "I had no data telling me that the leaders of eBay were unethical or evil. Why wouldn't I give them a chance?"

A snippet of the *Weekly Pal* from this period testified to the culture shifts. The teams had begun "integration meetings," and one recap showed both the challenge of mixing cultures—and some of the snarkiness that undoubtedly repulsed eBay employees:

> The PayPal/eBay Integration meetings on the product end have been going very well. The eBay folks have spent a lot of time preparing for these meetings, including lots of mock-ups. It's pretty awesome to see mock-ups of various eBay web pages with PayPal logos all over them.
>
> During one of the product integration meetings, they were asking if we could share IDs and passwords. We told them that obtaining PayPal passwords was like opening the doorway to that user's entire net-worth. David Sacks then proceeded to ask, "Has your site ever been hacked?" One of the innocent eBayians replied with a shrug, "Sure!" Sacks said, "Well, then it ain't happenin'." They agreed. =)
>
> And a few quotes:
>
> "Wow—you guys get free cold cuts!?"
>
> (At eBay), "we have to have our PRDs (a.k.a. specs) finalized for executive review by September 1 if we want these launched in January."
>
> Upon arriving at the front desk of eBay: "Who are you with?" ("PayPal") "Have you been here before?" ("No") "What's this regarding?" ("You acquiring us.") "Oh . . . OK . . . ummm . . . I guess you don't need to sign in."

Max Levchin stayed on as CTO longer than many had anticipated, but he struggled at eBay. He grew frustrated by big company life and found himself lacking a specific portfolio of responsibilities. John Malloy took his experience as a lesson for working with founders. "Because of Max . . . I'm so much more sensitive to the fact that, when my companies exit, I stay in touch with all my founders . . . because there's a loss," he said. "It's akin to depression . . . you have this thing fill your life every day and it's gone. You have to reinvent yourself."

Upon Levchin's departure from the company in November 2002, the team surprised him with a re-creation of the company's fabled IPO party. "The IPO Day was the best day of my life as far as I can remember," he said in an email to a small group afterward, "and [this] party was a faithful replica, complete with me making a fool of myself in front of lots of people. I am not sure what else to say about it . . . I loved the party, and I love all of you guys for putting it together and for your various other awesomeness :-)"

■ ■ ■

The rapid departure of Levchin and PayPal's senior-most leadership fed a narrative that eBay's culture was losing talent. But that telling overlooks the fact that many talented PayPal employees joined eBay post-acquisition and enjoyed lengthy, lucrative, and impactful careers there.

Katherine Woo arrived at PayPal in 2002, and as a result, she said, "I wasn't like dyed-in-the-wool, PayPal-or-bust. I wasn't there early enough." She stayed with the company and thrived after the eBay acquisition. Part of what kept her there, she noted, was deep respect for her manager, Amy Rowe Klement. "Amy cares about people," Woo observed, "and she wasn't caught up in this 'they're evil, and we're good.'"

For Klement, staying at eBay was driven by passion for a team she had helped to nurture from a handful of individuals above a bakery to an international financial firm. "I cared so deeply about my team (and for design, engineering, QA, content, etc.)," she explained, "and I had so much pride in what we had built. I wasn't ready to walk away. Related to this was my focus on my own leadership growth. I knew I had more to learn." She also felt the company had unfinished business. "We then immediately had to fight the narrative of being eBay's cash register," she noted. "We had to demonstrate that payments were bigger than any one marketplace."

Huey Lin was disappointed at the departure of the senior-most

PayPal alumni, but the exodus opened new opportunities for her and others. "Senior management all disappeared, and I had to shift my skills," she explained. Soon, PayPal's mid-level leaders earned fast promotions and learned how to manage people and navigate the mechanics of a larger organization.

eBay also offered instructional programs, including "learning and development" classes for managers—a new concept for PayPal employees. "[Management training] was not a thing at PayPal. You just kind of wing it," Lin remembered. She and others benefited from these offerings, and brought their newfound skills with them to later jobs.

Some PayPal alumni observed that success at eBay was, in part, a function of where an employee landed within the company. Early PayPal engineer David Gausebeck, for instance, joined the architecture team, where he stayed until 2008, six years after the acquisition. While he later founded his own start-up, he valued his time as an eBay employee. His team "was pretty insulated from anything about the eBay business. I was still working on the same problems and still building the same product and was still relatively happy doing that," he remembered.

Dozens of other PayPal alumni remained at eBay, and many credit eBay with providing professional development, teaching them how to scale a start-up into a mature organization, and rewarding them financially. Some still work at either PayPal or eBay as of this publication. For many, eBay's generous compensation made an impact. While Levchin, Musk, Thiel, and others benefited from both the IPO and the sale to eBay—in part because of an "accelerated vesting" of their equity, a common practice in such transactions—many of their colleagues had thousands of shares of unvested equity. Their years at eBay allowed them to earn a windfall.

■ ■ ■

Among others, Musk, Thiel, Sacks, Klement, and eBay's Jeff Jordan had all argued that PayPal could keep growing post-acquisition. History has proven those projections correct. In 2002, PayPal had more than 20 million users in dozens of countries; by 2010, it surpassed 100 million users in nearly every country in the world. As of this writing, PayPal counts more than 350 million users and conducted almost $1 trillion in transactions in 2020 alone.

The share of PayPal's business within the eBay ecosystem grew as well. Five years post-acquisition, PayPal accounted for a third of the company's total revenue; five years later, PayPal contributed nearly half. By some estimates, half of eBay's $70 billion 2014 valuation was attributable to PayPal.

In time, PayPal's impressive growth within eBay earned it a small chorus calling for its independence. In a 2002 talk at Stanford, a questioner asked Thiel what advice he had for PayPal. "The larger market is off eBay," he said, "and they should develop a lot of product features and functionalities that enable point-to-point payments in a non-eBay context."

The PayPal independence movement picked up steam, thanks to activist investor Carl Icahn. In 2013, Icahn took a significant stake in eBay and began to push it to spin off PayPal. In its January 2014 quarterly report, eBay responded: "Regarding Mr. Icahn's separation proposal, eBay's Board of Directors . . . does not believe that breaking up the company is the best way to maximize shareholder value."

Icahn and eBay sparred over the spring and summer, with Icahn levying charges of conflict of interest and lapses in corporate governance against eBay, in addition to his unceasing calls for PayPal's separation. "We have found ourselves in many troubling situations over the years, but the complete disregard for accountability at eBay is the most blatant we have ever seen," Icahn wrote in February 2014. In response, eBay called Icahn "dead wrong" in its own letter, titled "Stick to the Facts, Carl."

Icahn made his views public via lacerating open letters to shareholders and in press appearances. "PayPal is a jewel, and eBay is covering up its value," Icahn told *Forbes*. PayPal alumni weighed in on the debate as well. "It doesn't make sense that a global payment system is a subsidiary of an auction website," said Musk. "It's as if Target owned Visa or something . . . [PayPal] will get cut to pieces by Amazon payments, or by others like Apple and by start-ups if it continues to be part of eBay." Musk—who by this point was well into his dual-CEO-ship at Tesla and SpaceX—concluded that PayPal must either be spun out or sink entirely. "Carl Icahn can see it," Musk noted, "and he's not exactly super tech savvy."

Sacks agreed, arguing that PayPal, released from eBay's clutches, could offer a better experience than most banks. "If you allowed PayPal to pursue its destiny, there are moves it could make to become the largest financial company in the world," Sacks told *Forbes*. Sacks and Musk estimated that while PayPal's value had grown to an estimated $30 billion to $40 billion under eBay's ownership, it had the potential to become a $100 billion company on its own.

By summer 2014, PayPal president David Marcus departed for Facebook. A rising tide of interest in mobile payments followed the release of both Apple Pay and Alibaba's IPO, which raised awareness of Alipay, its payment product. All of this persuaded eBay to reverse course.

On September 13, 2014, eBay announced that it would spin off PayPal into an independent company. Reversing its January 2014 declaration that PayPal and eBay would remain one unit, PayPal CEO John Donahoe wrote, "A thorough strategic review with our board shows that keeping eBay and PayPal together beyond 2015 clearly becomes less advantageous to each business strategically and competitively." eBay shareholders would receive one share of PayPal stock per share of eBay stock they owned.

Thus PayPal went public for the second time in mid-July 2015, thirteen years after the announcement of its acquisition by eBay. As of this writing, eBay's market cap on the Nasdaq is more than $40 billion. PayPal is today worth more than $300 billion—more than 300 times its 2002 IPO valuation.

At twenty-plus-years old, PayPal has arguably become the worldwide payment system that its founders imagined. And yet, for some, even this scale of success is insufficient. "PayPal should be the world's most valuable financial institution by far," Musk argued. Years after they had left all of it behind, Musk proposed to Reid Hoffman that PayPal's founding team should reacquire the company and grow it into the world's financial nerve center.

Hoffman recalled the moment with humor: a musing of a compulsively ambitious friend whose to-do list included electric vehicles, space technology, mass transit, solar energy, bespoke flamethrowers, and much else. "It's like, Elon, let it go," Hoffman said.

■ ■ ■

Like PayPal itself, many of the company's founders and earliest employees have flourished. Several went on to build companies that are household names—such as YouTube, Yelp, LinkedIn, SpaceX, and Tesla. In several cases, the earliest investments in those firms came from the PayPal alumni network as well—Yelp, for instance, received its first investment from Levchin, who reportedly agreed to it the day after his birthday party, at which Yelp cofounders Jeremy Stoppelman and Russ Simmons mused about wanting localized reviews.

Even those who did not start their own ventures joined firms created by their PayPal brethren—Tim Wenzel, Branden Spikes, and Julie Anderson, for instance, all briefly joined Musk at his later ventures. Thiel later started a venture capital firm—Founder's Fund—that both hired many PayPal alumni and invested in their start-ups.

Not everyone hit the ground running, though. "I couldn't work for a year after that experience," Luke Nosek admitted. Instead, he traveled around the world following his exit. Others tried slower-paced, non-start-up environments. Both Bob McGrew and Levchin flirted with academic tracks. McGrew began a PhD program at Stanford. Levchin also sought a PhD in cryptography and spent a summer working with Confinity's early technical advisor, Dan Boneh. But then, Levchin recalled, Boneh pulled the plug on Levchin's burgeoning academic career.

"This is never going to work," Boneh said.

"Why? I'm loving this!" replied Levchin.

"No, no, because every time we talk, all you want to know is what is this going to get used for. You're just looking for your next thing. You're going to build your next company, not solve some complicated math problem," Boneh said. McGrew dropped out of his program as well. Thiel talked him into joining the big data analytics start-up Palantir Technologies as director of engineering.

Sacks's first post-PayPal effort took him, improbably, to Hollywood. Along with Levchin, Woolway, Thiel, and Musk, Sacks produced the satirical film *Thank You for Smoking*, which was nominated for two Golden Globes in 2007. Despite this success, he paused his production company soon after. "We created PayPal in three years, and we created a movie in three years," Sacks told a journalist in 2012. "They're both great experiences, but PayPal is a billion-dollar outcome that today has over one hundred million users . . . You can achieve things in technology on a scale you can't in movies." Sacks returned to Silicon Valley and created the corporate social network Yammer, which sold to Microsoft for $1.2 billion in 2012.

Some PayPal rivalries and fault lines have remained in place over the years and become well known in Silicon Valley circles. Some rifts, however, have unexpectedly healed. In 2010, Meg Whitman ran for governor of California. Among her backers: Peter Thiel, a former business adversary who contributed $25,900 to her campaign and advocated for her in the press.

■■■

By 2006, the story of PayPal's alumni network began to emerge in news stories, including a lengthy profile in the *New York Times*. But a 2007 *Fortune* magazine spread turned the group's linkages into legend. The piece's headline—the "PayPal Mafia"—stuck. The photos accompanying the article famously depicted Thiel, Levchin, and eleven other PayPal alums in mafioso regalia. Inspired by *The Godfather* films, the photo shoot took place at Tosca Cafe, an iconic San Francisco restaurant featuring plush leather couches and Italian murals.

Despite the photo's popularity, the image and description rankled many PayPal alumni, some who thought the mafia label was too calculating. "The 'mafia' [label] just kind of turned me off . . . That's not what PayPal was. Honestly, it was a big group of friends who thought they could do whatever they wanted, and just worked really hard, and were really smart, and willing to take risks and to lose. It's not like it was some grand plan," observed Kim-Elisha Proctor.

For some who knew and continued to work with the PayPal alumni, the moniker implied a polish and mystique missing from the company's roster of rough-hewn characters. "Almost everybody here feels like an outsider," Malloy observed. "There is no cool kid . . . The fact that now the PayPal people are the cool kids, they couldn't have been more opposite that."

Hoffman preferred the term "PayPal Network." "By grouping it as the PayPal Mafia, a lot of people assume that it's a whole bunch of people who think about the world in the same way," he told the *New York Times*. "In fact, it was a bunch of people who went through this really intense experience together . . . It's like the TV series *Band of Brothers*, a group of people who went to war together but were all heading in a variety of different directions."

Julie Anderson, employee number five at X.com, took issue with the mafia depiction of PayPal's founding network. When she first saw the photo—consisting of only male PayPal alumni—she said she felt "so nauseous. Because none of us were represented." Her criticism was justified: even as of November 2000, the company's 150-person phone list was one-third female, including several individuals—Julie Anderson, Denise Aptekar, Kathy Donovan, Donna Driscoll, Sarah Imbach, Skye Lee, Lauri Schultheis, and Amy Rowe Klement, among others—who worked in executive positions and played vital roles in the company's growth and success.

The iconography of the PayPal Mafia photo turned into a false idol—and a worrying one. As carefully documented in Emily Chang's book *Brotopia* and elsewhere, Silicon Valley has long had troubles with ensuring that women are treated equitably in hiring, fundraising, promotion, boardroom representation, and in the recognition of their achievements. The PayPal Mafia photo and mythology exacerbated this problem, and it gave photographic evidence of the "boys' club" critique.

For some PayPal alumni, the photo served as an unfortunate symbol of how a once-united team fractured in PayPal's aftermath. "The reality is that there is a very deep well of frustration & sadness & anger that while we (generally) did very well professionally," one alum wrote in an email, "the men stuck together, excluded us (generally) and became leaders of the world." She and others felt empowered at PayPal—but felt removed from much of the afterglow. These days, many of PayPal's alumni view the photo and the "mafia" label as a woefully one-sided depiction of PayPal's early team—and as the kind of image that reinforces damaging industry stereotypes.

SB Master, who birthed the PayPal name and thought a great deal about what companies and brands ought to dub themselves, believed that the "mafia" designation was a poor fit as well. She went on to consult for several of the early employees when they launched other companies and ventures, and knowing them as she did, she considered them a roster of offbeat nerds—rather than a tech mob. In thinking about the constellation of talent from PayPal's early years, she felt the name "PayPal Diaspora" spoke more powerfully to the offshoots of the original alumni.

Though included in the mafia photo, David Sacks also preferred the term *diaspora*. "It's not like a club. It's more like a diaspora movement," he said. "What basically happened is, you know, our homeland got taken over. They burned down our temple, and they kicked us out. We're more like the Jews than, like, the Sicilians."

■ ■ ■

Over time, the group hosted a number of reunions, including one at Sacks's home and another at Thiel's. Even those who had become distant from the core group marveled at how far their fellow alumni had come from their days on University Avenue. For Branden Spikes, the progress of his former colleagues was inspiring to witness. As he said later, "A lot of these people I sat next to in cubes writing code and building systems, and they went off to create some of the greatest companies that exist today. Getting back together with all these folks and hearing the stories was just so inspiring." Following one reunion, Spikes felt moved to raise funds to launch his own company.

Many held on to mementos from that period. More than one person interviewed for this book wore their X.com T-shirt or brandished a branded mug on screen. And several noted that their PayPal alumni status was powerful currency in technology circles—to this day they are peppered with questions about what they drew from those years.

Still, some have found the association stifling. "I don't want to just be 'the guy who created PayPal,'" Levchin said. So much has happened in the lives of the company's founders in the two decades since that one sympathizes. In the first email correspondence for this project, Musk wondered why anyone would be interested in the history of his second start-up. "It's a pretty old story at this point," he wrote.

But the old story casts a long shadow, and Musk himself betrayed a nostalgic streak. Decades after purchasing the X.com URL, he bought it again in 2017. Musk chuckled while retelling the story of his reacquisition of the domain. The broker who sold him the URL saw the deal as a crowning achievement. "[URLs] are his great passion in life, and he really knows his stuff . . . And he wrote me this long, heartfelt letter," Musk said.

Asked of his ambitions for the URL, Musk responded on Twitter. "Thanks PayPal for allowing me to buy back X.com!" he wrote. "No plans right now, but it has great sentimental value to me." At the time, a visitor to X.com was greeted merely with a single character, x. The rest of the page was left blank. Musk left an Easter egg on the bare-bones X.com site, though: Any other permutation of the URL—www.x.com/q or www.x.com/z, for instance—revealed the letter y instead.

In 2022, Musk purchased Twitter—and set about reviving his X.com ambitions. By 2023, he had renamed Twitter as X.com and rerouted the X.com URL. In interviews and posts, he'd elaborate on his conception for a super-app akin to China's WeChat, including a feature set that resembled his original, expansive X.com vision. To him, finance still hadn't taken full advantage of the information theoretic revolution. Decades later, he believed he could still bring that revolution to pass.

■ ■ ■

Though the founders engaged in little explicit talk about "company culture" at the time, PayPal's culture definitively shaped the approach of a generation of Silicon Valley talent. Today, the outsiders who built PayPal are among the most influential insiders in the world of technology and engineering, their utterances decoded, dissected, and debated. They are both leading and investing in companies, and they receive hundreds of pitches per week from up-and-comers full of ideas, ambition, and energy.

Inevitably—whether on podcasts, conference appearances, or in speeches—they share what they drew from their time at PayPal. This project benefited from those answers, but many were also quick to attach a disclaimer. "It's always unclear . . . what lessons to draw," Thiel explained, "because you can't really run an experiment in one of these companies twice."

Still, there is little doubt that the PayPal experience informed the group's future endeavors. Above all, PayPal proved to its founders that talented outsiders could upend an industry—something they've replicated in everything from professional social networking to government contracting to infrastructure. "What we learned from the PayPal experience was . . . that you could actually go and revolutionize an industry with people who were very smart, working hard, and deploying a technology that people hadn't seen before," Hoffman said. "And so, suddenly, which industries you might possibly go at becomes a much broader scope as a function of our experience at PayPal." Amy Rowe Klement echoed the sentiment: "If not us, then who? The idea that our motley crew of misfits could come together to build something out of nothing was really incredible."

The alumni also came to see inexperience as an asset. "Very few of the top performers at the company had any prior experience with payments," Mike Greenfield, a member of the fraud analytics team said, "and many of the best employees had little or no prior background building internet products." Had the company built its fraud process traditionally, he said, they "would have hired people who had been building logistic regression models for banks for twenty years but never innovated, and fraud losses would likely have swallowed the company."

Lauri Schultheis recalled specifically hiring *for* inexperience. "When we were looking to hire people for fraud, we were actually trying to find people that didn't have experience with fraud, because we didn't want them to have preconceived notions about what they would be doing at PayPal . . . We wanted them to be able to pivot and think outside the box and look at things from a different perspective, instead of saying, 'Well, you know, at such-and-such bank, this is how we did it, and that's how we should do it here.'"

Tim Wenzel recalled inviting a candidate in for a final interview with Thiel. After the candidate finished, Thiel walked him over to Wenzel's cubicle, and Wenzel saw the candidate out. By the time Wenzel returned from the door to his computer, a Thiel email awaited him: "That's it. Please, no more payments people."

Many were outsiders in another sense—the majority of the ten original cofounders of X.com and Confinity were foreign-born. "Immigrating is an entrepreneurial act," Sacks explained. "You take an affirmative step to leave your country, and you frequently leave everything behind. That's the ultimate entrepreneurial act. So it's not surprising that when people get to the US, they continue to try to do entrepreneurial things, to mold their own environment."

Levchin added an unexpected qualification for PayPal employees that he felt contributed to the company's success and the later achievements of its alumni: many of its earliest employees simply hated being employees. "The very best employee at any job at any level of responsibility is the person who generally believes that this is their last job working for someone. The next thing they'll start will be their own," Levchin said. "Having as many people like that as possible is what made the difference in the company, and it's what made it such a fertile ground for entrepreneurs later on." Board member Tim Hurd explained qualifications for PayPal employees more simply: "Were you an intellectual rock star? Number one. Could you do what we needed you to do really well? And would you work really hard to do it? Nothing else mattered."

To succeed in Silicon Valley is to become insulated from unorthodox outsiders who may shape the future. Today, several of PayPal's founders are likely closer to prime ministers than they are to the Tom Pytels of the world. "If you get to a certain level of comfort, it's hard to put it all on the line again and to appreciate the person who is putting it all on the line again," Malloy said. "Do you really understand that person that's sleeping on the floor?"

The founders—especially in their capacity as investors—have had to find ways of working around this challenge. To that end, Levchin takes regular meetings with smaller student organizations at the various colleges he visits, harkening back to his ACM days. Thiel is known for taking sit-downs well outside of his immediate orbit, including the occasional high school student who reaches out with a compelling note. Hoffman forces himself to regularly ask others: "Who is the most eccentric or unorthodox person you know, and could I meet them? They might be crazy—*or* they might be a genius." He's searching, it would seem, for the less than perfectly polished founder who resembles his once less than perfectly polished colleagues, a group that turned a "hot mess" into one of the world's largest public companies.

■ ■ ■

Still, these attributes of PayPal's employees explain only so much—late 1990s Silicon Valley was abuzz with offbeat "intellectual rock stars" willing to sacrifice social lives and sleep at the altar of start-up success. The company's achievements stemmed from other sources.

One was a relentless focus on the product itself—not just on the technology that underpinned it. "We were really very focused on building the best product we possibly could . . . We were incredibly obsessive about how do we evoke something that is really going to have the best possible customer experience," Musk said of his work on both Zip2 and PayPal. "That was a far more effective selling tool than having a giant sales force or marketing gimmicks or twelve-step processes or whatever."

Few epitomized that focus more than David Sacks and the members of the product team, many of whom would go on to distinguished careers in future product roles. Sacks himself carried product lessons from PayPal to his next endeavors, particularly regarding product distribution. At

PayPal, "we were starting from zero, with very few resources, and we had to figure out how to get distribution," Sacks said. "From the time that it was a PalmPilot thing . . . to the web product, it was always, how do we get anyone to discover this, so we can get anyone to use it?"

Designer Ryan Donahue remembered a team "obsessed with the distribution of their product. They had this very savvy and sort of really mature perspective on how important it was to be able to get your product into people's hands—and that that actually trumps the quality of your product and many, many other things." Amy Rowe Klement noted that the product team hired "high EQ leaders, who had customer empathy"— empathy that transmitted internally as well as externally. "We crafted the product management group to not just have empathy for customers and build great products," she observed, "but also to hold the company together."

Once that product problem was solved, PayPal's rapid growth led to another set of learnings that influenced the future work of its founders. Reid Hoffman's neologism "blitzscaling," for example, and Silicon Valley's obsession with fast growth can trace at least partial roots to the pair of start-ups on University Avenue. Russ Simmons remarked that one unintended side effect of that scale of growth was that it colored his view of future start-up experiences. "It definitely spoiled me for later, because it's like, 'Oh, you just launch a thing and then it takes off, right?'" he said.

■ ■ ■

That product and its proliferation were shaped through the crucible of the dot-com bust, and many alumni remarked on the generative power of external pressure. Born at the zenith of the dot-com boom, PayPal started to take off just as the wider industry tanked. "The majority of our experience," Jack Selby observed, "was after the bust."

PayPal came within a hair's breadth of a crash landing as well—in 2000, the company's burn rate left it with mere months of funding left. But those challenges inspired powerful outcomes: the team instituted fees and fought fraud, iterating rapidly on both fronts. Without outside financial pressure, many on the team suggest, those innovations may not have happened. "The best teams deal with meteors," Malloy observed. "Meteors that don't hit you create opportunity."

Even its tussles with eBay, alumni observed, evinced a fighting spirit. The team would have to build, release, iterate, and repeat as eBay challenged PayPal's use on the auction giant's home turf. "The thing that brought us really close together was battling eBay," Skye Lee noted, "because nothing brings a company together like having a mortal enemy."

Thiel points to this pressure as the defining characteristic of his PayPal experience. "If you're at a fantastically successful company like Microsoft or Google," he explained, "you will infer that starting a new business is easier than it is. You'll learn a lot of wrong things. If you're at the company that failed, you tend to learn the lesson that it's impossible. At PayPal we were sort of intermediate. We weren't as successful as some of the great successes of Silicon Valley, but I think people sort of calibrated it and learned the best lesson—that it's hard, but doable."

Their experience also made them stern judges of would-be start-up founders. "It's so much harder than people make it out to seem," Selby said of founding successful start-ups. In the group's work as investors, they judge the endurance of the founding team as much as the soundness of their ideas. How quickly will they move? How fast will they adapt to challenges? Will a team push to failure itself for the sake of learning? "If you're not redlining enough that you don't have some failures you're learning from," Hoffman observed, "then you're probably not learning at a fast enough speed."

There was, of course, a downside to such a pressurized environment. At times, fear of bankruptcy or eBay or a new competitor stiffened the spine; but it could also sap the spirit. Several employees half-jokingly referred to "PayPal PTSD"—the psychological toll of working round the clock in a company on the brink and with colleagues who could be intimidatingly intelligent.

In trying to explain the friction within PayPal, Levchin offered a compare-and-contrast between PayPal and his next venture, the photo-sharing service Slide, a meditation captured in published notes from a Stanford course about start-ups:

> The management team at PayPal was very frequently incompatible. Management meetings were not harmonious. Board meetings were even worse. They were certainly productive meetings. Decisions were made and things got done. But people got called idiots if they deserved it.
>
> The next time around, at Slide, we tried to create a nicer environment. The idea of having meetings where people really liked one another seemed great. That was folly. The mistake was to conflate anger with a lack of respect. People who are smart and energetic are often angry. Not at each other, usually. Rather, they're angry that we're 'not there yet,' i.e., that they have to solve x when they should be working on some greater problem. Disharmony at PayPal was actually a side effect of very healthy dynamics.
>
> If people complain about people behind each other's backs, you have a problem. If people don't trust each other to do good work, you have a problem. But if people know that their teammates are going to deliver, you're good. Even if they are all calling each other idiots.

Sacks observed that PayPal's culture of tension was also a culture of truth. "It was 'truth-seeking' . . . there was a lot of friction. We all respected each other and that's why it worked. There was a lot of yelling, and we just cared about getting to the right answer," he said.

David Gausebeck—a team member who didn't often raise his voice—left feeling that PayPal's culture was not predominantly one of conflict, but rather one characterized by high standards. Later, as the CTO and founder of Matterport, a 3D media platform, he drew on his mental model of the high-functioning team at PayPal. "You build certain expectations. Like when I'm working on a team, I expect all of them to be really good. That's my experience," he said.

■■■

For all their emphasis on hard work, intellect, product distribution, and bracing honesty, many PayPal alumni appreciated having been graced with something else: good fortune. "There's a lot of skill and smart people, but the bigger ingredient, by far, is a degree of luck," Selby reflected. "A confluence of events. The stars aligned. However you want to describe it. That allowed us to succeed."

"People always want it to be a simple narrative," Malloy said. "And that's not actually how it works. There's a tremendous amount of luck. I don't mean luck like you found a coin. You persevere in the face of changes, and you make your own luck. But even then, if the tide is going out on the idea, you may be doomed to fail."

For PayPal, luck came in several shades. The company was fortunate in its founding group coming together as it did. It was also fortunate in its timing. That the company didn't end up as just a forgotten PalmPilot accessory or a failed financial services superstore had as much to do with when it launched as what it offered. PayPal also managed to secure a vast, nine-figure round of funding in spring 2000—just before the bottom fell out of the market.

PayPal's product design was also appropriately timed—email addresses had become common, and the internet was essential by the time PayPal debuted. Had it arrived on the scene a year earlier or later, PayPal may have been too premature or too late, and the company may well have gone the way of eMoneyMail, PayPlace, c2it, or any of the dozens of the era's failed payment start-ups.

Its success worming its way into the eBay ecosystem, for all its hardship, also turned out to be felicitous. Had eBay fixed payments with Billpoint in the spring of 1999, PayPal may not have found its seed group of users later that year. eBay provided PayPal an active, vocal community of users who helped to spread the product. "There was an opening to start a company like PayPal, but even three years later, I'm not sure it would have been possible," Thiel said.

The company also went public and was acquired by eBay just before the internet's renaissance. PayPal alumni finished their tenure at the company as true believers in the internet amid a growing sea of skeptics. They had seen other companies die—casualties littered the field—but PayPal hadn't. Thus, they dove headlong into the "Web 2.0" movement, initiating and investing in the next generation of internet companies.

Because luck was at the heart of the story, PayPal alumni are quick to puncture any myths about inevitable success. "When you become famous in the Valley, you could be the ultimate outsider, but the Valley just co-opts you," Malloy said. "You become the fiction. The fiction takes over . . . We're all so damn good at spinning our own yarn. We lose sight of the humanity of it . . . who gets successful and who's not, boy, it's a thin razor's edge." That PayPal found the edge's fortunate side left some alumni with a commitment to expanding its breadth. "It's made me reflect on how we build this ability to dream in others," said Amy Rowe Klement.

PayPal's earliest employees reserve their highest praise for those who tread the same hard road—founders across varied fields of endeavor. "Those that bring the big ideas into hard, unpredictable reality are the practitioners, the high-leverage ones, and I admire them almost without reservation," Max Levchin wrote on a personal blog, years after PayPal. "One key ingredient of being this kind of a person is an almost irrational lack of fear of failure and irrational optimism, but there is a more tactical side there too: they manage to not get caught up in all the little details . . . while being remarkably aware of the really important ones."

By that point in his life, Max Levchin had ushered several ideas into "hard, unpredictable reality." And yet, he ended with an earnest request for advice: "There must be many more essential ingredients to being high-leverage. I'd love to understand this type of person better . . . so I can maximize my own leverage. Have any tips?"

Epilogue

In the process of completing this book, I set digital alerts for the phrase "PayPal Mafia." Like the people who lived the story, I arrived at a complicated relationship with the phrase itself. On one hand, it was a media-friendly descriptor, a quick way to explain what I was working on; on the other hand, the phrase was insufficient, as it explained later entrepreneurial efforts and connections, not the creation of PayPal itself. As I discovered, the term and the accompanying photo excluded many key players in the story—and portrayed the group as far more homogenous than they actually were.

While I strained to avoid contemporizing my subjects too much—obsessing over this or that modern Tweet or recent utterance—I did want to track the influence of the alumni group *as* a group. Unsurprisingly, the moniker "PayPal Mafia" was popular among the technology set. In the aftermath of an IPO or significant company acquisition, Twitter and other forums would light up with mentions of this-or-that would-be "mafia."

The term was especially popular abroad. In Europe, there was the "fintech Mafia" created by the success of Revolut and Monzo; in Canada, the alumni of Workbrain were similarly spotlighted. In Africa, the co-founders of Kenya's Kopo Kopo spoke explicitly about wanting to build the "PayPal Mafia of East Africa." In India, there was talk of how the success of e-commerce giant Flipkart had given rise to "the Flipkart Mafia." Some mafia references—"the Vegan mafia," for instance—weren't from the world of technology, but attaching the word *mafia* highlighted a similar sentiment and ambition: Could one seed group of talent nourish an ecosystem?

Dozens of these examples came my way through alerts and through friends, but I found the most interesting application of the "PayPal Mafia" in a world far removed from technology entrepreneurship. I hesitated to even share the story here, but it deserves to be documented, if only for posterity's sake. It is a singular tale—and it takes place clear across the country from Silicon Valley.

■ ■ ■

In December 1997, a white van delivered a teenager named Chris Wilson to the Patuxent Institution, a maximum-security correctional facility in Jessup, Maryland, just outside Baltimore.

Chris had grown up in Washington, DC, as the crack epidemic ripped through his community. Scores of young African American men fell victim to the mayhem all around them. By the age of seven, Chris had started sleeping on his bedroom floor instead of on his bed, to protect himself from stray bullets. By age ten, he had been to more funerals than birthday parties. By fourteen, he never left home without a gun.

Then Chris was given occasion to use it. Late one night, two men approached him outside a convenience store. "Chris, we got a message for you," one said. Chris wasn't about to wait to hear what it was. He pulled out his .38 caliber and fired six rounds. One man was killed instantly, the other ran away. Chris was tried as an adult and sentenced to life in prison.

It wasn't supposed to be this way, not for him. Chris had a family who cared about him. He loved to read; he played chess and the cello. He believed in his future. But he had been caught by the surging tides of carnage and criminality around him. If fear made him carry a gun, it was because Chris had seen things worth fearing.

One of his mom's boyfriends was a crooked cop. "One day," Chris said, "he knocked me out and raped my mom in front of me and bashed her skull in with his service weapon." His mother survived but neither she nor Chris was ever the same.

Walking to his grandmother's house one evening, he remembered stepping over dead bodies in the street. "How can you expect a kid to be normal," he asked, "when the people around him are dropping like flies?"

Prison was a shock, even to someone who had seen more than his share of shocking things. Upon arrival, he and nine other men were huddled into a room, stripped naked, and told to bend down for a cavity search. Chris recalls it as the most humiliating moment of his life.

Reality sank in: Patuxent was going to be his home for the rest of his days. One year passed in a depressive haze. Chris would wake up and wonder about how his promising young life had come to such a bitter, premature conclusion. He flirted with suicide. He smoked smuggled dope and cursed fate for bringing him here.

■ ■ ■

Stephen Edwards's path to incarceration in Patuxent resembled Chris's—a first-degree murder conviction handed down when he was sixteen. Before prison, Stephen's life had looked markedly different from Chris's. Stephen's parents were devout Christians, and he grew up with the gospel. He enjoyed a childhood of relative comfort and privilege: his dad worked for the Federal Reserve, and his family nurtured his considerable talents—which emerged early.

Stephen was a math whiz. His father would bring his work computer home at the end of the day, and Stephen would pass long hours learning how to program and play on the machine. He became especially interested in computer animation. Stephen devoted eight months to coding a five-minute animation of a NASA rocket launch. When the pixelated rocket blasted off successfully, Stephen beamed.

At twelve, Stephen began attending a public school in Washington, DC. There, his intelligence became a liability. He was bullied, constantly and cruelly. One evening, he was jumped by a dozen older boys. They smashed his head in with a crowbar and stabbed him in the rib cage. While his wounds healed, his psyche didn't. He grew paranoid about being attacked again and started carrying a gun for protection. At sixteen, he shot and killed a man who he thought was about to kill him. Stephen was sentenced to life.

■ ■ ■

Like Chris, Stephen had suffered through his first year in prison asking the same questions and finding few answers. But as the fog began to lift, Stephen turned back to his old love: computers. He thought that they might be able to sustain him through years of incarceration, if anything could.

Stephen's parents provided old programming books, and he began to teach himself new coding languages. Without access to an actual computer, he wrote out hypothetical programs longhand on yellow legal pads—same as young Max Levchin in Kiev. Lacking a computer to build the programs, he could only guess at their accuracy. But he enjoyed the puzzle solving of programming—and the satisfaction of building something from scratch.

Chris had been in prison for a year when he crossed paths with Stephen. "I met a guy who also was a juvenile who was serving a life sentence, and this guy was, like, super focused," Chris remembered. "He was studying to be a computer programmer. He had these goals and achievements that he wanted to get out of prison. I remember laughing at him, because he didn't even have a computer or access to a computer." They became fast friends and cellmates.

The self-improvement junkie in Stephen rubbed off on Chris. The two of them committed to a program of physical fitness, education, prayer, journaling, and reading—and held each other accountable. When Chris missed a math problem on his GED practice exams, Stephen would count out the push-ups Chris owed him.

Stephen's ambition set Chris's imagination alight. Inspired by Stephen's pursuit of computer programming without a computer, Chris wrote himself a list of stunningly ambitious life goals. He called it his "Master Plan," and among other things, it included learning Spanish, earning a college degree and an MBA, buying a black Corvette, and traveling the world. He mailed the document to the judge who had issued his life sentence.

■■■

Chris and Stephen became model prisoners. Within months, Chris had earned his GED, and Stephen had convinced the prison leadership to let him use the facility's lone office computer for his programming. In exchange, he agreed to build software to help lighten the prison's administrative load. A guard would stand watch nearby as Stephen coded away; prisoners "could not be near a computer unescorted," Stephen remembered.

The programming bug bit, and even the several hours a day Stephen managed to get behind the keyboard weren't enough to satisfy him. *I'd rather be doing this than anything else in this entire building! How can I get more time?* Stephen remembered thinking. As word of his skills traveled, the heads of other prison departments approached him to write "mini-programs," and Stephen lobbied for more computer access. Soon, Stephen became Patuxent's unpaid systems administrator. "I wrote fifty different applications while I was incarcerated," he recalled.

Before too long, prison leadership gave Chris and Stephen more responsibility. They were asked to teach classes to incoming prisoners, and they launched a book club and a career center. They also spotted a business opportunity—parents and families of prisoners wanted photos of their loved ones, so the pair convinced prison leadership to purchase a digital camera. They charged for the photos and donated the profits to the Inmate Welfare Fund, which helped to pay for various improvements to the prison.

Every year, Chris mailed the judge an update on his Master Plan progress, with the items he'd completed proudly crossed off the list. And every year, he heard nothing in return. But the Master Plan, which had begun as an exercise in fantasy, had led to meaningful achievements: Chris had finished multiple degrees, learned three languages, read a lengthy list of books, and built a business from scratch.

In his sixteenth year in prison, Chris's annual Master Plan update fell into the hands of a different judge. This new judge saw in his story exactly the type of improvement that the correctional system was supposed to facilitate, and she modified his sentence so he could be paroled.

"I didn't just have words of regret when I stood before the court; I came with the proof of my accomplishments in hand," Chris later wrote in the *Baltimore Sun*. "I had earned my high school diploma and an associate's degree. I had taught myself to speak Spanish, Italian, and Mandarin Chinese and mentored countless younger inmates as they arrived in prison. But most importantly for my judge, my master plan demonstrated ten years of consistency in achieving my goals."

"What you've done is nothing short of astounding," the new judge told him. He was granted his freedom at the age of thirty-two, sixteen years after first setting foot in Patuxent. His cellmate, Stephen, was released two years later, after a twenty-year sentence.

■ ■ ■

I became friends with Chris and Stephen in the course of writing this book, well after they had been paroled. After prison, Stephen used his programming talents to run a software consultancy, then built a start-up whose logistics technology helped schools, companies, and other venues remain open during the COVID-19 pandemic. Stephen even earned a patent—US10417204B2, "Method and system for creation and delivery of dynamic communications"—for his work on natural language processing.

Chris wasn't far behind. He started two businesses, wrote a widely praised book, and launched a second career as a globe-trotting artist—a remarkable post-prison trajectory culminating with an appearance on *The Daily Show* with Trevor Noah to promote his book, *The Master Plan*.

Both Chris and Stephen live life with a rare sense of urgency—an urgency that comes from a keen awareness of life's preciousness. Like many who met them, I wanted to know: How on earth had they done it? How had they overcome their circumstances and accomplished more behind bars than most of us do with all the freedom in the world?

Chris was honest about the role of luck—meeting Stephen when he did and, of course, finding a merciful judge—but he was also clear about the importance of individual effort. He set specific goals and stuck to them with religious conviction. He visualized and journaled about his

Master Plan every day for years, and he lived to cross items off the list. Affixed to his cell wall, the single-spaced sheet of paper was one of the first two things he saw when he woke up and one of the last two things he saw before going to bed.

The other piece of visual inspiration Chris woke up to every day, tacked up next to the Master Plan on the prison wall, was a photo—representing everything the Master Plan meant to him. Next to Chris Wilson's Master Plan on the wall of his cell in the maximum-security Patuxent Institution hung a clipped-out photo—from the November 2007 issue of *Fortune* magazine featuring the "PayPal Mafia."

■ ■ ■

Chris's and Stephen's interest in the story went well beyond the cover photo. Inside their Maryland prison, the two became amateur experts on the life and work of the PayPal founders.

It began when Stephen's family pitched in for some business magazine subscriptions to support his entrepreneurial interest—*Inc.*, *Entrepreneur*, *Forbes*, *Fortune*, *Fast Company*. In late 2007, when the issue of *Fortune* arrived, Stephen was the first to read the story, and he was captivated: before him was the road map for turning computer code into a successful life.

Stephen read the piece twice in one sitting, then passed the magazine to Chris. "Read that fucking article man," Stephen told him. Chris, too, was blown away: "I was like, 'Damn. This shit is crazy.' I thought, *This is how we do it when we get out. We gotta start grinding.*"

Chris remembered seeing the word *billion* in print and becoming entranced by the sum. "Even trying to quantify what a billion dollars is. A billion!" he said. "How could anyone be worth that? . . . I started reading about all of these PayPal folks who started from nothing and now were worth all of that. And then we started talking about 'What would we do with that kind of money? How could we change the world?' And then there was this picture of a few people who did it."

Stephen and Chris preserved the photo as inspiration. "I put a bunch of clear tape over in layers to laminate it," Chris recalled. "It looked a little funny, but it worked." The tape-laminated photo earned a place of privilege on the wall next to the life goals. "You wake up, you see it. You go to sleep, you see it," Chris said. "That was my motivation. I'm doing push-ups, I'm looking at 'em. During lockdown, I'm looking at 'em. It was like Robert De Niro in *Cape Fear* and shit." Stephen said that seeing the image every day "burned it into our psyche."

"I would tell people who saw the images I kept, 'I'm going to get out of prison. I'm going to live this kind of life. I'm going to be impactful in my community.' And they would tell me, 'Dude, you fucking crazy,'" Chris said.

■ ■ ■

The two clipped every nugget and scrap they could find about Elon Musk, Peter Thiel, Max Levchin, Reid Hoffman, and the other PayPal alumni. As the PayPal founders grew in their public profiles, Chris and Stephen amassed a large collection of clippings and treated the assembled packet like scripture. "These were the only things I cared about because they were the only things keeping me alive," Stephen admits. "That's the honest truth. To be reminded and have examples of people who are just as human as you and I."

Both began to think seriously about business and entrepreneurship as a viable life path after prison. "You already know society isn't going to receive you when you come out. There's no real 're-entry,'" Stephen explained. "The idea of re-entry right now is you come out on your knees, we'll give you some handouts, maybe you work at McDonald's or collect trash. But if you think you're going to live like the rest of us who haven't been in there, good luck. And so it was important for us to see that there's another path. Starting your own business is really the only path for which there's not a true ceiling that's imposed upon you."

Up to that point, neither Stephen nor Chris had known about businesses with ambitions the size of PayPal's, or about the networks that enabled such ventures. The networks Stephen and Chris had been exposed to dealt in laundered money, drugs, and violence and went by a different name: gangs. "The PayPal mafia was the positive example of a gang," Stephen said. "A lot of the guys in prison link up together for the wrong reasons. They don't have a lot of positive friendships."

■ ■ ■

The story spilled out of their cell. In their course for new inmates, Chris and Stephen titled their first lesson "What You Can Learn from the PayPal Mafia." They photocopied their article collection and distributed it, with the mafia photo as the cover sheet. "It's a really dark photo, and I used to get pissed off because people kept wanting to photocopy the original," Stephen said, "but I wanted them to photocopy a photocopy so that the original didn't get ruined!"

They would share how the members of the PayPal Mafia started at the bottom. About how many of them were immigrants. About how the founders were young—untried, unsure, and in some cases, unsuccessful. "We preached PayPal. We found synergy. The story connected," Stephen said.

And, of course, they talked about the money, contrasting it with examples of wealth their audience knew well. "If you thought you should follow a drug dealer, because a drug dealer—at risk to his life, with violence, guns, assault, incarceration, and death, and all that stuff—the most he's going to make is a million dollars. Let's be real. And that's after you've come through hell and back," Stephen said. "And then let me show you the opposite: guys who made billions without any of that stuff. What baffles the guys who heard the PayPal story was why no one had ever told them that was even an option."

The new inmates were dumbstruck by Musk's and Levchin's journeys. "They'd look at me, and say, 'Wait, I could have done that? How cool would that have been?'" Stephen recalled. The very idea that a start-up offered a path from the street to riches was a breakthrough— a map of the world that the inmates had never seen. "I used it to mentor everybody who said they wanted to be bigger than they currently were," Chris said. "Which was almost everybody in my midst, because we were in a maximum-security prison."

■ ■ ■

In their proselytizing of the PayPal story, Stephen and Chris consciously played up the "mafia" motif: the idea that PayPal's founders and employees had each other's backs. "When I talked to gang-affiliated young people, they can relate to that," Stephen said. They urged the prisoners to take action, to model themselves on the photo subjects, and to link up with like-minded people. "Study their backgrounds," Stephen would say, "so you can see that they're just like you . . . Look what they've done. And they're no different than you, in that they bleed the same blood as you, breathe the same air as you."

Stephen and Chris knew when their words hit home and when they didn't. They also knew their audience: They had grown up in the same rough neighborhoods, walked through the same prison gates. These inmates were skeptical of anything that seemed distant or phony; prisoners had keen ears for bullshit.

But when Stephen and Chris spoke about PayPal, the audience leaned forward in their chairs. This was real. The network was real. The photo was real. The money was real. "This story meant a whole lot to my life, and the lives of a lot of people in prison with us," Stephen said. "You can't deny what they've built, and what they stand for. You just can't deny it. It's an easy preach."

Debts

At their start, Max Levchin and Peter Thiel had thought the exercise of creating Fieldlink would be brief. Build the company, scale quickly, and sell it off to take advantage of the early internet gold rush. What was supposed to be a yearlong project for them turned into a five-year one—and a company that has remained in business for over two decades since.

This book, too, began as a roughly two-and-a-half-year project that swelled to five years. In that half decade, countless people helped to bring this book to life—and patiently endured stories and anecdotes about a late-1990s dot-com from an obsessed author. To my many indulgent friends, it will come as a relief to be able to write the following: yes, it's done at last, and I can finally shut the hell up about the PayPal book.

I would not be able to write that sentence if not for the hundreds of people who created and worked at PayPal, who took time to explain to a perfect stranger how they got to the company, what they did there, and what it meant to them. The great joy of this project was speaking for hours with these individuals, and I am grateful beyond measure for their time, candor, reflections, notes, and memories.

Simon & Schuster gave this project the green light because of my late editor, Alice Mayhew. Early on, she saw in it what I saw: that there was something about *this* company at *this* moment of time that cast a longer shadow than many appreciated—and that no one had a clue about its creation. She was this book's earliest champion, and more important, she was the person who bucked me up when my confidence in the project ebbed.

She also set a high bar for the book, as she did for all her projects. "Jimmy, you have to prove to me that what you write here is going to stand the test of time! Why is this story relevant fifty years from now? What's going to keep this on our backlist?" she pressed. Alice was an editor who wanted books to *last*—and she demanded her authors write books that did.

I can't know for sure if this text would meet Alice's lofty standard, but in her final communication with me, she hinted that we might be close. She had just read the earliest chapters of X.com's and Confinity's histories and remarked about the hothouse atmosphere: "Edison would be amazed." I hope Alice would be proud of the final telling of this tale, too. It would not have been possible without her.

When Alice passed in early 2020, I panicked. This book was a *massive* undertaking, not just for myself but for any editor brave enough to take up the challenge. Thankfully, Alice's baton passed to the brilliant, inimitable Stephanie Frerich. I had not communicated with Stephanie even once before her boss at Simon & Schuster handed this project off to her, and I had no idea what she'd make of it or how she would add it to an already full plate. She didn't know me from Adam, and she could have been forgiven for rejecting the assignment.

I'm glad she didn't. Stephanie Frerich's stewardship of this project was the greatest blessing. She read every line of this book several times, devotedly and doggedly pushed my thinking, and fought for this project in the face of delays and amid a global pandemic. There is not enough space to point out every error she corrected or weak sentence she strengthened, and if this book manages to tell the PayPal story faithfully and well, it is because of her efforts. She was what every author hopes for: an editor who cares about the project as much as the author does. I am moved to tears thinking about her efforts, and my gratitude to her is endless.

■ ■ ■

The person who "just knew" that it would all work out in the end is the person who seems to keep the faith in my book projects no matter how many times my own faith flags. Laura Yorke still tolerates me (one wonders why), and she guarded this book with all the passion of an agent who could see its potential. There are countless stories about authors wanting to chuck their drafts out the window and declare projects dead; then there are countless follow-up stories about agents who rescue those projects and set authors' heads on straight. Laura did that more times throughout this book than any agent should have to, and for that, and so much else, I am thankful.

My friend Justin Richmond endured the earliest versions of almost every paragraph and thought and quote in this book—usually sent by text message at some obscene early hour of the morning. He was my first phone call when the idea struck me to do this project, and he has been on the receiving end of thousands of messages, notes, and calls since. Talking every day with him made this project possible, and I thank him for that and the gift of his friendship.

Gregg Favre is many things—a fireman, a public safety official, a navy officer, a gifted athlete, and an old soul. He is also a friend who values the endurance it takes to finish projects of length, and I am grateful to him for the various moments in which he provided encouragement, dropped a dash of Stoic wisdom, or otherwise made sure that I pressed ahead. If I had a nickel for every time Gregg said "Stay in the fucking saddle!" (Jon Landau's advice to Jimmy Iovine in *The Defiant Ones*), I'd be rich. Thanks, Gregg. Now on to the next mountain.

Lauren Rodman is the person who made the hard exercise of finishing this book a joyful one. Lauren forced a celebration for each win—the earliest interviews, the first drafts, the significant revisions. At each stage, she required, at a minimum, a dinner to toast to small successes. Every person in the world should have a friend like Lauren Rodman, who reminded me throughout the years how far the project had come.

My friend Grace Harry saw the vision in this project and nurtured the flame of it in ways big and small. Grace has spent a lifetime as a muse for the most talented musical artists in the world—and she brought all of that intelligence and insight to bear in so many conversations about this book, its ambition, and its scope. She and her partner, Ahmir "Questlove" Thompson, helped me to notice the links between this company and clusters of creative people over the ages—artists, poets, writers, and musicians who came of age in a particular cultural stew. Grace also provided creative encouragement and perspective when I needed it most. We weren't in a music studio, but I now understand why so many legendary musicians *need* her to be in their studios. She midwifed this project, and it bears many of her imprints.

Endless thanks to my mentor, friend, and coach, Lauren Zander. In all likelihood, this book would still be an idea in my mind had she not demanded I get started and complete it. Nearly all writers face anxiety, impostor syndrome, fear, self-doubt, and related noise, and I am perhaps more than usually susceptible. Lauren was a shield against these, and she responded to all manner of crazy messages with firmness, focus, and compassion. A writer has had few better friends, and for her insistence and encouragement, I am grateful.

Many others helped to bring this book to life. Emily Simonson at Simon & Schuster helped to guide me through the editorial process with patience and kindness. Elizabeth Tallerico read the early chapters of this book voluntarily and provided support and advice throughout—including at the lower moments of drafting and redrafting. Marjie Shrimpton, Miranda Frum, and Rob Goodman all lent their editorial eyes to draft material, and the work is stronger for their interventions.

Caleb Ostrom came into this project late, and as I said to him dozens of times throughout our work, I only wish I had met him sooner. He was a first-rate thought partner, and I am grateful for everything he did to bring the text to life—including enthusiastically indulging my various stories, thoughts, and phone calls, some of which surely tested his patience. Thanks for putting up with it all, Caleb.

Authors need author-friends, and I am blessed with the best in the business. My friend Ryan Holiday made the first introduction to Peter Thiel that got the rock rolling down the hill. Allen Gannett indulged in our regular "author's therapy" dinners, and his conviction about this project made it worth doing. Ashlee Vance, the author of the definitive biography on Elon Musk, sat for a long meal with someone he had never met—and then made key contacts and offered editorial wisdom that only he could provide.

At the very start of this project, another "Alice Mayhew author," Walter Isaacson, made me believe in its importance and potential. At the very end, he provided the kind of advice that can only come from someone who has spent years laboring in the same fields. For his thoughts on everything from endnotes to fact-checking to interviewing, I am grateful.

My friends David and Kate Heilbroner offered their home when I needed to do the "cabin in the woods" routine, and David also fired up my enthusiasm for the project with his own passion for documentary storytelling and larger-than-life characters. Shir and Marnie Nir offered up their home when I needed another stretch off the grid to edit and revise, and they also provided just the right amount of hugs, lively conversations, and mac and cheese. To Chris Wilson, Andy Youmans, Leah Feygin, Bentley Meeker, Nadia Rawls, Brandon Kleinman, Katie Boyle, Parker Briden, Jacob Hawkins, Arthur Chan, Kevin Currie, Bryan Wish, Enna Eskin, Steve Veres, Mike Martoccio, Matt Gledhill, Matt Hoffman, Tom Buchanan, Miho Kubagawa, Trisha Bailey, Nikki Arkin, Alex Levy, Bronwyn Lewis, Kaj Larsen, Meagan Kirkpatrick, and Benjamin Hardy, thanks for the many, many words of encouragement (and for putting up with my many, many absences). No more texts about the book. I promise.

■ ■ ■

And finally, to Venice, to whom this book is dedicated. The idea for this project started when you were a one-year-old, and it was completed when you were six. The intervening five years have been among the happiest of my life, in large measure because you made them so. You, too, indulged my stories about Max Levchin and Elon Musk, and you offered wisdom of your kind in my moments of doubt about the project. You're unlikely to remember most of what happened these last five years. I will never forget them.

Authors of books like this should usually refrain from burdening readers with "lessons"—the reader is smart enough to figure those out for themselves. But there's a special acknowledgments-only exception to that rule for author-dads, and I'm going to take advantage of it to offer you a message in a bottle, for whenever you get around to reading these words.

Here goes: Your life will be shaped by the things you create, and the people you make them with. We tend to sweat the former. We don't worry enough about the latter. The story of PayPal isn't just about people banding together to shape a product—it's about how banding together shaped the people themselves. The founders and earliest employees of the company pushed and prodded and demanded better of one other.

I hope you find people like that, too, and that you make things with them. That sounds simple—but it's awfully hard. I've been fortunate: I have a sequence of those people in my life, many of whom have been named in the previous pages. You know them as "Auntie Lauren" and "Auntie Grace" and "Uncle Justin" and so on. They are the people who hold me to account. We don't just enjoy one another's company; we make each other better. Our friendship rests on productive discomfort, and we love each other enough to say what needs to be said.

In a funny way, I'm not sure I can play that role for you. There are lessons I love you too much to teach you, so you'll need to go out and learn them for yourself. Fellow travelers will help. Books need editors; lives do too.

As with all my advice, take it with a Very-Hungry-Caterpillar-sized grain of salt. Besides, I may not have to worry. If you cracked this book open at all, sat with it this long, and made it this far, maybe you'll be just fine.

J.S.
New York

A Note on Sources and Methods

I wrote this text roughly two decades after the events covered in these pages took place. My prior books were historical biographies, and I began this project in a fashion similar to those. To start, I created an extensive archive of every book, article, scholarly paper, and similar published reference to the company PayPal and to its antecedent companies Fieldlink, Confinity, and X.com.

Whenever possible, I tried to stick to those items published from 1998 to the mid-2000s. I also assembled a spreadsheet of every blog post, interview, and media appearance by the early founders and employees most closely associated with PayPal—then read, watched, or listened to each one of those appearances and mined them for nuggets. Those thousands of articles and hundreds of hours of footage proved essential, particularly recollections closer to the events in question.

Among the most valuable were talks at Stanford University by Elon Musk in 2003 and a tandem presentation by Peter Thiel and Max Levchin in 2004, as well as commentary from PayPal alumni on the question-and-answer platform Quora. Throughout this project, I have benefited immensely from the archival and cataloging efforts of universities, media outlets, libraries, and many other organizations. (It's no small irony that this book would have been impossible without YouTube—a digital video network built by those who began their careers at PayPal.)

I also benefited from the records warehoused in the Internet Archive. This nonprofit library does yeoman's work, and if and when an alien civilization wants to crack the code on our species, they could do worse than by starting with archive.org.

In addition to material gleaned from books, articles, and existing audio-visual content, I also reached out far and wide to former PayPal employees, investors, near-investors, competitors, and others in and around the PayPal universe. I attempted to contact several hundred people during the course of this project. More than two hundred responded and agreed to speak to me. I am grateful to the PayPal alumni I interviewed along the way, including many who are perpetually time-strapped and still made room for lengthy discussions. I hope the result is fresh and enlightening, even to those who lived the story.

For scenes or dialogue within the text, I have tried to interview at least two people who would have had intimate knowledge of the proceedings. I have tried to buttress those moments with paper or email records wherever possible, including board of directors' minutes, pitch documents, and internal memos. So many of the people I interviewed turned out to be pack rats, and I benefited from various notes, emails, documents, and correspondence they kept. In particular, I was able to dive into several gigabytes of email from this period, a volume totaling hundreds of thousands of pages. This helped me understand and capture moments big and small. I was particularly fortunate to unearth four years' worth of PayPal's company newsletter (i.e., the *Weekly eXpert* turned *Weekly Pal*) which lent my research a texture and immediacy that I hope is reflected in the text.

Quotations in the book are derived both from my interviews as well as from primary and secondary source material. For the sake of a readable book, I have refrained from noting every source within the text itself, but I have carefully compiled endnotes to account for quotations. I respected those moments in which sources wished to speak on background, and I did my best to limit my use of anonymous quotations.

This book endured several rewrites, editorial checks, and thorough read-throughs. There were the reads provided by several editors at the ace Simon & Schuster team, as well as a legal read through their contracted law firm, Miller Korzenik Sommers Rayman LLP. Independently, I also enlisted the support of a veteran fact checker, Benjamin Kalin, who brought a sharp eye to this text. Ben is relentless and cares deeply about the truth. I am grateful to have had him alongside me for this journey.

As with all projects of this length, there may be errors, and they are entirely my own. I wrote rough draft material for this project that totaled several hundred thousand words; my interviews alone constituted over fifteen days' worth of audio. What you hold in your hands is the product of a great many judgment calls and painful edits. The cutting room floor runneth over.

By design, this project suffers from the narrative fallacy: To write about a given company moment is to *not* write about whatever's happening in the next cubicle over. When Brad Stone sat down with Jeff Bezos to discuss Stone's first book on Amazon, Bezos asked how the author would deal with the limits of linear storytelling. "When a company comes up with an idea, it's a messy process," Bezos said. "There's no aha moment."

He's absolutely right—though Stone's response is correct, too: An author must take the narrative fallacy into account and "plunge ahead anyway." I would add that the point of books like this is to capture that messiness. Building anything (including this book) is a process fraught with blind alleys, roads not taken, and moments lost to the sands of time. Hopefully, this text illuminates that gritty, iterative effort as much as it reveals any grand insights about technology or business strategy.

In my writing, I tried to cover the topics that came up repeatedly in interviews, while also leaving room for those stories and ideas that moved or surprised me. But those are editorial choices, and a different set of choices would yield a different book. I would venture to guess that several versions of the PayPal history remain to be written—a future author may endeavor to explore this period again.

Hence my efforts to construct detailed endnotes that can be found at www.jim mysoni.com/foundersnotes. (The book's original 2022 hardcover edition included dozens of physical pages worth of notes. To condense the 2024 paperback, my publisher and I agreed to move these pages online and convert them from atoms to bits.) If some brave soul charts the PayPal waters anew, what you'll find in the notes are the rivers I found during my journey. I hope you map out some new ones in your search, and if I'm still kicking when you do, drop me a line. I will join you in nerding out on the PayPal years with gusto.

J.S.

About the Author

JIMMY SONI is an award-winning and bestselling author. His most recent book, *The Founders: The Story of PayPal and the Entrepreneurs Who Shaped Silicon Valley*, was a debut bestseller and has earned praise from the *Wall Street Journal*, the *New York Times*, the *Economist*, among many others. Described as "an intensely magnetic chronicle" (*New York Times*) and "engrossing" (*Business Insider*), the book explores PayPal's turbulent early days and the shaping of a generation of technological talent. *The Founders* was named one of 2022's must-read books by the *Financial Times*, selected as one of the year's best books by *The New Yorker*, and was a finalist for "Business Book of the Year" from the Society for Advancing Business Editing and Writing (SABEW).

Soni's previous book, *A Mind at Play: How Claude Shannon Invented the Information Age*, won the 2017 Neumann Prize, awarded by the British Society for the History of Mathematics for the best book on the history of mathematics for a general audience, and the 2019 Middleton Prize by the Institute of Electrical and Electronics Engineers (IEEE). The book explored the life and times of Dr. Claude Shannon, founder of the field of information theory and one of the twentieth century's forgotten geniuses. *Fortune* magazine called the book a "charming account of one of the twentieth century's most distinguished scientists . . . Readers will enjoy this portrait of a modern-day Da Vinci."

A prior work, *Rome's Last Citizen: The Life and Legacy of Cato*, shared the story of the ancient Roman Senator Cato the Younger, archrival of Julius Caesar and history's first stoic. Soni is also a coauthor of *Jane's*

Carousel, completed with the late Jane Walentas, which captured one woman's remarkable twenty-five-year journey to restore a beloved carousel in Brooklyn Bridge Park.

Soni began his career at McKinsey & Company, and he lives in Brooklyn, New York, with his daughter, Venice. He is an accomplished ghostwriter as well as sought-after keynote speaker for companies, conferences, and private events. Email hello@jimmysoni.com for more information about Soni's speaking engagements or writing projects. Follow him on Twitter/X.com or Instagram @jimmyasoni, and learn more about his work at www.jimmysoni.com.

EMAIL JIMMY

FOLLOW JIMMY ON
TWITTER/X.COM

SPEAKING
ENGAGEMENTS

PURCHASE BOOKS